# ENDORSEM

Brad Long and I have known each
teenagers together in Korea. I have been with him through a
number of strategic moments in his life. We know each other
very well. However, only in more recent decades, as I have
read his books and been heavily involved with the Dunamis
Project teaching on the Holy Spirit, have I come to realize
what an excellent researcher and instructor he is. When he
is convicted that something is important, he studies it in and
out, up and down until he is confident not only of what makes
up the subject but the why of it. He then presents his
understanding in very clear and logical lessons that are easy
to assimilate. He has done this with the whole Dunamis
Project teaching on the person and work of the Holy Spirit,
synthesizing Scripture and the teachings of admired mentors
and scholars as well as much personal experience. These
teachings on the Holy Spirit are so well organized and
presented, both biblically and theologically, that many
people, otherwise closed to or concerned about the
charismatic work of the Holy Spirit, have openly received
them without fear and with deep appreciation.

Brad has done it again with *Igniting Revivals in the Power of
the Holy Spirit*. Many people around the world are praying
for a mighty revival, a new outpouring of the Holy Spirit,
another great awakening. Many praying people feel that it is
drawing closer day by day, yet still wonder when it is going to
burst upon the world. Intercessors and preachers, teachers
and prophets all want to usher in that great world-
transforming work of the Holy Spirit. Brad has researched the
topic just as thoroughly as he always does and has discovered
markers, patterns, and keys for igniting revival. As he so often
does, he has developed his discoveries into logical sequences
and steps that we can take to bring revival closer.

While every age is different and the Holy Spirit is always doing surprising things that we don't expect, it is clear that there are things that we, the Church of Jesus Christ, can and must do to prepare the context for the Holy Spirit to work in powerful and new ways. Brad's book gives us steps that we can take. This is an important work that may well end up being a key used by the Holy Spirit to ignite the next great awakening.

**-Ben Torrey**
*Missionary Bishop for Korea,*
*Syro-Chaldean Church of N. America*
*Executive Director, The Fourth River Project, Inc.*
*Director, Jesus Abbey's Three Seas Training Center,*
*Taebaek, Gangwon, Korea*

Years ago, someone explained the Holy Spirit to me: "Satan's gonna try to keep you from getting up on that horse, but if he can't, he'll try to push you over on the other side."

There are two common stances for Christians where the Holy Spirit is concerned:
- Fear of going overboard.
- Going overboard.

For thirty-five years, Brad Long has led an organization that helps people get up on that horse without going overboard into weirdness, heresy, and offensiveness. He has done this by teaching the baptism in the Holy Spirit from within the context of Reformed theology and practice, fueled by the revival leadership of R. A. Torrey and his grandson, Archer Torrey of Jesus Abbey in Korea.

This book conveys the principles Brad has used in his leadership of Presbyterian & Reformed Ministries International. When I first met Brad in 1989, he was just starting as Executive Director of what had been the

Presbyterian Charismatic Communion, the tired remnant of a group of Presbyterians who had experienced the baptism in the Holy Spirit and were trying to survive in a denomination that didn't want them.

Brad has taken what was left of this organization and has built it into a vibrant international ministry with branches all over the world—truly a great accomplishment. And I have watched him do it from the beginning. The principles in this book are the principles he has used in thirty-five years of ministry at the helm of PRMI, and I can testify that these principles work."

**-Doug McMurry**
*The Clearing Where Eagles Fly*
*TheClearing.us*

Brad Long writes important books and articles, well researched and showing the leading of the Holy Spirit. This book is no exception. Get a hold of it, be inspired, and participate in revival.

**-Daniel Juster**
*Th.D., Restoration from Zion of Tikkun International*

"Let us rejoice and be glad and give him glory! For the wedding of the Lamb has come, and his bride has made herself ready. Fine linen, bright and clean, was given her to wear." (Fine linen stands for the righteous acts of God's holy people. Revelation 19:7-8 NIV)

In these last days, there is a call on the Body of Messiah/Christ to prepare for the Lord's coming. If you like, it is a partnership, first to pray, and to be involved in prayer with others in the

Ekklesia/Church, to have clean hands and a pure heart to seek out the Lord wholeheartedly. And to be actively involved in helping to build and promote the Kingdom of God however the Holy Spirit would lead us. It is our duty to be faithful to the Lord in His directives to each of us.

With this in mind, God has a plan to restore the Earth to Himself, for restoration in His family to transpire between Jew and Gentile, and between all races and peoples that will enable the Father to release the greater Glory on His Body to fulfill Yeshua/Jesus's prayer of John 17 and the great commission of Matthew 28. And to reform His Ekklesia/Church through function (gifts of the Holy Spirit and fivefold ministry) and governance.

This is where *Igniting Revivals in the Power of the Holy Spirit* can truly help us—enlighten and equip us—for the task and the partnership at hand, so the Body can help realize God's end-time plans to restore the Earth to Himself and establish Yeshua/Jesus's throne in Israel.

Over a lifetime in the Church, experiencing many revivals through the power and gifts of the Holy Spirit, Brad Long and Philip Noordmans have truly been equipped for this task by the Lord. This book is a must-read to better understand the end-time revival and awakening that is still to come.

**-Grant Berry**
Founder, Reconnecting Ministries
*Author and Producer, The Romans 911 Project*

For over a decade Brad has mentored me, and by extension the congregation I lead, in the practicalities and joys of co-laboring with Jesus as He grows His Church *in the power of the Holy Spirit*. His solid biblical teaching is corroborated by vast personal experience. His devotion to Jesus and passion for equipping the Church to do all that Christ commands to the glory of God the Father are inspiring. Partnered with his friendship, these have born much fruit in my life and ministry. If you are one who yearns to see the fulfillment of the prayer, "Your Kingdom come," I can't recommend this book highly enough.

**-David Westra**
*Pastor, Gold Avenue Church*
*Author, The Gospel Tool*
*gospeltool.org*

Now the world is full of chaos and confusion. And the situation seems to be getting worse and worse. People begin to be more aware of the signs of the end-time. And many theories and ideas, good and bad, are manifesting and presenting in all the fields, especially in education, politics, economics, social structures, even religious organizations. Especially in Christian world, we may see a lot of teachings and preachings which are related and pointing to the second coming of Jesus Christ. Yes, we Christians need to be more alert to the teachings.

I am very glad to see my spiritual brother and co-laborer in Christ, Rev. Dr. Brad Long, publish his new book *Igniting Revivals in the Power of the Holy Spirit*. In this book he indicates that although the world seems to be getting worse in its pace, our Lord Jesus Christ already admonished us, "Do not be frightened or dismayed." We still have a lot of work to do. And before His return, the Holy Spirit will ignite more great revivals before the door of salvation is closed (cf. Rev.

14:13-16.) In his book, Dr. Long provides several very important principles from the past about the patterns of revivals and how we can prepare for receiving and participating in the soon-coming great revivals. When we are ready to be involved in the revivals as God's instruments, then His Great Commission will be truly accomplished.

**-Rev. Dr. John C.H. Chang**
*Founding Pastor, Grace Christian Church in New York*
*Founding President, N.Y. Dunamis Theological Seminary*

# Igniting Revivals
## in the Power of the Holy Spirit

*Biblical Keys for Great Moves of God*

Zeb Bradford Long and Philip J. Noordmans
with Barbara Koob

PRMI

EXOUSIA
PRESS

PRMI EXOUSIA PRESS

*Igniting Revivals in the Power of the Holy Spirit:*
*Biblical Keys for Great Moves of God*

ISBN-13: 978-1-7339269-5-9

PRMI EXOUSIA PRESS

# THE MANDATE

In obedience to Jesus Christ, creating venues for God the Father to continue to fulfill Acts 1:4-8 until the gospel of the kingdom of God is preached to all nations.

This Good News of the kingdom shall be proclaimed in the whole world as a testimony to all the nations, and then the end will come. Matthew 24:14

While he was with them, he declared, "Do not leave Jerusalem, but wait there for what my Father promised, which you heard about from me. For John baptized with water, but you will be baptized with the Holy Spirit not many days from now."

So, when they had gathered together, they began to ask him, "Lord, is this the time when you are restoring the kingdom to Israel?" He told them, "You are not permitted to know the times or periods that the Father has set by his own authority. But you will receive power when the Holy Spirit has come upon you, and you will be my witnesses in Jerusalem, and in all Judea and Samaria, and to the farthest parts of the earth. Acts 1:4-8

# ACKNOWLEDGMENTS

Thanks to all those in the Presbyterian-Reformed Ministries (PRMI) and the Dunamis Fellowship International (DFI) who joined me in making contributions to this book. Specifically, I am indebted to the core leadership team of PRMI and the PRMI Board of Directors who provided the spiritual cover and support for me to write this book with all the lessons learned about igniting and sustaining outpourings of the Holy Spirit so they may be passed on to the next generation of believers. I am especially grateful to the Rev. Cindy Strickler (PRMI Director), the Rev. Martin Boardman, and the Rev. Paul Stokes who have taken part in discerning, affirming, and taking part in launching the Preparing for the Next Great Awakening Venture (NGA Venture).

Special thanks to the team who edited and formatted this book for publishing: Judy Cook, Rev. Lonnie Shields, Stephanie Ferguson, and Barbara Koob. You all did meticulous work on my dyslexic spelling and grammar, along with layout and preparation for publication. Judy, I am so appreciative of all the time you devoted to this project. As always, you patiently and tenaciously worked through the editing of this manuscript paying attention to every detail. Lonnie, I am grateful for your stepping in to help at the final hour. You are a great editor with keen insight which has greatly assisted me to ensure that biblical truths are expounded with the utmost clarity. I also want to add a special thanks to Stephanie for her editing skills as well as the beautiful design of the book cover, and to Barbara for managing this writing project with excellence.

In addition, I want to give a distinct recognition to Rev. Dr. Phil Noordmans, my coauthor, who has brought to this endeavor a pastor's heart and extensive experience of implementing teaching on the Holy Spirit within the local congregation. Thanks also to Rev. James Kearney, Bishop Ben Torrey, and others for their deep understanding, personal involvement, and prophetic insights of Holy Spirit outpourings and revivals. Also, I want to thank those who shared extensively from their firsthand pastoral experience. They are noted in the book, I highlight them here: Rev. David Westra with

Rev. Gina Dick, pastors of the Gold Avenue Christian Reformed Church; Rev. James Cubie, pastor of the three-hundred-year-old Mattituck congregation on Long Island; Rev. Rebecca Long Modrynski with Rev. Josh Modrynski, pastors of St. Giles Presbyterian Church in Richmond VA; and Dr. Craig Keener who was most helpful in giving insights into the Asbury University outpouring of the Holy Spirit.

Special thanks to Rev. Douglas McMurry, whose books *Glory Through Time Vol. 1 and 2* provide the historical affirmation of biblical patterns given in this book for preparing for, igniting, and sustaining revivals. His friendship, life of prayer, wisdom, and our partnership in the great move of the Holy Spirit, has been Jesus' means of guiding and sustaining me in fulfilling my leadership role in PRMI for over three decades.

And finally, I am so grateful to my wife the Rev. Laura Cole Long. She is also an anointed intercessor, spiritual leader, loving pastor, great preacher and teacher in her context of the local congregation. For these many years she has persistently, lovingly, Sunday by Sunday, in season and out, nurtured a PC(USA) congregation's biblical faith in Jesus Christ, and by cooperating with the Holy Spirit, she has provided a living laboratory showing that the revival patterns in this book apply to the local congregation as well as to vanguard moves of the Holy Spirit. Both venues work together to advance the kingdom of God and the gospel of Jesus Christ.

# Table of Contents

# Prologue

[Authors note: "I know that for some readers, describing in vivid details instead of bland and safe generalities, our following experiences of our cooperation with the Holy Spirit will be outside of their experience and worldview. Further I understand that what is described in this prologue, has as of this writing in October 2023, been taking place in real time. I am reporting this to you without the advantage of years or decades of hindsight to evaluate through objective verification to definitively determine if what we experienced is actually true and whether the prophetic visions that we saw were really from our God or just from ourselves. I understand we may lose some readers by giving you these reports in this vivid first-hand manner. However, the editorial team and I have decided to include this prologue because it is a glimpse into the spiritual and physical situation that we are presently in. These events provide a foretaste of the actual spiritual dynamics Jesus Christ is calling His Church and His people into. In this desperate hour there is not time for a long, less jolting nurturing of those whom Jesus is calling as His co-workers, to work with Him in igniting the global revival that will overcome this present darkness that is engulfing the world. – Zeb Bradford Long October 26, 2023]

As we have been preparing for publication of *Igniting Revivals in the Power of the Holy Spirit: Biblical Keys for Great Moves of God,* two events occurred in October 2023 which reveal the necessity of our cooperating with Jesus Christ in igniting outpourings of the Holy Spirit, which will bring waves of kingdom-advancing revival. The first event, on Oct. 7 was the invasion of Israel by the Islamic jihadist group, Hamas. The second event was the Mountain Top Equipping Camp conducted at Presbyterian and Reformed Ministries International's prayer and equipping center in Western North Carolina on October 11-15. That event was for equipping the saints for strategic intercession and spiritual warfare.

I believe that both events are revelatory—revealing God's plans and unmasking Satan's counterattacks. They are also "catalytic," for both events have the role of setting in motion these revealed plans of God and exposed schemes of Satan. These two events epitomize the true nature of our epoch fraught with the potential of global revival greater than the First and Second Great Awakenings and/or colossal demonic evil more terrible than World War II and the Nazi Holocaust.

## The Revelation of Satan's True Agenda and Method

Let's start with awful part—the revelation of Satan's plans for evil. On October 7, 2023, Hamas, the terrorist organization which controls Gaza, launched a massive, coordinated, surprise attack that came over land, sea, and air—with over 5000 rockets shot into Israel. The worst part was that the Islamic jihadists broke through the security barriers, entering many Israeli villages and kibbutzim, and murdering over 1300 men, women, and children. The number of victims continues to grow as more bodies are found. This is the worst atrocity against the Jews since the Holocaust during the Nazi reign of barbarism in the 1930s and 1940s.

Jihadists gunned down entire groups of innocent people, beheaded children and babies, gang-raped women and children, and burned alive whole families in their homes. Grisly evidence revealed children and families were tortured to death. Like marauding Orcs, they dragged several hundred men, women, and children back to Gaza. What is more, the murderers gleefully posted the graphic, gory atrocities on the internet, replete with the background screams of their victims and the Islamists shouting, "Allahu Akbar" "Allah is Greater!" [1] One particularly gruesome and disturbing picture was of a near-naked, bloodied woman, perhaps still alive, tied to the front of a car being paraded through the streets of Gaza with its citizens cheering. These are images of horror, pure hatred, and evil.

Many have observed that in the political and military realm, this was Israel's Pearl Harbor. It has united and mobilized the entire country into a declared war to destroy Hamas. At this point the United States has clearly sided with Israel, sending massive fire power and military assets into the region. However, this could quickly escalate to include the entire powder keg of the Middle East. With this new war, the world seems ready to explode into a global conflagration having the potential to ignite or aggravate other conflicts, including Europe (between Russia and Ukraine), Asia (between China and Taiwan), and the entire region of South China.

These October 7 events reveal to all with eyes to see that there is a relentless rise of very powerful demonic strongholds. This demonic evil is based on the hatred of God and of God's people, both Jews and Christians, and it is embodied in demonic strongholds based on Islam and Marxism in all their present permutations. This attack has unmasked the true evil intentions of Satan in these demonic strongholds. This is an opportunity for true moral clarity to reveal the end results of different ideologies and movements, exposing whether they are resulting in good or evil. It is also a revelation that behind these human expressions of evil, which may be dealt with by human means of military power, there is a radical, demonic, spiritual dimension. Further, this is a catalytic event which is intended to set in motion the diabolical plans of Satan. Already these events have inflamed hatred of Jews with the potential to escalate the outbreaks of evil worldwide. If you look closely at the protesters, many are Muslim and members of the radical left, and

---

[1] Allahu Akbar (Arabic: الله أكبر) is an Islamic phrase, called *Takbir* in Arabic, meaning "Allah is greater" or "Allah is [the] greatest".
https://en.wikipedia.org/wiki/Allahu_Akbar_(disambiguation)

they are chanting "gas the Jews," calling for Holocaust 2.0 to complete the work of Hitler, and "from the river to the sea," calling for the eradication of Israel as a nation. This rise of demonically energized and politically manipulated antisemitism is taking place in unlikely places such as China, and sadly on the elite college campuses of the United States and United Kingdom. It seems like the power of the antichrist is goading the world toward a global catastrophic war.

This evil manifestation is consistent with what Jesus Christ revealed as the birth pains of the end times of the world. Jesus Himself prophesied the growth of evil in the world with wars and rumors of wars. The attack against the Jews, like in the 1930s, is a harbinger of what Satan really has embedded in his hidden plans to include, not just a genocide of the Jewish people, but of Christians as well. Indeed, these terrible events which may have grown worse by the time you are reading this, is a revelation of Satan's plans made clear for all to see. This book assumes the reality of this evil and these evil days. We would certainly like to turn our heads away from such graphic and terrible displays of raw evil, but we must look, as it reveals the true state of our world, which is the context for the message of this book.

Without this revelation we will not understand the full extent of God's response to this great evil. No doubt, God will work through military power to destroy the human expressions of these demonic strongholds based on Islam and Marxism. Military power is required for the defeat of the strongholds whenever they acquire military means of implementing Satan's schemes as happened in World War II with the destruction of Nazism or the battle to destroy the Islamic Jahidi ISIS under the direction of President Trump. Further, unless we grasp the gravity of this evil, we will not understand the true urgency of the call for strategic intercession and spiritual warfare. This intercessory call must include a prelude of prayers for confession of sin, repentance, and forgiveness to prepare the ground where the Holy Spirit is leading. More importantly, if we do not grasp the gravity of this evil, we will not grasp the necessity of implementing the biblical keys for us to cooperate with the Holy

Spirit to ignite revivals. Global revival advancing the Kingdom of God is the only way to constrain and defeat this global evil.

## The Revelation of God's Global Revival Bringing Joy and Healing

The second revelatory event took place at the Mountain Top Equipping Camp. Here, God revealed to us His means of countering such radical evil and defeating Satan's genocidal plans.

In the week of October 11-15, 2023, about forty of us gathered for what we called our Mountain Top Equipping Camp, which was part of our Advanced Course on Equipping for Strategic Intercession and Spiritual Warfare[2] at the Community of the Cross. The group consisted of many experienced, anointed intercessors, as well as spiritual warriors and those with prophetic giftings. Messianic Jewish participants were part of this advanced course, which was of special importance for this crisis.

During this event we were led by the Holy Spirit to implement strategies and tactics for defeating the demonic strongholds through which Satan was working out his terrible plans, and to "pray in" an outpouring of the Holy Spirit.

## The Open Heaven and Holy Spirit Outpouring Manifesting Jesus Christ

I need to bring you into to this by saying that we spent several days in prayer engagements, dealing with the demonic strongholds exposed in the October 7 Islamic jihadist attack. We had also been teaching the tactics of intercession and conducting analysis of what was taking place in the world. In summary, we prayed the following to dismantle the demonic stronghold of Hamas.

---

[2] For more about this course please see the web site:
https://www.prmi.org/strategic-intercession-spiritual-warfare/

1. We prayed for the Lord to give us insight as to how to weaken and demolish the demonic stronghold through Hamas.

2. We felt the Lord say to specifically pray for the Hamas leader Khalid for his salvation and for the release of his anger/hatred of the Jewish people.

3. We prayed forgiveness, confession of sin and repentance, and then blessed Kahlid, praying for salvation. (This was all part of weakening the demonic stronghold. Readers need to understand that this is all part of the process of strategic intercession, following and cooperating with the Holy Spirit using His tactics.)

4. We also prayed for the empowerment and guidance of the military forces who were called to take part in defeating this stronghold of Islamic jihad while protecting innocent life.

On the evening of October 13, there was an outpouring of the Holy Spirit which I believe reveals the nature of the move of the Holy Spirit that God is calling us to take part in. We had already been through forgiveness, confession, repentance, recommitment to Jesus Christ, and prayer that the Holy Spirit would be poured out upon us for power and for gifts. For you to get a glimpse of this event, here is an excerpt from the After-Action Review of the event:

> In the team meeting at supper, I was led to suggest that my daughter Elizabeth, who was on the leadership team, should join me as my "wing woman," and that we should go into an extended period of worship. Lonnie, our worship leader, said that he would prepare a set of six praise songs.
>
> At about 7:00 pm we gathered in the main prayer room at the Prayer House. I was aware that the Holy Spirit was already moving and ready to take us into God's manifest presence. To call people together, Martin blew the shofar and Lonnie led in a worship song. Then, I was led to read the great Christ-exalting words of Philippians 2:5-11:
>
>> You should have the same attitude toward one another that Christ Jesus had, who though he existed

in the form of God did not regard equality with God as something to be grasped, but emptied himself by taking on the form of a slave, by looking like other men, and by sharing in human nature, He humbled himself, by becoming obedient to the point of death —even death on a cross! As a result God highly exalted him and gave him the name that is above every name, so that at the name of Jesus every knee will bow—in heaven and on earth and under the earth—and every tongue confess that Jesus Christ is Lord to the glory of God the Father.

I did this, not as a mere Bible reading, but as a proclamation into all spheres of reality, visible and invisible, of the Lordship of Jesus Christ. As I proclaimed the last verses, I saw these words opening the heavens. Jesus started to manifest Himself in our midst. I knew that it was a "kairos moment" and we were to step into it, first, by singing in the Spirit. We were caught up in an extended period of singing in the Spirit, which was just glorious. It seemed that we were joining the heavenly host and the vast chorus of redeemed from all the ages, in adoration of the Three in One and the One in Three.

We entered an extended season of the full, rich presence of God, in awesome majesty and power, and in love and tenderness as He was embracing all of us. Wave upon wave of the Holy Spirit washed over the group. The first wave that I observed from upfront leadership was **a time of holy laughter and profuse joy.**

As Elizabeth and I stood up in the front of the Prayer House in a leadership position, the Holy Spirt fell upon Elizabeth. She reported, "I first had a beautiful sense of God's love. Next, I saw the Holy Spirit dancing around with this playful joy." As she announced this to the group, I noticed the Holy Spirit falling upon Donna, Gerri and one other person, sitting right in front. They seemed to be manifesting holy joy, but also holding back. Then, I received the guidance to release Elizabeth to step out and to lay hands on people to pray for the joy of the Lord to fall upon them. As she stepped away, intercessor Sandy Doss stepped up behind me and laid hands on me for protection, as I had lost the covering provided by Elizabeth standing with me.

As Elizabeth laid hands on Donna, she was overcome with joy and burst forth with holy laughter. It spread like little rivulets of joy into the room. As Elizabeth saw the Holy Spirit moving upon people, she laid hands on them, and they too started to experience holy laughter. Grant, one of the Messianic Jewish brothers, with tears in his eyes, who just the night before had forgiven the Hamas leaders and jihadists for the murder of the Jews on Oct 7, was also caught up in holy laughter. It is important to note that during that night before we had laid the foundation for the strategic intercessory prayer session where the Holy Spirit led us into a time of confession, repentance, and forgiveness. And now God was suddenly moving us into His joyful holy presence. What a transition this had been! But so often in this type of strategic intercessory prayer focus, tears and laughter can be experienced in the Spirit. So as Grant was caught up in this holy laughter, even more people were caught in this refreshing, living joy of Jesus. However, not all experienced holy laughter. Bensie reported, "God was singing a love song to me. I was trying to move into the joy, and I just had to stay with the Lord singing His love over me." This went on for a long time and was profoundly restorative to many. We then moved into a time of powerful but gentle healing and deliverance ministry. Soon groups were praying for each other all over the room. My role was to have oversight over the entire room and to help direct people to join in praying for each other. People experienced inner healing from deep wounds incurred while living in a fallen world or from past prayer battles. There was also quite a time of deliverance as evil spirits who had gotten attached to people lost their ground and spontaneously left or, without much ado, were commanded to leave. I looked over the room with all the groups in ministry to each other and could see joy, peace, and quiet praise on people's faces as Jesus was at work in this healing ministry. Intermingled with the joy and healing, we also went into a time of commissioning for the battle and being called into different spheres of warfare. We knew that Jesus was restoring and healing us so we could join Him in the great work ahead of defeating demonic strongholds and igniting outpourings of the Holy Spirit.

It was getting late, and I could see that some people were finished, but the presence of the Lord was so heavy and the work in some groups was still intense. I gave a benediction and released those who needed to leave. Others stayed a long time.

The vibrant love, joy, healing, refreshment, reconciliation, and restoration of the fellowship between Jews and Gentiles as the one new humanity that we experienced on October 14, is in unequivocal contrast to the massacre of Jews and celebration of death that the world witnessed in vivid images of October 7. The revelation of October 7 is that the god named Allah, who apparently delights in the torture and murder of innocents, is none other than Satan, the great deceiver and bane of humanity. October 14 revealed the true character and purposes of the one true God revealed in the Bible, incarnated in Jesus Christ and active through the presence of the Holy Spirit. This amazing evening revealed that this great revival that the Lord is calling us to take part with Him in preparing for, igniting, and sustaining, will be characterized by the manifest presence of King Jesus, God the Father, and the Holy Spirit making real His kingdom on earth.

# Joining Jesus in Casting Flaming Coals of Revival Fire upon the Earth

This next revelatory event took place on Saturday Oct. 15, also at the Prayer House at the Community of the Cross. When we gathered that afternoon, we entered an extensive period of what we call the "intelligence preparation of the battle space." During this time people brought considerable intel from the small groups and from prophetic visions they had received. During this time, we identified the high-level demons who were at work in the world using the October 7 invasion of Israel and atrocities by Hamas to stir up a global catastrophe which could become World War III. After this time of discernment and confirmation, we then moved into a time of worship, which quickly became a period of glorious singing in the Holy Spirit which lasted a long time. Here is another glimpse with an excerpt from the After-Action Review of the event:

As we moved into worship, I knew that the Lord had anointed me for the overall command role. I was also intensively aware that the Lord had raised up just the right team around me to go into what we later realized was the decisive turning point in the battle. I was aware that the Lord was leading us into the war room in the third heaven. Through the Holy Spirit, this war room included us being both on earth and also sitting with Jesus Christ in the heavenlies. There Jesus grants us authority over all levels of demonic powers. As we started, I was aware that I was being called up into the third heaven and being granted the authority from Jesus to take part with Him in this engagement that He was initiating. Spreading out before me, I could see the entire multi-dimensional, visible and invisible battlespace. I was first aware of the five major high-level demonic spirits who were involved. Then, I heard the Lord saying that He was authorizing us to bind them, and command that their kingdom of darkness be divided and conquered so that they could not carry out their battle plans against God's kingdom and His chosen people. As I announced this to the group, we immediately went into battle with a rush of joy.

I was not called to give the commands but rather, I was in a position of standing with Jesus as the commander of the Lord's armies. Somehow from that position, through me Jesus was providing both the guidance as well as the authority for others to voice the commands that were actually His commands. I was seeing in the heavenly and earthly realms as these commands were going out as the Word of God, having their effect upon the demonic and earthly powers of darkness.

I will not go into details of this first phase of the prayer battle, which was exhilarating, as we were called into strategic level intercession and spiritual warfare. I expected this phase to last a long time and was anticipating that we would be brought into a battle in which the demonic powers would start to counterattack us through the air. This has happened many times before while engaged in such strategic intercession, but the Lord had other, better plans:

> "We had just spoken God's word, binding and dividing the archons. The intercessors, anointed by the Holy Spirit were boldly joining in, when to my surprise and great relief, the Lord said to me, 'That part is finished for now!' So, I announced that we needed to stop and wait upon the Lord, which quieted everyone down. (Looking out at the intercessors, I think some were a little disappointed!) Then in the few moments of silence, the Lord said, 'Now I am calling you to join Me in pouring out my Holy Spirit upon the earth to ignite revivals everywhere I choose. Now put up the world map so you may see from my perspective.' So, I put up the map."

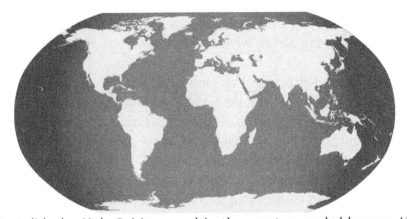

As I did, the Holy Spirit moved in the most remarkable way. He would come upon a particular person or group of people to have them pray for a particular place on the map where He was pouring out His Holy Spirit in revival fire. Frankly, I have no way to describe what happened when the map was put up. The atmosphere was thick with the presence of God, but it felt very different from the open heaven we had experienced the night before. Instead, it was like the entire Prayer House and all of us in it, while still rooted firmly on earth, had been transported into the third heaven. The prayer work that followed was not ordinary prayers being lifted up by people with prayer burdens for special locations. Rather Jesus, the Commander of the Lord's armies, was speaking through us, making prophetic proclamations. As these were being spoken, in my role as standing with Jesus in overall command, I could see the Word of God going forth and the fiery coals from the altar landing on the locations as they were named and identified on the map. Everywhere they landed, I could see the heavens opening, the fire of the Holy Spirt falling and revivals being ignited. I could also see that in these prophetic words, God was stirring up in His chosen people desperate prayers for revival as well as people being called into the obedience of implementing the keys that the Lord has given us for preparing for, igniting, and sustaining transformative outpourings of the Holy Spirit.

This was taking place in America, in Israel and the entire Middle East, in China and the Chinese-speaking world, in the

United Kingdom and in Canada. There were other nations and areas mentioned but these seemed to be the ones where, at that particular moment, God had chosen to pour out revival fire. It was as if I was there. I saw these flaming coals igniting in these locations with tributaries of mingled Holy Spirit fire and living water. I saw the Word of God and the Spirit all meeting and becoming a river of a great global awakening with millions upon millions of people being born-again and brought into the kingdom of God. I also saw the nations and peoples aligning themselves either with or against God's biblical plans, which have always started with His people, the Jews.

As we continued the prophetic work of naming locations and sending down from heaven the fire of the Holy Spirit, I suddenly saw battalions of demons gathering around the epicenters where the Lord was igniting the fire. They were plotting and raging against the people through whom the Lord was igniting and sustaining the streams of revival. Matching these images of the gathering demonic host, were echoes in my heart of the words recalled by the apostles, '...Why do the nations rage, and the peoples plot foolish things? The kings of the earth stood together, and the rulers assembled together, against the Lord and against his Christ' (Acts 4:25-26). I then heard the Lord say, 'Now I am sending the heavenly host of warrior angels to push back the armies of hell. Tell the intercessors to pray for sending this angelic host.' As we prayed, I saw and could feel clashes taking place in a multi-front battle in the heavenlies and on earth. In vision I saw the angelic host clearing away the demonic powers blocking the Lord's planned outpourings of the Holy Spirit.

As we continued to pray into this, I could feel that the Holy Spirit was shifting us out of this mode of prayer into the next phase which included going back into worship with another time of glorious praise to Jesus Christ. Next, we were led into giving thanks for the great revival that He was launching through His word that was sent out into those locations."

It was a little difficult for me to come down out of this war room in the third heaven. Gary Hixson came up to me and said, "You're not really here, are you?" I said, "No!" He and others prayed for me, and I felt like I was coming back down to earth. Later Gary told me that he had a vision of me being lowered down out of the heavens with golden cords. I think this had actually happened to the entire group. We all were left spiritually invigorated and physically worn out from this time of prayer.

## What Does All This Mean?

I believe that these October 2023 events are profound revelations of Satan's schemes for evil and God's kingdom plans for humanity. I believe that both Satan's and God's plans have been set in motion—plans that may be another stage in the events leading up to the End Times.

By the time you have this book in your hands, you will know from current events whether the worst-case scenarios of the unbridled evil have taken place or are still gathering for an even greater explosion of death and destruction. Or you may see the expressions of God's mercy as well as His divine vengeance against those who have launched this genocidal jihad against Israel and the Jewish people.

I hope that you will have seen that the Lord has answered the prayers of millions of people and constrained the high-level demonic spirits behind this chaos and carnage. All this is to be hoped for, but constraining evil is only part of the revelation of God's work revealed at the Mountain Top Equipping Camp. The second part is what I have attempted to describe above, when the Lord called us up into the heavenly places to pray for the flaming coals of Holy Spirit-empowered revival to be poured out upon the earth, which will not only overcome these demonic strongholds implementing Satan's plans but will bring the gospel of the kingdom of God to all nations on earth.

Another implication of this Mountain Top Equipping needs to be highlighted. It is the role of Jews who are born-again followers of Yeshua/Jesus. Their presence and full participation at this strategic intercessory prayer work is truly revelatory of God the Father's plans for igniting outpourings of the Holy Spirit in our present epoch. This revival will be enabled by and will result in the unity that Jesus prayed for His body to manifest on earth (John 17). This restoration of unity begins with the healing and restoration of the most fundamental fracture in the body which is between Jew and Gentile. Together as born-again Jews and Gentiles, as well as having representatives from other historic divisions of the body of Christ—Roman Catholic and Protestant, Pentecostal and Reformed, and others—we were functioning as the "one new humanity" (Ephesians 2:11-22). This unity, not just in theory but in practice, is the basis for our sharing in the authority of Jesus Christ over high-level demonic powers. This unity is foundational for the body of Christ to be in one heart and mind and to pray down from heaven the flaming coals for igniting revival.

The revelation of this Mountain Top Event is that God the Father is in our epoch putting in place this "one new humanity" unity, so that the biblical keys and patterns He has given to ignite these outpourings of the Holy Spirit will be effective. This great revival movement has already been launched. It is now up to us to follow up in prayer and obedience, as well as to continue to cooperate with the Holy Spirit so that the gospel of the kingdom may go to all nations.

# 1

# Restorative Outpourings of the Holy Spirit

In the two events described in the prologue that took place in October of 2023, the Lord has revealed to us the reality of the rise of demonic evil and His redemptive plans for constraining evil and advancing the gospel of the kingdom to all the nations.

From this recent revelation and from the last forty years participating in the glory of God, I am convinced that we are on the threshold of a Holy Spirit revival greater than anything we have ever seen in the past. This unprecedented global outpouring of the Holy Spirit has the potential to become an awakening which will advance the kingdom of God over Satan's empire of evil, completing the Great Commission of taking the gospel of Jesus Christ to all nations and peoples on earth. We are already experiencing these great movements of the Holy Spirit in multiple locations, which are all part of the great waves of the Holy Spirit advancing God's kingdom on earth that began with Pentecost.

These waves have moved through history in a generally westward direction around the globe and are now converging back on the city of Jerusalem, Israel, where it all started over two thousand years ago. All this is part of God the Father's master plan and method of fulfilling the mission command Jesus has given His body the Church:

> Then Jesus came up and said to them, "All authority in heaven and on earth has been given to me. Therefore go and make disciples of all nations, baptizing them in the name of the Father and the Son and the Holy Spirit, teaching them to obey everything I have commanded you. And remember, I am with you always, to the end of the age." Matt. 28:18-20

1

These moves of the Holy Spirit are written in the history of great revivals and awakenings which lead many—including myself—to the conclusion that we are approaching the climactic events heralding the End Times. Consistent with Jesus' descriptions in Matthew 24 of what to expect as we approach the End Times, we are seeing the global rise of demonic evil with the unleashing of the spirit of the antichrist.

## Signs of the End Times

In our present epoch, concurrent with the aggressive rise of demonic evil, there is the quantum advancement of God's kingdom. Over the last fifty years vast progress has been made in fulfilling the biblical prophetic harbingers of the End Times. Jesus tells us, "This Good News of the kingdom shall be proclaimed in the whole world as a testimony to all the nations, and then the end will come" (Matt. 24:14 TLV). This is happening to an amazing extent, and the impending outpouring of the Holy Spirit may provide the final push for its completion. In addition, we are witnessing the historically unprecedented fulfillment of the biblical prophecy of the Jewish people returning to the Land of Israel. Most remarkable of all, Jews are accepting Yeshua their Messiah. The prophet Jeremiah prophesied:

> "In those days, when your numbers have increased greatly in the land," declares the Lord, "people will no longer say, 'The ark of the covenant of the Lord.' It will never enter their minds or be remembered; it will not be missed, nor will another one be made. At that time they will call Jerusalem The Throne of the Lord, and all nations will gather in Jerusalem to honor the name of the Lord. No longer will they follow the stubbornness of their evil hearts. Jeremiah 3:16-17, NIV

Paul also looked to the day when the Jews would come to faith in Yeshua the Messiah (Jesus Christ), knowing it would mean the dawn of the completion of the kingdom of God. "For if their rejection leads to the reconciliation of the world, what will their acceptance be but life from the dead?" (Romans 11:15 TLV). We are seeing firsthand these harbingers of the End Times taking place in this present great movement of the Holy Spirit. Not only are we seeing all nations gathering in Jerusalem, but born-again Jews and Gentiles are coming into unity, forming the one new humanity. We are working together to do our part in fulfilling the Great Commission in the power of the Holy Spirit. This is not just a hope, but an actuality! It is, for instance, embodied in the partnership between Presbyterian Reformed Ministries and Tikkun America and Global. There are many other such partnerships reflecting this new reality of the emerging one new humanity.

We are entering an unparalleled time of outpourings of the Holy Spirit, advancing the kingdom of God with the potential for the completion of the Great Commission and the restoration of the kingdom of Israel (Acts 1:6-8). The wellspring and genesis for all this is in the heart of God the Father who, out of an all-encompassing love for corrupted creation and His fallen human family is acting out of His own sovereign initiative to send these waves of revival. However, in keeping with the Father's own vision of having not slaves and servants but sons and daughters who are also friends and co-workers, He is extending to us the invitation to join in the incredible last dance of cooperation with Him to complete the mission of the gospel of the kingdom going to all people.

This is the extraordinarily good news that gives us courage in the face of the extraordinarily bad news. We are beset on all sides with news of Satan's inevitable counterattacks. I am convinced both from biblical revelation and from discerning the signs of the times, that Satan is planning to unleash an even greater attack than in the 1930s and 40s, with a global tidal wave of evil on earth to prevent, divert, or at least delay these outpourings of the Holy Spirit. The demonic powers are moving at a frenzied pace in our time because they know that when these waves of the Holy Spirit reach their crescendo in the great End Times revival, Satan with his legions of fallen angels and deceived human beings will be annihilated in the lake of fire which is the second death (Revelation 20).

## God's History of "By My Spirit" Outpourings

For a history of outpourings as well as the signs that we are approaching this final End Times overthrow of Satan's kingdom and the return of Jesus Christ in glory bringing the restoration of all things (Acts 3:21), I recommend Douglas McMurry's teaching *Glory Through Time* in video and book form.[3]

The conclusion reached in McMurry's study is that outpourings of the Holy Spirit are God's method of overcoming the persistent tendency of the church to fall into political "power and might," instead of advancing God's kingdom God's way of "by My Spirit" (Zech: 4:6). McMurry demonstrates that every outpouring of the Holy Spirit resulting in genuine revival which advances the kingdom of Jesus Christ will result in a "by My Spirit" lifestyle.

This method of working with God—not by human power but only in God's power—was given, not just for Zerubbabel, but for all who are called to be God's co-workers on earth building God's kingdom. We see this "by My Spirit" basis operative first in the Old Testament prophets, priests, judges, and kings who were to have the Spirit of Adonai fall upon them for power. We see it again when the Holy Spirit came upon Jesus Christ at His baptism, empowering Him for His mission. Then in Acts 1:4-8 Jesus promises all of us who are called to be His witnesses this same equipping of the Holy Spirit's power.

Douglas McMurry, in his two volumes entitled *Glory Through Time*, traces the history of God sending waves of the Holy Spirit to establish His "by My Spirit" approach which for every generation must overcome Satan's deception of political "power and might." Waves of revival are essentially Jesus Christ as King showing up on earth! The

---

[3] Douglas McMurry, *Glory Through Time: Vol. 1 and 2*. (Tustin CA: Trinity Christian Publishers, 2021). Books: https://a.co/d/c5DVnTG, https://a.co/d/gwkf1oC; Videos: https://www.theclearing.us/video-teachings/glory-through-time/

result restores God's family to His "by My Spirit" mandate, empowering us as well as requiring us to live a "by My Spirit" lifestyle.

This By My Spirit lifestyle is described as follows:

1. Surrender to the King. (Jesus is King; we are not.)
2. Ask for the Holy Spirit. (Seek the power of God to accomplish God's goals.)
3. Let God write His laws on our hearts. (Let Him sensitize our consciences.)
4. Humility and servanthood. (Imitate the lifestyle of Jesus.)
5. Love and unity. (The ultimate goal of the Christian life is love as defined by Jesus.)
6. Cultivate the authority of prayer. (Jesus our high priest shares His authority with us.)
7. Maintain a direct connection with God. (Cultivate an ongoing daily relationship.)[4]

The ultimate result of revivals is to accomplish King Jesus' purpose and mission, which in Acts 3:21 is to "restore all things." Before this final objective is reached, the intermediate results in our fallen world are the constraining of human and demonic evil, common grace structures for the good of humanity and God's chosen people of biblical faith, living the kingdom lifestyle, which includes the empowerment for taking part in the mission of taking the gospel of the kingdom to all peoples.

However, during the struggles and ambiguities of our present epoch, let us keep our eyes fixed on Jesus Christ and the ultimate meaning and purpose of the revival waves that our Lord is calling us to take part with Him, in igniting and sustaining on earth.

"Revivals are an advance on this ultimate accomplishment of Christ, a down payment or "earnest money agreement"—in Greek,

---

[4]Douglas McMurry, *Glory through Time, vol. 2, The Forgotten Legacy of Transformational Revivals,* (Tustin CA: Trilogy Christian Publishers, 2022), 20-21.

*arrabon*—the word that the Apostle Paul uses when describing the work of the Holy Spirit in this present age (Ephesians 1:13, 2 Corinthians 1:22, 5:5). Through revivals, the glory of the King breaks through into our religious systems. Revivals are perennial epiphanies, Jesus reminding us, century after century of His ultimate destiny as Restorer of everything. His obligation in sending revival is not to us but to the Father. His assignment is to restore the creation to its pristine condition as He wanted it in the first place."[5]

## The Alpha Points of King Jesus' Revival Waves

Our focus in this book is on the beginning points of moves and waves of the Holy Spirit—the Alpha points! These are essentially when the fire falls from heaven igniting the movements of the Holy Spirit which manifest God's kingdom and presence on earth. The paradigm for this is the event of Pentecost described in Acts 2.

When the day of Pentecost arrived, they were all together in one place. And suddenly there came from heaven a sound like a mighty rushing wind, and it filled the entire house where they were sitting. And divided tongues as of fire appeared to them and rested [ESV footnote: Or *And tongues as of fire appeared to them, distributed among them, and rested*] on each one of them. And they were all filled with the Holy Spirit and began to speak in other tongues as the Spirit gave them utterance.  Acts 2:1-4, ESV.

Pentecost was a unique and singular event in that it was the first occasion for Jesus to baptize His followers with the Holy Spirit after His resurrection, ascension, and coronation. This event set the new covenant phase of the kingdom of God in motion within human history. However, it was followed immediately by other occasions

------

[5]McMurry, *Glory Through Time*, 2:452-453.

of the fire falling which set in motion new movements or tributaries of this great river of God.

We see this taking place in Acts 8 when the fire fell on the people of Samaria, and when the Spirit fell upon the Ethiopian eunuch through the anointed ministry of Philip (resulting in the gospel going to Africa). We see it again with the outpouring in the home of Cornelius through Peter in Acts 10, in which Pentecost occurs again, engrafting the Gentiles into the kingdom of God. The fire falls again in the one-man Pentecost in which Paul was filled with the Holy Spirit in Acts 9, and again with the outpouring in Ephesus in Acts 19 when the Holy Spirit fell upon twelve men. These are not random or accidental events; they are the intentional working out of God's master plan for advancing the gospel, a plan which is revealed in Acts 1:8: "You will receive power when the Holy Spirit has come upon you, and you will be my witnesses in Jerusalem, and in all Judea and Samaria, and to the farthest parts of the earth."

This naming of different geographical locations—Jerusalem, Judea, Samaria, farthest parts of the earth—represents the beginning points of successive waves of the Holy Spirit's work of advancing the kingdom of God. Each starting point was marked by the event of the fire of the Holy Spirit falling. The fact that they are described for us in the book of Acts confirms their strategic importance within God the Father's master plan for advancing the gospel to the ends of the earth. They are important because they reveal God's method. This method is essentially, again and again, fulfilling the promise of Acts 1:4-8, repeating with different groups of people in different locations the igniting events described at Pentecost, and in Samaria, in the home of Cornelius, and in Ephesus. It is important to note that what is described are actual events that took place. While there may be the preaching of the gospel or teaching of biblical truth, these biblical passages are describing actual historical events that have been objectively observed to have taken place and are starting points in the advancement of the kingdom of God on earth. They each have resulted in a group of born-again Christians being able to step into and live the seven aspects of the "by My Spirit lifestyle" which resulted in the advancement of the gospel of the kingdom of God.

## Why Start with the Beginning Points of Revival?

I believe that the Holy Spirit has given us the model or paradigm for these igniting events. He shows us how we are to take part with Him in His mission of redeeming humanity and completing the restoration of all creation. Therefore, the focus of this book will be on these igniting events when the fire first falls. This will be our focus for five reasons:

First: We are in a season when the Lord is moving again where this igniting work is necessary for the advancement of God's kingdom plans. We are in a period parallel to that of the opening chapters of Acts with the launching of the great waves of the Holy Spirit which reached from Jerusalem to Rome. Our present epoch is also comparable to what many of us in frontlines of anointed leadership experienced firsthand when the fire of the Holy Spirit fell in the 60s in the Charismatic Renewal, in the 1980s in the Vineyard movement, or in the 1990s in PRMI's own stream of launching the Dunamis Project. Going even further back beyond our recent memory, but vividly recorded in history, is the evidence that our epoch is similar to the time when the igniting work of the Holy Spirit proceeded the First and Second Great Awakenings. Or again, we are at a period similar to 1890-1910 when D.L. Moody and R.A. Torrey were called to ignite outpourings of the Holy Spirit which resulted in worldwide revivals. We are at a time which is a kairos moment of great opportunity, when our Lord Jesus Christ is calling us to take decisive actions which He will use to fulfill our prayers of, "Thy kingdom come, thy will be done on earth just as it is in heaven."

The present parallels to other eras when God was on the move are found in the manifestations of the Holy Spirit—people being saved, churches growing, signs and wonders manifesting the kingship of Jesus

Christ, but also in the manifestations of the antichrist who always opposes the moves of God. We now see multiple demonic strongholds centered in different locations around the globe are growing in demonic power and are coupled with the political, economic, cultural, and military means to oppose the advance of the gospel of the kingdom on earth. The pervasive influence of powerful demonic strongholds (along with the emergence of the occult) are bringing anti-God, totalitarian ideologies, and inflaming demonic strongholds that are similar to their 1930s counterparts. Their inexorable rise will again breed global tyranny, destruction, and genocide, starting with the Jews but including Christians, but this time it will be unfathomably more devastating.

So, the first reason for focusing on igniting outpourings of the Holy Spirit which may become revivals, is not only that the need is desperate, but it is in fact what God is doing! Born of desperation and no doubt in answer to the faithful prayers of many for decades, we are now faced with an extraordinary moment of opportunity— a kairos moment for the greatest revival of all times—a moment that, if we miss, will be catastrophic, not just for the kingdom of God but for all humanity.

Second: There have been numerous prophecies (many of which have already been fulfilled) going back for decades, some even for centuries, that God is going to send another great outpouring of the Holy Spirit. For instance, there is the remarkable 1947 prophecy by the famous Yorkshire plumber Smith Wigglesworth. This prophecy given shortly before he passed away is so important that I want to include it in its entirety. This was profoundly significant for the role of Presbyterian Reformed Ministries (PRMI). His focus is the United Kingdom which he foresees as a starting point for the rest of the world.

"During the next few decades there will be two distinct moves of the Holy Spirit across the Church in Great Britain. The first move will affect every church that is open to receive it and will be characterized by the restoration of the baptism and gifts of the Holy Spirit.

9

"The second move of the Holy Spirit will result in people leaving historic churches and planting new churches. In the duration of each of these moves, the people who are involved will say, 'This is a great revival.' But the Lord says, 'No, neither is this the great revival, but both are steps towards it.'

"When the new church phase is on the wane, there will be evidence in the churches of something that has not been seen before: a coming together of those with an emphasis on the Word and those with an emphasis on the Spirit.

"When the Word and the Spirit come together, there will be the biggest move of the Holy Spirit that the nations, and indeed, the world have ever seen. It will mark the beginning of a revival that will eclipse anything that has been witnessed within these shores, even the Wesleyan and Welsh revivals of former years.

"The outpouring of God's Spirit will flow over from the United Kingdom to mainland Europe, and from there, will begin a missionary move to the ends of the earth."[6]

Aspects of this prophecy have already been fulfilled with the outpouring of the Holy Spirit in the Charismatic renewal, the Word of Faith movement, the Vineyard movement and so forth. However, it is the last word, the merging of those streams that emphasize the Word (i.e., the Presbyterian and Reformed) and those that emphasize the Holy Spirit (i.e., the Charismatic and Pentecostal) that signals the beginning of the greatest revival of all time.

In recent decades, prophecies about a coming great revival have been given to many in diverse streams of the Christian as well as the Messianic Jewish movement. We have also received similar prophecies given to us in the Presbyterian and Reformed stream, one of which was given by Douglas McMurry in 2019 that, "God has prepared PRMI to be a key player in the Third Great Awakening." This has taken place through our Dunamis Project Equipping

---

[6] https://byfaith.org/2021/11/22/smith-wigglesworths-revival-prophecy/

process which connects the Word and Spirit. PRMI is also directly connected to the Smith Wigglesworth prophecy through active branches in in the United States, Canada, and the United Kingdom. These branches are mutually sharing in igniting and sustaining these global moves of the Holy Spirit.[7]

There are many indicators that we are indeed seeing the beginning of the fulfillment of these prophecies combining Word and Spirit in the very hopeful outpourings that we are already experiencing. The fulfillment of all these prophecies of a great revival leading to a great awakening all depends on the initial igniting of Pentecost-like events. This is why we shall be honing our focus on these events.

Third: There is however another reason why we must focus on the initial igniting events. It has to do with the nature of contemporary prophecy. Such prophecies, like the ones given by Smith Wigglesworth or Doug McMurry, are not a replacement of the Bible, nor necessarily a prediction of the future, but rather God's invitation for us to join Him in accomplishing His purposes on earth in our own time and place. While Holy Spirit fire falling upon the earth is a sovereign act of God the Father, Jesus calls us, His friends and co-workers, to have an essential role in cooperating with Him to prepare the way for Him to pour out the fire of the Holy Spirit. In the following chapters, we will be providing practical guidance for our role in this dynamic dance of cooperation with the Father, Son, and Holy Spirit in this work of igniting outpourings of the Holy Spirit. There are key principles that we can learn from the book of Acts and other periods when God was doing His igniting work. The Holy Spirit is calling us to put in place these key principles today. These principles provide our human part in cooperating with God the Father, Son, and Holy Spirit in preparing for, then igniting,

---

[7] For PRMI's connection with the British Isles please see the web page for The Dunamis Fellowship in Britain & Ireland (DFB&I) https://www.dunamis.org.uk/

and then sustaining these moves of the Holy Spirit. This is how these prophetic words will indeed be fulfilled.

Fourth: Igniting outpourings of the Holy Spirit is the essential key to the Church of Jesus Christ continuing to be alive and faithful to its mission. Without new infusions of life and power coming from this igniting work of the Holy Spirit, bringing the living presence of God and empowerment to witness to Jesus Christ, the church either calcifies into lifeless orthodoxy and/or legalism, or she falls into apostasy from biblical faith. Most often the "by My Spirit" lifestyle is lost, and the people of God are deceived into trusting "power and might" approaches to fulfilling God's mission mandates. Either way the Church ceases to be the embodiment of the kingdom of God on earth and the means for God to accomplish His redemptive purposes. So, preparing for such igniting events is the urgent and necessary work of our present time.

Fifth: Participating with God's plans of igniting outpourings of the Holy Spirit is not the calling for everyone. The ongoing work of growing the Church in the power of the Holy Spirit, making and nurturing disciples of Jesus Christ, providing pastoral care, teaching, and taking part in fulfilling the missions mandate must continue to move forward, but I do believe that Jesus is calling into this initiatory, igniting work those in the apostolic, prophetic, and evangelistic offices as well as those called to strategic intercession and spiritual warfare. These offices and roles in the Body of Christ have always been the vanguard of the advancement and expansion of the kingdom of God on earth and the fulfillment of the Great Commission of making disciples of Jesus Christ from all nations. This continued advancement of the gospel and the continued vitality of the Church of Jesus Christ depends on the ongoing fulfillment of Acts 1:4-8 in new Pentecosts for each new area, each generation, and indeed for each person who is born again.

## The Biblical Keys to Igniting Outpourings of the Holy Spirit

Having limited our focus to igniting outpourings of the Holy Spirit leads us to the next practical and urgent question: How is God the Father calling us, His friends and co-workers, practically to cooperate with Him in preparing for and taking part in this igniting work?

Is this not the urgent question of our times? We yearn for true biblical revival to take place. We are expectant that God is on the move bringing a great awakening that could complete the Great Commission and usher in the return of our Lord Jesus in glory. We are immensely encouraged by the history of past outpourings of the Holy Spirit and the resulting global revivals. We are sure that God is about to do it again!

We also must confront the rise of demonic evil in the world, in our own nations, and even in the Church of Jesus Christ. We know that there truly is no hope of reversing these pernicious trends toward evil and a catastrophe in the geopolitical realm except for a great awakening, but how does this happen? The short answer, at least from my Presbyterian and Reformed as well as biblical perspective, is that all things flow from God the Father who is creator and Lord over all. Outpourings of the Holy Spirit come out of His sovereign will. However, we do have a role! We believe that role has been revealed to us in the Bible, especially in the book of Acts. It has also been revealed through the history of two thousand years of outpourings of the Holy Spirit which have manifested and advanced God's kingdom on earth. We will introduce several biblical and historical patterns that are both the preparation for, as well as the result of, igniting outpourings of the Holy Spirit.

The application of these keys and foundations is not some new program that we implement and—presto!—it will happen accordingly. Nor is this like a baking recipe where you measure out the right amounts of various ingredients, mix them together, put them in the oven for just the right amount of time at the right heat and then out comes your perfectly baked cake. No! The essence of igniting outpourings of the Holy Spirit centers on cooperating with the Father, Son, and Holy Spirit in a loving, living relationship. We are in a dynamic dance with each of the three Persons of the Holy Trinity as well as with Jesus' friends and co-workers. These biblical patterns which we will be presenting are the dance steps that the Lord is calling us to take with Him in what could be the last great dance of the End Times.

In summary, the purpose of this book will be to prepare us as individual disciples of Jesus Christ, congregations, and mission groups, to play our part by cooperating with the Holy Spirit as Jesus' friends and co-workers, igniting outpourings of the Holy Spirit. These outpourings, if we are faithful in following the "by My Spirit" way of taking part in the Father's master plans, which is making disciples of all nations, have the potential to result in the greatest revival of all times, bringing the completion of the Great Commission in the power of the Holy Spirit and the "restoration of all things" in Jesus Christ.

In the next chapter we must make sure that we are completely grounded in Jesus Christ, who has received all authority in heaven and on earth and has poured out the Holy Spirit so that we may be empowered to take part in fulfilling the Great Commission of making disciples of all nations.

# 2

# King Jesus Receiving All Authority

Jesus Christ sending waves of revival (His master strategy for accomplishing His mission of restoring all things) depended upon Him entering His kingdom and receiving all authority in heaven and on earth.

In this chapter, let us ponder the event of Jesus' coronation and its staggering implications not just for our own eternal salvation but for the destinies of the nations and the entire creation. To help us conceive what is frankly humanly inconceivable, let us follow Jesus' own words as He reveals to His disciples His plans.

In Matthew 16 Jesus provided a series of prophecies that laid out the plan that God the Father had chosen for Him to accomplish — the mission of redeeming humanity which culminated in His coronation as King of Kings.

> From that time on Jesus began to show his disciples that he must go to Jerusalem and suffer many things at the hands of the elders, chief priests, and experts in the law, and be killed, and on the third day be raised. (Matt. 16:21)

This revelation that Jesus will be killed and the unbelievable promise that He will be raised from the dead was so distressing to His disciples that Peter in deep love and concern took Jesus aside privately and said, "This must not happen to you!" This earned Peter a stern rebuke from Jesus:

> But he turned and said to Peter, "Get behind me, Satan! You are a stumbling block to me, because you are not setting your mind on God's interests, but on man's."  Matt. 16:23

After giving some more teaching on both the radical cost and the blessings of discipleship, Jesus gives another startling prophecy predicting His imminent ascension which would mean stepping into His kingdom.

> The Son of Man will come with his angels in the glory of his Father, and then he will reward each person according to what he has done. I tell you the truth, **there are some standing here who will not experience death before they see the Son of Man coming in his kingdom**. Matt. 16:27-28 (bold is mine)

When was this extraordinary event of the Son of Man coming into His kingdom to take place? There are different interpretations of these verses. In seminary we learned that this was one of those end-times prophecies related to the second coming and that Jesus sort of got the timing wrong. Others see that there were really three different time frames contained in this prophecy. The first is verse 27 which does indeed seem to relate to the second coming, but then what about verse 28? One very feasible interpretation is that this refers to the transfiguration, which is recorded in the next verses, which is a prefiguring of Son of Man coming into his kingdom. There, Peter, James, and John actually saw Jesus in the glory of the Father. Another interpretation, the one I favor consistent with Jesus' promise that "some would not experience death before they saw the Son of Man coming into his kingdom," is the third time frame which I believe took place at His ascension which led to His coronation. They did not actually see this event because Jesus was obscured by the clouds of heaven, but they would have understood from the prophecy by Daniel, which we will look at shortly.[8]

To His disciples with their understanding of Jewish prophecies, His use of the term, "Son of Man" was laden with End Times meaning and anticipation. He had previously applied the term to Himself on numerous occasions (Luke 9:18-22). They knew from the Hebrew prophets, whose promises of the coming Messiah burned in them, the astonishing claims that Jesus was making about Himself. He was the long yearned for Messiah! They fully anticipated that they would see this great event of the Messiah coming into His kingdom.

They were not disappointed! After telling them not to leave Jerusalem until they were clothed with power from on high, and giving the promise that they would be baptized with the Holy Spirit (Luke 24:49, Acts 1:4-8), the Ascension event took place.

> After he had said this, while they were watching, he was lifted up and a cloud hid him from their sight. As they were still staring into the sky while he was going, suddenly two men in white clothing stood near them and said, "Men of Galilee, why do you stand here looking up into the sky? This same Jesus who has been taken up from you into heaven will come back in the same way you saw him go into heaven. Acts 1:9 -11

---

[8] Mark 9:1 And he said to them, "I tell you the truth, there are some standing here who will not experience death before they see the **Kingdom of God come with power**." Some have suggested this verse is referring to the outpouring of the Holy Spirit at Pentecost when the Kingdom of Jesus Christ on earth was manifested in power. John Calvin, in his commentary on Matthew 16:28 affirms this, **"**Coming in his kingdom. By the coming of the Kingdom of God we are to understand the manifestation of heavenly glory, which Christ began to make at his resurrection, and which he afterwards made more fully by sending the Holy Spirit, and by the performance of miracles; for by those beginnings he gave his people a taste of the newness of the heavenly life, when they perceived, by certain and undoubted proofs, that he was sitting at the right hand of the Father." https://www.bibliaplus.org/en/commentaries/3/john-calvins-bible-commentary/matthew/16/28

But what happened when Jesus arrived in heaven? He was established as King! However, although the disciples could not see what happened at Jesus' arrival in heaven, they knew what took place because they were familiar with Daniel's prophecies. In the book of Daniel, we find a prophecy of the coming of a King who would rule over an eternal kingdom.

> In the days of those kings the God of heaven will raise up an everlasting kingdom that will not be destroyed and a kingdom that will not be left to another people. It will break in pieces and bring about the demise of all these kingdoms. But it will stand forever. Dan. 2:44

Now when would this everlasting kingdom be established on earth? McMurry adds the following profound observation of when this would happen, which corresponds to the time of the birth of Jesus:

"Through the prophet Daniel He prophesized the next four empires that were about to happen in world history after the sixth century BC. Then, he added, after those four empires will have come and gone (count them Babylonian, Medo-Persian, Greek, Roman), He would send a 'king whose kingdom will crush all other kingdoms and bring them to an end, but it will itself endure forever' (Daniel 2:44). He insists on the word kingdom specifically by prophesying four world empires which it will replace. And his thinking is amazingly consistent throughout the Bible: A king."

Later Daniel gives the vision of the coronation of the King of Kings—the "Son of Man," which is a prophetic glimpse of what happened at the ascension when the disciples lost sight of Jesus because He was covered by a cloud. Let's take a sudden shift of perspective from the disciples' view from earth to the perspective of heaven when Jesus arrived on the clouds. Read these full verses because they are so amazing! Ask the Lord to take you into these realities which establish Jesus as King.

> "I was watching in the night visions. Behold, One like a Son of Man, coming with the clouds of heaven. He approached the Ancient of Days and was brought into His presence. Dominion, glory, and sovereignty were given to Him that all peoples, nations, and languages should serve Him. His dominion is an everlasting dominion that will never pass away, and His kingdom is one that will not be destroyed. Dan. 7:13-14 TLV

The cloud that obscured Jesus from the disciples' view must not have been an ordinary cloud but the "clouds of heaven," an irradiation of God's glorious presence carrying Jesus into this ultimate reality of the third heaven.

Let's take one more shift of perspective to that of John on Patmos, caught up into the heavens in Rev 5:11-13. Here he observed the coronation prophesied in Daniel 7:13-14 actually taking place. This event so transcended anything that the human mind could grasp that it was given to John in a mystical vision and through symbols.

After the vision of the scroll sealed with seven seals that no one could open, Jesus Christ, who was crucified and raised from the dead, arrives in heaven in the image of the "Lamb who was slain." Here was the greeting of the resurrected Jesus Christ as He arrived in heaven and was then crowned, "the blessed and only Sovereign, the King of kings and Lord of lords."[9]

> "Then I looked and heard the voice of many angels in a circle around the throne, as well as the living creatures and the

---

[9] 1Tim. 6:15 -16 ". . . whose appearing the blessed and only Sovereign, the King of kings and Lord of lords, will reveal at the right time. He alone possesses immortality and lives in unapproachable light, whom no human has ever seen or is able to see. To him be honor and eternal power! Amen."

elders. Their number was ten thousand times ten thousand—thousands times thousands—all of whom were singing in a loud voice: "Worthy is the lamb who was killed to receive power and wealth and wisdom and might and honor and glory and praise!

Then I heard every creature—in heaven, on earth, under the earth, in the sea, and all that is in them—singing: "To the one seated on the throne and to the Lamb be praise, honor, glory, and ruling power forever and ever! And the four living creatures were saying 'Amen,' and the elders threw themselves to the ground and worshiped." Rev. 5:11-13

This is the coronation of Jesus as the King of the kingdom. This is when Jesus, the Son of Man, came in His kingdom and was given all authority in heaven and on earth. According to what Daniel saw, "To him was given ruling authority, honor, and sovereignty. All peoples, nations, and language groups were serving him. His authority is eternal and will not pass away. His kingdom will not be destroyed."

The ascension followed by the coronation, is the fulfillment of Jesus' prophetic word that those disciples standing there with Him would still be alive, when they would, "see the Son of Man coming in his kingdom" (Mattew 16:28). Judas Iscariot was the one disciple who had tasted death, and so was not present when Jesus came into His kingdom.

## All Authority in Heaven and on Earth

Ponder for a moment this authority which will be the basis for Jesus pouring out the Holy Spirit on earth to advance His kingdom. Meditate upon the vast extent of Jesus' authority before moving to the practical application. Make Paul's prayer for the Ephesians your own!

I pray that the God of our Lord Jesus Christ, the glorious Father, will give you spiritual wisdom and revelation in your growing knowledge of him—since the eyes of your heart have been enlightened—so that you can know what is the hope of his calling, what is the wealth of his glorious inheritance in the saints, and what is the incomparable greatness of his power toward us who believe, as displayed in the exercise of his immense strength. This power he exercised in Christ when he raised him from the dead and seated him at his right hand in the heavenly realms far above every rule and authority and power and dominion and every name that is named, not only in this age but also in the one to come. And God put all things under Christ's feet and gave him to the church as head over all things. Now the church is his body, the fullness of him who fills all in all. Eph. 1:17-23

Where do you suppose Paul got glimpses of the supremacy and majesty of King Jesus Christ after His coronation? While certainly they are Holy Spirit inspired majestic poetry depicting spiritual realities, I believe they are based on actual firsthand eyewitness encounters that took place when Paul was caught up into the third heaven. Recall that the Damascus Road encounter took place after Jesus' was crowned as King. Paul is reporting what he personally saw and experienced!

Just as Paul needed to have a firsthand encounter with King Jesus before he could receive his humanly impossible mandate of being Jesus' "chosen instrument to carry my name before Gentiles and kings and the people of Israel," (Acts 9:15) so too we also need to grow in an intimate relationship with Jesus Christ and be fully grounded on the reality that all authority in heaven and on Earth has been given to Him as King of the universe.

I must share a personal note as to how these verses came alive for me, becoming the basis for both having faith that Jesus Christ really was raised from the dead, and that He is truly King of the universe. For years I had prayed, "Lord, show me who you really are! Lord, show me yourself!" My mentor Archer Torrey also prayed for me for several years that I would have a very direct encounter with Jesus Christ in His total glory and majesty as the one who received all authority in Heaven and Earth as the basis for the mission that I had been given. He prayed that I would be caught up into the presence of God at the center of the universe as Paul was when he was caught up into the Third Heaven. Archer's prayer was that I would be able to see the same visions through direct encounter. This happened to me twice! I was caught up into what must have been the Third Heaven where I had a face-to-face encounter which profoundly changed me. There I experienced the reality of God the Father, Son, and Holy Spirit and the Heavenly City, the River of Life, and received from King Jesus the calling and mandate to take part in advancing the kingdom of God in the power of the Holy Spirit that I have been seeking and following with all my mind and heart over these years. This gave me the basis of experiential faith which confirmed the revelations of the Word of God, to trust completely in Jesus' authority and to be able to step out in faith and obedience to the Lord's calling again and again. I believe that the Holy Spirit's work is to give each of us who are called, a confirmation of Jesus having received all authority in heaven and earth, which will be the steadfast basis for each of us saying yes to King Jesus' invitation to take part in this great outpouring of the Holy Spirit which has the potential to complete the Great Commission.

## Jesus' Kingship Includes Both the Redeemed and the Unredeemed—The Church and Society

Jesus himself said, "All authority in heaven and on earth has been given to Me," (Matt. 28:18). To grasp the vast extent of what this may practically look like, the great Dutch Reformed statesman and theologian Abraham Kuyper stated, "There is not a square inch in the whole domain of our human existence over which Christ, who is Sovereign over all, does not cry, 'Mine!'"[10]

Kuyper stated what Danial predicted of the Son of Man. "Dominion, glory and sovereignty were given to Him that all peoples, nations, and languages should serve Him. His dominion is an everlasting dominion that will never pass away, and His kingdom is one that will not be destroyed (Dan. 7:13-14 TLV). But how practically does Jesus Christ express this Kingship over all dimensions of human reality? Much depends on having a clear, biblical answer to this question. I believe that from a Reformed understanding of what the Bible teaches about God's sovereignty and His way of working to bring salvation to fallen humanity, that there are two different means through which Jesus expresses His kingship. These are separate but interconnected.

The first way is revealed on Mount Sinai to the Hebrews just freed from Egyptian bondage. God (Adonai) made a covenant with them through the Law revealed to Moses.

> "Look! I have set before you today life and prosperity on the one hand, and death and disaster on the other. What I am commanding you today is to love the LORD your God, to walk in his ways, and to obey his commandments, his statutes, and his ordinances. Then you will live and become numerous and the LORD your God will bless you in the land which you are about to possess. Deut. 30:15-16

Through the covenant people of Israel, God's kingdom overcame the power of death and brought a way of life embodied on earth.

---

[10] Abraham Kuyper, *Sphere Sovereignty,* qtd. in *Abraham Kuyper, A Centennial Reader,* ed. James D. Bratt (Grand Rapids, MI: Eerdmans, 1998), 488. For further commentary on this affirmation, see *Kuyper's Inch* by Roger Henderson. https://digitalcollections.dordt.edu/cgi/viewcontent.cgi?article=1380&context=pro_rege

This way of life and blessing is fulfilled in the coming of the Messiah, Yeshua, Jesus Christ, that through faith in His Name salvation is extended to all people. Now, after the coming of Yeshua, God's presence and kingdom on earth is expressed through the fellowship of those who have been born-again through faith in Yeshua as the Messiah and have entered God's eternal kingdom.

In this book we shall be focused on how King Jesus is working within the fellowship of those who have been born-again and empowered by the Holy Spirit, igniting outpourings of the Holy Spirit, God's chosen method of advancing His kingdom.

However, we cannot do that without acknowledging that there is another entire sphere in which Jesus' kingship is being expressed. Neither King Jesus' sovereign rule nor His love stop at the borders of the fellowship of those who have been born-again. It extends to all creation, and all created in God's image who are not yet born-again into the everlasting kingdom. All through the Bible we find that God's sovereign rule is not just over the covenant people of Israel but over all nations and over all peoples.

> All you nations, clap your hands! Shout out to God in celebration! For the sovereign LORD [Adonai Elyon] is awe-inspiring; he is the great king who rules the whole earth! He subdued nations beneath us and countries under our feet. Ps. 47:1-3

This universality of King Jesus' rule is affirmed also in the New Testament. Consider, for example, the words of Paul: "Let every person submit himself to the governing authorities. For there is no authority except from God, and those that exist are put in place by God," (Romans 13:1 TLV). Recall that Paul is speaking of a Roman government which was not at all redeemed. So how was Jesus' kingship expressed outside of the redeemed? The answer from our Reformed perspective is that the Kingship of Jesus is expressed through God the Father's universal law written in the Ten

Commandments and written within the human conscience.[11] On this basis, systems of philosophy, morality, social systems, political systems, judicial and governmental structures have been formed. When these are in the service of God's kingdom and consistent with His natural law, they constrain both demonic and human evil and provide for the flourishing of human life. Jesus' love and kingship extending to all people and including all people is summed up in His command to us:

> "You have heard that it was said, 'You shall love your neighbor and hate your enemy.' But I tell you, love your enemies and pray for those who persecute you, so that you may be children of your Father in heaven. He causes His sun to rise on the evil and the good, and sends rain on the righteous and the unrighteous. Matthew 5:43-45, TLV

These spheres of government, society, and politics are all part of the "human domain" and included in the "every square inch" over which Jesus Christ exerts His kingly rule. When we pray, "Thy kingdom come, Thy will be done," we are asking Jesus to impact both the Church and the world in accord with His kingdom. All are included under the Kingship of Jesus Christ, and all are included in the master strategy chosen by God the Father for fulfilling His redemptive plans for fallen humanity. From the Day of Pentecost until the End Times, Jesus has sent, and is sending, waves of the Holy Spirit which manifest the Kingship of Jesus, first among the redeemed in the Church of Jesus Christ, but then reaching out to include all dimension of human life. This is the reason why all true

---

[11]Romans 2:14-16 For whenever the Gentiles, who do not have the law, do by nature the things required by the law, these who do not have the law are a law to themselves. They show that the work of the law is written in their hearts, as their conscience bears witness and their conflicting thoughts accuse or else defend them, on the day when God will judge the secrets of human hearts, according to my gospel through Christ Jesus.

revivals will ignite the Church of Jesus Christ and transform society and the nations bringing them into alignment with God's kingdom values and reality.

This is how every revival which has become a great awakening has not only ignited the church in biblical faith and brought a "by My Spirit" lifestyle but has also transformed human society to overcome the structures of evil and come into alignment with biblical kingdom values. Review the history of the social and political impact of great awakenings for this. It was the First Great Awakening which paved the way for the American Revolution and the birthing of a democratic republic, a government based on biblical Judeo-Christian values which constrains tyranny and optimizes human freedom. This great move of God also led first to the abolition of the slave trade in the British Empire, and later to the abolition of the millennials-old evil institution of slavery worldwide. (At least everywhere except in those areas still under the sway of the demonic strongholds of theocratic Islam and godless totalitarian ideologies of Marxism.)

We shall fully explore in another volume how Jesus as King sending revivals which may become great awakenings impacts and transforms the nations, but here our focus is on igniting outpourings of the Holy Spirit which is the beginning of all kingdom-advancing, world-transforming revivals.

In this next chapter we review how King Jesus, having received all authority in heaven and on earth, makes two decrees to launch His kingdom providing a way of redemption for fallen humanity.

# 3

# King Jesus Advancing His Kingdom to All Nations

Receiving "all authority" (Matthew 28:18) describes a state of being or an office that Jesus Christ now occupies as King of Kings. This rule and authority must be activated and expressed in actions.

Two commands embodying Jesus' plans are directly related to understanding the role of igniting outpourings of the Holy Spirit in the Father's master strategy. Jesus wants us to know about this and play a strategic role in accomplishing it.

Jesus gives these two commands before His official coronation and in anticipation of receiving all authority, apparently so that He could deliver these commands to his beloved disciples while still face-to-face. I think those first disciples and all of us who have come after them needed to hear these words directly from the mouth of the resurrected Jesus Himself. The first decree is giving all who are born-again into the kingdom of God our mission: we are to be His witnesses and to make disciples of all nations. The second decree, which is coupled with the first, provides the **means** to accomplish this mission—not in human power and might, but by the Holy Spirit.

Jesus considered these two decrees so essential for launching His kingdom on earth that He repeated them on several occasions. Each iteration has nuances of meaning and application that when considered as a whole present the mission of redeeming humanity, defeating Satan's empire of evil, manifesting God's kingdom on earth, and leading to the restoration of all things in a new heaven and a new earth. All this will take place through King Jesus who has received all authority in heaven and earth.

Along with the commission goes the promise of the authority and empowerment to accomplish this work. This is essentially the same empowerment that Jesus received when the Holy Spirit came upon Him when He was baptized by John the Baptist. This is the same preparation from the Holy Spirit empowering the Old Testament prophets, kings, and judges. Jesus summarizes this empowerment with the words that we would be baptized with the Holy Spirit (or in the Jewish version, immersed with the Holy Spirit.) This is described in Acts 1:4-5 and then further defined in Acts 1:8 as "you shall receive power when the Holy Spirit has come upon you, and you will be my witnesses..."  This is so that we may fulfill God's work, NOT by human "power and might," but, "by My Spirit!"

Here are the verses of these combined decrees. We need to hear them from the Jewish Messianic version as they depict aspects that are often missed with other versions of the Bible. The commission is in bold black, and the promise of empowerment and authority to carry out the commission is in italics and underlined.

Now the eleven disciples went to the Galilee, to the mountain Yeshua had designated. When they saw Him, they worshipped; but some wavered. And Yeshua came up to them and spoke to them, saying, **"All authority in heaven and on earth has been given to Me. Go therefore and make disciples of all nations, immersing [baptizing] them in the name of the Father and the Son and the Ruach ha-Kodesh [Holy Spirit], teaching them to observe all I have commanded you. And remember!** *I am with you always, even to the end of the age.*" Mat 28:16-20 TLV

Later He appeared to them, the eleven, as they were reclining at the table. He rebuked them for their unbelief and hardheartedness because they did not believe those who had seen Him after He had been raised. He told them,

"Go into all the world and proclaim the Good News to every creature. He who believes and is immersed [baptized] shall be saved, but he who does not believe shall be condemned. *These signs will accompany those who believe: in My name they will drive out demons; they will speak new languages; they will handle snakes; and if they drink anything deadly, it will not harm them; they will lay hands on the sick, and they will get well*." Mk. 16:14-18 TLV. This is also confirmed in Luke 10:19.

Then He said to them, "These are My words which I spoke to you while I was still with you—everything written concerning Me in the Torah of Moses and the Prophets and the Psalms must be fulfilled. Then He opened their minds to understand the Scriptures, and He said to them, "**So it is written, that the Messiah [Christ] is to suffer and to rise from the dead on the third day, and that repentance for the removal of sins is to be proclaimed in His name to all nations, beginning from Jerusalem. You are witnesses of these things.** And behold, I am *sending the promise of My Father upon you; but you are to stay in the city until you are clothed with power from on high."* Luke 24:44-49 TLV

It was evening on that day, the first of the week. When the doors were locked where the disciples were, for fear of the Judean leaders, Yeshua came and stood in their midst! And He said to them, "Shalom aleichem!" ["peace be upon you"] After He said this, He showed them His hands and His side. Then the disciples rejoiced when they saw the Lord. Yeshua said to them again, "Shalom aleichem! **As the Father has sent Me, I also send you.**" And after He said this**,** *He breathed on them. And He said to them, "Receive the Ruach ha-Kodesh! [Holy Spirit] If you forgive anyone's sins, they are forgiven; but if you hold back, they are held back."* John 20:19-23

Now while staying with them, He commanded them not to leave Jerusalem, but to wait for what the Father promised— which, He said, "you heard from Me. *For John immersed [baptized] with water, but you will be immersed in the Ruach ha-Kodesh [Holy Spirit] not many days from now."* So when they gathered together, they asked Him, "Lord, are You restoring the kingdom to Israel at this time?" He said to them, "It is not your place to know the times or seasons which the Father has placed under His own control. ***But you will receive power when the Ruach ha-Kodesh [Holy Spirit] has come upon you; and you will be My witnesses in Jerusalem, and through all Judah, and Samaria, and to the end of the earth."*** Acts 1:4-8

This connection with fulfilling the mission of God in the power of the Spirit of God is consistent with God's method all through the Bible when He calls people to take part in His work on earth. There is only one way to work with God, and that is on His terms and not on ours. God clearly established this foundation over 2500 years ago in His prophetic words spoken through the prophet Zechariah speaking to Zerubbabel the Governor of Judea after the return of the exiles from Babylon.

The angelic messenger who had been speaking with me then returned and woke me, as a person is wakened from sleep. He asked me, "What do you see?" I replied, "I see a menorah of pure gold with a receptacle at the top. There are seven lamps at the top, with seven pipes going to the lamps. There are also two olive trees beside it, one on the right of the receptacle and the other on the left." Then I asked the messenger who spoke with me, "What are these, sir?" He replied, "Don't you know what these are?" So I responded, "No, sir." Therefore he told me, "This is the LORD's message to Zerubbabel: 'Not by strength and not by power, ***but by my Spirit***,' says the LORD of Heaven's Armies." Zech. 4:1-6

While spoken to Zerubbabel, facing the daunting challenges of returning from the 70-year exile and beginning the building of the temple in 536 B.C. (Ezra 2:2; Neh. 7:7; 12:1), these words are a mandate given to all who would take part in building God's kingdom. Advancing God's kingdom can only be done in the power and by the direction of the Holy Spirit, not by our own human power and might.

This is why the mission mandate to take part in building the kingdom is always matched by God's provision of the equipping empowerment of the Holy Spirit and the abiding presence and authority of Jesus Christ.

## Acts 1:4-8 The Two Streams of the Holy Spirit Advancing God's Kingdom Vision

Embedded in Acts 1:4-8 is a profound revelation of God the Father's strategic plan for our redemption. The first concerns God's chosen people, the Jews, which in the Zechariah's vision are symbolized by one olive tree. The second part of God's redemptive plan includes the non-Jewish peoples, the Gentiles, the "wild olive tree" whom God the Father through Jesus Christ is engrafting into His original covenant people, the Jews (Rom 11:17). Both great streams are fulfilled by the power of the Holy Spirit poured out at Pentecost in Jerusalem.[12]

### The Jewish Stream – Restoring the Kingdom to Israel

So when they had gathered together, they began to ask him, "Lord, is this the time when you are restoring the kingdom to Israel?" He told them, "You are not permitted to know the times or periods that the Father has set by his own authority." Acts 1:6 –7

---

[12] To learn more about the reconnection between Jew and Gentile, check out Reconnecting Ministries and the Romans 911 Project at https://reconnectingministries.org/romans-911/

This is the part that I always used to skip over. I thought those Jewish disciples of Jesus just missed it. They were still thinking that the Jews would return to the Land of Israel and that the City of Jerusalem would be the center of the kingdom when Jesus returned in glory. Then a Presbyterian Jewish believer, Dan Juster, the founder of Tikkun International, pointed out something I had never noticed before. Jesus did not say that the kingdom would NOT be restored to Israel. He just said not yet! And in the meantime, they had the mission of taking the gospel of the Jewish Messiah to the ends of the earth in the power of the Holy Spirit. This shifted my way of understanding in that I realized I had only been seeing this from the Gentile perspective, and not the Jewish perspective. The true biblical vision includes Jew and Gentile. So, I changed my language and added Yeshua to Jesus and Hamashiach or Mashiach to Messiah.[13]

This hope for the kingdom being restored to Israel as part of God's master plan for redemption is confirmed in the sermon that Peter gives the Jewish audience in Acts 3:11-25. This is after the man born lame was healed at the Gate Beautiful. This was all incomprehensible to me as a Gentile Christian. The meaning of this is not obvious until we add to it other verses where the Lord is specifically speaking to the Jewish people:

> Therefore, repent and turn back so that your sins may be wiped out, so that **times of refreshing** may come from the presence of the Lord, and so that he may send the Messiah appointed for you—that is, Jesus. This one heaven must receive until the time **all things are restored**, which God declared from times long ago through his holy prophets. Acts 3:18-21

This points to the new heaven and new earth. But before that final completion and restoration, it will include the fulfillment of all

---

[13] Hamashiach is the Hebrew word for "The Messiah" or "The Anointed One." And so, "Mashiach" is used for Messiah.

the Old Testament promises of the kingdom restored to Israel. There is a mission to fulfill to bring us to that point. This earthly work has two parts or two great intermingled streams:

The first one is for the Jews, the "olive tree" of God's chosen covenant people. This includes the Jews returning to the geographic place promised to them by God through Abraham—the Land of Israel. It most importantly includes receiving Yeshua the Messiah in faith, being born again, and fulfilling God's vision of the "one new humanity" (Eph. 2:14-16). This will also include the restoration of the kingdom to Israel, in that as we approach the End Times, Jerusalem will be called the "throne of Adonai," and the gathering place of all the nations (Jer. 3:17).

## The Non-Jewish Gentile Stream—To the Ends of the Earth

The second great stream of the Holy Spirit which is launched with the fulfillment of Acts 1:4-8 is the Gentiles, which includes all the nations of the world who are the "wild olive branch," grafted into the Jewish trunk through Jesus Christ/Yeshua Mashiach. This great move of God, while starting in Jerusalem with the Jewish people, moved in the Jewish world into Judea, Samaria, and then starting with the Holy Spirit falling upon the Roman Centurion Cornilious in Acts 10-11 moving to the rest of non-Jewish humanity (Romans 11:17).

The non-Jewish believers, the Gentiles, were grafted into God's covenants made with the Jewish people through faith in Jesus Christ. This is the same basis upon which the Jews were joined into the New Covenant—faith in Jesus who provided the way of salvation through His crucifixion, resurrection, ascension, and coronation as King.

In God's vision both Jew and Gentile as distinct but mutually supportive intermingled streams will be working together as the "one new man." This started first in Jerusalem in the first Pentecost among the Jewish believers (Acts 2), and then in Caesarea among the Gentile believers (Acts 10). Both outpourings launched great waves of the Holy Spirit which were God the Father's means of fulfilling His redemptive plans for all humanity. These waves of the Holy Spirit, as they return to Jerusalem where they began, will result in the "restoration of all things" promised in Acts 3:21: "This one heaven must receive until the time all things are restored, which God declared from times long ago through his holy prophets." Restoring all things takes place through the Jews coming to faith in Jesus the Messiah, the kingdom being restored to Israel AND the gospel being preached to all the Gentile nations.

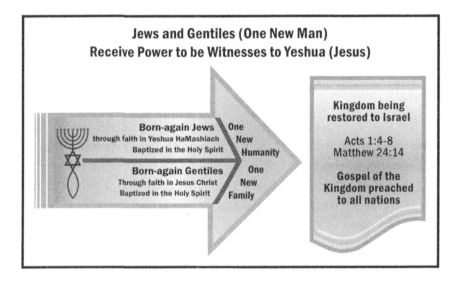

## The End Goal – Accomplished through Sending Waves of the Holy Spirit

In this vast plan of God when the nations are reached with the gospel of Yeshua Mashiach/Jesus Christ AND the Jewish people come to salvation through Yeshua Mashiach/Jesus Christ, we shall see the "restoration of all things" in the return of Jesus Christ! This is affirmed by Yeshua/Jesus himself when he provides the final condition for His return: "This Good News of the kingdom shall be proclaimed in the whole world as a testimony to all the nations, and then the end will come" (Matt. 24:14 TLV). Paul confirms the role of the Jewish people coming to faith in Yeshua the Messiah as a decisive sign of the End Times.

"For if their rejection leads to the reconciliation of the world, what will their acceptance be but life from the dead?" (Romans 11:15 TLV)

And if there is any doubt about the way into the kingdom of God, it is through Jesus Christ alone! And faith in Christ alone!

Jesus replied, "I am the way, and the truth, and the life. No one comes to the Father except through me. John 14:6

And there is salvation in no one else, for there is no other name [Jesus Christ] under heaven given among people by which we must be saved. Acts 4:12

Let us now step out of these vast plans of God and return to the method that He has chosen to implement them. It is through pouring out the Holy Spirit, which means that people are first born-again through faith in Jesus Christ, and then they are baptized with the Holy Spirit and begin to be empowered witnesses of Jesus Christ. This is essentially the fulfillment of Acts 1:4-8. Under certain conditions (which we will be exploring later in this book), these outpourings of the Holy Spirit, in which people are empowered to be witnesses to Jesus Christ, will launch a wave or pulse of the Holy Spirit. Think about the many multiple outpourings of the Holy Spirit described in the book of Acts from the first Pentecost (Acts 2) to when the Samaritans received the Holy Spirit (Acts 8), the Ethiopians in Africa (Acts 8:26-40), and how the outpourings continued grafting in the Gentiles (Acts 10-11).

Each of these igniting events, while all part of the same river of God, formed a wave or pulse of the Holy Spirit which advanced the kingdom of God in a particular area and among different groups of people. This pattern is given to us in Acts 1:8. "....and you will be my witnesses in Jerusalem, and in all Judea and Samaria, and to the farthest parts of the earth."

At the conclusion of the writing of the book of Acts, the farthest part of the earth was Paul's journey to Rome. Now, some two thousand years later, we see this pattern down through the centuries. The empowerment for witness to Jesus and people being brought into His kingdom moves forward in successive outpourings of the Holy Spirit.

## Westward Waves of Holy Spirit Revivals through the Centuries Advancing the Kingdom of God

The great reformed theologian Jonathan Edwards discerned this dynamic of the Lord advancing the kingdom through pulses or waves of the Holy Spirit. Dr. Richard Lovelace[14] an historian of revival offers the following summary of God's master plans revealed in Acts 1:4-8.

---

[14] Richard Lovelace, professor of theology at Gordon Conwell Seminary. He wrote a great book intitled *Dynamics of Spiritual Life*.

"Edwards conceived of the Christian movement as a kind of army of spiritual liberation moving out to free the world from an occupying force of demons that had already been defeated in principle at the Cross. According to Edwards' postmillennial optimism, Christianity is destined to sweep outwards in a series of such pulsations until the whole earth is full of the knowledge and the glory of God, as the waters cover the sea."[15]

We find that in our present epoch, these waves have been moving in a westward direction around the world and are converging back on the city of Jerusalem in fulfillment of the Old and New Testament prophecies of the End Times and the return of Yeshua Mashiach/Jesus Christ.[16]

Now we have a biblical grid to see the big picture of how God has chosen to advance His kingdom down through the ages. It is through outpourings of the Holy Spirit which become western waves or pulses of what are often called revivals. Under certain conditions these moves of the Holy Spirit may become what may be identified as a great awakening in which the body of the church restored to its biblical foundations and empowered to live a kingdom lifestyle makes disciples of Jesus Christ of all nations. Further, in these awakening waves of the Holy Spirit, the kingdom of God advances overturning evil and bringing entire societies and

---

[15] Montgomery, Warwick ed., *Demon Possession* (Minn. MN: Bethany Fellowship Inc., 1976), 87.

[16] The Holy Spirit moving in generally a Westward direction is a description of the history of revivals. For instance, Paul's missionary journeys did not continue to take him to Asia but West to Rome. See my article *The Four Great Waves of the Holy Spirit* Jan 23, 2020 https://www.prmi.org/the-four-great-waves-of-the-holy-spirit/

nations into alignment with God's redemptive plans for all humanity. This vast plan flows from the reality that Yeshua Mashiach/Jesus Christ as King has received all power and authority, and that we take part by being obedient to the King's two great decrees of advancing His kingdom to the far ends of the earth and accomplishing this mission "by His Spirit."

## The Church's Role: Jews and Gentiles in a Circle of Love

However, as these two great steams come together, I must share with the help of our Messianic Jewish partners, and specifically Grant Berry[17] what they have identified as the "Circle of Love," which is an update on the Jerusalem Council of Acts 15. In the first century Jerusalem Council, the Jews who were born-again through faith in Yeshua Hamashiach/Jesus the Messiah welcomed the born-again Gentiles in love. They were called to recognize that they were being engrafted into Israel through faith alone in Jesus Christ. In other words, they did not have to become Jewish as marked by the rite of circumcision. Now two thousand years later, and after seasons of rejection and persecution of the Jews first by the Church of Jesus Christ and later by Islam seeking to replace both Judaism and Christianity, the tables have turned. Christians are now being called through Jesus Christ to love and welcome the Jews back into the family. Grant observes:

> We the Ekklesia, Yeshua's church of born-again Jews and Gentiles have a huge role to play for this new season. We are to partner with God and prophetically proclaim the salvation of Israel. The circle began with the Jews who shared Jesus Christ to the Gentiles, now the Gentiles are to take this gospel back to the Jewish people sharing their Yeshua Mashiah to them such that we will all become one family of

---

[17] Grant Berry, founder of Reconnecting Ministries and author/producer of the Romans 911 Project, https://reconnectingministries.org/romans-911/

God, beloved sons and daughters. This may be called God's circle of love and envisioned as follows:

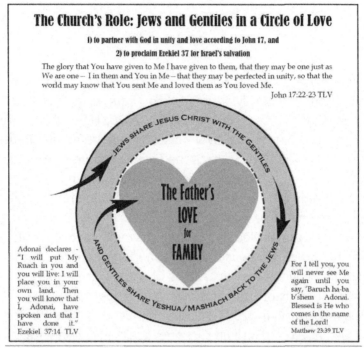

At the beginning of each outpouring that may become a wave, there is always an igniting Pentecost type event that initiates the entire dynamic. These outpourings come from King Jesus and His full authority but require our preparation and participation. Now, in our epoch, fraught with harbingers of the End Times, the combined streams of born-again Jews and Gentiles (the "one new man") that was ignited first in Jerusalem with Jesus' Jewish disciples and then included the Gentiles in the home of Cornelius in Caesarea, is surging back to Jerusalem and in its wake gathering people of all nations, bringing us closer and closer to the fulfillment of the Great Commission.

This is not just a prophetic hope to be fulfilled sometime in the distant future. It is taking place right now on this Pentecost, May 28, 2023, as I am reviewing this chapter! Born-again Jews and Arabs, all citizens of Israel, gathered on the Southern Steps of the Temple Mount. They were joined by representatives from all over the world, including some representing PRMI, to celebrate Pentecost and to pray for a great wave of revival.

## Pentecost Outpouring on the Temple Mount Southern Steps

Grant Berry, the founder of Reconnecting Ministries Intl., attended the PRMI Mountain Top Equipping event at the Community of the Cross on May 8-12, 2023. He and his wife Hali were to take part in a prayer meeting scheduled for Pentecost Sunday on the Southern Steps of the Temple Mount which may have been the site of the first Pentecost. This prayer gathering was to be the culmination of the twenty-one days of fasting for the salvation of Israel that had been called by Mike Bickle, Jason Hubbard, and other global prayer leaders in which millions of people were praying for Israel. This was to be a gathering of the "one new man" brought by Yeshua Mashiach/Jesus Christ toward a ten-year focus to reach the ends of the earth with the gospel to celebrate Jesus' 2000 anniversary in 2023. Gathering at this location on this Pentecost 2023 and praying in one heart and mind for a great outpouring of the Holy Spirit were born-again Jews, Israeli Arab Christians, and representatives of the international church through the prayer and missions' movement.

As we laid hands on Grant and prayed for him, the Lord very clearly told me to give him my yamaka—the precious one that I had

bought on my last visit to the Western Wall. I asked him to please represent us born-again Gentiles who are part of the one new humanity formed in Jesus Christ, and to represent my prayer and commitment to work together to pray in this revival—a revival which will include both great streams, Jews and Gentiles, together in the one new humanity in Yeshua to fulfill the mandate of taking the gospel of the kingdom to all nations.

Grant returned from the event on the Southern Steps with the following testimony:[18]

> "First, really strong WINDS were blowing the night before the event (in Judaism, the day begins after sunset). Then in the light of day during the event a beautiful light RAIN was given. (It hardly ever rains in MAY in Jerusalem, so this was highly unusual. Two DOVES were seen flying over the Southern Steps. And finally, a small PORTAL OF LIGHT appeared in the clouds above the Southern Steps. In addition to these signs in the physical realm, there was the gathering itself. The manner in which all of these meetings in Jerusalem over Pentecost weekend were organized was unprecedented, with so many international prayer and mission organizations coming together in love and unity and partnership with Israeli (Jewish and Arab) leadership—laying down their own ministry foci for the greater call of the Body of Messiah/Christ to unite under the Gospel banner, first to the Jew and then to the nations. This order in the Gospel was reaffirmed and honored by all (see Romans 1:16)."

---

[18] Grant Berry, What Are the Next Steps After the Southern Steps for the Ekklesia/Church and Israel?, https://reconnectingministries.org/southern-steps/

### High Winds, Light Rain, Portal of Light, and Jews and Gentiles Together:   WHAT DOES THIS MEAN?

Grant, who was there, gives the following interpretation:[19]

"I believe that the physical phenomena that we witnessed were signs of great spiritual significance, revealing that what Adonai is doing in this great Holy Spirit outpouring will include the restoration of Jew and Gentile. In the Bible the WIND speaks of power which was poured out at the first Pentecost. The RAIN symbolizes refreshing and restoration of the presence of God. The DOVE is a sign of the descent of the Holy Spirit as well as of Shalom/peace drawing us together into Jesus' love and the intimacy with the Father. Finally, one other sign was given, and that was the very tiny portal of light in the thick clouds above, emphasizing the FIGHT that lies ahead for the Kingdom to come and the great need for an informed repentance throughout His Church.

I believe the tiny portal over Jerusalem is an indication of the intensity of darkness over Israel and the nations and the greater need now for much more prayer, worship, and repentance support to be sent from the nations to

---

[19] Grant Berry, What are the Next Steps After the Southern Steps for the Ekklesia/Church and Israel?, https://reconnectingministries.org/southern-steps/

42

join the body in the land to help clear the skies spiritually over Israel so the greater GLORY can be released.

I (Grant) believe the RESTORATIVE PIECE in the Body of Messiah/Christ opens the doors to a pathway and journey of this love, deference, and cooperation through the reunited Bride that will lead us to the greater power the Father wants to pour out on us to shine His light to a lost and deluded world. There is no replacement for it. All of this was beautifully demonstrated through the Prayer and Mission movements in the Church in the nations connecting with Israeli and Arab leaders in the land. We are experiencing today, through Messiah/Christ Jew and Gentile, and all nations coming together in God's circle of love as one big happy family."

In summary, I (Brad) believe that this Pentecost Sunday 2023 event held on the Southern Steps of the Temple Mount in Jerusalem, as well as the igniting events that we are experiencing in PRMI which include born-again Jews as well as representatives from all nations, are just a few of the forthcoming igniting events that embody the distinctive nature of this present great outpouring that we are called to take part in. These igniting events reveal the essence of God's plans and means for sending revivals with the potential to become the great End Times awakening. The vanguard of this present revival is the restoration of God's original plans for advancing the gospel of the kingdom to all the nations, as revealed in the book of Acts in chapter 15. These revivals are the two distinct rivers of the Holy Spirit launched at the first Pentecost, but now they include both Jew and Gentile yet remain distinct through Jesus Christ/Yeshua Hamashiach as they come together as the one new humanity, and that is the one new family of God. The result will be the restoration of the kingdom of Israel as well as the all the nations of the earth coming into the kingdom of God.

# 4

# Markers 1-3 of all Pentecost Events

As we prepare to take part with God in His work of igniting outpourings of the Holy Spirit, we must understand how God connects with our human and material world. We will identify these connections as "markers" of God's presence and work within our sphere of reality. There are many such examples of God, who is Spirit, interfacing with our human and material spheres. Some obvious indicators of God's presence and activity recorded in the Bible are signs and wonders, healing, joy, creativity, fire, holiness, and so on. Many of these indicators, such as signs, wonders and spiritual gifts will be found each time there is an outpouring of the Holy Spirit. However, in this chapter we identify the five most essential markers which enable us to discern that the Father is preparing to ignite an outpouring of the Holy Spirit and is calling us to take part or has indeed ignited a move of the Holy Spirit. These are important indicators of the way that God has chosen to work within our human time and space. These become evident if we look for them in the event of Pentecost which provides the model for all future outpourings of the Holy Spirit.

These five markers are as follows:

1. The Holy Spirit always pours out His grace and power on **prepared individuals and/or groups.**
2. Outpourings of the Holy Spirit always have a **physical address.**
3. Outpourings of the Holy Spirit always have a **time stamp**.
4. **Jesus Christ baptizes people with the Holy Spirit.** This happens directly or is mediated through His anointed co-workers.

5. These outpourings result in individuals and groups becoming **empowered witnesses to Jesus Christ.**

Each of these distinctive markers has profound and practical implications for how we take part in God's work of igniting outpourings of the Holy Spirit. They also provide a means of discerning genuine Pentecost events. In this chapter we shall explore the first three, and then the last two in the next chapter.

## First Marker: A prepared individual or group of people

At Pentecost, the group of about 120 disciples of Jesus Christ had been prepared and were gathered in a set-apart location. We see a partial list of who was there and how they were being prepared.

> Then they returned to Jerusalem from the Mount of Olives (which is near Jerusalem, a Shabbat day's journey). When they had entered, they went up to the upper room where they were staying—Peter and John and Jacob and Andrew; Philip and Thomas, Bartholomew and Matthew; Jacob son of Alphaeus and Simon the Zealot and Judah son of Jacob. All these with one mind were continuing together in prayer— along with the women and Miriam, Yeshua's mother, and His brothers. In those days, Peter stood up among the brothers and sisters (the number of names all together was about a hundred and twenty) and said, ... Acts 1:12-15

The picture: Detail of El Greco – 1596
Pentecost, Museo del Prado, Madrid,
Spain. Public domain

Certainly, those named above and many unnamed had already spent nearly three years following Jesus and listening to His teaching. Their immediate preparation for the event of Pentecost was that they were following the command of Jesus. He told them,

"Do not leave Jerusalem, but wait there for what my Father promised, which you heard about from me. For John baptized with water, but you will be baptized with the Holy Spirit not many days from now." Acts 1:4-5

Their act of obedience put them in the geographic location that the Lord had chosen for the outpouring of the Holy Spirit. They were continuing in prayer and worship. This was preparing their hearts as individuals, and as a fellowship in the designated location. They were also given a hint that this event would take place at a certain point in time that they were to wait for, which they would be doing anyway as they were preparing for the Jewish Festival of Weeks (Shavuot). This was to take place five weeks after the second night of Passover commemorating Adonai giving the Torah to Moses on Mount Sinai.

Peter's sermon after Pentecost adds some further instructions to Jesus' original directives for preparing an individual or group for the outpouring event.

Now when they heard this, they were acutely distressed and said to Peter and the rest of the apostles, "What should we do, brothers?" Peter said to them, "Repent, and each one of you be baptized in the name of Jesus Christ for the forgiveness of your sins, and you will receive the gift of the Holy Spirit. Acts 2:37-38

Repentance from sins and accepting Jesus Christ as Lord and Savior, which are expressed in the public sacramental action of being baptized with water in the name of Jesus Christ, are added by Peter as necessary preparations for Jesus to baptize people with the Holy Spirit.

## The Preparation for the Gentile Pentecost

Pentecost, described in Acts 2, took place entirely among the Jewish believers. This launched the waves of the Holy Spirit which were a part of the Father's master plan of, "restoring the kingdom to Israel." (Acts 1:6) This was of course the ardent expectation of Jesus' first Jewish disciples. Jesus does not reject their sincere question, but radically expands their vision that the empowerment of the Holy Spirit was to equip believers to be His witnesses to advance the gospel of the kingdom to all nations. Paul sums up this master plan of God in the words, "For I am not ashamed of the gospel, for it is God's power for salvation to everyone who believes, to the Jew first and also to the Greek." (Rom. 1:16)

Those of us who have seen the gospel of Jesus Christ going to the non-Jewish (including ourselves), have often taken this part of the promise of Acts 1:4-8 for granted. But for those first Jewish believers to include the non-Jewish (the Greeks) was inconceivable. Because of this, launching waves of the Holy Spirit beyond the narrow confines of the Jewish world required a series of dramatic outpourings of the Holy Spirit (Pentecost events) in locations beyond the city of Jerusalem. The first expansion took place among the Samaritans through Philip. The expansion into the non-Jewish/Greek world required another distinctive Pentecost event.

This time not in Jerusalem, the center of Jewish life and history, but in the town of Caesarea,[20] a Roman garrison town. Extraordinary preparation was required for this outpouring of the Holy Spirit to take place in the home of Cornelius, both for him and for Peter, a Jew through whom God was to ignite this outpouring. Cornelius, even though he was a Roman centurion and a pagan, is described as follows: "He was a devout, God-fearing man, as was all his household; he did many acts of charity for the people and prayed to God regularly," (Acts 10:1-2). He was instructed by an angel to send men to Joppa to get Peter. When the delegation from Joppa found him, they informed him, "Cornelius the centurion, a righteous and God-fearing man, well-spoken of by the whole Jewish nation, was directed by a holy angel to summon you to his house and to hear a message from you," (Act 10:22). This Roman centurion's preparation must have taken years. He must have admired the Jewish people. We can see that he was a man of prayer and one who was seeking God with all his heart. He also did many acts of charity as an expression of his personal piety. These things must have been communicated to his entire household. The Holy Spirit was working on him, preparing him, not just to accept Jesus as the Messiah, but also to be filled with the Holy Spirit as the Jewish believers had been at Pentecost. What is more, through Cornelius God was preparing his whole household, for they joined in the prayers as well. His piety must have also had an impact on those who were under his military command. This is evidenced by him sending as one of the messengers, a "devout soldier." We do not know his name, but surely, he was also a God-fearing man and was among those who were there with the whole household when the Holy Spirit was poured out.

Peter also had to be prepared so that he, a Jew, would be able to set foot in the home of a Gentile who was considered unclean, and eat food that was considered unclean. There was such a vast

---

[20] Caesarea, a city name derived from the Roman title "Caesar", was the name of numerous cities and locations in the Roman Empire...
https://en.wikipedia.org/wiki/Caesarea

chasm between Peter the Jew and Cornelius the Gentile that it took an angelic visitation and a vision from heaven to prepare them both to bridge this gap. For Peter, it took a direct command from the Lord that he was to go with them and that what God had made clean he was not to call unclean.

> Then a voice said to him, "Get up, Peter; slaughter and eat!" But Peter said, "Certainly not, Lord, for I have never eaten anything defiled and ritually unclean!" The voice spoke to him again, a second time, "What God has made clean, you must not consider ritually unclean!" This happened three times, and immediately the object was taken up into heaven. Now while Peter was puzzling over what the vision he had seen could signify, the men sent by Cornelius had learned where Simon's house was and approached the gate. They called out to ask if Simon, known as Peter, was staying there as a guest. While Peter was still thinking seriously about the vision, the Spirit said to him, "Look! Three men are looking for you. But get up, go down, and accompany them without hesitation because I have sent them." Acts 10:13-20

Peter's preparation was as stunning as Cornelius'!

We see that often those whom Jesus calls as ignitors of outpourings of the Holy Spirit need to go through an intense time of preparation, just as Peter and his companions, and Cornelius and his household did.

## Paul's Pentecost

The preparation of Saul, the Pharisee, to encounter Jesus and to be filled with the Holy Spirit was extreme. His intensive study of the Hebrew scriptures must have been used by the Holy Spirit to make him hungry for God and zealous for the truth. His encounter with the resurrected Yeshua the Messiah on the road to Damascus had left him blind, but he must have experientially connected the dots of all the prophetic promises of the Messiah. This encounter with the One he was persecuting must have shattered all Saul had believed about this heretical sect. Being blind for three days was a deep, terrible, and accelerated preparation of his soul and entire belief system to receive the baptism with the Holy Spirit which empowered him for his humanly impossible mission.

We shall discuss these preparations further in a later section. The critical take-away from this review of these examples in Acts is that the outpourings of the Holy Spirit took place among people who were prepared. Their preparation included being gathered in God's chosen place at a particular time which connected with a kairos moment. This introduces two other decisive markers.

## Discovering that this location may be "cyberspace."

During the Covid 19 Pandemic in 2020, PRMI was unable to offer our normal Pentecost gatherings, but the Lord led us to offer an "Upper Room" in Cyberspace over the internet. People joined from many parts of the globe to pray together for an outpouring of the Holy Spirit. It was amazing! People received the baptism with the Holy Spirit and were knit together in community in Jesus Christ across multiple time zones. While the means of connection was the internet, which meant that we could gather in "one place" in cyberspace, each of us was still in our unique geographical location, some in Johannesburg, South Africa, others in Clinton, South Carolina, USA, others in the United Kingdom, and others in China and various locations around the world.

## Second Marker: A Physical Address

Outpourings of the Holy Spirit always have a **physical address**. In other words, they occur at a particular location on earth.

Then they returned to **Jerusalem** from the Mount of Olives (which is near Jerusalem, a Shabbat day's journey). When they had entered, they went up to the **upper room** where they were staying—Peter and John and Jacob and Andrew; Philip and Thomas, Bartholomew and Matthew; Jacob son of Alphaeus and Simon the Zealot and Judah son of Jacob. All

51

these with one mind were continuing together in prayer—along with the women and Miriam, Yeshua's mother, and His brothers. Acts 1:12-14 TLV

These verses have led many to see the Upper Room as the venue or physical location where the Pentecost event took place. This location can be visited today in the southern part of the Old City of Jerusalem on Mount Zion.

This Photo by Unknown Author is licensed under CC BY-SA-NC

This room has been the traditional location of the Last Supper. However, Acts 2:1 does not name this place as the location of the Pentecost event. It just says they were "in one place." "When the day of Shavuot [Pentecost] had come, they were all together **in one place**." (Acts 2:1 TLV).

Based on this lack of naming the specific place and taking into account the large number of people who witnessed the Pentecost event and became believers, others have argued that it was in one of the rooms in the sprawling temple complex. Some have suggested that it was perhaps the southern side of the temple where the ritual baths were located, which would have made it possible for 3000 people to have been baptized.[21]

(Southern Stairs Today with Excavated Mikvehs)

We have included these two possible locations for the outpouring of the Holy Spirit because such outpourings of the Holy Spirit always have a location on earth—a physical address.

Another example of a physical address for an outpouring of the Holy Spirit is the home of the Roman Centurion of the Italian Cohort in Caesarea (Acts 10:1). I am sure that the fact that he was of the Italian Cohort would have been enough to identify the exact location of this military unit as well as the location of the officer's home. This marked the location where the Holy Spirit fell upon the centurion and all those gathered.

Saul encountered Jesus on the road to Damascus. Three days later he was in a particular physical location when Ananias was sent to pray for him to receive his sight and to be filled with the Holy Spirit. Ananias was directed to go to a specific address.

"Get up and go to the **street called 'Straight,'** and **at Judas' house** look for a man from Tarsus named Saul. For he is praying, and he has seen in a vision a man named Ananias

---

[21] https://acts242study.com/pentecost-where-were-the-disciples/

come in and place his hands on him so that he may see again." Acts 9:10-12

Other locations in Acts when the Holy Spirit fell upon people may not be as specifically identified but are assumed, such as in Acts 19 when Paul prayed for the twelve men and the Holy Spirit fell upon them with the manifestations of tongues and prophecy. This event took place somewhere in the city of Ephesus.

### "Pentecosts" in the New Testament: An Overview

| Marker 1 Upon Whom did the Holy Spirit Fall? | Marker 2 The Location | Marker 3 Time Stamp | Text |
|---|---|---|---|
| Jesus' "Pentecost" | Jordan River | | Mt. 3:13-17 |
| Apostles' Pentecost | Jerusalem | 9am | Acts 2:1-4 |
| Samaritan "Pentecost" | Samaria | | Acts 8:4-25 |
| Saul's "Pentecost" | Damascus | | Acts 9:1-19 |
| Gentile "Pentecost" | Cornelius in Caesarea | | Acts 10:1-48; 11:1-18 |
| Ephesian "Pentecost" | Ephesus | | Acts 19:1-7 |
| Your / Our "Pentecost" | | | |

This concept, that the outpouring of the Holy Spirit always has an address, is confirmed again and again in the Bible and in the history of other outpourings of the Holy Spirit. Such addresses are given because they are the nexus—the connection point between heaven and earth when God has acted decisively within geographic space.

After the coming of Jesus Christ, these places can be anywhere, not just Jerusalem or Samaria, but anywhere that people gather and worship the Lord in spirit and in truth (John 4:21, 24). However, the Lord has chosen to set apart particular places for His activity, which seems to include a process of gathering those who worship Him in spirit and in truth, and having their presence and prayers sanctify and set apart the place. It also seems that there are certain places where God has sovereignly chosen to manifest His presence.

I know that when we were led to the twenty-four acres upon which we were called to build the Community of the Cross, the place just felt set apart and chosen by God. We found out later that the river running along the lower side of the property had been the baptismal place for the first congregation in the valley starting in 1825, with hundreds of people having been baptized there. In addition, there was some evidence that the location could have been significant to the two local warring Indian tribes, the Catawba and the Cherokee, as a type of a meeting place—a sort of a DMZ.[22] Also, the intercessors have discovered and closed several "portals" on the land. There are indeed places where there are openings to the spiritual world—both the "light" side and the "dark" side. What we are sure of is that we are given dominion to set locations apart for God's use. In some cases, it is through the prayers of God's people that the barrier between heaven and earth has been worn thin. There is a complex interrelationship between a place set apart by God and a place sanctified through the activities of God's people worshipping in spirit and in truth.

## Third Marker: A Time Stamp

Added to this idea of an address which is a specific location, we find that outpourings of the Holy Spirit take place at a particular time. These actions by God within our human time frame are like a package that is delivered to our doorstep, with a time stamp that

---

[22]DMZ is a "demilitarized zone."

shows when it was delivered. In other words, the fire of the Holy Spirit falls at a specific time. The Pentecost event took place at 9:00 in the morning.

We know that the Holy Spirit fell in this igniting event at a specific time because of Peter's reply to those who accused them of being drunk.

> Others, poking fun, were saying, "They are full of sweet new wine!" But Peter, standing with the Eleven, raised his voice and addressed them: "Fellow Judeans and all who are staying in Jerusalem, let this be known to you, and pay attention to my words. These men are not drunk, as you suppose—for it's only the third hour of the day! Acts 2:13-15 TLV

This experience of the Holy Spirit falling upon people is subjective in that it may be inwardly felt. People may feel joy or physical sensations like heat or electricity, but it is also an objective, observable, and verifiable event. It is an occurrence taking place in a particular location at a point in time.

In the book of Acts we are not told the specific time the other outpourings of the Holy Spirit took place. For example, the outpouring at Cornelius' home must have taken place after Peter and the other disciples left Jerusalem and traveled about thirty miles to Caesarea. The important thing is that this took place at a particular time at a specific location.

In the history of outpourings of the Holy Spirit after the book of Acts, there is often the mention not just of the people and the place but of the time the Pentecost event took place. Two are reported by Jonathan Goforth in his book *By My Spirit*.

> Perhaps no movement of the Spirit since Pentecost has been so productive of results as the Moravian Revival of the eighteenth century. We read that **about noon, on Sunday, August 10th, 1727,**

> "While Pastor Rothe was holding the meeting at Herrnhut, he felt himself overwhelmed by a wonderful and

56

irresistible power of the Lord and sank down into the dust before God, and with him sank down the whole assembled congregation, in an ecstasy of feeling. In this frame of mind they continued till midnight, engaged in praying and singing, weeping and supplication."[23]

Goforth then notes the impact of the Moravian fire starters in igniting what would become the First Great Awakening:

"The accounts that we have of "the Love Feast in Fetter Lane," London, **New Year's Day, 1739**, give us an insight into the beginnings of another great movement which originated in that same period. We are told that there were about sixty Moravians present at the meeting, together with seven of the Oxford Methodists, namely, John and Charles Wesley, George Whitefield, Wesley Hall, Benjamin Ingham, Charles Kinchin and Richard Hutchins, all of them ordained clergymen of the Church of England. Of that meeting Wesley writes: '**About three in the morning as we were continuing instant in prayer, the power of God came mightily upon us**, insomuch that many cried for exceeding joy, and many fell to the ground. As soon as we were recovered a little from that awe and amazement at the presence of His Majesty, we broke out with one voice -- 'We praise Thee, O God; we acknowledge Thee to be the Lord!'"[24]

We shall be giving many other examples from our own experience in this book where the time stamp for the Pentecost event is given. However, here let us consider the reasons why this time stamp is important.

_____

[23]Jonathan Goforth, D.D., *BY MY SPIRIT*,
https://www.gospeltruth.net/bymyspirit.htm

[24]Ibid.

The first is that these are events that take place within human time and space. The outpouring of the Holy Spirit is not just about believing the right things, though there are correct biblical doctrines to believe. Instead, they are events that happen to people and happen at a particular time and place, such as the Holy Spirit falling upon Mary and expressing His power through the miracle of her conceiving Jesus. The incarnation—the Word becoming flesh—took place at a particular time and place with the angelic visitation. Then there is the example of Jesus being born in a particular physical location, a stable in Bethlehem, at a particular moment in time. These events are not myths or fantasies which may communicate timeless truths, but actual historical events in which eternity intersects with our time and space creating timeless truths.

In themselves these times are significant just as one's own birthday is significant. However, they are also markers of God's activity in the human historical realm which are part of His master redemptive plans. These are designated in the Greek as "kairos time," which means the time is fulfilled—the moment for God's activity which touches earth and human life has arrived. We see this type of time in Jesus' words, "Now is the fullness of time [kairos]," He said, "and the kingdom of God is near! Turn away from your sins and believe in the good news!" (Mk. 1:15 TLV).

"Kairos" is distinct from what we have been speaking of as the time stamp of 9:00 am for the outpouring of the Holy Spirit at Pentecost. This 9:00 in the morning is what is called "chronos" time, or chronological time that you keep track of by a chronograph which is the technical term for a clock which records the passing of seconds, minutes, and hours. However, what makes the "chronos" time stamp of 9:00 am important is that it connected with the "kairos moment" of God's intervention on earth. We shall see later that when this conjunction of "kairos" and "chronos" takes place, there will be certain activities that God calls us as His friends and co-workers to do, that result in God's presence and kingdom being manifested within human lives and history.

An outpouring of the Holy Spirit taking place at a particular time and place is rooted in the nature of Jesus' promise of the baptism with the Holy Spirit as a definite experience. R.A. Torrey gives the full biblical basis for why there must be a geographic address and a time stamp in his teaching on the baptism with the Holy Spirit.

> In the first place *the baptism with the Holy Spirit is a definite experience of which one may and ought to know whether he has received it or not.* This is evident from our Lord's command to His disciples in Luke xxiv.49 and in Acts i.4, that they should not depart from Jerusalem to undertake the work which He had commissioned them to do until they had received this promise of the Father. It is also evident from the eighth chapter of Acts, fifteenth and sixteenth verses, where we are distinctly told, "*the Holy Spirit had not as yet fallen upon any of them.*" It is evident also from the nineteenth chapter of the Acts of the Apostles, the second verse, R. V., where Paul put to the little group of disciples at Ephesus the definite question, "Did ye receive the Holy Ghost when ye believed?" It is evident that the receiving of the Holy Ghost was an experience so definite that one could answer yes or no to the question whether they had received the Holy Spirit. In this case the disciples answered, "No," that they did not so much as hear whether the Holy Ghost was given. ...[25]

We shall return to the biblical teaching on the baptism with the Holy Spirit as this is the essence of all outpourings of the Holy Spirit and the key to all true revivals of biblical faith that advance the gospel of Jesus Christ.

---

[25] R.A. Torrey, *The Person and Work of the Holy Spirit: As Revealed in the Scriptures And in Personal Experience* (New York, Chicago, Toronto, London and Edinburgh: Fleming H. Revell Co., 1910), 130-131. (In the original 1910 version, 173-174.)

# Two Illustrations of the First Three Markers

## Holy Spirit Outpouring at the Young Life Camp in Nicaragua

In 2002 I was invited to bring a team to Central America. This was in cooperation with Presbyterian Church USA (PC(USA)) and Reformed Church of America (RCA) missionaries in these countries. Johnny Alicia Baez, who spoke Spanish and was on staff of the RCA global mission unit, accompanied me. Our longest visit was to Nicaragua.

The first week was at the Young Life Camp located in Santa Lastenia during January 2002, where we joined Jim and Sarah Hornsby, the Presbyterian missionaries who had invited us.[26] They were part of my Presbytery in North Carolina and had been baptized with the Holy Spirit years before at Presbyterian Charismatic Communion events. [27] They invited me to bring systematic biblical teaching on the gifts and power of the Holy Spirit from a Reformed perspective. They had provided some basic teaching on the Holy Spirit but did not feel that they were called or anointed to pray for people to be baptized with the Holy Spirit. This was a situation like what happened to Philip in Samaria. God had used Philip to prepare the way though the powerful preaching of the gospel of Jesus Christ with signs and wonders. However, when it came time to pray for people to receive the infilling with the Holy Spirit, he apparently needed to call in the anointed apostolic leaders Peter and John (Acts 8:14-15).

Jim and Sarah had prepared the way! They had faithfully led many to faith in Jesus Christ and had nurtured many as faithful disciples. They moved in the gifts of the Holy Spirit themselves and had provided teaching for others. They had sacrificially served the people by building the Young Life Camp. They had also worked to

---

[26] https://lafinca.younglife.org/home/   Vida Joven (Young Life) Camp located in Santa Lastenia

[27] The Presbyterian Charismatic Communion (PCC) founded in 1966 was later renamed as Presbyterian-Reformed Ministries International (PRMI) and is based in Black Mountain, NC.  www.prmi.org

help provide financial income through growing fair-trade coffee to relieve their desperate poverty. They had shaped Young Life as a Christ-centered organization grounded in the Bible and had certainly grown the fruit of the Spirit. However, they did not have the anointing to ignite the outpouring of the Holy Spirit upon the group of Young Life leaders. Other onsite participants were Earl and Bev Rutledge, who were with World Outreach Fellowship and had joined Jim and Sarah in the work with Young Life as mentors and teachers. Earl translated for me on several occasions, and they both demonstrated gifts of prayer, healing, and teaching. That they were not used to ignite a movement of the Holy Spirit does not represent a failure on their part at all. Rather it is God's method to involve people with different giftings in preparing for, igniting, and then sustaining an outpouring of the Holy Spirit, which is why all five of the equipping anointings (apostle, prophet, evangelist, pastor, and teacher) are needed to grow the church into its full mature expression. This is also an application of the principle of I Corinthians 3:6 where Paul, says, "I planted the seed, Apollos watered it, but God has been making it grow." God does it this way so that He gets the glory.

This Young Life camp where I was invited to teach was part of the regular equipping for several hundred Young Life leaders who were forming Young Life groups in very difficult locations, challenged with poverty as well as crime.

The markers of God at work took place as follows:

### A prepared group of people

Jim and Sarah, Earl and Bev, as well as other Young Life leaders, had already done much preparatory work among those gathered. My role, with Johnny Alicia Baez, was to provide systematic teaching on the Holy Spirit. The leaders, who were facing desperate situations, were hungry for the empowerment of the Holy Spirit. It was clear that the Lord was already at work in them. As we gave the biblical basis for the baptism with the Holy Spirit and shared our own personal experiences of His work, the hunger grew. As another form of preparation, we had several times of prayer for various needs in which we experienced the Lord blessing, healing, and delivering people from evil spirits. We were beginning to see the Lord working in power. We had also offered several occasions during the event for participants to reaffirm their faith in Jesus Christ. I was told that some made professions of faith for the very first time, but for most it was a time of recommitment to following Jesus Christ.

## Address and Time Stamp of the Outpouring

On the last full day, I had been teaching all morning and was wrapping up. I could tell that the audience was losing interest. They were accustomed to teaching that just ended with suggestions for application. It was also noon and getting close to lunch time at 12:30. The weather was hot and sultry, and I think everyone, including myself, was ready for an afternoon nap.

I received the guidance within my spirit that this was a "kairos moment of opportunity" and that God had set apart the ball field on the top of the hill as the nexus place where He would encounter us—that is, if we stepped into both the moment and the space.

I said to everyone. "Ok, I am finished teaching. You have heard the steps to asking for and receiving the baptism with the Holy Spirit. I want you to spend some time, not talking to each other, but talking to Jesus, and asking Him what He wants to give you for you to be a better Young Life Leader. As part of your preparation also ask the Lord to show you if there is anything that you need to confess to him or if there is anyone that you need to forgive. Speak it out to Jesus. If you need more prayer, then Jim and Sarah and Earl and Bev will be here after I leave for follow up. If Jesus tells you that He is going to baptize you with the Holy Spirit to empower you to be His witness, then I want you to come up to the ball field on the top of the hill. There, Jim Hornsby and I will be ready to lay hands on any of you that the Lord speaks to."

Jim prayed for the entire group in Spanish. Then we walked up the hill to the ball field. We really did not expect anyone to come up. As we started up the hill, the Holy Spirit fell upon us. We were praying in tongues and asking Jesus to send the Holy Spirit upon these young leaders to empower them as witnesses to Jesus, according to Acts 1:4-8. The Lord also gave me the gift of faith to trust him to work. After what seemed like a long time of waiting in the piercing sun, to our surprise, first one, then a few and then nearly the entire group walked onto the field.

As they walked up onto the field, they were all crying out to God, asking for His power and grace.

Jim and I then prayed in English and in Spanish for the Holy Spirit to fall on them. We started to lay hands on them. As we did the Holy Spirit fell upon the whole group with all sorts of manifestations.

The time stamp of the moment the Holy Spirit arrived at the address of the ball field at the Young Life camp was January 12, 2002, about 12:20 pm. This is the moment when chronos and kairos connected, and heaven touched earth.

In that moment Jesus baptized those young people with the Holy Spirit. This reality points to the fourth marker which we cover in the next chapter. Here it must be noted that, while mediated through Jim and me, it was clear to all that it was Jesus Christ who was igniting the fire of the Holy Spirit and not us. After we laid hands on a few people and because there were too many for us to get to, Jim just started crying out to Jesus to send the Spirit upon all of them. As he did the Holy Spirit suddenly fell upon many with outreached hands and they fell to the ground either weeping or with holy laughter. Others just started speaking in tongues without anyone specially praying for them or for that gift. The entire group, including Jim and me, was overwhelmed by the overflowing love and presence of King Jesus.

Jesus baptized that prepared group, at that time and place, but leading to the fifth marker, we must ask what was the lasting fruit? On that hot afternoon on the ballfield, I could see that there were many manifestations of the Holy Spirit taking place. By the looks on their faces, I could tell that something profound was taking place. But had they demonstrated the fifth marker of becoming empowered witnesses for Jesus Christ? As is often the case, the full answer to this question was not in evidence until much later.

Jesus used Jim and me to ignite the fire. I left shortly after this outpouring took place.[28]

These on-fire witnesses to Jesus were then nurtured by Jim and Sarah Hornsby, and Earl and Bev Rutledge as well as PRMI teams led by Chris Walker, Susan Fink Lockheart, Sam Hale and many others who spoke Spanish and continued the ministry in Young Life. For several years, Earl Rutledge served the PRMI teams as translator and later as a teacher with Chris Walker. The amazing, verifiable fruit of this outpouring was that many of those who experienced this outpouring on the ball field became key leaders, not just for Young Life in Nicaragua, but as leaders taking this evangelistic movement to other parts of Latin America.

## Outpouring in Alaska at Victory Bible Camp

---

[28] This was just one of the outpourings of the Holy Spirit that the Lord ignited on that trip. Everywhere we went, which included the Mosquito Coast and other areas where the Reformed Church of America had partnerships or missionaries, we experienced similar outpourings of the Holy Spirit.

It is so exciting to see Jesus at work! Please allow another report demonstrating these three markers. This took place in a radically different location from the Young Life Camp.  Spruce Lodge at the Victory Bible Camp north of Palmer, Alaska in February/March 2007 was extremely cold with deep snow.[29]

The Dunamis Project equipping series was being conducted in Alaska. This was Unit #2 *In the Spirit's Power,* on how to cooperate with the Holy Spirit. This five-day intensive equipping event focuses on the gifts of the Holy Spirit. This is the second event of the six units featuring different topics that take place in the same location. After the first Dunamis event, word gets out that God is really at work through these events, and so we always have new people joining the series in mid-course. To bring them in and get them on the same page with a biblical understanding of the work of the Holy

---

[29] Victory Bible Camp mile 95 on the Glenn Hwy, 64741 S. Victory Road, Glacier View, AK 99674 https://vbcalaska.org/

Spirit, we always offer a make-up, abbreviated version of this basic teaching. Also, at each Dunamis Project event we call people to a recommitment to following Jesus Christ and offer a time of prayer with laying on of hands for the infilling with the Holy Spirit.

This Dunamis event was packed out. We must have had around a hundred and twenty people there from many different churches. Most notably, we had several native people, some from villages in the far North.[30]

One of those attending was a lovely lady named Marjorie, who arrived at the camp in a pink Mary Kay Cadillac. She was an anointed woman of God, an intercessor, filled with the Holy Spirit. She attributed her success in the Mary Kay business entirely to Jesus. She introduced me to her son whom she had prevailed upon to fly up from the lower forty-eight to take part in the Dunamis event. He was obviously skeptical of the Holy Spirit stuff, but, with dry humor, had complied with his mother's wishes. We prayed for him to have a powerful experience with God.

Apparently, there were many other first-time participants who were also skeptical of the supernatural gift-giving work of the Holy Spirit. This was especially true of some of the Presbyterian pastors who had come to check us out. They had come because they had been promised rational, systematic, biblical teaching. At meals I could hardly eat as I was peppered with theological questions from the pastors. As the team and I provided teaching on spiritual gifts and taught the make-up class on the basic doctrines of the Holy Spirit, I could feel the ice of skepticism starting to thaw. Finally, we came to the concluding Saturday afternoon and evening, time to pray that Jesus would baptize for the first time or fill again with the Holy Spirit all those He was drawing into His kingdom work.

That afternoon others were teaching. Despite the cold, and the pale sun quickly setting, I donned cross country skis and went out alone to pray on the trails. I made my way out to my favorite prayer place at the camp, at the end of the snow-covered landing strip,

---

[30] Some were from St. Lawrence Island where we had previously conducted a series of Dunamis equipping events.

overlooking the vast panorama of mountain peaks golden in the setting sun and the Matanuska glacier. I was praying for Jesus to pour out his Holy Spirit upon everyone so they would be empowered to do His work. I also spent some time confessing my sins. I felt Jesus say, "Just trust me; I will manifest my glory tonight."

Let me tell you what happened; it was amazing!

All week long the Lord had been preparing the group and they were ready and eager. I could feel the faith and expectation. I was not the only one who had spent time in confession and preparation. Many had spent time alone in confession and in meditation upon Jesus' promises of the baptism with the Holy Spirit. Also, apparently the pastors had their theological and biblical questions answered and were ready to see if this was real by asking Jesus to empower them for ministry.

I do not even remember how we moved into the invitation to come forward to receive the baptism and infilling with the Holy Spirit. I just remember that suddenly the Holy Spirit fell upon me! It was like Jesus was reaching through me and my hands to bless everyone that I touched or got near to. Many were being rested in the Spirit. At first this was so unexpected that no one caught anyone. It was just happening. Others did not fall, but as they stood there in expectant faith, I could see the Holy Spirit starting to move upon them. When this happened, I asked those around them just to lay hands on them. Often the whole group would go down under the power of the Holy Spirit. I came up to Marjorie's son, who was standing there with a stoic look on his face. He had that look of, "There is no way I am going down." I reached out to pray for him, but before I could lay hands on him, a surge of power went through me. The next thing I knew he seemed to have been lifted off the floor a foot or two and seemed to fly horizontally about ten feet in front of me. I had no time to clearly see what was happening to him because a wave of the Holy Spirit hit me, nearly knocking me down. I would have gone down, but the Lord said "No! Stay standing. I am not finished working through you yet." It seemed that at that very moment the river of God was streaming through me like an unbounded cataract throughout the whole room. At this point, the whole group was caught in praise. I looked over at Marjorie's son and saw him caught up in an ecstasy of joy and astonishment—a look that was shared by many!

As I was seeing all this it was as if the river of the Holy Spirit surging through me was just getting to be too much. I was blazing hot and felt like I would explode. At that moment I heard the Lord say, "Now step outside! Now!" So, without turning over the oversight of the room to anyone, I headed out the side door. I stepped out into what looked and felt like a psychedelic drug-induced trip. The sky was ablaze with dancing color! It was the northern lights—a curtain of brilliant, moving, irradiant light, that seemed to be descending right upon the building we were in. I was astonished. It seemed that this was a physical manifestation of the descent of the Dove upon us. I stepped back into the building which was still going full blast with everyone engaging in ministry to one another. I picked up the microphone and said, "Step outside and see what God is doing!" Many stepped outside into the withering cold with no boots or jacket and stood in wonder at this magnificent display of the northern lights. Many were saying that they had never seen such a display except in the very far North. It was the native people, however, who were moved most. They stood looking up with their hands raised in praise. One said, "Yes! That is the Holy Spirit showing that He really fell! He really loves showing off like this!"

We went back into the meeting room which erupted into glorious praise. All of this took place at about 8:30 to 9:30 on that winter evening. That was the time stamp and our equivalent to 9:00 in the morning. In the debriefing that followed the next morning, we heard reports of what had taken place within people that matched the external signs. We also talked at length about the manifestation of the northern lights. On this topic the natives, who are usually very reticent, were quick to share. It turns out that they had experienced this type of manifestation through nature several times when there were outpourings of the Holy Spirit in their villages. They told about unusual manifestations of the northern lights and storms subsiding at the very moment they had been filled with the Holy Spirit. They said that once at a Dunamis Project event on St. Lawrence Island, at the very moment the Holy Spirit fell another sign through nature had taken place. Jesus had sent a small whale to come right up to the shore of the village. This had never happened before! With rejoicing, the men had hurried out, climbed into their seal skin kayaks, and brought in the whale. This was food for at least a year. Thinking back, there have been several natural phenomena like sudden rain showers, rays of sunlight bursting through the clouds, gusts of wind on windless days, and more! Why not? Is not Jesus King over all creation, who can still the wind and the waves? To show forth His presence while falling upon us, the Holy Spirit could well cause ripples through the natural order. These natural expressions when matched by our own subjective experiences are intended to bolster our faith in the Holy Spirit who is the Third person of the Trinity, sharing in power and authority with the Father and the Son.

These two astonishing events clearly demonstrate the first three markers of a prepared group of people, a set apart place, and a time stamp. The fruit of both outpourings has persisted over the years. The revival streams ignited by them continue to this day to various degrees.

In the next chapter we shall go deeper describing the final two markers of a true Pentecost event that advances the kingdom of God: Jesus is the Baptizer with the Holy Spirit, and there will always be the good fruit of people empowered to be His witnesses.

# 5

# Markers 4 and 5—All for Jesus!

In this chapter we must continue these markers of the interface between God's kingdom and our human sphere.

## Fourth Marker: Jesus Christ Baptizes People with the Holy Spirit

The essence of all Pentecost events is that born-again individuals, or a fellowship of born-again believers, are baptized by Jesus Christ with the Holy Spirit. This is clear from Acts 1:4-8.

For John baptized with water, but you will be baptized with the Holy Spirit not many days from now." Acts 1:5

For John immersed with water, but you will be immersed in the Ruach ha-Kodesh not many days from now." Acts 1:5 TLV

Using the Jewish Messianic translation of "immersed" helps us get past much of the controversy around the term *baptism with the Holy Spirit.* This is an initiation into the reality of the Holy Spirit falling upon us for power as Jesus himself experienced when the Holy Spirit fell on Him, empowering him for ministry.

We shall return repeatedly to this reality that the baptism with the Holy Spirit is the essence of all revivals. The point I want to make here is that of agency as the marker of a Pentecost event. The question is, "Who baptizes us with the Holy Spirit?" From the biblical witness it is clear that it is the resurrected, ascended, and coronated King Jesus who baptizes us with the

Holy Spirit. This is clear from the words of John the Baptist in all the Gospels: (Underlining added for emphasis.)

> John answered them all, "I baptize you with water, but one more powerful than I am is coming—I am not worthy to untie the strap of his sandals. **He will baptize you** with the Holy Spirit and fire. Luke 3:16

Jesus' own words suggest that the ultimate source of the Holy Spirit coming upon us for power is God the Father. (Acts 1:4 "...what my father promised...") In our Reformed understanding of the Trinity, God the Father is the source and initiator of all things. However, it is Jesus Christ who accomplishes the will of the Father. So, in this case it is Jesus who baptizes us with the Holy Spirit in accord with God the Father's will. In Acts 2, without the need for any intermediaries, Jesus, after His ascension, directly baptized those gathered with the Holy Spirit.

> Suddenly a sound like a violent wind blowing came from heaven and filled the entire house where they were sitting. And tongues spreading out like a fire appeared to them and came to rest on each one of them. Acts 2:2-3

No one laid hands on any of those gathered. King Jesus from His place in Heaven at the right hand of God the Father, without human mediation, directly poured out the fire upon them. Like the cloud from heaven that transported the resurrected Jesus into the throne room of heaven, this wind coming from heaven was no ordinary wind, nor were the tongues of fire ordinary fire. It was in fact the Third Person of the Trinity, manifesting Himself at a particular time and place on earth with that specific group of prepared people.

In the Pentecost event recorded in Acts 2, the Holy Spirit fire fell directly from the resurrected King Jesus because at that time there were no other people on earth upon whom the Holy Spirit had fallen with the specific purpose of being witnesses to Jesus Christ. The group gathered in Jerusalem was the first group of born-again, set apart and anointed witnesses to be the means through whom Jesus would pour out the Holy Spirit upon others.

Another unmediated outpouring of the Holy Spirit took place in the home of Cornelius the centurion. While it is true that Peter had been baptized with the Holy Spirit and was no doubt preaching in the power of the Holy Spirit about Jesus, there was no offer to lay hands on them. I do not think he or the other Jewish believers who accompanied him had any expectation that Yeshua the Messiah would pour out the Holy Spirit upon the Gentiles as He had upon the Jewish believers at Pentecost. This is evident in their astonishment at what took place. (Bold added for emphasis.)

> While Peter was still speaking these words, the Holy Spirit fell on all those who heard the message. The circumcised believers who had accompanied Peter were greatly astonished that the gift of the Holy Spirit had been poured out **even on** the Gentiles, for they heard them speaking in tongues and praising God. Then Peter said, "No one can withhold the water for these people to be baptized, who have received the Holy Spirit just as we did, can he?" Acts 10:44-47

After Pentecost and after the Holy Spirit falling upon the Gentiles gathered in the home of the Cornelius, the Holy Spirit still comes from the Father through Jesus Christ and falls on prepared people, but Pentecost events are now frequently mediated through Jesus' Holy Spirit empowered co-workers. Jesus Christ is the original fire starter, but now He often works through His co-workers who lay hands on people and pray for them. In the book of Acts we see examples of Jesus Christ both directly and indirectly igniting the work of the Holy Spirit. A paradigmatic example is in Acts 8:

> Now when the apostles in Jerusalem heard that Samaria had accepted the word of God, they sent Peter and John to them. These two went down and prayed for them so that they would receive the Holy Spirit. (For the Spirit had not yet come upon any of them, but they had only been

baptized in the name of the Lord Jesus.) Then Peter and John placed their hands on the Samaritans, and they received the Holy Spirit. Acts 8:14-17

King Jesus baptized the Samaritans with the Holy Spirit, but he did it through His anointed co-workers Peter and John. In these situations when Jesus decides to work through other people, it is easy for the person receiving the Holy Spirit as well as the observers to get confused as to who is doing the baptizing. This is what happened to Simon the magician.

Now Simon, when he saw that the Spirit was given through the laying on of the apostles' hands, offered them money, saying, "Give me this power too, so that everyone I place my hands on may receive the Holy Spirit." Acts 8:18-19

He thought the power came from Peter and John, and he was swiftly corrected. No! The baptism with the Holy Spirit comes only from Jesus and cannot be bought nor manipulated.

## Through Whom Did Jesus Baptise People with the Holy Spirit?

| Marker #1: Upon Whom did the Holy Spirit Fall? | Marker #2: The Location | Through Whom? | Marker #3: Time Stamp | Text |
|---|---|---|---|---|
| Jesus' "Pentecost" | Jordan River | Direct from the Father | | Matt. 3:13-17 |
| Apostle's Pentecost | Jerusalem | Direct From Jesus | 9am | Acts 2:1-4 |
| Samaritan "Pentecost" | Samaria | Peter and John | | Acts 8:4-25 |
| Saul's "Pentecost" | Damascus | Ananias | | Acts 9:1-19 |

| Gentile "Pentecost" | Cornelius in Caesarea | Direct from Jesus while Peter was preaching | | Acts 10:1-48; 11:1-18 |
|---|---|---|---|---|
| Ephesian "Pentecost" | Ephesus | Paul | | Acts 19:1-7 |
| Your / Our "Pentecost" | | Through Whom? | | |

All through history and up to the present, Jesus has continued to baptize people with the Holy Spirit both directly and mediated through others.

Examples of Holy Spirit fire falling unmediated from heaven upon individuals and groups abound all through history where no one was laying on hands or even teaching on the baptism with the Holy Spirit or expecting this event to take place. However, in many of these cases the group had been prepared through facing some great challenge, or they had been crying out to God for help.

One historic example is the Moravian Pentecost. This took place during a time of great dissention and confusion among the refugees from persecution who had gathered at the safe haven of the Zinzendorf estate.

It is said that at Herrnhut, Zinzendorf visited all the adult members of the deeply divided community. He drew up a covenant calling upon them 'to seek out and emphasize the points in which they agreed' rather than stressing their differences. On May 12, 1727, they all signed an agreement to dedicate their lives, as he dedicated his, to the service of the Lord Jesus Christ.

The Moravian revival of 1727 was thus preceded and then sustained by extraordinary praying. A spirit of grace, unity, and supplication grew among them.

On July 12, many of the community covenanted together on their own accord to meet often to pour out their hearts in prayer and hymns.

On August 05, Zinzendorf spent the whole night in prayer with about twelve or fourteen others following a large meeting for prayer at midnight where great emotion prevailed.

On Sunday, August 10, Pastor Rothe, while leading the service at Herrnhut, was overwhelmed by the power of the Lord about noon. He sank down into the dust before God. So did the entire congregation. They continued until midnight in prayer—singing, weeping, and praying.

On Wednesday, August 13, the Holy Spirit was poured out on them all. Their prayers were answered in ways far beyond anyone's expectations. Many of them decided to set aside certain times for continued earnest prayer.[31]

Notice the other markers of a genuine outpouring of the Holy Spirit. The physical address was at Herrnhut in Saxony, Germany. The time stamp was August 13, 1727. It must have been around noon or when they had their normal prayer service. Jesus poured out the Holy Spirit upon those gathered in answer to their desperate and persistent prayers.

This unmediated way of the fire falling may happen to individuals as well as to groups. Judy, one my editors added, "When I watch the crusades of Reinhard Bonnke in Africa, frequently the Holy Spirit will fall upon thousands with no one touching them. I've been in meetings where the Holy Spirit fell upon people healing and delivering with no one touching them. It is more common than we think." By comparison, the Holy Spirit often falls in mediated ways. First, there is teaching on the empowering work of the Holy Spirit. Then, people are invited to ask Jesus to fill them with the Holy Spirit, and their asking is accompanied by the laying on of hands. This is the most common way I have found that Jesus baptizes people with the Holy Spirit. However, there are times when Jesus Christ will choose to

---

[31] /moravians.net/en/joomla/en/about-us/34-moravian-moments/276-moravian-moment-169-moravian-revival-a-modern-pentecost-part-3  This is in the newsletter and web page of the Moravian Church Eastern West Indies Province.

baptize people with the Holy Spirit in an unmediated way to make sure that there is no confusion that He is doing it.

## Unmediated and then Mediated Outpouring of the Holy Spirit at the Halleluiah Church near Seoul, Korea

This happened at the first national Dunamis event sponsored by PRMI in South Korea in March of 2008. PRMI worked with Ben Torrey (the son of Archer Torrey of Jesus Abbey and the Fourth River Project) and other partners in Korea. One of these was Rev. Daniel Bei who was the originator of the idea to offer a major event at the megachurch known as the Halleluiah Church near Seoul, Korea. We had a team of anointed leaders coming from America including Peyton Johnson (Archer Torrey's nephew), John Chang (who headed our Chinese ministries), and me. The setting of a famous mega church with its impressive buildings was a major temptation to be confused as to the source of the power. Also, all the publicity about the gathered team offering the event was not helpful, with its focus on me and others being promoted as anointed leaders.

There were about 200 pastors from throughout South Korea in attendance from many different denominations. The team was anointed to provide the basic teaching on the baptism with the Holy Spirit. I was the primary teacher with a reputation for being used in many locations for igniting outpourings of the Holy Spirit. I was also providing biblical teaching on the Holy Spirit that was based on the exegetical work of R.A. Torrey and Archer Torrey that had been written in our PRMI Dunamis Project equipping process. This teaching was bridging the gaps between the different denominational groups represented.

As I was teaching, the team could discern—and I could feel—that all eyes were on me. The expectation was shifting away from Jesus as the One who baptizes with the Holy Spirit to me! So, when the evening came to offer to pray with laying on of hands for the outpouring of the Holy Spirit, the team confirmed what I had already been feeling—that Jesus did not want me, nor anyone else in leadership, to lay hands on anyone. Frankly, I was disappointed with this guidance because I love laying hands on people and watching God work. I guess my ego was also involved because it was most flattering to have all the attention and adoration, but my older brother in the Lord, Ben Torrey, said strongly, "If we offer for you to lay hands on them, they will all flock to you!" This was delivered sternly, but with love and wisdom confirmed by the rest of the team. However, I knew the anointing was on me, so I went off by myself and asked Jesus what to do. He told me that I was to tell the team and to announce publicly to all those gathered that He [Jesus] was the one who baptizes with the Holy Spirit, and that when they were ready for Him to do that, they were just to stand up and ask Him to empower them. Then the Lord also said, "And you are to publicly turn the leadership over to the rest of the team and then, before I can do anything, you must immediately leave the room and go up to the parking place above the mega building and pray."

On that night the room was filled with intense excitement and the expectation that there would be the laying on of hands, but even before we started to worship, I stood up and announced what Jesus had told me to say. As I did, I could hear an audible sigh of disappointment go over the crowd that had grown even larger for that night. I then publicly handed the meeting over to Ben Torrey, John Chang, and Peyton Johnson with Ben leading in Korean. Then I just walked out of the auditorium. It was one of the hardest things I ever did! I wanted the glory, but I knew that there was only one way of working as Jesus' co-worker—radical obedience. As I went out into the dark and climbed up the steps, I felt a swarm of demons coming after me. I called Cindy back in the States who was interceding herself and mobilizing intercession. She had originally planned to be on the trip but had been disinvited by the Koreans because it was thought to be culturally unacceptable to have an ordained anointed woman on this initial leadership team. So, she had had to stay home and intercede from afar. With this intercessory prayer cover, I was called into the breach to hold open the doors of heaven against the demonic powers seeking to shut them. As I struggled alone in the dark, up there, I felt buffeted by demonic powers, and even tripped over some unseen object and nearly fell over the edge into the ravine below. This struggle with the powers and principalities lasted for what seemed forever. Suddenly I felt a breakthrough and had a vision of King Jesus in majesty and glory, standing over the church and pouring out the Holy Spirit. It was like there was a raging river of the Holy Spirit flowing through me into the building and all those in it. I was praying in tongues at the top of my voice but also my physical being was reaching the limits of what I could contain of the Holy Spirit surging through me. Right when I was reaching the point of physical exhaustion, John Chang found me and put his arms around me and joined in the extraordinary intercession. He told me that after I had left, after some time of intense waiting upon the Lord, he and Ben had called the pastors to repentance and confession of sins. This had taken place individually and in small groups and, for many, included tears and crying out to God. After this time of confession followed by forgiveness and healing prayer, Ben Torrey called them to gather in groups of four and lay hands on each other to receive the Holy Spirit. This was a true Pentecost event. In reflecting on this, Ben Torrey reported to me: "I don't remember anything about you leaving; it was not very dramatic. The whole meeting was, in my memory, very quiet. I don't remember any major evidence of outpouring at the time but over the years since, I have heard quite a few people testify that they did receive the Baptism at that time, and that they were moved by Brad's not being the one to lay on hands. This was precisely the thing that lowered barriers to receiving for a number of people. Further it was a great confirmation of what we had been teaching—that receiving the baptism with the Holy Spirit is not based on some emotional experience or on manifestations, but by asking, receiving in faith, and then stepping out in obedience to the guidance of the Holy Spirit."

What is so interesting is that the next day when we were commissioning the pastors and the church leaders to return home, the team received the guidance that we as a team were to lay hands on each of them. Ben, Peyton, John, and I laid hands on them. John and I were a team. As we prayed, we saw the Holy Spirit fall upon them, giving gifts and manifestations. It was now safe to do this because it was clear that Jesus as King is the one who baptizes us with the Holy Spirit. However, the Lord worked through us to bless them with the gifts that they needed to be Jesus' empowered witnesses and co-workers.

That outpouring launched a movement of the Holy Spirit that bore great fruit over time. Revival was ignited in a number of congregations. Further, Dunamis Fellowship Korea was birthed to provide continued equipping and fellowship for those called into this great move of God.

Baptism with the Holy Spirit, whether mediated or unmediated, is a critical, defining event in every authentic outpouring of the Holy Spirit. If the people involved do not directly and clearly attest to King Jesus as the ultimate source of baptism with the Holy Spirit, then it is not a true Pentecost event that will advance the gospel of the kingdom. Those whom Jesus appoints, calls, and equips with the grace to serve as fire starters must be prepared to follow King Jesus' directions, and if so directed, get themselves out of the way.

## Fifth Marker:  Baptism with the Holy Spirit Will Result in Individuals and Groups Becoming Empowered Witnesses to Jesus Christ

This final marker is given to us in Acts 1:8.

You will receive power when the Holy Spirit has come upon you, and you will be my witnesses in Jerusalem, and in all Judea and Samaria, and to the farthest parts of the earth. Acts 1:8

After the story of Pentecost in Acts chapter 2, the rest of the book chronicles how the gospel advanced to the then-known world in the power of the Holy Spirit as people witnessed to Jesus Christ by preaching the Word and living out the gospel of the kingdom.

The focus here is not to discuss all the various manifestations of the Holy Spirit falling upon people, but to focus on another marker of each genuine outpouring of the Spirit: People who are empowered by the Holy Spirit will be witnesses to Jesus Christ. This is all part of the Father's master plan to ignite waves of the Spirit that will propel the gospel forward to the nations. "This gospel of the kingdom will be proclaimed throughout the whole world as a testimony to all nations, and then the end will come," Matt. 24:14, ESV.

This is marker of a true outpouring of the Holy Spirit: Jesus Christ preached, lived, and embodied in His people, the Church, as the One He revealed Himself to be. Jesus declared, "I am the way, and the truth, and the life. No one comes to the Father except through me" (John 14:6).

If Jesus Christ becoming real and present as the One HE says He is, is not evidenced in the outpouring event and in the long-term fruit, then I doubt whether it was a true Pentecost event that was coming from Jesus Himself. True Pentecost events will start revival waves of the Holy Spirit which advance Jesus' kingdom on earth.

81

A word of caution is in order. Many moves of God have been started with these five markers, but they have gone off the rails due to deception. Some have done what Paul accused the Galatians Christians of doing:

> The only thing I want to learn from you is this: Did you receive the Spirit by doing the works of the law or by believing what you heard? Are you so foolish? Although you began with the Spirit, are you now trying to finish by human effort? Galatians 3:2-3

## Reflections on the Five Markers of an Outpouring of the Holy Spirit.

Outpourings of the Holy Spirit come at the initiative of God the Father. However, God's sovereign decrees include our participation and cooperation with the Father, Son, and Holy Spirit. These five distinctive markers help us cooperate with the Holy Spirit and do our part. As we explore this dynamic, we are faced with the question of which marker is the starting point? We have listed them above as: **A physical address, a time stamp, a prepared individual or group of people, Jesus doing the baptizing, and people empowered to live and witness to Jesus and the gospel of the kingdom.** This order in actual practice may be arbitrary, as they are very interwoven in the actual outpouring event. They are given, not as a prescription of an order to be followed rigidly, but as a description of God's actions, to help us discern what the Lord is doing, and to help us participate in what He is doing.

All these markers are important to discerning whether the Lord is about to pour out the Holy Spirit and then confirm that a true biblical Pentecost event has indeed taken place. We will have the role of discerning what God is doing in a particular place, among a specific group of people, to prepare for these outpouring events. Our role then becomes discerning how the Lord is calling us to cooperate with Him. As an example, let's take the marker of a **prepared Individual or group.** This marker confirms that we do indeed have a role in getting ourselves ready for the event. This marker leads to a prayer: "Lord, show us where and whom You are preparing for an outpouring of the Holy Spirit." One piece of evidence that God is preparing a group, or an individual is **seeing people coming to salvation in Jesus Christ.** This preparation is the internal work of preparing our hearts and minds through accepting Jesus Christ as Lord and Savior. An outpouring of the Holy Spirit is essentially when an individual or group is baptized or filled with the Holy Spirit, so the preparation consists of all the factors that prepare a person for receiving this empowerment. An encounter with Jesus Christ in which we accept Him as Lord and Savior, making King Jesus not just ruler of the universe but of us, is essential. This prepares the way for the initiatory experience of the Holy Spirit falling upon the group of people or person.

This was the model of the first disciples, who first were born again and then later baptized with the Holy Spirit. However, after Pentecost there is the possibility that these two events may happen simultaneously, which is what happened in the case of Cornelius. He was born again and immersed in the Holy Spirit all at once. Later in Acts 8 and 19, the accepting of Jesus Christ apparently took place first and was followed by the Holy Spirit falling upon them later.

The point here is that the most basic preparation must be people being brought to salvation! This primary preparation would need to be supplemented by teaching on how to walk as a disciple of Jesus Christ, and how to pray for and receive the empowering work of the Holy Spirit. We shall provide practical models of how to prepare people in a later chapter. (Later when we discuss what R.A. Torrey names as the biblical pattern for revival, we shall see that accepting Jesus Christ as Lord and Savior is the first key to revival.) So, a sign of God's preparation is: Are there people coming to faith in Jesus Christ?

Another sign that God is preparing people for an outpouring of the Holy Spirit is **a divine restlessness, deep hunger for more of Jesus and a deeper relationship with Him, and a deep yearning to be useful in**

**God's kingdom.** While not explicitly stated, I think we see this restlessness and yearning for God in Cornelius the centurion in Acts 10.

Often, such yearning for more of God and a desire to be more useful in His kingdom do not really come until a person or a group has been through a time of "wilderness testing." We see this in the lives of people, particularly pastors and church leaders, who come to PRMI teaching events on the Holy Spirit. They are usually desperate.

Another sign that we are reaching a kairos moment for outpourings of the Holy Spirit right now in many locations around the world is **an increase of evil in society and the powerlessness in the church.** When the church has been deceived into the same anti-God movements that we see in society, it ceases to be salt and light.

The growing influence of Marxism and the occult through such anti-God movements as Black Lives Matter and the GLBTQ+ social trends are fueling a growing desperation and hunger among the remnant of those for whom the Bible is the Word of God and Jesus is not only the only way of salvation but also King over every dimension of reality. Compromise with evil and the powerlessness of the church are the prevailing and growing conditions within western society. We need Jesus! We need to be empowered to witness to Jesus! We need to be baptized with the Holy Spirit! Our sense of desperate need leads to desperate prayers for all of Jesus and all that God the Father has promised us through Jesus!

Another major indicator that God the Father is preparing for an outpouring of the Holy Spirit in a particular place with a particular group is the following: **People are already praying for an outpouring of the Holy Spirit.**

Perhaps they are just crying out for revival or an increase in faith or for God to act. The important thing is that these expressions of desperation are taking the form of urgent and consistent prayer. Usually, this prayer for revival starts with just one person who gathers a few others to unite in prayer.

We shall see later in this book that concerted intercessory prayer is always the key to revival. With limited time and resources, we will need to focus on those whom God seems to be preparing rather than on those who are not interested. This is what is implied in the words of Jesus to his disciples:

> He sent them out to proclaim the kingdom of God and to heal. And He said to them, "Take nothing for the journey— no walking stick, no travel bag, no bread, no money, nor even to have two shirts. Whatever house you enter, stay there and depart from there. And whoever does not receive you, when you leave that town, shake off the dust from your feet as a witness against them." Luke 9:2-5 TLV

Outpourings of the Holy Spirit take place where they are welcomed and invited. This is rooted in our Creator having given us free will. Jesus will not force us to love Him; love that is compelled is not truly love.

We shall return to these five markers throughout this book. They are the parameters within which God the Father has chosen again and again to fulfill His promise given in Acts 1:4-8, so that disciples of Jesus Christ may be empowered to advance the Kingdom of God. They will also provide a discernment grid to help us determine whether such an experience is a true Pentecost event with the potential to ignite and set in motion revival that will advance the Kingdom of Jesus Christ.

In the next chapter we add to these five markers another dynamic that is revealed to us in the book of Acts that helps us cooperate with Jesus as the Father prepares for, ignites, and then sustains outpourings of the Holy Spirit. This dynamic is what R.A. Torrey described as the biblical pattern for igniting revivals.

# 6

# The Biblical Pattern for Igniting Revivals

In this chapter I need to bring you into some of the back story of how the Lord called me personally and PRMI as a ministry into this strategic work of praying for a great revival which may become the next great awakening. I also need to make explicit the process that led me to identify these different biblical patterns for igniting and growing revivals in which God the Father has called us to take part.

What follows will be a very personal part of the story of how I was grafted into the R.A. Torrey-Jonathan Goforth revival streams through becoming a part of the Torrey family. I must tell you these personal stories because outpourings of the Holy Spirit and the revival streams that they birth are always personal and to some extent, family affairs. The reason is that the Father, Son, and Holy Spirit are persons. When we are born-again, we are brought into God's family. When we are baptized with the Holy Spirit, we are empowered to work in fellowship with other members of God's family. Often these are bloodlines of natural families that have been brought into God's family by the blood of Jesus. For me this was being grafted into Jesus' blood line that flows through R.A. Torrey and his descendants. I share this with you because you may be called by Jesus to join this or other streams of revival with their distinctive family connections.

# The Vision of Jesus Igniting Revival Fires by Casting Flaming Coals Upon the Earth.

In June of 2021, I was praying in the Prayer House which was still under construction at the Community of the Cross (COC). My prayer was born of desperation! Both the ministry of PRMI and I personally were going through a refining fire. We were under spiritual attack. We were also in the middle of a truly global crisis of demonic strongholds growing in great power to block the advancement of the gospel of the kingdom of Jesus Christ. There were, and at this writing still are, ominous and growing existential threats against the biblical Judeo-Christian values system that upholds the Western nations, especially the United States, Canada, and the United Kingdom. This values system has provided the framework for our great nations to be in the vanguard of both advancing the Kingdom of God and of constraining totalitarian evil. From about 2019 until 2022 I had been called to be the point intercessor with a prayer cohort engaged in strategic level intercession and spiritual warfare. These prayer battles left me physically and spiritually exhausted and wounded. [32]

In addition to these global, high-level intercessory prayer battles, Laura and I had also been through a tough year with some medical issues, which, by God's grace we came through. Another stressful factor was the great adventure of building the Prayer House at the Community of the Cross based on faith, which means sharing the vision and praying for provision. God's provision, which I am sure in His eyes is always right on time, was not on time to keep the construction crews working. So, we had to put a stop to the work. This drove us to prayer. Added to all this was the fact that I had just turned seventy and was wondering if the Lord was done with me. So, I was in the Prayer House walking around,

---

[32] I have defined these threats against God's Kingdom in the following books: *Exposing the Trojan Horse of BLM*, and *Days of Infamy: The Demonic Invasion of the United States – November 2020 to January 2021* both published by PRMI Exousia Press, Black Mountain NC, 2021and 2022 respectively.

praying and having a time with the Lord. Feeling helpless and stymied on all fronts, I was crying out to the Lord for help. I was also reminding the Lord of the prophetic words that we had received in 2019 from Douglas McMurry–that 30 years of teaching the Dunamis Project for equipping people to cooperate with the Holy Spirit in working with Jesus Christ the Lord had prepared PRMI to be a key player in the Third Great Awakening.

I was struggling with all this and crying out to the Lord when suddenly I was caught up into His presence. I had a vision of Jesus reaching into the altar in front of the throne of the Father. He had hands full of blazing coals and was casting them upon the earth. In all the places those fiery coals landed there were outpourings of the Holy Spirit—waves of revival, all converging into the great End Times revival. These vast global rivers of God's fire were returning to Jerusalem where it all started with the outpouring at Pentecost.

Then I saw those flaming coals landing on the Community of the Cross, right in the unfinished Prayer House. I saw that this was to be one of those places the Lord had chosen to be a landing pad of the Holy Spirit. In all this Jesus seemed to be saying, "I am fulfilling My word! 'I have come to bring fire on the earth, and how I wish it were already kindled!'" (Lk. 12:49 NASB) I heard him say, "I am kindling this fire of revival, and I am calling you and PRMI to take part in it. I am calling you and PRMI to prepare for the next great awakening in the power of the Holy Spirit."

## Launching the NGA Venture in the R.A Torrey Stream

I shared this vision of the landing and launching pad with my co-workers and the PRMI Board of Directors. When Rev. Becki Newman, an Anglican priest on our PRMI Board of Directors, heard this vision that we were a "landing pad" for the coals of the Holy Spirit, she added, "Yes, and also a launching pad for all those people who will come to the COC and be empowered by Jesus Christ to be sent out as His witnesses." This is consistent with the original vision of the COC received at Jesus Abbey in 1975-76—that this would be a place of encounter with Jesus Christ for prayer, equipping, and sending. They confirmed that this vision and calling was from the Lord, and we have launched a formal initiative: Preparing for the Next Great Awakening in the Power of the Holy Spirit. We call it the "NGA Venture."

After receiving this vision and having it confirmed by the PRMI Board, I spent two weeks at the beach in prayer. I was asking the Lord to reveal the next steps of how He intended to fulfill the vision. I had already developed the teaching material for the entire Dunamis Project, but I knew that the Lord wanted to add to it some keys for igniting revival for this present epoch. Then there was the great challenge of how to move from an outpouring of the Holy Spirit initiated by a Pentecost event, which may awaken and transform local congregations, into a global awakening that transforms entire societies and leads to the fulfillment of the Great Commission. It was at this point that the Lord spoke to me saying, "Just stay in the stream you are in to take part in igniting my pouring out the Holy Spirit for this next great awakening." This stream of revival and kingdom advancement that PRMI is called to embody may be traced back to R.A. Torrey and the outpourings of the Holy Spirit world-wide from 1890-1910. These revivals centered in the English-speaking world, Korea, and China. In these great moves of God, two of the key figures were the American evangelist and teacher of the Holy Spirit, R.A. Torrey (1856-1928), and the Canadian Presbyterian missionary to China, Jonathan Goforth (1859-1936). They were assiduous students of the Bible and, both having been baptized with the Holy Spirit, were anointed and empowered witnesses to Jesus Christ. They were both men of great faith matched with great intellects and had firsthand experience in great moves of God. The Lord used both to ignite outpourings of the Holy Spirit that were global in scope, advancing the Kingdom of God and transforming societies. In their writings and practice they pass on to us foundational principles for cooperation with the Holy Spirit.

The R.A. Torrey and Jonathan Goforth streams of revival ran through the English-speaking world, but then expanded to include Korea and China, eventually merging and mingling with the

Charismatic Renewal movement ignited by the Holy Spirit in the 1960s. Recently other connections have formed with various streams of the Holy Spirit within the Body of Christ, especially the Messianic Jewish movement and the Roman Catholic charismatic stream. These join with the great river of Presbyterian and Reformed theology going back to Geneva with John Calvin, to Scotland with John Knox, and to the Netherlands with Abraham Kuyper. Acting upon this guidance, I was led to explore biblical patterns for igniting outpourings of the Holy Spirit. These patterns have their origins in the book of Acts but have continued throughout the entire history of revivals.

## My Own Personal Story

To provide the reason for this choice of Torrey and Goforth and this segment of revival history, I must start with my own personal story of being grafted into the R.A. Torrey, Jonathan Goforth, and China-Korea stream. It involves my relationship with the stream of the Holy Spirit that the Lord released through the great evangelist, D.L. Moody (1837-1899), and the anointed teacher and evangelist, R.A. Torrey, and my participation in the great outpourings of the Holy Spirit that have taken place in Korea and China. The fire of the Holy Spirit, falling in waves that transform the church as well as society, is always mediated through people knit together in a relationship with Jesus Christ and in loving and Spirit-led relationships with each other. This is consistent with the nature of the Holy Spirit as the Third Person of the Trinity. His work among us will always be personal as we are grafted into Jesus' family.

I need to pause to provide some background of how all this took place and how it came about that I was in Korea in the first place! In September of 1965, my family moved to South Korea as my father had been appointed to the foreign service as the advisor for economic development, in answer to my mother's prayers. She had a great love for Korea, born of her association with many missionaries from Korea. This was because we had a summer home in Montreat, North

Carolina, the center of the Presbyterian Church in the USA missionary training and sending base. This love for Korea led her to sponsor a Korean war orphan in 1951, the same year I was born.

I am extremely dyslexic; I could hardly read and write. So, rather than getting on the airplane with my family to go to Korea in September, I had to stay in the United States to complete a remedial reading/writing program. So, I spent four months in the home of Hank Wilson, my best friend who lived down the street from us in Falls Church, Virginia. Hank was the son of Henry Hall Wilson who was part of the Kennedy/Johnson administration.[33] Those four months in their home included visits to the White House and an introduction to government and politics, but that is another story! In early January 1966 I flew alone to South Korea, arriving in the dead of winter! It was shortly after my arrival that my parents met some old friends at the airport—Archer and Jane Torrey. Archer graduated from Davidson College in 1939. My father had attended Davidson College before and after the war. My mother had known Jane Gray Torrey through the guild of Charlotte Artists. My father knew of Jane Gray's brother, Bernie, while at Davidson College. The family connections were deep! This is important to note because the Holy Spirit often moves through these deep personal friendships and family relationships.

Archer Torrey had been called to reestablish the Anglican seminary in Seoul following the Korean War. He served as director of the seminary from 1957 to 1964. In 1964 the Lord called the Torreys to leave the seminary and to launch out in a great, very risky experiment of building a prayer community. Archer was influenced by the Benedictine model. The Lord had led them to an isolated valley in the rugged east coast mountains of South Korea. Most of the English and American missionaries in Korea thought Archer, his son Ben, and ten Korean men were completely crazy

---

[33] https://www.ncpedia.org/biography/wilson-henry-hall-jr

when they set out to live in a tent on the side of a mountain to start building what was to become Jesus Abbey.

Archer Torrey's grandfather was R.A. Torrey, a great teacher on the Holy Spirit. He and a Canadian missionary, Jonathan Goforth, had been used by God to ignite the Manchurian Revival of 1907-08. Goforth was heavily influenced by the Pyongyang Revival of 1907 and prayed for God to do the same in China. The Pyongyang Revival can be traced back to Torrey's influence from his first international tour starting in December 1901. In early 1902 he was in Suzhou, China. Whenever Torrey would campaign at a mission station, he would speak to the foreign missionaries in the morning, the Chinese workers in the afternoon, and the public in the evening. He always emphasized the importance of prayer for worldwide revival in his morning talks. Another favorite topic was the necessity of praying for and receiving the baptism with the Holy Spirit as God's preparation for service. The following year a young Methodist missionary, Mary C. White, stationed in Suzhou since 1901, took her 1903 summer break in Wonsan, Korea with her friend, Presbyterian missionary, Frances McCully. While there, she encouraged McCully to join her in prayer for revival. They were joined by the station chief, Dr. R.A. Hardie. This concerted prayer led directly to the 1903 Wonsan revival, which led to the even greater outpouring of the Pyongyang Revival three and a half years later.

In the 1920s R.A. Torrey took trips to China accompanied by his son R.A. Torrey Jr. Later R.A. Torrey, Jr. became a missionary to China, and when the communists took over in 1949, he went to South Korea. R.A. Torrey Jr. had lost an arm in China in the war with Japan and went to Korea to help with the many thousands of Koreans who had suffered amputations during the Korean war with the communists. Reuben Archer Torrey III was born in China on January 19, 1918. When he was 17 years old, he returned to the United States to attend Davidson College in North Carolina.

## My First Meeting with Jane and Archer Torrey

When my parents met Jane and Archer Torrey (R.A. Torrey III) with their daughter Bunny at the Kimpo Airport, my mother promptly invited them to come to our home on the American embassy compound in Seoul. They were there for supper and spent the night before taking the train back to Hwangji (now Taebaek City) the next day. This providential encounter at the airport led to many family visits to Jesus Abbey as well as my becoming close friends with Ben, their son who was one year older than me. Archer became my spiritual father and mentor. I left Korea in the summer of 1970 to return to America to enroll in my father's and Archer's alma mater, Davidson College, located outside of Charlotte, NC. In the fall of 1974 I began Union Seminary, where I met and married fellow student Laura Cole.

## While in Korea Jesus Baptized Laura and Me with the Holy Spirit

In June of 1976, Laura and I went to South Korea as short-term PCUS missionaries. This was part of the requirements for our Doctor of Ministry Degree at Union. We taught theology and English at the Presbyterian seminary in Seoul, and led an English-speaking college group at the famous Young Nok Presbyterian Church which had sixty thousand members. The important transformative event that happened to us that amazing year was that we were both engrafted into the movement of the Holy Spirit that is embodied in R.A. Torrey and Goforth and into the Korean/Chinese connection.

In February of 1976, while staying at Jesus Abbey, I received the baptism with the Holy Spirit when Archer and Jane Torrey, with other members of the Abbey community, laid hand on me. When the Holy Spirit fell upon me, I was caught up in visions in which Jesus called and empowered me to take part in this R.A. Torrey/Jonathan Goforth move of the Holy Spirit with the

Anglo/American, Korean, and Chinese flavor, advancing the gospel of the kingdom worldwide. (Looking back now, decades later, I give praise that Jesus has worked to fulfill much of what I saw that remarkable night in prophetic vision. The part that is yet to be fulfilled, which is doing my part in leading this ministry in preparing for the next great awakening which will complete the Great Commission, is taking place as I am writing this book.)

Two months later, while at a special prayer meeting for missionaries in the home of Presbyterian missionaries Ellen and David Ross, Laura was also baptized with the Holy Spirit. Jesus Himself just poured the Holy Spirit out upon her as a surprise like Christmas. No one laid hands on her and she was not even praying to receive this empowering work of the Holy Spirit. This was the turning point in our lives and ministries. In June, before returning to the United States, Laura and I spent another month at Jesus Abbey. During that time, I had a mystical experience in which I had an encounter with Jesus Christ. He birthed in me the vision of building a place like Jesus Abbey for prayer, equipping, and sending in the mountains of western North Carolina. We called the vision Jesus Abbey II in North Carolina. This later became the vision for the Community of the Cross, a place of encounter with Jesus Christ for prayer, equipping, and sending.[34]

When we finished Union Seminary in VA in 1978, we said "Yes" to a call to serve Presbyterian congregations in eastern North Carolina. In August of 1980 we moved with our 4-month-old daughter, Elizabeth, to Taiwan as Presbyterian missionaries. We served at the Presbyterian Bible College located south of Taipei in the city of Hsinchu until August of 1989 when we returned to the United States for me to become the Executive Director of Presbyterian Reformed Ministries International in January of 1990.

---

[34] I have written about this year in Korea as well as the long relationship of being mentored by Archer Torrey in the book, *Growing in Friendship with Jesus Christ*, (Black Mountain, NC: PRMI Exousia Press, 2003).

# 1984 Outpouring of the Holy Spirit at the Presbyterian Bible College in Taiwan

While in Taiwan we were called to take part in igniting and nurturing a great outpouring of the Holy Spirit which swept through the churches of Taiwan. This is how I first learned about what R.A. Torrey called the biblical pattern for igniting outpourings of the Holy Spirit. In 1984, when Archer Torrey came to Taiwan from South Korea to conduct the teaching event on the Holy Spirit at the Presbyterian Bible College, we experienced a tremendous outpouring of the Holy Spirit. This outpouring ignited a move of the Holy Spirit in Taiwan among the Taiwanese Presbyterian churches. I will use the grid of the five markers of all outpourings of the Holy Spirit to describe this great outpouring.

## Marker #1: A Group of Prepared People

For several years I had taken groups of Presbyterian pastors and American and Canadian missionaries to Jesus Abbey in Korea and introduced them to the work of the Holy Spirit. The first trip to Jesus Abbey took place in 1982 when Laura and I first started work at the Bible College. I took my co-worker and academic dean, Timothy Huang, to Korea to explore different educational models that we could introduce at the Bible College. At least that was our idea, but the Lord had something very different in mind. After visiting the flourishing theological seminaries and congregations in Seoul, we traveled across to the east coast to visit Jesus Abbey. In those days, life there was very basic, with what those of us from Taiwan considered terrible food and primitive living conditions. There was no electricity at Jesus Abbey. I took Timothy there because this is where I had received the baptism with the Holy Spirit in 1976. I wanted him to see a model of a Holy Spirit-empowered prayer community which was grounded in the constant study of the Bible and sacrificial Christian living. Archer gave us a personal, one on one, crash course on the teaching of R.A.

Torrey with his own additions. (This teaching later became the basis for the Dunamis Project, which I developed for PRMI in the 1990s.) On this first trip, not only did we spend time going point by point through the Bible with Archer, but we also spent hours in intensive prayer. Timothy was an eager student and spiritually hungry. His English was excellent which was just as well as I was still growing in my Chinese, and Archer's Chinese was so rusty, with a heavy Henan accent, that he was nearly incomprehensible to us from Taiwan. Then one night after Archer and I laid hands on Timothy to receive the baptism with the Holy Spirit, we were all awakened about midnight, with loud shouting in tongues. Now I had my first co-worker!

We returned to Taiwan on fire. Our starting place at the Bible College was a small group of faculty members. We did not know it at the time, but I learned much later that R.A. Torrey had affirmed that the beginning place for revival is a small group gathered in prayer.

> "Let a few of God's people, they don't need to be many, get thoroughly right with God themselves—the rest will count for nothing unless you start right there; Let them band themselves together to pray for a revival until God opens the heavens and comes down. Then let them put themselves at God's disposal to use them as He sees fit. That will bring a revival to any church, any community." [35]

We started to pray for an outpouring of the Holy Spirit. We also grew in love and trust of each other. The Lord led us to start this way in praying together, which was a powerful confirmation of the truth of R.A. Torrey's direction of the role of prayer.

------

[35] Quoted in the devotional "A Prescription for Revival" by Greg Laurie May 16, 2019. Speaking at a conference in 1917, R. A. Torrey gave this prescription for revival. https://harvest.org/resources/devotion/a-prescription-for-revival/

The Lord started to answer our prayers! For the next two years there were small beginnings. First, I would take small groups of Bible College students to a prayer mountain that was founded outside the town of Miaoli (苗栗). This prayer mountain, with its rustic facilities, was only about an hour's drive from the Bible College. It was based on the Pentecostal Korean model and involved prayer and fasting. The services at the Prayer Mountain drew hundreds of people, but there was a lot of emotionalism as well as doubtful biblical theology, and it was scorned by the Taiwan Presbyterian Church. However, when I would take small groups of Bible College students to pray and fast, many had profound encounters with Jesus Christ. Some were baptized with the Holy Spirit and became co-workers. One of my wife's English students named Charity Chen took part in these very first trips to the prayer mountain. She had polio as a child and was slightly crippled in one leg. In that culture being both female and crippled meant great rejection. She was also the only Christian in her family. At the prayer mountain she was baptized with the Holy Spirit and became another faithful co-worker. During this period, I also arranged many trips to South Korea. These were groups of 15-30 students, faculty, Taiwan Presbyterian Church pastors, and often Canadian and American missionaries. After visiting the famous churches in Seoul (which were far bigger and more vibrant than anything we had in Taiwan), we would go to Jesus Abbey for a week of teaching on the work of the Holy Spirit. Part of the experience was joining in the community's life of prayer and work. A part of the experience was eating kimchi for three meals a day. We would often go in the late fall and early spring when there was ice and snow on the ground, which was always a first-time experience for us from tropical Taiwan.

Once a group of Presbyterian pastors asked for permission to pray and fast. I advised them that they could of course pray, but because of the cold and the rigors of work and life at the Abby, they needed to keep their strength up by eating. After their first meal, they came back to me and said that the food was so awful compared to Chinese food that eating it was even better then fasting.

These were glorious and happy times and were all preparation for what the Lord was planning for Taiwan. I could write an entire book just on this phase of preparation. The trips to Korea built a team of co-workers with deep friendships. Especially important to Laura and me, as personal friends as well as accountability partners, were Paul and MaryBeth McClean, sent to Taiwan by the Presbyterian Church of Canada. They were working among the Hakka people. Their two boys and our two girls were about the same age, and they were the core of the house church that we had in our home at the Bible College. It was deep and lasting friendships like these with the McCleans that sustained us all through the challenges on the mission field. Many others, both missionaries and those in the expat community in Taiwan, could be mentioned. However, while their names are in our hearts it would be tedious to name them all for those who do not know them.

## Marker # 2: The Address of the Outpouring

On each of these trips to Korea, nearly everyone would experience the Holy Spirit falling upon them. Miracles of inner and physical healing happened, and many were set free from evil spirits. Once I took Laura's English student Charity Chen as part of the group to Jesus Abbey. She had already been baptized with the Holy Spirit, but at the Abbey through the loving ministry of Jane and Archer, Jesus healed her of the many deep emotional wounds from the family rejection she experienced because of her handicap. She became a radiant and powerful witness of Jesus Christ despite her leg braces and later wheelchair.

As people like Charity and others went back to Taiwan, everyone could see that they had changed. The result was that I started to get requests to bring Archer Torrey to Taiwan for a teaching event. So, in June 1984, we did our first equipping and teaching event on the Holy Spirit at the Bible College in Hsinchu. When we announced this event for pastors and church leaders, we honestly did not expect much response. However, this announcement touched a deep hunger. Word had spread throughout the Presbyterian churches in Taiwan of the transformation that had taken place among those who had been on the trips to Korea.

On opening day, we were surprised and daunted when about 120 (mostly pastors from the Presbyterian Church of Taiwan but also some from other denominations) came to register for the event. Additionally, some American, Canadian, Australian, and British missionaries attended. All were hungry for the empowering work of the Holy Spirit. We packed out the Bible College chapel. Rev. Archer Torrey offered five days of intensive systematic teaching.

## Marker #3: The Time Stamp of the Outpouring

It was 11:55 am on Friday, the last day of the teaching event, when Archer finished the teaching. He had nearly put everyone to sleep with a dry, methodical review of all the Greek words for the two controversial terms of "baptism" and "filled" with the Holy Spirit. It was time for lunch. Everyone was hungry and restless to conclude the meeting. However, I was aware that something was beginning to stir. At that time, I did not have a word for it, but now I do: It was a "kairos moment" of the Holy Spirit starting to hover over the group. I had no idea what to do but Archer did! He said, "Well that concludes my teaching on the baptism with the Holy Spirit. I know we need to conclude this event with lunch." He looked around at the packed chapel. Some people in the back of the room were already gathering their belongings and getting ready to leave. They had trains to catch. Then Archer said, "I believe that Jesus Christ Himself is saying, 'Now is the time, and that if any of you ask Jesus, He will gladly baptize you with the Holy Spirit.' Jesus is saying to you, 'I want you to have the Holy Spirit falling upon you to give you power to be My witnesses.'" Archer continued, "Jesus Christ is here, and He is ready to fulfill His promise to each of us!" That stopped all movements to the door. I could feel the room was beginning to become heavy with the presence of God. Archer continued, "Now asking to be baptized with the Holy Spirit is not about feelings but about your will. It is about asking and receiving in faith." Then he told a story about how he had not felt anything when he was baptized with the Holy Spirit and had not received the gift of tongues until long after this event. He then told another long story about how he had experienced the power of the Holy Spirit. I could feel the emotional excitement drain out of the room. Then Archer said, "Now after you have asked, you can expect Jesus to call you to some action of obedience. Remember the Bible says the Holy Spirit is not about feeling but rather it is a matter of obedience. That is what the Bible says in Acts 5:32, 'We are witnesses of these events, and so is the Holy Spirit whom God has given to those who obey him.'" Again, all the emotional excitement drained out of the room. I looked at my watch and noticed that it was almost 12:25 and thought to myself, "Well it looks like Archer has just kept talking too long and we have missed the opportunity." Then Archer, in the middle of another story, suddenly said, "Now is the moment! If anyone wants to ask Jesus to baptize you with the Holy Spirit, then come forward and Dr. Long and I will lay hands on you. But remember it is Jesus who does this work; we are just His co-workers." (Actually, Archer used the term "Jesus' bag boys delivering the groceries", but I could not translate that well into Chinese, so I translated it "co-workers".) There was a moment's pause. Then the entire group stood up and came forward. The fire fell! It was like Pentecost with everyone being baptized in the Holy Spirit, with amazing manifestations of the Holy Spirit's power and presence. Many received gifts of tongues and prophecy and other gifts of the Holy Spirit. Healings took place. Demons were cast out. Others had visions of ministry and calling. I had not experienced anything like this. The room was filled with the majesty, power, and presence of God the Father, the Son, and the Holy Spirit.

## Markers #4 and #5: It was Jesus who Baptized People with the Holy Spirit and Empowered Us to be His Witnesses

For me this was another transformative experience. One thing I vividly learned was that cooperating with the Holy Spirit does not depend on feeling but on obedience. Archer pounded home this lesson during this extraordinary outpouring. I was translating for him as he was going from person to person laying on hands. I was having a cyclone of feelings of joy, wonder, amazement, as well as sensations like electricity surging through my whole body. At one particularly dramatic manifestation—the pastor from a prominent Presbyterian church in Taipei received tongues, burst out with a prophecy, and then fell to the floor overcome with holy laughter—I turned to Archer and said, "Wow! Do you feel that?" He whipped around and sternly said, "Feel what? I am not feeling anything at all! This is not about feelings but faith and obedience! Learn this and learn it well! Walking with Jesus is about obedience, obedience, obedience! Got that?" I think I had some idea of what Peter must have experienced when he was rebuked by Jesus. I said, "Yes Sir!" With all my feelings having been quenched, I turned and continued in obedience, translating for Archer. The extraordinary manifestations continued unabated, and I felt nothing. That lesson has stuck with me!

Above all, what I saw demonstrated constantly was that while King Jesus chose to mediate this outpouring through Archer's teaching and through both of us laying on hands, Archer kept pointing back to Jesus. Through the Holy Spirit, Jesus' presence filled the room with love, majesty, and power. He was really there!

# R.A. Torrey's Pattern for Igniting Outpourings of the
# Holy Spirit

After this outpouring, Archer stayed at my home at the Bible College for several more days before returning to South Korea. So, several of my co-workers and I had hours of uninterrupted time to debrief the event. He was very much in the teaching and mentoring mode with me. During this debriefing, I asked Archer if this outpouring was comparable to what had taken place during the outpourings of the Holy Spirit with R.A. Torrey's global evangelistic tours. The answer was essentially "Yes" but with some differences that were distinctive to what the Lord was doing with each of the different locations in the USA, Canada, Great Britain, Korea, and China. He said,

When my grandfather was in Australia in 1902 the focus there on evangelism packed out meetings with men. There, hundreds accepted Jesus Christ and were born again. Later, in Korea and China, he often started with smaller meetings with the foreign missionaries. They would gather from different parts of Korea or China where they had been laboring, often without much fruit. They were exhausted and discouraged from their work. He would focus on the need for prayer and the baptism with the Holy Spirit. It was from there that Torrey would accompany the missionaries in doing larger public meetings with the Koreans or Chinese people. These meetings were often evangelistic, with reports of many repenting and accepting Christ.

My grandfather on these missions, always held together what he believed was the biblical pattern or biblical keys for revival – evangelism, baptism with the Holy Spirit, and prayer but the emphasis he gave them depended on the audience and context. He was rooted in the Bible as the Word of God, but listened to the Holy Spirit for guidance, and was an astute observer of his context and audience. Led by the Spirit he was able to adapt his teaching to be used greatly by God everywhere he went to ignite and sustain waves of the Holy Spirit.

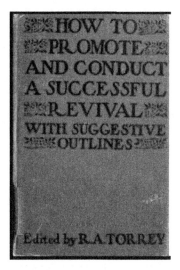

This is what I have been trying to do here with these pastors. I had to give them that long boring lecture on the different meanings in Greek for being filled with the Holy Spirit. With those theologically trained pastors you need to get to their hearts through their minds!

Then, the Lord led us into a conversation about the keys to the astonishing effectiveness of the R.A. Torrey evangelistic missions that ignited revival moves of the Holy Spirit globally. This led to the following conversation that planted in me the seminal idea of the three R.A. Torrey keys for igniting outpourings of the Holy Spirit.

## Brad: "Archer, what was the key for the Lord using R.A. Torrey in igniting revivals all over the world?"

**Archer**: "I look to his practice which is supplemented by what my grandfather wrote. For instance, he edited a book entitled, *How to Promote and Conduct a Successful Revival: With Suggestive Outlines*. But the rest is found in his other books which have proved to be more timeless, such as *The Person and work of the Holy Spirit,* and *The Power of Prayer and Prayer of Power."*

First was the preparation for each of the events which always included **a lot of prayer**-people getting their hearts right with God and praying that the Lord would pour out the Holy Spirit and bring people to salvation. In some situations, this prayer preparation would take place for months or even years before the actual event took place. He never let the logistical preparation needed for accommodating crowds of thousands of people, which was enormous, take the place of the prayer preparation. Usually, as I understand it, there were teams dedicated to each aspect, with the prayer preparation paramount.

Second, my grandfather, especially after D.L Moody died, was a great evangelist from the pulpit, but also in personally leading people to faith in Christ. He had this burning passion to "win souls for Christ." Further, for each of the missions that he conducted, hundreds of people were equipped in what Reuben called "personal work," the one-on-one leading people to faith in Jesus Christ. He always insisted that the people doing personal work be born-again, baptized with the Holy Spirit, and earnestly praying for the lost. They were also put through rigorous equipping of how to witness. Their training always concluded with laying on of hands for them to be baptized with the Holy Spirit or filled with the Holy Spirit so they could be empowered witnesses to Jesus. He put this practical equipping in a book he wrote entitled *Personal Work*. This is based on excellent biblical teaching but also contains practical instructions on how to lead people to faith in Christ. There is a section that deals with objections. I think you ought to make sure that book is translated into Chinese. You could use it to equip your own workers here.

While my grandfather was certainly greatly anointed in powerfully presenting the gospel to the crowds and calling for commitment, the effectiveness of these presentations was greatly enhanced by the hundreds of personal workers who would come alongside those to whom the Holy Spirit was bringing conviction. I remember when Dr. Billy Graham came to Seoul, Korea in 1973 to conduct his largest crusade ever. I, along with Presbyterian missionary David Ross, was part of the team equipping the hundreds of "personal workers" who followed up Dr. Graham's powerful evangelistic preaching. Thousands of people came to faith in Jesus Christ in that crusade." (Then Archer said with a big smile) "By the way, this was the great part about that crusade, but the part that Dr. Graham missed—the teaching on the baptism with the Holy Spirit. But David and I snuck it in any way with the groups we were equipping which is why they were so effective.

Third, the two main topics of his teaching while working with D.L. Moody, which Moody always wanted him to teach on, were the "Power of Prayer" and the "Baptism with the Holy Spirit." For my grandfather, it was not enough for people to come to faith in Jesus Christ. He always followed what he saw as the biblical pattern—which was after people were born-again, they needed to be baptized with the Holy Spirit as in Acts 1:4-8 so that they could have the Holy Spirit falling upon them for power to effectively witness to Jesus Christ. You see it was not enough for them to experience the Holy Spirit's "inward work" of bringing them to faith and growing in sanctification. They always needed the "outward work" which provides the power and gifts to be effective in expanding the Kingdom of God. This leading people into the outward work of empowerment is the key to these great evangelistic meetings bringing people to faith and igniting great revival movements."

So, looking back, when my grandfather first started doing the missions with D.L. Moody around 1890, Moody was the main evangelist. Moody died, Christmas 1899, and the mantle came upon Reubin as the main leader of these evangelistic crusades. From then on, as I understand it, the three themes of every crusade were:

1) Evangelistic preaching and soul winning,
2) Teaching on and leading people to be baptized with the Holy Spirit, and
3) The power of prayer and the prayer of power.

"Each of these was based on what the Bible teaches. As far as I know, I do not think anyone else put those three themes together the way my grandfather did. I think that was the key to why, everywhere he went (which was worldwide) God used him to ignite outpourings of the Holy Spirit, like what we have just experienced here in Taiwan. These resulted in the great revivals that set the church on fire, brought thousands of people into the Kingdom of God, and expanded missions. These revival movements transformed entire societies, emptying the jails in Wales, laying the foundations for Sun Yet Sen (孫中山) to establish the Republic of China on biblical values as in the American Constitution, or overturning the Baal-system of land ownership with land reform based on biblical principles here in Korea.[36]"

**Brad: So, it looks like the Holy Spirit led us to implement these three keys to igniting an outpouring. Is that why He blessed us with this amazing outpouring?**

**Archer:** "Yes! You see you were doing the work of prayer. You were preaching and teaching Jesus and were working to win souls to Jesus Christ. Then I came and did the teaching on the baptism with the Holy Spirit. You see! Jesus really is in charge and even if we do not always know what we are doing, if we listen, He will guide us to apply these foundations that are revealed to us in the Bible and enable us to work with Him on earth. It has often been like that for me too, as I just sort of blunder along, often a little confused, with my mind, heart and soul fixed on following Jesus! He is the one who works the miracles and builds our Father's Kingdom. We are just the bag boys, delivering the groceries."[37]

Looking back now, decades later, to that amazing outpouring of the Holy Spirit that took place in 1984, I can

---

[36]I must confess that it was not until much later that I understood what Archer was saying about the results of true revival impacting and transforming society. At the time I just thought he was meddling in politics. I did not understand that God's Sovereignty included every dimension of reality.

[37]From personal conversations with Archer Torrey while debriefing the outpouring of the Holy Spirit in 1984 at the Presbyterian Bible College in Hsinchu, Taiwan ROC.

affirm that these three R.A. Torrey keys did indeed come together, and God used them to ignite a great move of the Holy Spirit which had tremendous impact on the churches in Taiwan. This outpouring launched the equipping ministry of the Presbyterian Lay Training Center at the Bible College which was to thrive for the next five years with thousands of lay people and hundreds of pastors and church leaders being filled with the Holy Spirit. So, this is the fifth marker of a genuine Pentecost event—the gospel of the kingdom of God was advanced and indeed continues to advance in many tributaries to this present day.

## What Do We Call These Three Themes?

What is the best way to describe these three essential elements that the Lord uses to ignite revival? What would R.A. Torrey himself name them?

In reflecting on the great success of the evangelistic missions in Manchester and Birmingham England, Kennedy Maclean noted that Torrey attributed the great success to, **"The people working on the biblical pattern—upon the plans of God's Model for Revival laid down in Acts 2— everyone filled with the Holy Ghost, and everyone going to work!"**[38]

These three keys to revival are indeed the **"biblical pattern"** that we see in the book of Acts—the wonderful effectiveness of the R.A. Torrey model. While he may have been the upfront preacher and teacher who presented the Word and was anointed to call people to accept Jesus Christ as Lord and Savior, as well as to be baptized with the Holy Spirit, he was backed up by hundreds of others who were empowered by the Holy Spirit for preparing the context for the movement of the Holy Spirit to take place.

---

[38]Dr. Roger Martin, *R.A. Torrey Apostle of Certainty* (Murfreesboro, TN: Sword of the Lord Publishers, 1976), 169.

While some did the work of prayer, a massive administrative and logistical work enabled the gathering of thousands of people. Armies of "personal workers" were ready to speak to people one-on-one in personal evangelism. This intense Holy Spirit empowered and directed activity is described as follows:

> "Scarcely had he [R.A. Torrey] given out the invitation the first night in Birmingham when the great hall became a beehive of activity. Christians spoke to others near them and went out on the streets to reach others." [39]

So, while we must honor R.A. Torrey, who was the great anointed teacher, evangelist, and apostolic ignitor of outpourings of the Holy Spirit, these three keys resulted in revival because of all those others who were also cooperating with the Holy Spirit.

## R.A. Torrey Combined These Three Elements in the Biblical Pattern

These three elements of winning souls, leading people to pray to receive the baptism with the Holy Spirit, and teaching on and leading people into the work of empowered prayer are identified by Archer Torrey, R.A Torrey's grandson, as three interwoven essential strands. It is important, however, to confirm that R.A. Torrey, not only in his practice but also in his written statements, combined these three essential elements. When they are intentionally combined, they create a synergy that God uses to ignite outpourings of the Holy Spirit which become movements which bring people into the Kingdom and

------

[39] J. Kennedy Maclean, *Triumphant Evangelism: The three years mission of Dr. Torrey and Mr. Alexander in Great Britain and Ireland,* (London: Marshall Brothers, 1907), 61.

advance the gospel. These passages from R.A. Torrey's writings point to an integration of these essentials.

- "When any church can be brought to the place where they will recognize their need of the Holy Spirit, and take their eyes off from all men, and surrender absolutely to the Holy Spirit's control, and give themselves to much prayer for His outpouring, and present themselves as His agents, having stored the Word of God in their heads and hearts, and then look to the Holy Spirit to give it power as it falls from their lips, a mighty revival in the power of the Holy Ghost is inevitable."[40]

- The first great revival of Christian history had its origin on the human side in **a ten-day prayer meeting.** We read of that handful of disciples, "These all with one accord continued steadfastly in prayer." (Acts 1:14, RV) The result of that prayer meeting was that we read in the second chapter of the Acts of the Apostles, "**They were all filled with the Holy Ghost**, and began to speak with other tongues, as the Spirit gave them utterance" (2:4). Further on in the chapter we read that "**there were added unto them in that day about three thousand souls.**" (v. 41, RV) This revival proved genuine and permanent. The converts "continued steadfastly in

---

[40]R.A. Torrey, *How to Promote and Conduct a Successful Revival: With Suggestive Outlines* (Chicago, New York, and Toronto: Fleming H. Revell Co., 1901), 18.

the apostles' teaching and fellowship, in the breaking of bread and the prayers" (v. 42, RV) "And the Lord added to them day by day those that were being saved." (v. 47, RV)[41]

- Every **true revival from that day to this has had its earthly origin in prayer**. The great revival under Jonathan Edwards in the eighteenth century began with his famous call to prayer. The marvelous work of grace among the Indians under Brainerd had its origin in the days and nights that Brainerd spent before **God in prayer for an enduement of power from on high for this work**.[42]

At all the R.A. Torrey meetings which began after the death of Moody in December of 1899, a combination of these components ignited the great outpourings of the Holy Spirit. These are the three unique aspects of R.A. Torrey's ministry. These three provided the conditions needed for the Lord to ignite great outpourings of the Holy Spirit, which in turn became revivals. Others who have been greatly used by God have been called to focus on one or more of these elements, but R.A. Torrey seems to be unique in putting them all together.

In the next chapter we will go deeper into each of these three keys of the biblical pattern.

------

[41]Ibid., 19.

[42]Ibid.

# 7

# Going Deeper—Three R.A. Torrey Revival Keys

We have identified what R.A. Torrey identified as the biblical pattern for igniting outpourings of the Holy Spirit which historically resulted in great waves of revival advancing the Kingdom of God and fulfilling the Great Commission.

## Summary Concepts: The Three R.A. Torrey Revival Keys

**Key #1:  Evangelism**

**Key #2:  Baptism with the Holy Spirit**

**Key #3:  Empowered prayer**

In this chapter we will explore further each of these three keys and establish the biblical foundation for why Torrey was used by God to ignite outpourings of the Holy Spirit from 1900 to 1910, and why we may be used by God in our epoch for the same purpose.

## Key #1:  Evangelism (Matt. 28:18-20)

When we review the other keys, which are the baptism with the Holy Spirit and prayer, we may think that there are better starting points for igniting outpourings of the Holy Spirit than evangelism and missions. "Soul winning" is after all such a dated term for our present era.  Why not start with what appears to be the more logical point of the work of prayer?  This seems a lot easier for many people and congregations than winning people to Christ. Starting with this call to evangelism will push many beyond their comfort zone, but this must be our starting point. The reason is that this is God the Father's heart and King Jesus' fundamental mission; it is the reason for His incarnation and coronation in the first place. This is confirmed in Jesus' own words:

> "No one has ascended into heaven except the one who descended from heaven – the Son of Man. Just as Moses lifted up the serpent in the wilderness, so must the Son of Man be lifted up, so that everyone who believes in him may have eternal life." For this is the way God loved the world: He gave his one and only Son, so that everyone who believes in him will not perish but have eternal life. For God did not send his Son into the world to condemn the world, but that the world should be saved through him. John 3:13-17

This is the core mission that Jesus Christ gave His first disciples and all of us who, through believing in Jesus Christ have been born-again into the Kingdom of God. Further, and most importantly, this first work of evangelism and mission is rooted in the fundamental mission of Jesus Christ as confirmed in His own words:

> He said to them, "Go into all the world and preach the gospel to every creature. The one who believes and is baptized will be saved, but the one who does not believe will be condemned. Mark 16:15-16

> Then he opened their minds so they could understand the scriptures, and said to them, "Thus it stands written that the Christ would suffer and would rise from the dead on the third day, and repentance for the forgiveness of sins would be proclaimed in his name to all nations, beginning from Jerusalem. You are witnesses of these things. And look, I am sending you what my Father promised. But stay in the city until you have been clothed with power from on high." Luke 24:45-49

You will receive power when the Holy Spirit comes on you; and you will be my witnesses in Jerusalem, and in all Judea and Samaria, and to the ends of the earth." Acts 1:8

An essential step in God the Father's entire enterprise of redeeming fallen humanity is sharing the gospel so that people may accept Jesus Christ as Lord and Savior and be born-again into the Kingdom. The process of growing as Jesus' disciples and as His empowered witnesses all depends upon new birth into the Kingdom. Returning to this most basic starting point of evangelism is crucial in our own age when so many churches have been compromised by liberal theology and lost the biblical faith that Jesus Christ is the only way of salvation. Many have lost the passion that comes from the awareness that, "Salvation is found in no one else, for there is no other name under heaven given to mankind by which we must be saved," Acts 4:12.

R.A. Torrey's starting point was a driving passion for winning souls for Jesus Christ, summed up well in the famous quote below:

"I would rather win souls than be the greatest king or emperor on earth; I would rather win souls than be the greatest general that ever commanded an army; I would rather win souls than be the greatest poet, or novelist, or literary man who ever walked the earth. My one ambition in life is to win as many as possible."[43]

This is not just an inspirational quote or an aspiration. R.A. Torrey put it into practice in his own life and ministry. He also equipped others to take part in winning souls for Christ. The basis of this passion was rooted in his vital all-consuming faith in Jesus Christ. He had a profound awareness that there was no other way of salvation than Jesus Christ. Further, he lived with the deep awareness that Jesus had personally called and commanded him to go out and be His witness, bringing people to be born again into the Kingdom of God. This passion for winning souls

---

[43] https://www.inspiringquotes.us/quotes/hw2G_QISHDAFN

for Jesus Christ was rooted in a total, living, personal relationship with God the Father, Son, and Holy Spirit. Torrey was also grounded in the Bible as the Word of God that revealed both God's heart as well as direction for each individual and the master plan for humanity.

This focus on winning people for the Kingdom of God also provides the basis for the other keys for revival. This becomes clearer when we see the conditions that R.A. Torrey lists as the criteria to be a successful soul winner.

1. The one who would have real success in bringing others to Christ must himself be **A THOROUGHLY CONVERTED PERSON**. Jesus said to Peter, "When thou art converted strengthen thy brethren."

2. The one who would have real success in bringing others to Christ must have a **LOVE FOR SOULS**, i.e., a longing for the salvation of the lost. If we have no love for souls, our efforts will be mechanical and powerless. First of all, a love for souls like every other grace of Christian character is the work of the Holy Spirit.

3. The one who would have real success in bringing men to Christ must have a **WORKING KNOWLEDGE OF THE BIBLE**. The Word of God is the sword of the Spirit (Eph. vi. 17). It is the instrument God uses to convict of sin, to reveal Christ and to regenerate men.

4. The one who would have real success in bringing men to Christ must **PRAY MUCH**. Solid work in soul winning must be accompanied by prayer at every step.

5. The one who would have real success in bringing men to Christ must be "**BAPTIZED WITH THE HOLY GHOST**." "Ye shall receive power after that the Holy Ghost, is come upon

you," said Jesus to his disciples after having given them the great commission to go out and bring men to Himself.[44]

Torrey calls these, "General conditions, the fulfilment of which is absolutely essential to real success in bringing men to Christ."[45] We shall see that the other two keys, the baptism with the Holy Spirit and the work of prayer for igniting revival, flow directly from these essential conditions. This is to be expected if the Father's purpose in igniting outpourings of the Holy Spirit which may become waves of the Holy Spirit advancing God's Kingdom with the only doorway in being that one must be born-again.

Soul winning was the beginning of R.A. Torrey's work, and it must be the beginning of our work of preparing for a great awakening. The reason is that this goal connects us to the fundamental purpose of Jesus coming in the first place. If we start anywhere else, such as trying to help the poor and oppressed, building the Church, seeking a more just society, or seeking to push back Satan's evil empire, while all these are good things, we are already off to the wrong start and will end up deviating from the core mission of Jesus and the Church. God the Father's starting point is given in John 3:16, so missions and evangelism with the purpose of winning souls to Jesus Christ must be our starting point.

The challenge before us in this epoch is how to reach the younger generations with the gospel of Jesus Christ. The world is a very different place now in the second decade of the 21st century than it was in the first decades of the 19th century. However, human nature remains the same and Satan has the undeviating purpose of keeping humanity in eternal darkness. The need for Jesus as the only name under heaven by which we must be saved is as great as ever. We shall return to the urgent

---

[44]R.A. Torrey, *How to Bring Men to Christ* (Chicago, IL: The Bible Institute Colportage Association, 1893), 7-13.
https://www.gutenberg.org/files/51931/51931-h/51931-h.htm

[45]Ibid.

question of how we are called to implement these keys for igniting revivals in later chapters.

## Key #2: Baptism with the Holy Spirit (Acts 1:4-8)

We in PRMI have taught extensively on the baptism with the Holy Spirit in the Dunamis Project; thus, we are assuming that most people who have been associated with us are familiar with this teaching. However, as we prepare for this next great outpouring of the Holy Spirit, we need to make sure that we are on solid biblical ground. Satan has persistently and effectively opposed this biblical teaching on the empowering work of the Holy Spirit. Satan's designs have always been to deceive the Church into a "power and might" instead of "by my Spirit" approach to being a witness to Jesus and the embodiment of the Kingdom of God on earth. Frankly, it is this focus on the baptism with the Holy Spirit which has often been neglected by others who have done the work of evangelism or worked for church renewal. In many mainline conservative, as well as liberal denominations, this neglect has included hostility and rejection of streams like PRMI and the charismatic and Pentecostal movements which have embodied the "by my Spirit" approach. The result is a loss of the power of the Holy Spirit for accomplishing the work of fulfilling the mandate that Jesus Himself has given the Church of making disciples of all nations (Matt. 28:16-20).

This is not surprising among liberals who have rejected the Bible as the Word of God, but it has been no less harmful for those in the evangelical stream who reject or neglect the teaching and practice of the baptism with the Holy Spirit. Both have yielded the same result: a powerless Christianity.

For instance, as far as I know the great Dr. Billy Graham did not include in his highly effective evangelistic crusades teaching on receiving the baptism or infilling with the Holy Spirit as promised in Acts 1:4-8. I had several personal conversations with Dr. Graham about this.[46]  Accompanying me in one of these personal meetings at his home in Montreat, NC, was the anointed evangelist from Uganda, Peterson Sozi. Peterson had translated for Dr. Graham for one of his crusades in Africa.  During the jihad against Christians by Idi Amin, Peterson had been the vanguard of a great move of the Holy Spirit with signs and wonders bringing many into the Kingdom. We had worked together in Uganda to provide teaching on the Holy Spirit to their leaders and had continued to conduct evangelistic missions in which there were manifestations of the Holy Spirit. I mentioned to Dr. Graham that it was obvious that he was anointed and empowered by the Holy Spirit, otherwise he could not have done what he did. I asked why he did not include the teaching on the empowering work of the Holy Spirit as part of his public crusades as a follow up for those who had made decisions for Jesus Christ. He affirmed to us that yes indeed he had had an experience of the Holy Spirit falling upon him, anointing him for the work of evangelism. He also said that it was the key to the great effectiveness of his preaching, but then he told us that he felt that it was just too controversial at that time to teach on this topic. He stated that he was concerned that this teaching on what at that time were very contentious topics of the baptism and infilling with the Holy Spirit would be used by Satan to destroy the wonderful Christian unity of people of all denominations coming together to make possible the crusades which brought so many worldwide to saving faith in Jesus Christ. He then personally affirmed that it may be our role to provide

---

[46] These conversations took place on several occasions when I had personal meetings with Dr. Graham. The most recent took place about a year before he passed away on Feb. 21, 2018.  The Rev. Peterson Sozi who had translated for Dr. Graham in one of the African Crusades and I spent almost two hours in prayer and conversation with Dr. Graham at his home in Montreat, North Carolina. It was in that conversation that he affirmed that our (Peterson and my) calling and anointing was to provide the teaching on the baptism with the Holy Spirit. As we were leaving Dr. Graham made an interesting comment. He said, "Thank you for sharing with me, this old man for so long.  By the way, getting old is for the birds! You know President Obama was here and rushed off after less than 30 minutes."

the biblical teaching from the Presbyterian and Reformed perspective, which he agreed was an urgently needed topic. Dr. Graham laid hands on Peterson and me and prayed that we would continue to be anointed to advance the gospel of Jesus Christ in the power of the Holy Spirit. Lest we be too critical of this great man of God, we need to consider that Philip the great evangelist to Samaria was not anointed to lay hands on people to receive the baptism with the Holy Spirit. This required the arrival of Peter and John from Jerusalem who had the apostolic anointing for igniting Pentecost events. Also, we need to consider that during this period, the prevailing theological construct for understanding the baptism with the Holy Spirit was based on the traditional holiness Pentecostal teaching. This was the unbiblical teaching that one had to have a second work of grace which led to being entirely sanctified. This qualified one for the baptism with the Holy Spirit, with the initial evidence of speaking in tongues. Satan indeed used this teaching to bring division and disunity in the body of Christ.

A great tragedy is that in reaction against the Pentecostal movement birthed at Azusa Street in 1905-6, many of the mainline denominational churches rejected the biblical teaching on the baptism with the Holy Spirit. Frankly I think that much of this reaction was not related to the Pentecostal movement at all but to the fact that starting in the 1920s the great protestant denominations had already started to be deceived by liberalism. In fact, the last decades of R.A. Torrey's life were spent in North America combating the liberal movement that was rejecting the authority of scripture, the divinity of Jesus Christ, that Jesus is the only way of salvation, and the need for the empowering work of the Holy Spirit. On mission trips he took to China in the early 1920s, Torrey had to deal with the corrosive effects of liberalism on biblical faith, which included quenching the great revival and evangelistic moves of the Holy Spirit.[47]

In any event, I received this word of affirmation and encouragement from this truly great man of God—that Peterson and I were called to this role of teaching about the baptism with the Holy Spirit and leading people to receive it. We both took this affirmation as coming from Jesus.

As we emphasize the critical role of the baptism with the Holy Spirit, we must be careful to present a clear biblical definition of this often distorted, rejected, and misunderstood term. For this we must cut through layers of controversy and return to what Jesus meant when He gave His disciples and us this precious promise. So, let's start with Jesus' words, which is where R.A. Torrey started:

> While he was with them, he declared, "Do not leave Jerusalem, but wait there for what my Father promised, which you heard about from me. For John baptized with water, but you will be baptized with the Holy Spirit not many days from now." Acts 1:4-5

If we want to know what baptism with the Holy Spirit means, we just need to go to verse eight which defines what this experience is and the purpose for which it is given. It is, "...when the Holy Spirit comes upon you, and you will be my witnesses ..."

I believe R.A. Torrey provides the definition of the baptism with the Holy Spirit that is most consistent with what Jesus meant by the promises given in Luke 24:44-49 and in Acts 1:4-8. Here is a summary definition and list of the results of the baptism.

---

[47]R.A. Torrey was the leading biblical scholar and theologian in developing a series of essays called the "Fundamentals" to resist this advance of liberalism. https://sharedveracity.net/2020/05/08/fundamentalist-rueben-a-torrey-and-the-faith-healing-controversy-at-the-moody-bible-institute/

- "The baptism with the Holy Spirit, is the Spirit of God falling upon the believer, taking possession of his faculties, imparting to him gifts not naturally his own, but which qualify him for the service to which God has called him."

- In the first place the baptism with the Holy Spirit is a definite experience of which one may and ought to know whether he has received it or not.

- In the second place it is evident that the baptism with the Holy Spirit is an operation of the Holy Spirit distinct from and additional to His regenerating work.

- The next thing which is clear from the teaching of scripture is that the baptism with the Holy Spirit is always connected with, and primarily for the purpose of testimony and service.

The definition of the baptism with the Holy Spirit that is consistent with what Jesus intended is filled out with the further explanation by R.A. Torrey of the results that we see in the Bible of having been baptized with the Holy Spirit. These results are consistent with what we experience today as we receive and personally experience this promise of Jesus Christ. These are summarized from R.A. Torrey:

1. The specific manifestations of the baptism with the Holy Spirit are not precisely the same in all persons. This appears very clear from 1 Cor. 12:4-13.

2. While there are diversities of gifts and manifestations of the baptism with the Holy Spirit, there will be some gift to everyone thus baptized. (1 Cor. 12:7)

3. It is the Holy Spirit who decides how the baptism with the Spirit shall manifest itself in any given case. (1 Cor. 12:11)

4. While the power may be of one kind in one person and of another kind in another person, there will always be power, the very power of God, when one is baptized with the Holy Spirit. (Acts 1:5, 8)

5. Another result of the baptism with the Holy Spirit will be boldness in testimony and service. (Acts 4:31)

6. The baptism with the Holy Spirit causes the one who receives it to be occupied with God and Christ and spiritual things. (Acts 2:4, 7, 8, 11)

7. To sum up, the baptism with the Holy Spirit is the Spirit of God coming upon the believer, filling his mind with a real apprehension of truth, especially of Christ, taking possession of his faculties, imparting to him gifts not otherwise his but which qualify him for the service to which God has called him.

R.A. Torrey's understanding of the baptism agrees with the teaching of the New Testament. It is also in continuity with the Spirit of God falling upon people in the Old Testament for power for action, which in turn is consistent with the promise given Zechariah as the means of taking part in God's redemptive and Kingdom building work on earth.

Therefore, he told me, "This is the LORD's message to Zerubbabel: 'Not by strength and not by power, but by my Spirit,' says the LORD of Heaven's Armies." Zec. 4:6

This linking back to the Old Testament is critical, as this outpouring of the Holy Spirit and what we believe will be the next great outpouring of the Holy Spirit in our epoch, will combine both the Jewish and the Gentile streams of biblical faith as never before, and will represent the practical fulfillment of the restoration of all things foreseen in Ephesians 2:11-16.

Therefore, remember that formerly you, the Gentiles in the flesh—who are called "uncircumcision" by the so-called "circumcision" that is performed on the body by human hands— that you were at that time without the Messiah, alienated from the citizenship of Israel and strangers to the covenants of promise, having no hope and without God in the world. But now in Christ Jesus you who used to be far away have been brought near by the blood of Christ. For he is our peace, the one who made both groups into one and who destroyed the middle wall of partition, the hostility, when he nullified in his flesh the law of commandments in decrees. He did this to create in himself one new man out of two, thus making peace, and to reconcile them both in one body to God through the cross, by which the hostility has been killed. Eph. 2:11-16

We shall return to how we may pray for and receive the baptism with the Holy Spirit in the chapter on igniting outpourings. However, let's here just establish that it is an essential key to igniting outpourings of the Holy Spirit. We identify various essential characteristics of all revivals as the R.A. Torrey three keys. Although each of these will be shown to be essential, a greater emphasis may be given to any one of them as determined by the context as well as the neglected areas of biblical doctrine and experience. However, those who took part in the great outpourings of the Holy Spirit from 1900-1910 identified the baptism with the Holy Spirit as the essence, not just for that great season of revivals but for all revivals.

The baptism with the Holy Spirit as essential to all revivals is confirmed in the writings and testimonies of those who were the leaders in the great revivals that were ignited by R.A. Torrey's missions to Great Britain, to Korea, and to China. These are Jessie Penn Lewis, who took part with Evan Roberts in the Welsh Revival of 1905, and Canadian Presbyterian Missionary Jonathan Goforth through whom God ignited the 1907-8 outpouring in Manchuria, China. Both great outpourings on opposite sides of the globe and in different cultural settings were part of the Holy Spirit wave which was ignited through R.A. Torrey. They emphasize a dimension that is not elaborated upon by Torrey but certainly consistent with his teaching. The baptism with the Holy Spirit is essential to all revivals starting in Acts because this is the only way that born-again people are enabled to be co-workers with God the Father, Son, and Holy Spirit to advance the Kingdom on earth.

**Jessie Penn Lewis makes the following profound summary of this second key:**

"The baptism of the Holy Spirit is the essence of revival," for revival comes from a knowledge of the Holy Spirit, and the way of co-working with Him to enable His work in revival power.

The primary condition for revival is, therefore, that believers should individually know the baptism with the Holy Ghost. This term is being used as a convenient expression for describing a definite influx of the Holy Spirit which thousands of believers throughout the Church of Christ have received as a definite experience. **Such an infilling of the Spirit was the cause not only of the revival in Wales in 1904-5, but of all other revivals in the history of the world."**[48]

---

[48]Jessie Penn-Lewis with Evan Roberts, *War on the Saints,* 1912 unabridged original edition (New York: Thomas E. Lowe, Ltd, 1973), 287.
www.victory4you.net

Let us confirm this essential role of the baptism with the Holy Spirit for raising up Jesus' co-workers by another participant in the great revivals that took place in China in 1908—Canadian Presbyterian Missionary Jonathan Goforth (1859-1936).

Jonathan Goforth had labored for years in China preaching the gospel of Jesus Christ with little fruit of souls birthed into eternal life. Then he heard about the great revival taking place in Wales in 1905. This stirred a deep hunger in him and in other missionaries to start praying for a powerful move of God in China. In 1907 he went to Korea to see firsthand the wonderful outpouring that was taking place there, which was another tributary of the revival river God had ignited through R.A. Torrey.

At some point in this process, Goforth and his wife Rosaleen were baptized with the Holy Spirit and were used to ignite the great outpouring in Manchuria China. I had looked for a long time to determine when the event of their baptism with the Holy Spirit took place. I thought it was in China, but it turns out that this event took place in a Reformed Church outside of New York City that was having a revival.[49] This must have been when they had to flee China during the Boxer Rebellion of 1900.[50]

---

[49]This information came from Rev. Dr. John Chang in a personal conversation. Rev. Chang is the past president of the RCA General Synod and a leader in the great outpouring of the Holy Spirit in the Chinese world.

[50]"In 1900, the Goforths had to flee for many miles across China during the Boxer Rebellion. Jonathan was attacked and injured with a sword, but they both survived and escaped to the safety of one of the 'Treaty Ports.' The Goforths returned to Canada for a year."
https://en.wikipedia.org/wiki/Jonathan_Goforth

The reason why the baptism with the Holy Spirit is the key to all revivals is that until we have this experience with the Holy Spirit, we are unable to engage fully and be fully equipped as co-workers with God to advance His Kingdom on earth. Regarding the first disciples, Goforth says:

"Our Lord did not permit His chosen followers to witness a word in His name until endued with power from on high. It is true that before that day [of Pentecost] they were the "born-again" children of the Father and had the witness of the Spirit. But they were not the Lord's efficient co-workers and never could be until Spirit filled. [51]

This is a powerful affirmation of this second key, and the reason why the baptism with the Holy Spirit is the essence of all revivals. This is the means that Jesus has promised us to enable us to become "co-workers" with Him in advancing His kingdom on earth. This is why Jesus tells his born-again disciples to wait in Jerusalem until they were clothed with power so they could be His witnesses. It is this step of becoming empowered co-workers which leads to outpourings of the Holy Spirit resulting in growing the Church and advancing the Kingdom of God. Until born-again disciples of Jesus Christ experience the baptism with the Holy Spirit, they remain friends of Jesus, which is a wonderful thing and of course results in their eternal salvation. This is a static condition which may produce deep loving fellowship among these friends of Jesus. However, it is like a closed clique of best friends which does not grow or welcome newcomers into their shared intimacy, but when they are baptized with the Holy Spirit, they become co-workers with Jesus and the means that Jesus deploys to bring others into His Kingdom. This is when the Church of Jesus Christ becomes a dynamic vanguard movement of the Kingdom of God on earth which will transform human hearts as well

---

[51]Goforth, *By My Spirit,* 11.

as entire nations. The fellowship of friends centered in Jesus Christ now grows and expands!

A word from Jonathan Goforth which may serve as a prophetic glimpse into what happens when this second key—the baptism with the Holy Spirit is neglected:

"On another occasion, I was asked to address a meeting of the Presbyterian Synod in Toronto. I took as my theme the revival at Changtehfu in 1908. (出生于 Changtehfu, Honan China) I look back to that revival as perhaps the mightiest of the Spirit that I have ever been through. During those wonderful ten days there were seven different times that I was prevented from giving an address owing to the great brokenness among the people. While I was addressing the Synod, a theological professor, sitting at a table nearby, looked anything but happy. My account of the Holy Spirit's convicting power over a Chinese audience seemed to put his nerves all on edge. I understand that there was another professor from the same seminary who was sitting in another part of the building, and that he, too, fidgeted in his seat most uneasily. It seems that he finally turned around and hissed, "Rats!" That came perilously near being a sin against the Holy Ghost. By the most liberal allowance, could such prophets be expected to send out from their school young prophets filled with a Holy Ghost message? Can we wonder that spirituality is at so low an ebb throughout Christendom? Thirty-two percent of the Protestant churches in the United States report no increase in membership for 1927. The church attendance in Britain is not half of what it was twenty-five years ago. **There can be no alternative; it is either Holy Ghost revival or apostasy.**" [52]

---

[52] Goforth, Jonathan, *By My Spirit* , Marshall, Morgan & Scott, LTD, London and Edinburgh, 1929. pgs. 14-15

Has this not proven to be the case when we look back at the sad history of those once great denominations which rejected revival? This has been the long sad story of my own denomination, the Presbyterian Church in the USA. I and many other leaders in the renewal movements that God had sent to call this denomination back to biblical faith were rejected. While of course none of us leaders were perfect and our ministries had their own flaws and shortcomings, the leadership of the PC(USA) rejected both the earthen vessels as well as the treasure who was the Holy Spirit. The result has demonstratively been apostasy from biblical faith.

We shall return later in the book for more detailed teaching on how to receive the baptism with the Holy Spirit as the key to igniting all movements of the Holy Spirit that enable Christians to be co-workers with Jesus advancing the Kingdom and fulfilling the mission mandates. We shall also return to the role of Jonathan Goforth, who from his experience in China adds two "indispensable factors for revival" to these three keys.

## Key #3:  Empowered Prayer (John 14:12-14)

R.A. Torrey says, "Great revivals always begin first in the hearts of a few men and women, whom God arouses by His Spirit to believe in Him as a living God: as a God who answers prayer, upon whose heart He lays a burden from which no rest can be found except in importunate crying unto God."[53]

---

[53]R.A. Torrey, "How to Pray" Chapter XII
(https://www.ccel.org/ccel/torrey/pray.i_1.xv.html

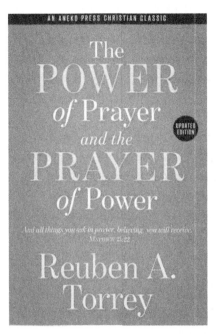

This work of prayer is essential for taking part in God's work. It is the essential first step to preparing for and enabling the outpourings of the Holy Spirit. The great Reformed theologian Jonathan Edwards saw the role of "extraordinary prayer" as the key to God the Father sending outpourings of the Holy Spirit. This is evidenced in His famous passage:

"It is God's will, through his wonderful grace, that the prayers of his saints should be one great and principal means of carrying on the designs of Christ's kingdom in the world. When God has something very great to accomplish for his church, 'tis his will that there should precede it the extraordinary prayers of his people."[54]

The call to extraordinary prayer as the chief means of God working on earth presents the possible misunderstanding that it is an entirely human-centered activity, which we can work up ourselves, but that is not the case. The fuller context of Edward's biblical and Reformed theology rooted in the Sovereignty of God, which takes into account our human activity and participation, is well explained by Mark Rogers in the following: (The bullet points are mine.)

- Edwards was convinced from scripture that God would send revival as an answer to the prayers of his people.

---

[54]Johnathan Edwards, *The Works of Jonathan Edwards Series, The Great Awakening*, ed. C. C. Goen (New Haven: Yale University Press, 1972), 4: 516.

Therefore, he labored to promote a widespread movement of prayer.

- While Edwards published and organized, he did not think God had left it in human hands to work or program this prayer movement. Edwards explained, "From the representation made in the prophecy . . . it will be fulfilled something after this manner; first, that there shall be given much of a spirit of prayer to God's people, in many places disposing them to come into an express agreement, unitedly to pray to God in an extraordinary manner." People were not first in the process, God was.

- Of course, he gave the desire to pray first, or the people would never possess it. The prayers would be extraordinary, but that's because God would make it so.

- In other words, the Bible says revival will follow "extraordinary prayers." Therefore, people should gather and pray for revival.[55]

---

[55]Ibid.

131

As explained above, there is considerable nuance and creative tension between the two realities of God's sovereign will and human freedom.

These two realities, which are both revealed in the Bible, have, in Calvinism and Arminianism, hardened into cold doctrinal statements which have severely divided the body of Christ.[56]  In the intellectual and rational sphere, I struggled for a long time with these conflicting doctrines. However, these intellectual and doctrinal issues resolved for me when I was baptized with the Holy Spirit. Jesus called me into this extraordinary dynamic of being His friend as well as co-worker. When I said, "Yes!" to Jesus' invitation and call, these logical contradictions and doctrinal impasses were resolved in the dynamic of a living loving, divine-human community.

While I personally start from the writings of John Calvin as consistent with the revelation of the Sovereignty of God in the Bible, I prefer to see this as more of a dynamic dance of cooperation that the Lord has invited us into. As sovereign over all creation, God liberates us from the tyranny of ourselves, and grants us the extraordinary freedom of freely and willingly taking part in this great dance. This is also biblical, beginning in the book of Genesis with God giving our first parents dominion over the earth, as well as the freedom to eat of every tree in the garden except the tree of the knowledge of good and evil. After their disobedience, in relaunching the way of redemption, God continued to invite human beings into a dance of cooperation—first with Noah to build the ark, and later with Abraham to set in motion the way of salvation which culminated in Jesus Christ.

Experiencing firsthand this interplay between God's sovereignty and our freedom leads me to do what Edwards did, which is to, by

---

[56] For a summary of these two positions, see the following:  Mary Fairchild, "Calvinism Vs. Arminianism." Learn Religions, Aug. 31, 2021, learnreligions.com/calvinism-vs-arminianism-700526

the grace of God, let Him bend my will to following Jesus Christ and to cooperate with the Holy Spirit. Practically, this means ardently praying for and working for revival, which includes writing this book and implementing these patterns of how God has ignited outpourings of the Holy Spirit. All while recognizing that it is all from God and the only way for me or any of us to do our part in this great dance, is "by Thy Spirit."

So, we must follow the example of R.A. Torrey and intentionally and vigorously work to implement these three keys of doing evangelism, teaching on and praying for Jesus to baptize believers with the Holy Spirit, and doing the work of earnest prayer. When we do, and our efforts are by the Holy Spirit and not in our own strength (which is "power and might"), we may expect to see God at work through us. We work as Jesus' friends and co-workers using these three keys in an extraordinary synergy which will bring kingdom advancing, world-changing revival.

**Summary of How the Three Work Together to Form an Extraordinary Synergy, Bearing the Fruit of True Revival.**

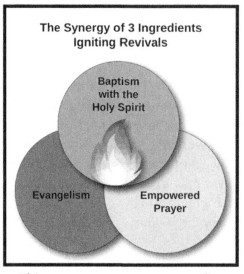

This combination of evangelistic preaching, emphasizing the need for the baptism with the Holy Spirit and prayer, meant that those who were born-again were empowered by the Holy Spirit to do the work of intercession as well as to witness to Jesus Christ. Those who are born-again are then equipped as witnesses to Jesus Christ to bring others into the kingdom and join the dance.

This generates an extraordinary synergy of divine-human activity that, once ignited, starts a conflagration of Holy Spirit empowered and prayer-sustained Kingdom advancement that goes viral and transforms not just hearts and minds of individuals, but entire societies. I believe that the Lord God intended the result to be the fulfillment of the Great Commission of making disciples of Jesus Christ of all nations. This is all most exciting, and we believe that the fruit in the worldwide revivals that took place from about 1900 to 1910 is evidence of how God greatly used these three keys.

However, we must pause and consider that however effective these three keys have been, are there not some things missing? In my own journey of growing in this process of seeking the Father's guidance for preparing for the next great awakening, for a while I got stuck on these three R.A Torrey keys. Their application by Torrey had borne such extraordinary fruit of worldwide revivals that they seemed to be all that was needed. However, as I continued to study the way the Holy Spirit had used R.A. Torrey to ignite other outpourings, I realized that while essential, these keys are incomplete. There is more needed to ignite outpourings of the Holy Spirit that would exalt Jesus Christ and would truly advance the Kingdom of God.

In the next chapter we will explore further the work of the Canadian Presbyterian Missionary to China, Jonathan Goforth. God used him to ignite the Manchurian revival of 1908. We will introduce what Goforth identified as the "indispensable factors for revival." This will complete the picture of what the Lord is calling us to put in place for igniting outpourings in our epoch.

# 8

# Two Jonathan Goforth Foundations

Jonathan Goforth, (1859-1936) and Rosalind [Bell-Smith] (1864-1942) - First Canadian Presbyterian missionaries to mainland China

The three keys established by R.A. Torrey are certainly essential, but they do not represent the whole of what the Bible reveals to be God the Father's required ingredients for igniting outpourings of the Holy Spirit. A review of the great revivals in China ignited by the Holy Spirit through Jonathan Goforth necessitate the addition of two more ingredients.[57]

We have already introduced Jonathan Goforth (顧約翰) and noted the weight that he added to the second R.A. Torrey key of the baptism with the Holy Spirit. I want to further introduce this remarkable missionary couple to you because they are of special significance to the revival streams that flow from Korea to China and the back-to-Jerusalem movement. This is all part of the work that God is doing presently through PRMI to prepare for the next great awakening. When we pause to connect the dots, PRMI's strategic role in this great move of God becomes evident. From PRMI's founding in 1966, we have had a role in the great stream of the Holy Spirit flowing through R.A. Torrey, Archer Torrey, Taiwan (Formosa) Korea, and China. We also find that Canada, the United Kingdom, and the United States all benefited from the same dynamic moves of the Holy Spirit in the British Isles, especially within the Presbyterian expression of biblical faith.

## God's Hand in the Life of Jonathan Goforth

A short biographical sketch of this great missionary's life sets the context for his ministry and connects this anointed couple to our present Presbyterian and Reformed, as well as R.A. Torrey stream of the Holy Spirit.[58] Jonathan Goforth's father, John Goforth of Yorkshire, England, immigrated to Canada in 1840, where they

---

57 https://www.bu.edu/missiology/missionary-biography/g-h/goforth-jonathan-1859-1936-and-rosalind-bell-smith-1864-1942/

58 I have summarized these biographical facts from the following articles: "Jonathan Goforth, Radiant Soul-Winner of North China" by Thomas John Bach, https://www.wholesomewords.org/missions/bgoforth4.html and "THE GOFORTHS: The First Canadian Presbyterian Missionaries to China" by Tongjal Wungakha, https://walkingtogether.life/jonathan-rosalind-goforth/

settled near Thorndale in western Ontario. They were pioneer farmers. Jonathan was born February 10, 1859. At age 18, through the biblical, evangelistic preaching of a Scottish Presbyterian pastor named Lachlan Cameron, Jonathan accepted Jesus Christ as Lord and Savior and immediately had a passion to win people to Christ. He entered Knox College in Toronto. While a student, the Canadian Presbyterian missionary George Leslie Mackay of Formosa visited the campus. Mackay was the founder of the Presbyterian Church of Taiwan, and from his own journals I have read that he prayed for and received the baptism with the Holy Spirit for empowerment for missions. When he preached to the students at Knox College, it must have been in the power of the Holy Spirit for the young Jonathan Goforth heard the Lord speaking to him: "I heard the voice of the Lord saying: 'Who will go for us and whom shall we send?' and I answered: 'Here am I, send me.' From that hour I became a foreign missionary."

In the year 1885, Goforth received a copy of Hudson Taylor's book, *China's Spiritual Need and Claims*. He was deeply impressed and from that time on, with renewed dedication, he began to pray that a door would be opened for him to go to China. At the General Assembly of the Presbyterian Church of Canada in June 1887, a new missionary vision came to that body of Christians with the result that Jonathan Goforth was appointed their pioneer missionary to North China. On October 25 of the same year Goforth was ordained, and the same month he was married to Florence Rosalind Bell-Smith.[59] On February 4, 1888, they sailed for China.

---

[59]Florence Rosalind Bell was born in London, England, and had grown up in Montreal, Quebec, Canada. https://en.wikipedia.org/wiki/Jonathan_Goforth

By the middle of September of the same year they were looking over their new mission field in the Province of Henan.

This newly married couple were sent to pioneer the mission station in the northern part of Henan province ( 河南省) in 1888. This was a season of effectiveness but also great hardship and refining fire. They lost five of their eleven children to sickness during their pioneer work there. The Boxer Rebellion broke out in 1900 with attacks against foreign missionaries. "Jonathan was attacked and injured with a sword, but they both survived and escaped [across China] to the safety of one of the "Treaty Ports."[60]

This simple factual statement "injured with a sword" and "lost five children to sickness" may just go by most readers, but not me! I shall never forget visiting one of the mission stations in Korea where, like every such station in Korea and China, usually on the top of a hill or in a secluded corner of the compound, would be the cemetery. This one was like a mountain meadow, overgrown with flowers and long grass. As I pushed back the flowers gone wild and found the worn lichen-covered gravestones, I started reading. My oldest daughter's name is Elizabeth, so this one really arrested me! "Our Precious Baby Elizabeth born 1900. Now in the Arms of Jesus."  As I read the inscriptions on the gravestones, I realized that they were mostly children from babies to about ten or eleven years old. A few were adults who had died of disease, but others had been martyred. On all, etched in the stone, were the biblical promises of the resurrection in Jesus. I was overcome with tears as I touched

---

[60]https://en.wikipedia.org/wiki/Jonathan_Goforth

the grief of those young parents laying their children in the ground so far from their native soil. I was also struck that they had come from England, Scotland, Canada, and America. Truly the gospel was planted in Korea, China, and other mission fields by the blood of the martyrs and the tears of mothers and fathers losing their precious children.[61]

Despite all this hardship, or perhaps because of it, the Goforths were effective in pioneering the mission station in Henan. However, the Holy Spirit seems to have been working on him and stirring in him the yearning for the empowering work of the Holy Spirit. A summary of this time which may be deduced from his life and writing is given by David Smithers:

> "You must go forward on your knees," was the advice Hudson Taylor gave to a young Canadian missionary named Jonathan Goforth. Mr. Goforth faithfully and fervently followed this advice throughout all his missionary endeavors in China. Yet, after thirteen years of faithful praying and preaching, and what most would consider a very successful ministry, Goforth became restless and dissatisfied. It was at this time an unknown party from England began sending pamphlets on the Welsh revival of 1904. Goforth was deeply stirred as he read these accounts. . ... He then gave himself to much more prayer and Bible study. Goforth now found

---

[61]This sketch is a composite of the mission stations I have visited in Kwangju, Chonju, and Tae Chun in South Korea.

himself being driven by a fresh vision, a vision for a mighty outpouring of the Holy Spirit."[62]

The outpourings of the Holy Spirit in Wales were ignited by the flaming embers from the great Torrey evangelistic missions to England. Later Jonathan Goforth heard about the great moves of God that started coming in waves in Korea in 1903, 1905 and 1907. These outpourings of the Holy Spirit were directly traced to the streams of the Holy Spirit ignited through R.A. Torrey in his global tours of 1903 which included Great Britain, China, Japan, Australia, and India.[63] In all these locations, R.A. Torrey, in his teaching as well as practice, implemented the biblical pattern of evangelism, the baptism with the Holy Spirit, and the work of prayer. The result was that moves of the Holy Spirit were ignited in all these locations.

In 1907 Jonathan Goforth visited Korea to view firsthand the great outpouring taking place. His participation in this outpouring in Korea sparked the fire that he took back to China. He wrote about this in a short report entitled "When the Spirit's Fire Swept Korea."

It was in the year of the great revival, 1907, that I visited eight of the chief mission centers of Korea. On returning to China, I told the facts to the Chinese Christians at Mukden[64], and they seemed deeply moved. I went to Pei Tai Ho and told the missionaries there how the Lord had

---

[62]David Smithers, https://www.revival-library.org/prayer_makes_history/goforth_jonathan.shtml

[63]https://en.wikipedia.org/wiki/R._A._Torrey

[64] Mukden which is a major city in the Northen part of China that used to be called Manchuria is now known as **Shenyang"** (simplified Chinese: 沈阳; traditional Chinese: 瀋陽; pinyin: *Shěnyáng*), formerly known as **Fengtian** or by its Manchu name, **Mukden**, is a major Chinese sub-provincial city and the provincial capital of Liaoning province, in north-central Liaoning. – https://en.wikipedia.org/wiki/Shenyang

blessed Korea; and I heard some in tears vow that they would pray until a like blessing came to China. Afterwards I was invited to go to Chi Kung Shan, another health resort, to talk about Korea. I told the story on a Sunday evening. As I finished it occurred to me that I had been too long, and immediately I closed with the benediction. But no one moved. The stillness of death reigned. This lasted six or seven minutes, and then suppressed weeping broke out over the audience. Sins were confessed; forgiveness was asked for bad temper and quarrels, and the like. It was late when the meeting broke up, but all felt that the Holy Spirit had been among us, refining as by fire. Then we had four days of conference and prayer. It was the most wonderful time I have ever seen among missionaries. We resolved that we would pray every afternoon at four o'clock until the church of China was revived. That autumn we began to see the power of God manifested among the people, but it increased in mighty measure after the beginning of 1908 in Manchuria and elsewhere."[65]

## How the Holy Spirit Spreads Revival Fire

The lesson from the example of Goforth is that revival spreads by people hearing about it. It also spreads when those who are touched by the revival pray for others. This includes both men and women. An often underplayed but critical aspect of these outpourings is the role of women. Another lesson is once again the strategic role of prayer.

After going to Korea in 1907 where he saw the Holy Spirit moving in great power, Goforth returned to China on fire. Apparently, he began to meet daily with other missionaries to pray for revival. This prayer group, "vowed to God and to one another that they would pray until revival came to China."[66] These prayers were answered in 1908 when

---

[65]Jonathan Goforth, *When the Spirit's Fire Swept Korea* (Kingsley Press, 2013), 2. https://www.kingsleypress.com/

[66]Ibid.

the Holy Spirit started to be poured out in China through the preaching and testimonies of Jonathan Goforth.

He wrote a book on that experience entitled *When the Fire Swept Korea*. His second book *By My Spirit* is about how the fire of the Holy Spirit spread to Manchuria, China. This is more analytical and reflective, and he develops the core factors that are involved in the great outpouring of the Holy Spirit. It is to this book that we shall return for the foundations that need to be added to R.A. Torrey's three keys.

## R.A. Torrey's Connection to PRMI and the Call to Prepare for the Next Great Awakening in the Power of the Holy Spirit

Before adding these foundations to R.A. Torrey's biblical pattern, we must connect some dots between R.A. Torrey, Goforth and PRMI's present role in this next great outpouring of the Holy Spirit.

The first connection is the Welsh Revival starting in 1904 and the Korean revivals of 1903–1905 and 1907. All were directly ignited by the work of R.A. Torrey and those who had been a part of his missions in England and in Asia. In the studies I have done, I have found no direct mention of R.A. Torrey by Jonathan Goforth. However, in a biography by Roger Martin, *R.A. Torrey: Apostle of Certainty,*[67] there are reports of later trips to China in which we find mention of their relationship.

---

[67]Roger Martin, *R.A. Torrey: Apostle of Certainty* (Murfreesboro, Tennessee: Sword of the Lord, 2000).

In 1921, R.A. Torrey visited China and was at the Hunan Bible Institute 湖南聖經學校, which was a branch of BIOLA, [68] founded in 1916 and closed by the communists in 1952. On this and other trips to China his topics included "The Baptism with the Holy Spirit." There in China he had to counter the corrosive effects on biblical faith and practice by higher criticism and the social gospel upon the church in China.

Martin notes that while doing these conferences for both missionaries and Chinese speakers, "it was a real joy for him [R.A. Torrey] to meet his warm friend, the well-known missionary Jonathan Goforth, who shared the conference platform with him." This suggests that they had known each other before this meeting in 1921 and formed a friendship, but I have not been able to find any direct links. Another notable fact about these trips to China in 1919-1921 was that his son Ruben (R. A. Torrey II) accompanied him.[69] Later, Ruben returned to China as a Presbyterian missionary where his son Archer (R. A. Torrey III) was born in 1918.[70] I cite this history to demonstrate that when I became Executive Director of PRMI in 1990, the R.A. Torrey, China and Korea streams of the Holy Spirit was grafted into PRMI. This ministry was founded as Presbyterian Charismatic Communion (PCC) in 1966 and has become Presbyterian Reformed Ministries International (PRMI). The connection of this stream embodied in Presbyterian

---

[68] BIOLA (the Bible College of Los Angelos) "established in 1908 by Lyman Stewart, founder and president of the Union Oil Company, and the Rev. T.C. Horton, two men of extraordinary vision and commitment to Christian higher education."   "... In 1912, the school had grown sufficiently in its outreach and constituency to call R.A. Torrey, a leader in the field of Christian education, as its dean." https://www.biola.edu/about/history

[69] Ibid., 244.
[70] https://www.prmi.org/archer-torrey-the-life-of-an-intercessor/

Charismatic Communion and PRMI preceded by 18 years my role which began in 1990. In 1972, the Rev. Brick Bradford, Director of PCC, took a trip to Asia, visiting Presbyterian Missionaries in Taiwan, Korea, and Japan. In each location God used Bradford to ignite outpourings of the Holy Spirit. Brick's visit to Korea was especially fruitful igniting outpourings of the Holy Spirit among Presbyterian Missionaries and among Korean Presbyterian churches. Brick also prepared the way for the outpouring that took place at the Presbyterian Bible College by a visit to the school and meetings with Presbyterian missionaries. That is another exciting story, but not for here!

## Revivals are often "family affairs"

All this history may seem like a digression for those who are eager to get on with the work of igniting moves of the Holy Spirit, but this history confirms that revivals are really "family affairs" in which the fire of the Holy Spirit is passed from person to person through people who are knit together in Christian love and fellowship. In some cases, as in the Torrey family, we see actual blood lines, but it is also through the blood line of those who are bought by the blood of Jesus. The Holy Spirit flowing through personal relationships is to be expected as He is the Third Person of the Trinity. He, like the Father and the Son, is a person, and the transfer of His power and gifts, while falling from heaven, take place through the medium of personal relationships among those who have been born-again into the kingdom of God and are in love and fellowship with each other and with the Father, Son, and Holy Spirit. In this present outpouring of the Holy Spirit, I believe it is God the Father's great intention to engraft many more people worldwide not just into His kingdom, but into this stream of the Holy Spirit that is embodied in the spiritual family lines of Torrey and Goforth.

Jonathan Goforth's Four "Indispensable Factors in Revival"

Upon Goforth's return from his 1907 visits to Korea, the Lord started igniting a great move of the Holy Spirit in Manchuria in 1908. A report of this is written in his book *By My Spirit*.[71] In the concluding chapter Goforth identifies the indispensable factors in revival. This anointed man of God has provided this summary for future generations so that we will know the keys to taking part in God's kingdom-advancing plans. These are completely consistent with R.A. Torrey's three keys, but they provide some additional elements that are critical to true revival.

Goforth's definition of revival: "If God the Holy Spirit is not glorifying Jesus Christ in the world today, as at Pentecost, it is we who are to blame. **After all, what is revival but simply the Spirit of God fully controlling in the surrendered life?**"[72]

Goforth also commented on:

1. **The role of prayer**: "The history of revival shows plainly that all movements of the Spirit have started in prayer."[73]

"What is the secret of revival?" a great evangelist was once asked. "There is no secret," he replied. "Revival always comes in answer to prayer."[74]

---

[71]Jonathan Goforth, *By My Spirit*, (Grand Rapids, MI: Zondervan, 1948).
[72] Ibid., 131.
[73] Ibid., 132.
[74] Ibid., 134.

2. **The role of the Bible as the Word of God**: "We wish to affirm, too, that we can entertain no hope of a mighty, globe-encircling Holy Spirit revival without there first being a back-to-the-Bible movement."[75]

3. **Exalting Jesus Christ**: "Finally, the call to revival must be a call to exalt Jesus Christ in our hearts as King of kings and Lord of lords." He is like an Everest Peak, rising from the level plain. There must be room only for Him if we would have Him dwell with us all. Every idol must be smashed..."[76]

3. **The Baptism with the Holy Spirit**: This is assumed everywhere in what Goforth writes: Missions can only be done God's way, which is, "by My Spirit."

He concludes his book reporting on the move of God in China addressing clergy and the church (apparently Presbyterians in Canada):

"But, brethren, the Spirit of God is with us still. Pentecost is yet within our grasp. If revival is being withheld from us, it is because some idol remains still enthroned; because we still insist on placing our reliance in human schemes; because we refuse to face the unchangeable truth that "it is not by might but BY MY SPIRIT."[77]

R.A. Torrey would agree completely with these indispensable factors. Let's focus on the two that are implicit in all of R.A. Torrey's teaching as well as in the biblical patten for igniting revival. These need to be added as foundations for igniting this present movement of the Holy Spirit.

---

[75] Ibid.
[76] Ibid., 136.
[77] Ibid., 138.

## First Goforth Foundation: The Bible as the Word of God

That the Bible is the word of God was assumed by R.A. Torrey and the basis of all his teaching. The three keys of revival which he identified as the biblical pattern for revival, are based on what the Bible teaches. R.A. Torrey wrote brilliantly and persuasively on the topic of the Bible as the Word of God in a booklet, "Ten Reasons why I Believe the Bible is the Word of God."[78] It is my assumption too that the Bible is the Word of God. My point in these pages is not to argue this assumption, but to establish that all true revivals that advance the gospel of the kingdom are based on the Bible as the Word of God. Often the result of a true Pentecost event will be that the Bible is received, honored, and obeyed as the Word of God. The result of being filled with the Holy Spirit will be the birthing of Bible studies as well open ears to receive what the Bible teaches as the truth.

The Bible when received as the Word of God provides the guard rails for the movement of the Holy Spirit in which people are usually open to receiving guidance from the Holy Spirit and to experiencing manifestations of the Holy Spirit. As these manifestations and experiences are largely subjective in nature, they open people up to the possibility of deception. People may focus on their experience, or receive guidance from their own imaginations, or from evil spirits. The Bible as the Word of God provides an objective check against these deceptions. As Goforth says, revival must be preceded by and result in a "back to the Bible movement."

---

[78]R.A. Torrey, "Ten Reasons Why I Believe the Bible is the Word of God"
https://bibleportal.com/sermon/RA-Torrey/ten-reasons-why-i-believe-the-bible-is-the-word-of-god

## Second Goforth Foundation: Jesus Christ as King

In chapter 2 we established this firm foundation that Jesus is King. Jesus is the Lord and the One who baptizes us with the Holy Spirit in order that we will be exclusively His co-workers and witnesses.

But how do we know who Jesus is and that He is King and the only way of salvation? It is the Bible, the Word of God, which reveals to us Jesus Christ as King. Of course, after coming to faith and being baptized with the Holy Spirit, we may experience Him as King, but it is God's self-disclosure in the Bible that guides our subjective experiences and speculations and binds them to objectively revealed truth.

### Yes! This History is Inspiring, but it is not 1900.

How do we put these three keys and two foundations together now, over a hundred years after they were so effectively applied by Torrey in his missions worldwide starting in 1900 and Goforth in China starting in 1907? The world of that era was so different from our present age. How could it work? Are these principles dated? Or were they perhaps contingent on the unique personality and giftedness of R.A. Torrey and the faith and missionary zeal of Jonathan Goforth?

This takes us to the problem of forming new "wine skins", or what we will identify as "containers," needed for igniting and sustaining outpourings of the Holy Spirit for our present epoch of the 2020s. We turn to this urgent question in the next sections of this book.

In the next chapter we bring together the three R.A. Torrey keys and add the Goforth foundations as a biblically grounded and historically proven pattern for how we are called to cooperate with Jesus Christ in igniting Pentecost events with the potential to become great revivals advancing the kingdom of God.

# 9

# Intro to the Meta Pattern and Phase #1

These *Five Markers of Pentecost Events*, *The Three Keys,* and the *Two Foundations*, when put in place, become what the Lord uses to ignite outpourings of the Holy Spirit which set in motion revivals that grow the Church, advance the Kingdom of God, and fulfill the Great Commission.

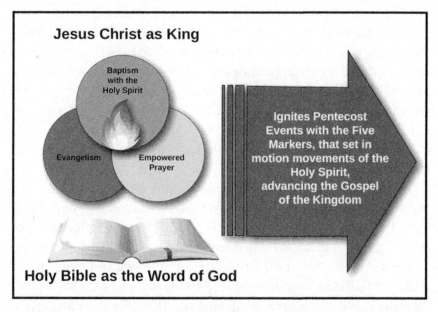

**Jesus Christ as King**

Baptism with the Holy Spirit

Evangelism

Empowered Prayer

Ignites Pentecost Events with the Five Markers, that set in motion movements of the Holy Spirit, advancing the Gospel of the Kingdom

**Holy Bible as the Word of God**

The Lord has used these elements to ignite the moves of the Holy Spirit that we see in the decade of revivals from 1900 until 1910. This has also been our experience as illustrated by the firsthand experiences recounted in this book. As we have insisted throughout this book, outpourings of the Holy Spirit are actions of the Sovereign God. However, He has called and equipped those who have been born-again into His Kingdom to work with Him as friends and co-workers. So, we have an important role of cooperating with the Holy Spirit in these dynamics.

However, these dynamics may seem like woefully complicated dance steps that we need to master if we are to keep in step with the Holy Spirit's work on earth. This complexity may make it difficult to draw these different factors together into coherent programs and/or ministries that may be implemented in widely different venues so they may be become transferable to others.

For instance, how does all this get implemented in a local congregation, or into regions, or into people groups which have not yet been evangelized? I have wrestled with this problem for decades and have been led by the Holy Spirit to put together various programs which have been greatly used by God for igniting and sustaining moves of the Holy Spirit (some of these programs have been referred to in this book) but while we may learn from past programs that God may have greatly used, like the evangelistic missions of R.A. Torrey or the PRMI Dunamis Project, my goal has always been to introduce the biblical principles and the deep dynamics of cooperating with the Holy Spirit that lie behind any of these fruitful programs. Leaving you with ready-made programs that you can copy or imitate is not my purpose. That would be a matter of just putting new wine in old wine skins—that is, wine skins that worked for a particular group or time period, but may not work for what the Lord is doing for you in your own context.

As we review the book of Acts, revival history, and our own first-hand experiences with being used by Jesus to ignite outpourings of the Holy Spirit, is there a "meta pattern" that provides a framework for how God may be calling us to combine all these separate elements intentionally?

Let us refine this question: Has God revealed to us His "meta pattern" to guide us in identifying and doing our part in the five markers and implementing these three keys and two foundations in different contexts which will not quench the Holy Spirit or be an attempt to manipulate God, but still provide enough of a framework for developing an effective, transferable program?

## Discerning the Meta Pattern of Outpourings of the Holy Spirit

I believe there is! To discern and understand this meta pattern we must return again to the model for all outpourings of the Holy Spirit—the examples of Pentecost events in the book of Acts. Here we find a three-phased dynamic which we have identified as follows:

**Phase #1: Preparing the Altar--**God the Father prepares an individual or a group whom He has called to bring into His great salvation and Kingdom plans.

**Phase #2: Igniting the Fire**—This happens when Jesus baptizes prepared individuals and groups with the Holy Spirit, initiating them into the dance of cooperating with the Holy Spirit to be witnesses and co-workers with Him.

**Phase #3: Sustaining the Flame**—Once the Holy Spirit is poured out upon the individuals and/or group who took part in the Pentecost igniting event, they must continue to grow as the body of Jesus Christ and as empowered co-workers and disciples of Jesus Christ, extending the kingdom of God.

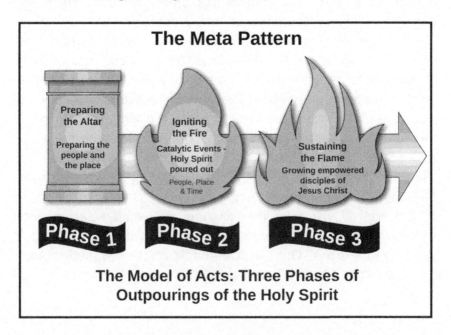

**The Meta Pattern**

Preparing the Altar

Preparing the people and the place

Igniting the Fire

Catalytic Events - Holy Spirit poured out

People, Place & Time

Sustaining the Flame

Growing empowered disciples of Jesus Christ

Phase 1    Phase 2    Phase 3

**The Model of Acts: Three Phases of Outpourings of the Holy Spirit**

These three phases are present in the book of Acts and have taken place all through history in a vast variety of different contexts whenever God has chosen to pour out the Holy Spirit in a particular time and place with a unique group of prepared people. Together they provide a framework and a context for these crucial elements that have been essential for all revivals. We shall also see that, at the leading of the Holy Spirit, we may be called to give each of these phases a programmatic expression which the Lord will use to ignite and sustain outpourings of Holy Spirit in His chosen locations and people.

I am convinced that the Lord has showed us this meta pattern, (the five markers, the Torrey keys, and the Goforth foundations) so that we may take part with God the Father, Son, and Holy Spirit in their redemptive plans. Indeed, these principles and the biblical pattern of revival are given to us as the actual means that we, as Jesus' friends and co-workers, will take part in. I believe they are given to us in our epoch for a reason. There are many indications that we have entered a kairos season of Jesus igniting Pentecost events worldwide which are setting in motion revivals with the potential to become a great global awakening.

Keep in mind that phases are not to be seen as rigid structures or formulas with guaranteed outcomes. Instead, they are descriptive of the dynamics of our cooperating with the Holy Spirit. When the two foundations of the Bible as the Word of God and Jesus as King, and the three keys to revival are embedded in these phases, they become a dynamic, synergistic cycle. In this cycle more and more people are born again into the kingdom of God, the Church of Jesus Christ grows, the kingdom of God is increasingly manifested on earth, the Great Commission of making disciples of Jesus Christ draws closer to completion, and the time of the return of Jesus Christ restoring the kingdom and all things draws nearer and nearer.

The biblical vision of the kingdom of God advancing both geographically and over time is contained in the hymn "God is Working His Purpose Out," which is based on the prophetic visions of Isaiah 11:8 – 10, and Habakkuk 2:14.

God is working his purpose out,
As year succeeds to year:
God is working his purpose out,
And the time is drawing near;
Nearer and nearer draws the time,
The time that shall surely be,
When the earth shall be filled
with the glory of God
As the waters cover the sea.[79]

## Phase #1: Preparing the Altar

Before the fire of Pentecost will fall, an altar must be prepared. How can we cooperate with God the Father, Son, and Holy Spirit to prepare the altar for the fire of the Holy Spirit to fall?

Preparing the altar necessitates preparing the people and preparing the place for the Holy Spirit to fall in power. This includes implementing the R.A. Torrey's three keys for revival and the Goforth foundations, along with additional insights we have gained over the years.

God the Father takes the initiative in the preparation process, and He beckons us to join Him as His co-workers. Here are five ways that our King may call us to cooperate with Him to prepare the altar for the fire of the Holy Spirit to fall. These are given in the following order, but in actual practice may take place simultaneously or with priority given according to the circumstances.

---

[79]Arthur Campbell Ainger (1894), "God is Working His Purpose Out."
https://hymnary.org/text/god_is_working_his_purpose_out

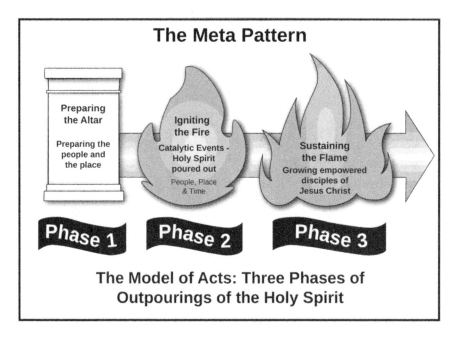

## The Meta Pattern

**Preparing the Altar**

Preparing the people and the place

**Igniting the Fire**

Catalytic Events - Holy Spirit poured out

People, Place & Time

**Sustaining the Flame**

Growing empowered disciples of Jesus Christ

**Phase 1**    **Phase 2**    **Phase 3**

### The Model of Acts: Three Phases of Outpourings of the Holy Spirit

1) **Evangelism In the Power of the Holy Spirit** - Bringing people into the kingdom of God through faith in Jesus Christ and submitting to Jesus as Lord.

As you recall, this is R.A. Torrey's first key to revival—evangelism through the empowered preaching of the gospel of Jesus Christ. This is necessary because, as already pointed out by Torrey, the baptism with the Holy Spirit is for those who are already born-again, have been brought into God's kingdom, and are being formed as living stones into the body of Christ.

In this chapter we shall go further into the specific type of evangelism that is most conducive for preparing the altar.

2) **Teaching on the Biblical Theme of Baptism with the Holy Spirit**

This is R.A. Torrey's second key to revival: teaching on the baptism with the Holy Spirit and inviting people to receive this baptism that Jesus promised. Jesus Christ models this preparatory teaching on the Holy Spirit as part of preparing the first disciples for the outpouring of Pentecost. This preparation starts with the teaching of John the Baptist who announced in Luke 3:16, "I baptize you with water, but one more powerful than I am is coming—I am not worthy to untie the strap of his sandals. He will baptize you with the Holy Spirit and fire."

Then Jesus provides the example of not moving into His public ministry of empowered preaching, teaching, and signs and wonders, until after the Holy Spirit fell upon Him (and remained on Him) during his water baptism in the river Jordan by John (Luke 3:21-22). It was only after this Pentecost event of the Holy Spirit falling upon Jesus, that we find that Jesus is now "full of the Spirit" and "in the power of the Spirit" (Luke 4:1, 4:14).

Jesus adds clear teaching to modeling life in the Spirit. In John 16:4-15 and Luke 24:46-49 Jesus tells His disciples about the role and work of the Holy Spirit. Then after his resurrection, He explains their role in the mission that He is giving them and the need for the equipping of the Holy Spirit.

> [Jesus] said to them, "Thus it stands written that the Christ would suffer and would rise from the dead on the third day, and repentance for the forgiveness of sins would be proclaimed in his name to all nations, beginning from Jerusalem. You are witnesses of these things. And look, I am sending you what my Father promised. But stay in the city until you have been clothed with power from on high." Luke 24:46-49

This teaching preparation is very clear and specific leading up to His ascension.

> To the same apostles also, after his suffering, he presented himself alive with many convincing proofs. He was seen by them over a forty-day period and spoke about matters concerning the kingdom of God. While he was with them, he declared, "Do not leave Jerusalem, but wait there for what my Father promised, which you heard about from me. Acts 1:3-4

This is then followed by very explicit teaching and promises about the work of the Holy Spirit as it connects with the mission given in Acts 1:5-8. All this teaching, which is associated explicitly with empowerment to witness to Jesus Christ alone, is essential if we are to be prepared for these Pentecost events, for without the connection to Jesus and to the Bible, we will inevitably be deceived. We will be led by our own emotional experiences or lack of experience or fall prey to unbiblical human ideologies, doctrines, and philosophies.

3) **The Work of Intercessory Prayer—Praying "Thy Kingdom Come"**

Preparing the altar necessitates that we implement R.A. Torrey's third key to revival—intercessory prayer. We pray for God to send workers into His harvest field; we pray for unbelievers to be brought into the kingdom of God; we pray that new converts will be baptized with the Holy Spirit; we pray strategically for the defeat of Satan's strongholds which are blocking the advance of the kingdom of God; and much more.

4) **Nurturing Born-again People as Disciples of Jesus Christ**

We teach on basic spiritual disciplines that help Christians grow, such as prayer, Bible study, and being a member of a local fellowship of believers (a church).

5) **Standing Firm as Individuals and as Groups in the Face of Refining Fires and Testing in the Wilderness**

Just as Jesus did not allow the test in the wilderness to distract or detour Him, so we must put on the full armor of God and stand firm. In the refining terrain of the wilderness, we come to know by experience that persecution is painful, but God is greater. God advances His kingdom, not by human might or power, but by His Spirit (see Zech. 4:6).

These five ingredients will all need to be built into every program or ministry that is part of preparing for an outpouring of the Holy Spirit. The ministry of PRMI over the last fifty years has developed several very effective programs embodying these five processes that are critical for creating the venue for fulfilling Acts 1:4-8. There are many other ministries that God has greatly used. I suggest that you check them out. Let's be intentional and strategic in preparing the altar, but even more, let's trust and obey our King.

Before concluding this chapter, let's take a closer look at the first R.A. Torrey key to revival, namely, evangelism in the power of the Holy Spirit.

# Evangelism—Bringing People into the Kingdom of God Through Faith in Jesus Christ and Submitting to Jesus as Lord

As a biblical model for evangelism that is led and empowered by the Holy Spirit and advances the kingdom of Jesus Christ, we may observe Philip. The way Jesus worked through Philp embodies a practice of evangelism that is especially effective.

## Model of Philip Doing Holy Spirit-Empowered Evangelism

### Philip – A Born-again Disciple of Jesus Christ Who Had the Holy Spirit in Him, Bearing the Fruit of the Holy Spirit.

To understand the form of evangelism embodied by Philip, we must start with the facts given us in the Bible.  First, he must have been with those who had already come to faith in Jesus Christ and gathered in Jerusalem on the day of Pentecost. We do not know this for sure but can assume that he was a part of the group who was baptized with the Holy Spirit on that day and was part of the newly birthed fellowship of believers. What we definitively know about Philip is that he was "full of the Spirit and wisdom." The Greek here for "full" is the word used to describe the indwelling, sanctifying work of the Holy Spirit which results in wisdom as well as the fruit of the Spirit and is reflected in changed character. This work of the Holy Spirit is distinct from the Holy Spirit falling "upon," giving power for witnessing to Jesus Christ, and results in gifts and manifestations. The empowering work of the Holy Spirit began at Pentecost among the group gathered in the Upper Room who were already born again (i.e., the Holy Spirit already lived in them and was changing their character.)

We meet Philip in Acts 6. Conflicts and disagreements developed within the new community of believers. In this case it was between the widows of the Greek speaking Jews and the native Hebraic Jews over the distribution of food. To solve this problem seven men were chosen to serve as deacons, Philip being one of the seven (Acts 6:5-7). The criteria used to select these individuals included evidence that they had good character and were full of the Spirit and wisdom. The phrase "full of the Holy Spirit" in this case refers to the long-term, inward work of the Holy Spirit that produces Christ-like character qualities.

These were important qualifications for a ministry role that required the just distribution of wealth and expressions of compassion. What was needed was not power, but love, wisdom, and good character. All this prepared Philip for the work of evangelism because, through the indwelling of the Spirit, he not only had a vibrant faith in Jesus Christ, but embodied the character of Jesus Christ—His love, compassion, and servanthood.

**Philip Had Been Baptized with the Holy Spirit, Who Fell Upon Him in Power with Gifts and Manifestations.**

As we noted above, it is likely that Philip was baptized with the Holy Spirit on the Day of Pentecost. Later, Philip and others were forced out of Jerusalem due to persecution. Somewhere in that transition the Holy Spirit called Philip to go and preach the gospel of the kingdom. The Holy Spirit, who had baptized Philip with power to witness, fell on him again, filling him and equipping him to witness to Jesus. Signs and wonders accompanied his evangelistic efforts.

Now those who had been forced to scatter went around proclaiming the good news of the word. Philip went down to the main city of Samaria and began proclaiming the Christ to them. The crowds were paying attention with one mind to what Philip said, as they heard and saw the miraculous signs he was performing. For unclean spirits, crying with loud shrieks, were coming out of many who were possessed, and many paralyzed and lame people were healed. So there was great joy in that city. Acts 8:4-8

We see the wonderful fruit of this empowered ministry. Many were born again through faith in Jesus Christ and were baptized. The emphasis is on the reality that not just men were baptized, as would have been in keeping with the Jewish tradition, but women as well (Acts 8:12)! This points to the radically new thing that God was doing through Jesus Christ in which these traditional barriers were broken down in the new reality of the kingdom of God. People were set free from demons, and indeed the demonic strongholds in the areas were being overcome by the kingdom of God. Even Simon the sorcerer was set free from the demonic stronghold of witchcraft.

> But when they believed Philip as he was proclaiming the good news about the kingdom of God and the name of Jesus Christ, they began to be baptized, both men and women. Even Simon himself believed, and after he was baptized, he stayed close to Philip constantly, and when he saw the signs and great miracles that were occurring, he was amazed. Acts 8:12-13

In due time Philip's responsiveness to the Holy Spirit's nudges led him to leave Samaria and travel down the road toward Gaza where the Spirit led him to witness to an Ethiopian who eventually carried the gospel to his homeland. Propelled by the Spirit, the kingdom of God advanced across cultural and geographic barriers.

All this activity was part of a move of the Holy Spirit, manifesting the reality of Jesus Christ and the kingdom of God. What was taking place was the gospel going forth, advancing the kingdom of God, with signs and wonders (Hebrews 2:3-4). As people were brought into the kingdom through faith in Jesus, they were set free from evil spirits who were coming out of them with shrieks. The love of Jesus was being expressed through all sorts of healings taking place, the most obvious of which was the physical healing of those who had been lame or paralyzed. What is not so obvious but no doubt was taking place was relational healing, in which people's sins were forgiven. No doubt they were also forgiving each other. All these manifestations of the presence of God were leading to the greatest miracle of all, which is that people were being born again into God's eternal kingdom! We do not know how long this season of empowered evangelism lasted; it may have been a few days or weeks or months.

It Is important to recognize that this is not the actual Phase #2 of people being baptized with the Holy Spirit, but rather the preparation for what was to take place later when the apostles came down and laid hands on the converts. While all this is but the start of the revival, it is a most important start—bringing people to be born again into the kingdom of God and Jesus Christ manifesting His majesty and power.

# Summary

Evangelism that is empowered by the Holy Spirit is a major form of preparation of the altar upon which the fire of the Holy Spirit may fall. Indeed, these manifestations demonstrate that the Holy Spirit is already moving and preparing the people and the place.[80] I believe this is the biblical model of how God the Father intends evangelism to take place.

The basic reason why this work of evangelism is so crucial is that the promise of the baptism with the Holy Spirit is given to those who have already been born-again and are members of the kingdom of God. It is also important to note that this type of Holy Spirit-empowered evangelism can only be conducted by those who have already been born-again, are growing as disciples of Jesus Christ, and have been baptized with the Holy Spirit, thereby being enabled to serve as co-workers with Jesus, equipped to cooperate with the Holy Spirit.

Before we move on to Phase #2, Igniting the Fire, let's pause to consider a contemporary example of revival.

---

[80]The PRMI Dunamis Project Unit #6 *Evangelism and Missions in the Power of the Holy Spirit* (or *Listening Evangelism*) deals with the dynamic of evangelism that is empowered and directed by the Holy Spirit. You may find this teaching on PRMI's web page. www.prmi.org

# 10

# The Outpouring at Asbury University in 2023

Does God work in our day like He did 2000 years ago through Philip the evangelist? Do God's love and power still bring people into the kingdom of God? The answer is a resounding "Yes!"

Many times I have experienced signs and wonders occurring in settings in America and around the world while the gospel was being preached, resulting in people being born again into the kingdom of God. Rather than telling stories from the past, let's consider an illustration of God at work right now!

While I am writing this chapter, February 17, 2023, an outpouring has been taking place at Asbury University in Wilmore, Kentucky. In fact, my wife Laura has been listening to the live stream of the praise, prayer, worship, and prophetic words taking place. All this is happening now, in real time! So, I want to take the risk of sharing with you what is taking place because I think it demonstrates Phase #1, Preparing the Altar, especially the work of evangelism and of prayer for revival and for the outpouring of the Holy Spirit. I found out later that Jesus was apparently baptizing and/or refilling some of the students with the Holy Spirit which is Phase #2 Igniting the Fire. Commenting on an outpouring of the Holy Spirit as it is taking place is always risky because there has not been time to assess the long-term results. By the time you read this book, this will be old news and we will be able to assess whether our initial observations were in fact true.

As I am listening to this live stream of worship and praise from Hughes Auditorium, I believe the Holy Spirit spoke to me saying, "Now stop work on the book and mobilize the PRMI intercessors. Call them to pray that this outpouring of the Holy Spirit that I am sending, will be protected and will continue to spread." So, I wrote the following Prayer Communique[81] to our team of intercessors. It is so exciting when the Lord calls us to take part in His present work! This process of cooperation with the Lord is often dynamic and can be a little confusing with multiple things taking place concurrently.

## Prayer Communique February 17, 2023
### from Brad Long and Martin Boardman

For years there has been prayer for a great outpouring of the Holy Spirit that could be the next great awakening. Anointed intercessors like Doug and Carla McMurry have prayed for this for forty years. In the last few years, there has been a great symphony of prayer for revival, which seems to be worldwide in scope.

In 2021 PRMI was led to formally launch the Next Great Awakening Venture (NGA Venture). We believe Jesus called us to pray for and prepare for this next great outpouring. A part of this has been praying for this outpouring among the younger generations. We have joined this great symphony of prayer for revival in the

---

[81]The PRMI *Prayer Communique* is an occasional, when needed publication that is sent out to a select team of intercessors. We must often deal with strategic level intercession and spiritual warfare, so these are usually kept confidential.

Discerning the Times war room, the Next Great Awakening catalyzers group, and other PRMI prayer cohorts.[82]

I had been hearing about the outpouring of the Holy Spirit that was starting to take place at Asbury University in Wilmore, Kentucky. Many people had sent me reports on this event. At the Discerning the Times war room meeting,[83] we were led to pray about this outpouring, that the Lord would protect them from deception, and that it would be used to ignite other outpourings of the Holy Spirit, especially among the younger generations.

On February 15, 2023, after our prayer time, I believe I heard the Lord say that the fiery coals of revival were landing there at Asbury University among the college students, and that we were to send a group to the University. This group could be on site to discern what was taking place, but also to help bring the fires of revival to these younger generations back to the Community the Cross and into PRMI as part of our igniting the NGA among younger generations. I felt the Lord say that we needed to do this right away at the beginning of this present move of God at Asbury, before the Emerging Adult Consultation that will take place March 2-4 at the COC.

---

[82]These are special prayer cohorts of PRMI intercessors under the oversight of Rev. Martin Boardman, Prayer Mobilizer for PRMI and the Dunamis Fellowship Canada.

[83]This gathering of intercessors from Canada, United Kingdom and the United States takes place weekly over Zoom. This meeting has been going since the prayer engagements of 2020 over the demonic invasion during the US Presidential elections. I describe these strategic level prayer engagements in my book, *Days of Infamy: The Demonic Invasion of the United States – November 3, 2020 to January 7, 2021*. Available through PRMI at www.prmi.org

We have representatives flying in from Canada, the UK, and the USA for that set-apart event.

I sent this guidance out to a team of intercessors on February 16. I also called Cindy in the UK, who was there for the DFB&I annual meeting. We discerned that this might be a *kairos* moment.

At the same time, JuleAnn (our prayer coordinator for the Community of the Cross) had been led through a powerful dream in which she was standing among young people in a revival where she was to go. We also strongly felt that Victoria Geurink (the PRMI office manager) should go as she is of that age group and is leading our Upward Challenge Program at the COC this summer. The purpose is to ignite a movement of the Holy Spirit in young teens.

Victoria and JuleAnn left yesterday at about 5:00 pm to get

*Victora and JuleAnn at Asbury*

as close to Wilmore, KY, as possible. They could only find a vacant hotel room in Beria, Kentucky, about an hour away. People are flooding into the meetings, and buses have been bringing students from other Christian and secular colleges to the revival. Already there are reports of the move of God spreading to other colleges.

Praise God!!

To help us pray into this great outpouring, here are some pictures from my daughter Rebecca, pastor at St. Giles Presbyterian Church in Richmond, VA. She sent it from Craig

Keener's Facebook post. She has been watching the live stream all day and is joining the prayer work.

Please pray for the outpouring that is taking place and pray for Victoria and JuleAnn as they enter into what is taking place. It is urgent that we step into this tremendous kairos moment of opportunity. Also, we must, in the name of Jesus Christ, block any plans that Satan must surely have to subvert or to hinder this gracious work of God. Thanks so much.
**END of First Part of the Prayer Communique –**

When JuleAnn and Victoria arrived at Asbury I started to receive a steady stream of reports from them about what was taking place. These were also passed on to the PRMI intercessors and I include them in the book to provide a flavor of what is taking place.


Initial Reports from JuleAnn

12:45 –We are inside. It's so holy in here. Amazing. We stood in the cold from 8:30 until about 12:15. Snow and frigid but we're ok. This is worth it.
1:06 –I'm seeing ppl [people] praying for each other. There is such a gentle love and reconciliation encouragement

167

amongst "strangers" all ages and races. This is really happening. I'm hearing the LORD saying I'm here and I'm pouring My love over thirsty souls.

1:09 –This is genuine. No showiness. Sweet holiness. Stunning. Beautiful. I keep seeing His goodness and gentleness sweeping back and forth over the ppl as ppl are pouring their hearts out in worship.

1:43— It's so wonderful. The Spirit gently is moving throughout the room in gentle waves. Ppl are being touched deeply. Jesus is clearly here. All 4 questions of discernment are being checked. Thank you for inviting me to do this. This is really a fulfillment of the dream the LORD gave me. This is really happening.

BRAD 1:44 – Thanks keep sending the reports. We are watching the live stream. Amazing!

1:55 – It's all Jesus. This guy is prophesying and praying over us that the Holy Spirit breaks our heart for the lost.

1:56 – This is an anointing of evangelism and intercession. Break our hearts!

1:58—Hearts are breaking. There is an outcry. A new wave is moving.

1:59—Worship pray and testify.

2:06— It's full. Jam-packed. They have prayer teams. At the altar. Victoria and I are so excited to bring it back. They have worship and then reading scripture simply no exhorting just reading and then saying this is the word of God and we believe it.

2:46—Praying for prodigals.

2:59— Crying out for Jesus—pressing into the kindness of God. Repentance and reconciliation. Confession just leave it here. Holy Spirit looking deeply into hearts. Worship, Word and the Youth--we are covering and blessing them. The Holy Spirit is empowering the young. Blessing them encouraging. Breaking off things. This is amazing. Honoring and blessing the young.

3:05—Praying for the church now.

3:32—This is nonstop open heaven. I'm seeing Holy spiritual fire Holy Spirit fire!!!3:57—Praying for awakening over the US and then the world. Powerful. The room is roaring. **Stopping with JuleAnn reports. But they keep coming!**

I have presented this to you in the unrefined raw form to just give you a flavor of the dynamic of the working of the Holy Spirit. However, I think it is important to add some reflections on the revival and to place the vivid firsthand reports by JuleAnn and Victoria in their larger context. Dr. Craig Keener[84] is a professor and prolific author at Asbury Seminary. He places the events that took place at Asbury University in the historical context of past revivals and points to the way that this outpouring is a harbinger of more outpourings to come. Dr. Keener is well qualified to offer this discernment. First, he was there on site when the Holy Spirit fell! Further he is also a student of global revivals and a New Testament scholar.

Dr. Keener has been a great influence on my own writing and teaching on the Holy Spirit. Of special importance for me and the Dunamis Project is his two-volume work entitled *Miracles: The Credibility of the New Testament Accounts,* which provides a biblical,

---

[84] Dr. Keener did his Ph.D. work in New Testament and Christian origins at Duke University and is known for his work as a New Testament scholar on Bible background (commentaries on the New Testament in its early Jewish and Greco-Roman settings). Well over a million of his thirty-plus books are in circulation and have won thirteen national and international awards. His award-winning, popular-level IVP Bible Background Commentary: New Testament (now in its second edition [2014], and available in a number of languages) has sold over half a million copies.

philosophical, theological, and historical basis for the continuation of the empowering gift-giving of the Holy Spirit as promised in Acts 1:4-8.

Here are some excerpts from an interview with Dr. Keener by David Shedlock in the blog, Caffeinatedthoughts, published March 6, 2023.[85] Dr. Keener places what happened at Asbury in its historical context.[86]

*David - What are your thoughts on the First Great Awakening? and the Second Great Awakening? The Azusa Street Revival?*

**Dr. Keener** –That Calvinists (such as Whitefield and Edwards) dominated the First Great Awakening on this side of the Atlantic and Armenians dominated the Second Great Awakening should warn us against supposing that God pours out his Spirit only on his children with this or that theology. He blesses us because we are his children in Christ, not because we merit it on our own account. There have also been different kinds of awakenings or revivals in history.

What has happened at Asbury is closer to the template of college awakenings, including past Asbury revivals. (I think also of the postwar revival in schools in Nigeria in the 1960s; in the US, the Haystack Prayer Meeting propelled workers into missions.) Some events we call awakenings consisted of various revivals, and altogether lasted for decades. The Second Great Awakening was like that; indeed, the Methodist Church then grew from Francis Asbury's arrival in the US until the time of his death 40 years later, 1000 times. And of course, the Azusa Street Revival, though only a few years at its height, propelled so many workers into mission that there are now estimated to be more than half a billion Pentecostals and charismatics in the world. Admittedly, those so classified by

---

[85]Published on March 6, 2023 David Shedlock , *Professor Craig Keener on the Recent Asbury Outpouring:* "The reality of what some of us call revival is initiated by God. It is not initiated by us."
https://caffeinatedthoughts.com/2023/03/professor-craig-keener-on-the-recent-asbury-outpouring/

[86]The pictures of the Asbury outpouring as well as the following comments from Dr. Craig Keener are used with his permission.

sociologists are an amorphous group, but even at minimal estimates they remain the second largest block in Christendom next to the Roman Catholic Church, with which they overlap.

**David** –*Were the recent events at Asbury precipitated by a particular sermon? During the time of these services, was there regular preaching, or was it primarily prayer and singing?*

**Dr. Keener**—Prayer and singing dominated, as in the Welsh Revival, but because of a sense of God's awesome majesty that was too palpable to do otherwise than to give God honor. When you're in God's presence, you can't boast. It humbles you. A chief characteristic of this experience was what the leaders called "radical humility" and unity before the cross. They kept those up front nameless, preserving the revival's sanctity by honoring the Lord alone. While that was the focus, however, there were regular moments of scripture readings from students, testimonies of how people had been touched, and preaching (including preaching the gospel of Christ and calls for consecration and reminders of God's love and healing for those who know they need him). ...

**David**— *While there is no way to know where the Spirit will blow, is there any reason to think this will last? And if it does, what will that look like?*

**Dr. Keener**—One pattern in Luke-Acts is that outpourings of the Spirit, individual or collective, often follow prayer (cf. Luke 3:21-22; 11:13; Acts 1:14; 4:31; 8:15). That has often been true in subsequent history as well, for example, concerts of prayer during the First Great Awakening that led to the Second. People in the Asbury community had not forgotten the earlier Asbury revivals, such as 1905, 1908, 1950, and 1970, and prayer for another one has continued over decades. What happened on the university campus has not happened on this scale here for 50 years. It's not about the place, but an ethos that *welcomes* the outpouring of the Spirit and honors God's holiness is far likelier to experience it than a place resistant to it. If we look at past Asbury revivals as a template, those who experienced the heart of it were never the same and went out to change the world for Christ, our worthy king, often in intercultural missions. – End of Interview

Dr. Keener in personal notes to us added some further insights to the above published interview:

"I am so grateful I was in town—I had always prayed that I would be here when a significant outpouring would come. I had to travel a lot in March and April and the university let out for summer by the time I could slow down. I would like to add to your assessment the following:

First, I think, different revivals/outpourings take different shapes even as they did in Acts. I did hear from some students that a number of students at Hughes Auditorium were praying in tongues (certainly I was) but everything was respectful, and nobody was seeking attention, so the public worship was in English (and occasionally Spanish or some other language from some of the worship leaders). Of course, tongues have not happened at all revivals, much as I love to pray in them :-)

Second, concerning follow up: The university is on summer break now and I was not around much after February to observe what was happening. The public meetings ended officially on Feb. 23 (except for those under age 25), impossible to sustain logistically (I myself didn't realize how exhausted I was until the public meetings stopped, and then I was ready to collapse!) Some people still arrived, and we prayed for/with them but that was by the Lord's arrangement rather than anything official. (At the height of the outpouring there were twice as many visitors in town as residents, and the strain on the local community resources became so great that the police blocked the road into town! But hundreds of people were feeling led to donate food, etc., so that as long as Hughes Chapel remained open to the public there was enough food available.)

One of the campus pastors, however, shared that everyone he talked with said they'd never forget this experience. That's not the same as saying that everybody is still experiencing outpouring per se; my wife and I have talked with students both at the university and the seminary who have been deeply touched and some others (a smaller number) who are bewildered and don't know what to make of what happened. That has happened in past outpourings as well (not least on the day of Pentecost). The university has Bible studies planned for the dorms this coming year (I'm not sure if that's every year or something new) and they will be studying the book of Acts.

The idea of concluding the public meetings on Feb. 23 was to pass the torch beyond Asbury. Over a year in advance Feb. 23 had been scheduled as the collegiate day of prayer—with Asbury as its host campus and hundreds of other campuses connected by videoconference. It looks like God was getting the campus ready to pass the torch. The focus at Asbury now is mostly discipling the students. Previous Asbury revivals have lasted just 1-2 weeks, but the impact coming out of them has been missionaries and servants of the gospel around the world. I expect the same will be the case here. But again, Asbury was just a place where the spark exploded; God is working around the world."

Dr. Keeners' observations connecting the events at Asbury University to the history of revivals is most helpful! Let's make some further connections to the patterns of the Holy Spirit's ways of working that we have identified in this book.

First the five markers of outpourings: The "address" and "time stamp" are suggested as follows:

"The revival was sparked by students spontaneously staying in Hughes Auditorium following a regularly scheduled chapel service on February 8, 2023." [87]

Chapel attendance is mandatory for students on certain weekdays. On Wednesday, February 8, 2023, a handful of students remained in the

---

[87]https://en.wikipedia.org/wiki/2023_Asbury_revival

chapel following a regularly scheduled service. Student body president Alison Perfater was one of them, and in an interview with Tucker Carlson, said it was after a fellow student decided to openly confess some of his sins to the small group that 'the atmosphere changed'."

The "prepared group" were the students who had been nurtured in biblical faith and Methodist-Holiness spirituality in the context of the history of outpourings of the Holy Spirit that had already taken place at Asbury. In 2011, with Rev. Cindy Strickler and a PRMI healing team, I was invited by Dr. Steve Seamands[88] to teach on healing at conferences at Asbury. I was greatly impressed at the spiritual atmosphere of the university and seminary campus; it was infused with the presence of Jesus Christ. I could see that this would be a fertile ground for an outpouring of the Holy Spirit.

Where does this fit in the meta pattern? It seems clear that the altar has been prepared, and the fire is falling. In many ways from my perspective at a distance, this seems very much in accord with what was taking place in Acts 8 with the manifest presence of God bringing repentance, commitment to Christ, and working in signs and wonders, bringing the Samaritans into saving faith. God is truly manifesting His presence at Asbury. The revival move of the Holy Spirit is already spreading to other Christian colleges and, most remarkable for this generation, is going viral over the internet. A report confirming this:

---

[88]Dr. Steve Seamands, Professor of Christian Doctrine, Asbury Theological Seminary. M.Div., Asbury Theological Seminary, 1972 Ph.D., Drew University, 1983.  https://thrive.asburyseminary.edu/dr-steve-seamands/

"Responses to the revival have been reported at other university campuses, such as Samford University, Cedarville University and University of the Cumberlands. The revival notably is ecumenical in its expression, with Methodist, Baptist, Episcopal, and Roman Catholic groups participating in its spread. Visitors told The Washington Post stories of "miracles and healing" they witnessed at the event, along with unparalleled hospitality by locals and students." [89]

This is all wonderful, but are they moving to Phase #2 which is the fulfillment of Acts 1:4-8, of students receiving the baptism with the Holy Spirit and being empowered to be witnesses to Jesus Christ? It seems so, but we shall see from the lasting fruit! Also, at this point so soon after the initial move of God, it remains to be seen whether they will be able to enter Phase #3 and to sustain the flame. We have every hope and expectation that this revival will continue to grow and spread among this generation.

I believe that we are called to pray for their protection against the demonic counterattacks that often follow the manifest presence of God. We must also pray for this work of the Holy Spirit not just to continue there, but to spread.

The events at Asbury University in 2023, are a very hopeful sign that God the Father is, in our epoch, reaching to incorporate into His eternal kingdom the younger generations. I believe this is a harbinger that we are in the preparatory phases of a global revival with the potential to become the Third Great Awakening which may well complete the Great Commission. We now must turn to the crucial second phase of Igniting the Fire, which is Jesus baptizing with the Holy Spirit those who have been brought into His kingdom.

---

[89]https://en.wikipedia.org/wiki/2023_Asbury_revival

# 11

# Phase #2 Igniting the Fire— The Dunamis Project

Before moving into this chapter, let's pause for an overview and review of major concepts. We have identified these as the apostolic biblical blueprint for preparing and igniting revivals.

**Five Distinctive Markers of All "Pentecost" Events**

1. The Holy Spirit always pours out His grace and power on **prepared individuals and/or groups.**

2. Outpourings of the Holy Spirit always have a **physical address.**

3. Outpourings of the Holy Spirit always have a **time stamp**.

4. **Jesus Christ baptizes people with the Holy Spirit.** This happens directly by Jesus or is mediated through His anointed co-workers.

5. The outpouring results in individuals and groups **becoming empowered witnesses to Jesus Christ.**

To discern whether you are experiencing a genuine "Pentecost" event in fulfillment with Acts 1:4-8, look for these five markers.

**R.A. Torrey's Three Keys to Revival**

1. Evangelistic preaching and soul winning

2. Teaching on baptism with the Holy Spirit and praying for people to be baptized with the Holy Spirit

3. The work of prayer

**Jonathan Goforth's Two Foundations**

1. The Bible as the Word of God

2. Jesus Christ as King

The Five Markers of Pentecost Events, The Three Keys, and the Two Foundations, when put in place, become what the Lord uses to ignite outpouring of the Holy Spirit, which in turn set in motion revivals that grow the Church, advance the kingdom of God, and fulfill the Great Commission.

All this may take place within the context of what we are calling the meta pattern.

## The Meta Pattern

**Phase #1: Preparing the Altar:** God the Father prepares an individual or a group whom He has called into His master salvation and kingdom plans.

**Phase #2: Igniting the Fire:** This occurs when Jesus baptizes with the Holy Spirit the prepared individuals and groups, initiating them into the dance of cooperating with the Holy Spirit to be witnesses and co-workers with Jesus Christ.

**Phase #3: Sustaining the Flame:** Once the Holy Spirit is poured out upon the individuals and/or groups who took part in the Pentecost igniting event, they must continue to do the work of intercessory prayer as well as nurturing believers as disciples of Jesus Christ and standing firm in the face of the world, the flesh, and the devil.

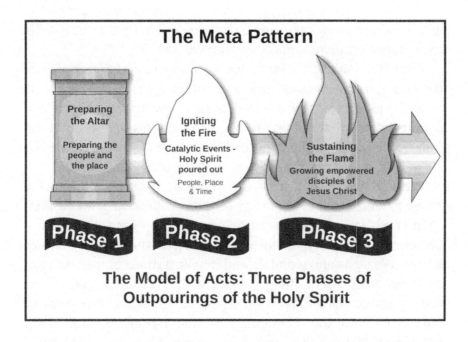

# The Meta Pattern

**Preparing the Altar**

Preparing the people and the place

**Igniting the Fire**

Catalytic Events - Holy Spirit poured out

People, Place & Time

**Sustaining the Flame**

Growing empowered disciples of Jesus Christ

**Phase 1** **Phase 2** **Phase 3**

## The Model of Acts: Three Phases of Outpourings of the Holy Spirit

In this chapter I want to focus on the actual igniting of the fire of the Holy Spirit in the Pentecost event. I believe that in our present epoch of hoping for and praying for revival, we have entered a kairos season in which God intends to ignite these Pentecost events.

## Phase #2: "Igniting the Fire" is an Event and Not a Process

Whereas Phase #1 and Phase #3 are usually extended processes, Phase #2 is an event. Why? Because of the nature of the baptism with the Holy Spirit. It is an occasion when people experience the

Holy Spirit falling upon them, initiating them into the empowering work of the Holy Spirit as Jesus' co-workers. This initiatory event is a concrete occurrence that the person or group experiences. As R.A. Torrey confirms from the biblical witness: "The baptism with the Holy Spirit is a definite experience of which one may and ought to know whether he has received it or not."

Following their baptism, the Holy Spirit's empowerment occurs episodically, that is, again and again as needed. Only Jesus lived in a permanent state of empowerment; we do not.

After this initiation experience a person begins to experience the Holy Spirit falling upon him or her or filling them. The result will often be expressions of the Holy Sprit's power through gifts and manifestations that witness to Jesus Christ. This operation of the Holy Spirit, which is referred to in Acts 1:4-8, is distinct from the indwelling, saving, and sanctifying working of the Holy Spirit.[90]

We see this moving from the Phase #1 process and into the Phase #2 Pentecost event in the reports of Philip in Samaria (Acts chapter 8). We do not know just how long Phase #1 lasted in Samaria, but it was marked by preaching of the gospel in which there were signs and wonders and manifestations of the reality of the kingdom of God. The greatest miracle is that people by the droves were coming to faith in Yeshua the Messiah and were being born-again into the kingdom, with the biblical sign of water baptism. All this, while accompanied by many manifestations of the power of the Holy Spirit through Philip, was part of the inward work of the Holy Spirit. People became disciples of Jesus Christ and then began the process of growing as disciples.

At some point during all this wonderful and exciting activity of people being set free from bondages, confessing and repenting, experiencing Jesus' healing power, and entering salvation, the text notes the following:

---

[90]See the PRMI Dunamis Project, Unit #1 *Gateways to Empowered Ministry* teaching on the distinctions between the inward and outward workings of the Holy Spirit. www.prmi.org

Now when the apostles in Jerusalem heard that Samaria had accepted the word of God, they sent Peter and John to them. These two went down and prayed for them so that they would receive the Holy Spirit. (For the Spirit had not yet come upon any of them, but they had only been baptized in the name of the Lord Jesus.) Then Peter and John placed their hands on the Samaritans, and they received the Holy Spirit. Acts 8:14-17

The clear import of these verses is that the Samaritan believers were not yet baptized with the Holy Spirit according to the model of Acts 1:4-8 so that they may be initiated into becoming witnesses and co-workers with Jesus Christ. Their baptism with the Holy Spirit took place when Peter and John laid hands on them.

What happened next is not recorded for us. There may have been all sorts of manifestations comparable to the first Pentecost event, but we don't know if that was the case. We may surmise, however, that something very definite and observable took place because Simon, the newly converted wizard, saw something.

Now Simon, when he saw that the Spirit was given through the laying on of the apostles' hands, offered them money, saying, "Give me this power too, so that everyone I place my hands on may receive the Holy Spirit." Acts 8:18-19

After the Samaritans were initiated into the empowering work of the Holy Spirit, they could continue the evangelistic and discipling work in that location. Peter and John returned to Jerusalem but spread the fire of the gospel along the way there. Philip, through whom Jesus had launched the first phase of bringing the people into the kingdom of God, was then called out of Samaria for his next assignment, to bring the Ethiopian eunuch into salvation. After the Pentecost event, the revival in Samaria moves to Phase #3, Sustaining the Flame, which will entail growing the church and fellowship there. That this took place is suggested in the reports after Saul was converted and became the Apostle Paul:

> Then the church throughout Judea, Galilee, and Samaria experienced peace and thus was strengthened. Living in the fear of the Lord and in the encouragement of the Holy Spirit, the church increased in numbers. Acts 9:31

It seems that Paul himself may have been a part of the discipling process. This is suggested in Acts 15:3 where in Samaria and in other locations "... they were relating at length the conversion of the Gentiles and bringing great joy to all the brothers." Evidently a type of ongoing discipling and teaching was taking place.

At this juncture one may ask an important question: "Why did not Philip, who was so obviously anointed by the Holy Spirit for evangelism with signs and wonders, lay hands on the Samaritans resulting in them receiving the baptism with the Holy Spirit? Why did the apostles have to come down from Jerusalem?" Hold that question until the chapter on becoming a fire starter.

We will find some redundancy with the two foundations and the biblical pattern for igniting outpourings. There will also be some differences in sequencing and emphasis between the first Pentecost event and those that follow, including our experiences.

### A. For the Fire to Fall at the First Pentecost Event, Those Gathered in the Upper Room Had to Have Been Born-again.

This took place through faith in Jesus Christ. They were fully convinced that Jesus was indeed raised from the dead and was indeed their Lord and Savior. I believe that those first disciples and the others in the core group following Jesus were already born-again by the indwelling of the Holy Spirit. **This is why the first R.A. Torrey key is preaching the gospel of Jesus Christ so that people may be born into the kingdom of God.**

After the first Pentecost event, the Lord worked through empowered preaching of the gospel of Jesus Christ with signs and wonders that manifested the presence and power of God. These took place after the disciples were filled with the Holy Spirit. For example, the Holy Spirit manifested powerfully through the ministry of Philip.

### B.  The Model of Philip—Doing Evangelism in the Power of the Holy Spirit with Jesus Manifesting in Signs and Wonders.

Philip was part of the first outpouring that took place. He had been baptized with the Holy Spirit along with the other 120.  He was first called as a deacon helping with the growing community. Then when this wonderful community of believers were forced to flee under persecution, he moved into being a Holy Spirit-empowered evangelist.

Philip went down to the main city of Samaria and began proclaiming the Christ to them. The crowds were paying attention with one mind to what Philip said, as they heard and saw the miraculous signs he was performing. For unclean spirits, crying with loud shrieks, were coming out of many who were possessed, and many paralyzed and lame people were healed. So there was great joy in that city. Acts 8:5-8

But when they believed Philip as he was proclaiming the good news about the kingdom of God and the name of Jesus Christ, they began to be baptized, both men and women. Even Simon himself believed, and after he was baptized, he stayed close to Philip constantly, and when he saw the signs and great miracles that were occurring, he was amazed. Acts 8:12-13

Signs and wonders are taking place for two reasons: First, they are showing the validity of the gospel. Second, they are the actual manifestations of the kingdom of Jesus Christ.

### C. Teaching and preparation for the baptism with the Holy Spirit.

Jesus had already provided teaching on the Holy Spirit for the disciples.

To the same apostles also, after his suffering, he presented himself alive with many convincing proofs. He was seen by them over a forty-day period and spoke about matters concerning the Kingdom of God. While he was with them, he declared, "Do not leave Jerusalem, but wait there for what my Father promised, which you heard about from me. Acts 1:3-4

We see in John 16:4-15 and Luke 24:46-49 that Jesus Christ does provide teaching on the Holy Spirit. After giving a version of the Great Commission that they were called to preach, He then commanded them to wait until they received power. (Bold added for emphasis.)

[Jesus] said to them, "Thus it stands written that the Christ would suffer and would rise from the dead on the third day, and repentance for the forgiveness of sins would be proclaimed in his name to all nations, beginning from Jerusalem. You are witnesses of these things. And look, I am sending you what my Father promised. But stay in the city until you have been **clothed with power from on high**." Luke 24:46-49

### D. They were growing together in unity and prayer

All these continued together in prayer with one mind, together with the women, along with Mary the mother of Jesus, and his brothers. In those days Peter stood up among the believers (a gathering of about one hundred and twenty people) and said ... Act 1:14-15

The ability to pray in "one mind" was based on the unity forged through their common experiences of having walked with Jesus, witnessed the horror of His arrest, trial, crucifixion and his burial, which included not just Jesus' tortured body, but all their hopes that He was the promised messiah. Their unity of one mind was sealed, as together they were the eyewitnesses to the most astonishing, unparalleled events in human history—Jesus was resurrected from the dead, appeared to them on numerous occasions, announced that He had received "All authority in heaven and on earth," and then ascended into heaven in a cloud of glory.

This shared experience of the reality of Jesus Christ was the basis of their preparation to receive the Holy Spirit. However, the basis of their unity in this common experience of Jesus was not perfect nor based on total conformity. For even at this point in their firsthand encounters with Jesus it is noted that, "When they saw him, they worshiped him, but some doubted" (Matthew 28:17). I find that one line that "some doubted" to be the greatest confirmation that all of what is recorded in the Gospels and the book of Acts are actual historical events that took place, and the people who witnessed them were people just like us. These are not myths nor made up stories, but real events to which any group of people, including us today, would have had a diversity of reactions, including doubt and unbelief.

### E. Lastly, they were obedient to Jesus Christ and the directions that He had given them.

While he was with them, he declared, "Do not leave Jerusalem, but wait there for what my Father promised, which you heard about from me. For John baptized with water, but you will be baptized with the Holy Spirit not many days from now." Acts 1:4-5

They obeyed Jesus and stayed in Jerusalem, thus putting themselves in the geographical location the Lord had chosen where, at the appointed time, the Holy Spirit was to be poured out.

**Summary of the Different Ways that God Will Prepare the Altar that May Be Put into Program Expressions**

Extrapolating from the experience of the first followers of Jesus preparing for the first Pentecost event, we find the following basic conditions for preparing the altar. These are supported through the other outpourings that took place, are recorded in the book of Acts and backed up by our own contemporary experience.

- Concerted persistent prayer for the outpouring of the Holy Spirit.

- Teaching on the baptism of the Holy Spirit by an anointed teacher.

- Teaching/preaching a vision of the kingdom of God and His sovereignty over every aspect of society because Jesus Christ has received "all authority in heaven and on earth."

- Growing in John 17 love and unity within the Church. Acts 1:14

- Evangelism that shares the gospel and calls people to saving faith in Jesus Christ.

- Making disciples of Jesus Christ who love Jesus and are growing in intimacy with Jesus, are called to holiness, and are living into the Great Commission.

- Acting in obedience to Jesus Christ to gather in one place in fellowship which includes prayer and praise.

- The Lord may also allow persecution of the fellowship which drives us to face our powerlessness and fall on our faces, crying out to God.

- Preparing the altar for the Holy Spirit to fall connects with preparing the set-apart group of people, which is the third marker of God's activity.

## At the First Gateways Dunamis Event in 1991

I have already shared with you several Pentecost events that have taken place. Here I need to tell you the story of Holy Spirit falling at Lake George, New York in 1991, which ignited the Dunamis wave of the Holy Spirit. Over the past thirty years this has taken the programmatic form of the Dunamis Project. Everywhere this equipping process has been implemented, it has prepared people to experience Pentecost events. This has taken place in many locations in North America, Central and South America, UK, Europe, Eurasia, Africa (especially Uganda, Nigeria, and South Africa), the Middle East, Japan, Korea, China, Hong Kong, Indonesia, New Zealand, Eastern Europe, and more. In some locations these have become significant tributaries of the great revival of God, empowering people for growing the Church and fulfilling the Great Commission. This movement has been sustained for over thirty years, and, at the writing of this book continues to grow and expand. We shall return later to Phase #3 Sustaining the Flame and explore the dynamic of how this movement has been able to continue. For now, we need to understand how it all began. Come with me to a Pentecost event in Lake George, New York, at the Silver Bay YMCA Conference Center in March of 1991.

### Phase #1: Preparing the Altar for the Pentecost Event at Lake George, New York

Preparing the altar for the fire of the Holy Spirit to fall at Lake George in 1991 was a long process. This preparation included not only the preparation of individuals but also the ebbs and flows of the Charismatic Renewal movement and the development of the ministry of PRMI. I need to give some brief history to set the stage for this outpouring,

Presbyterian Reformed Ministries International (PRMI) was founded in 1966 as Presbyterian Charismatic Communion (PCC). This is a great story of how five Presbyterian ministers received the baptism with the Holy Spirit and moved into empowered witness to Jesus Christ, igniting fires of renewal of Biblical faith within their congregations. They were all rejected by the leadership of the Presbyterian Church. Some lost their ordination.

After this rejection by the denomination, instead of joining the independent church movement, they received God's call to stay in the Presbyterian Church with the intent of igniting fires of revival within the church. They formed the PCC to welcome and to nurture into empowered discipleship the many thousands of Presbyterians who, like them, were experiencing the baptism with the Holy Spirit and becoming empowered witnesses to Jesus Christ. This ministry grew and expanded under the anointed leadership of the Rev. Brick Bradford and his associate, Rev. Carter Blaisdell. Theirs is an amazing story of how God worked, and the Charismatic Renewal spread through large conferences and to hundreds of Presbyterian and Reformed congregations in North America. As I have already noted, God also used Brick Bradford to ignite Pentecost events in Korea, Taiwan, and Japan. The "Spirit Alive" program directed by Carter Blaisdell had ignited charismatic renewal in hundreds of congregations within the Presbyterian and Reformed denominations in the USA and Canada. All this is a wonderful history and a firm foundation upon which their successors could build, but by the time I came on as Executive Director in January of 1990, the Charismatic Renewal was at an ebb. This ministry was essentially bankrupt and in need of new vision. A number of the big-name leaders in the charismatic movement who could be counted on to pack out conferences, had gone into retirement. Some had died and others had fallen into sin or gone off the rails into unbiblical doctrines, bringing division and confusion. Frankly, it was a huge shock and disillusionment, having come from Taiwan where the move of the Holy Spirit was at full tide, to be called into leadership in a receding and fragmented movement and a ministry that was in debt, without enough financial gifts to pay the office rent, the office staff, or my own salary. Later I found that it had only been through heroic efforts and great personal sacrifice that Brick and Carter had held the ministry together until my arrival.

On a personal note, this first year as Executive Director was a time of terrible refining fire for Laura and me. Our three children were unhappy having to adapt to Oklahoma western culture. There was no money to pay my salary, so we were using up our savings to live and pay rent. The local Presbytery that we were in— Indian Nations Presbytery—was suspicious of us and not just unwelcoming but vocally hostile.

I remember one night I was in complete despair and ready to quit. To get away from the children, Laura and I took a long walk in which I asked my wonderful wife, "Now tell me why we are here and how did we get here?" As we talked and prayed, we surrendered ourselves to the Lord and said, "Lord we can do nothing! You're in charge completely!" I think the Lord had to get us to the point of complete surrender and giving up on ourselves before He could start His work.

This desperate, bleak situation drove the Board of Directors and me as the newly called Executive Director into urgent prayer. As we cried out together to the Lord, clear guidance came.

First, He birthed in me a new vision for the ministry—a vision which was approved by the PRMI Board of Directors and has been our guiding vision statement (with some modifications) for three decades. This vision statement put us on the right track of what we were to be doing: "Exalting Jesus Christ, igniting the Church in the power of the Holy Spirit, and doing this under the authority of the Holy Bible as the Word of God..."[91] There is more, but what I think the Lord did was to establish the two Goforth foundations for outpourings of the Holy Spirit—Jesus as King, and the Bible as the Word of God.

Second, God led the PRMI Board to make a profound policy change. We were not to charge for ministry nor were we to utilize coercive fund-raising techniques. Rather we were to pray for God's guidance, step out in obedience, and follow Jesus' directions as He

---

[91]The complete vision statement is as follows: Exalting Jesus Christ, Igniting the Church in the Power of the Holy Spirit, and doing this under the Authority of the Holy Bible as the Word of God; Through Prayer, Leadership, Development, Growing the Church and Mission Outreach, So that the Church may be Empowered to Do all that Christ Commands for the Glory of God the Father.

called us to work with Him to do our part in creating venues for the Father to keep on fulfilling Acts 1:4-8. We were to pray for the people and financial provisions needed to do what the Lord was calling us to do, and to trust the Lord for provision. We were to share the vision of what the Lord was doing and present the opportunity for people to take part through prayer, participation, and financial giving. This put us as a ministry, and me personally, on the right track of doing God's work in God's way, which is, "Not by strength and not by power, but by my Spirit,' says the LORD who rules over all" (Zechariah 4:6).

This has been hard to follow. But over the years, it has resulted in God's amazing provision of people, finances, and open doors, which usually were not on our timetable but His! This put us in the place where we could receive God's vision and direction, and trust Him to walk it out in obedience. Above all He has given us the gift of mountain-moving faith, which is a fundamental condition for praying in Pentecost events.

Third, the Lord said, "Do what you did in Taiwan as the beginning! Start Korean style Prayer Mountains with prayer and fasting. Call the people to pray for Me to send a new outpouring of the Holy Spirit." I thought to myself that it would never work to gather Americans and Canadians together for days of prayer and fasting. But to my amazement I found that we were not the only ones desperate for a move of God: Thousands were! In 1990 we offered a series of Prayer Mountain events in various conference centers around the United States—in California, Pennsylvania, North Carolina, and Toronto, Canada. People came! Often there were two to three hundred people praying and fasting for three to five days. The Lord anointed me to call for these gatherings and to lead them; I also invited other anointed prayer leaders to join me in these events.

This was fulfilling the third R.A. Torrey prescription for revival, which is a few people gathered in prayer. At these Prayer Mountains the Holy Spirit started to move, manifesting Jesus' power and presence. There was healing ministry, effective intercession, and even some people being filled with the Holy Spirit. Mostly, however, the focus was on praying for an outpouring of the Holy Spirit in the congregations. I believe without doubt that it was those Prayer Mountains that prepared the way for the great outpouring and wave of the Holy Spirit that this ministry was to experience for the next thirty years.

Fourth, the other word of guidance that we received was to gather a group of seasoned leaders in the charismatic movement to ask God to reveal a new wineskin, not just for reigniting outpourings of the Holy Spirit, but for equipping leaders to provide anointed leadership for the movement. So, we gathered a small group in 1990 in Oklahoma City to seek God's guidance. Among them were Doug McMurry and Carter Blaisdell, the Associate Director of PRMI, as well as some others who had been touched by the Vineyard movement taking place through John Wimber.

As we prayed together, the Lord gave us the vision of a process for fulfilling Acts 1:4-8 and equipping leaders who had been baptized with the Holy Spirit to continue to cooperate with the Holy Spirit in advancing the kingdom of God. The result of this meeting was that we designed the entire program called the Dunamis Project.[92] This was partly based on my experience of equipping

---

[92] The PRMI Dunamis Project is a series of six five-day equipping events generally conducted in a set-apart location. These equipping events take place over a period of three years. The six units each accompanied with an extensive manual are as follows: *Gateways to Empowered Ministry* (Introducing the Person and work of the Holy Spirit), *In the Spirit's Power* (Learning to cooperate with the Holy Spirit and growing in the gifts of the Holy Spirit), *The Power of Prayer*, *The Healing Ministry of Jesus*, *Spiritual Warfare for Kingdom Advance*, and *Listening Evangelism: Evangelism and Missions in the Power of the Holy Spirit*. For more information and to register for an event near you in the USA,

leaders for the move of the God that had taken place in Taiwan. Doug McMurry, a gifted author, teacher, and intercessor, and I started to write the first of the six manuals which were to accompany each of the five-day events.

The first one was entitled *Gateways to Empowered Ministry*. This was based on R.A. Torrey's biblical exposition of the person and work of the Holy Spirit. We added teaching from Charles Kraft on worldview.[93] We also brought in Doug's study of revival history, and I included practical lessons from being on the frontlines of the move of the Holy Spirit in Korea and Taiwan. The first five-day event was scheduled for March of 1991 at the Silver Bay YMCA Conference Center in Lake George, New York. We chose this location because the Bay Road Presbyterian Church, pastored by Rev. Dick Byrd, was an on-fire charismatic congregation that could provide prayer and logistical support. This pastor had been involved for years in PRMI's Spirit Alive program that ignited outpourings of the Holy Spirit in hundreds of congregations.

I invited my mentor Archer Torrey to come from Korea to join Doug and me in teaching this first Dunamis event. (As already reported, he was the one through whom God had ignited the Taiwan move of the Holy Spirit in 1984.) One hundred and forty

---

www.prmi.org   In Canada www.dfc.org In Korea www.dfk.org Chinese speaking world  and other locations go to  www.dfc.cc.

[93]In 1985-89, Dr. Charles Kraft, a professor of Fuller Theological Seminary, led several teams to Taiwan to teach on healing and deliverance ministry. I had also taken teams of leaders from Taiwan to Fuller Seminary for further teaching and had visited the Anaheim Vineyard led by John Wimber where we experienced Jesus moving in signs and wonders.

people from the United States and Canada showed up for this first five-day event. Many of them had been participants in the Spirit Alive events and Prayer Mountains and were hungry to keep growing in the Holy Spirit.

Many participants were like the Reverends Cindy and Steve Strickler. Cindy, a hospital chaplain and CPE instructor, and Steve Strickler, the pastor of a Hungarian Reformed congregation, were exhausted from ministry and needed rest and refreshment. Because of the teaching and outpouring that took place at this event, Steve was anointed for pastoral work in the power of the Holy Spirit and later in renewal work in the PC(USA) through the Presbyterian Lay Committee. Cindy was called into an anointed leadership role in PRMI.[94] This was true of several people who attended the first Dunamis event at Lake George, NY; they formed the core leadership team for PRMI.

**Phase #1: Preparing the Altar at the Gateways Dunamis Event at the Silver Bay Conference Center.**

At the event itself the preparation of the altar took place in the following ways: First, the Lord had already been preparing the people long before they arrived at this event. Each had their own story of how they were led to take part and how God had called them. We spent the first five days in systematic teaching, mostly by Archer Torrey, on the person and work of the Holy Spirit and the promises that Jesus had given concerning the baptism with the Holy Spirit. Torrey carefully built the theological and biblical understanding of what the Bible taught on the Holy Spirit. Ample time for questions and answers allowed the many pastors with theological and biblical questions about the Holy Spirit to ask them. We were having to deal with the common Reformed view that the

----

[94]The Rev. Cindy Strickler has served as president of the PRMI Board of Directors, and later in 2002 joined me in launching the PRMI Dunamis Fellowship International. She was the Pastor of the DFI and later the Director. She now in 2023 serves as the Director of PRMI.

gifts of the Spirit had ceased. Further, there were major issues with the Holiness Pentecostal teaching which had made its way into the Charismatic Renewal, that one had to have a "second work of grace" and that the initial physical evidence of the baptism with the Holy Spirit was that one spoke in tongues. There was lots of controversy! Doug shared the history of revivals within the Presbyterian Church of Scotland. I taught an entire new addition to the teaching on the Holy Spirit about the role of worldview which I had learned from Dr. Kraft of Fuller Theological Seminary when he had brought teams to Taiwan. I had gone through the process of having my own worldview expanded to include the present-day working of God in signs and wonders as well as gifts and manifestations of the Holy Spirit. All this was presented in a pragmatic and systematic way, always with Jesus Christ as the center and the Bible as the authoritative Word of God. However, it was Archer Torrey whose careful, erudite teaching on the Bible in both Greek and Hebrew plus his vibrant faith and experience that helped break through all these theological objections.

In addition to teaching, Doug and Carla McMurry led worship. We had times of great fellowship together, and while I did not know it at the time, a little group from Bay Road Presbyterian Church were off hidden away interceding. They were urgently and in agreement praying for Jesus to send a great outpouring of the Holy Spirit.

**Moving to Phase #2, Igniting the Fire**

On the last full day, as the morning teaching began, Archer told me that he would not be at the teaching times. I was upset because I was feeling insecure, but he insisted. He smiled at me and slipped out. Doug and I kept on teaching, but we felt like the real anointed teacher had abandoned us and we had been called in as the second string just to fill in. We broke for lunch—no Archer. After lunch I went back to my room. In Archer's room, which was next to mine, I heard a low murmuring noise. In that old wooden building, there were lots of strange noises, so I did not pay much attention. In the bright, sunny, bitterly cold day, (it was 20 below zero), I went out cross-country skiing. When I returned to my room to get thawed out, the murmuring noise continued. I thought it was the ancient water pipes. I went and taught on the R.A. Torrey steps for praying to receive the baptism with the Holy Spirit, then came back for a nap before supper. In that state between sleep and wakefulness, I had a vision of angels and incense rising before God making a pathway, an open heaven, for the descent of the Holy Spirit. I awoke with the realization that the murmuring noise was Archer praying in the Spirit. I knew then that I had not been dreaming but was seeing a vision of the crucial role of prayer in the outpouring of the Holy Spirit.

That Saturday night was a moment of opportunity, like in 1984 in Taiwan. As we gathered after supper, I was greatly relieved when Archer showed up for the evening session. I could feel the presence of God filling the room and the faith and expectation of all those gathered. Together we explained that we would be praying for the baptism with the Holy Spirit. He did some teaching on asking and receiving in faith. He said that you receive the baptism with the Holy Spirit not out of your emotional experience, but just by trusting God's Word, asking, and then receiving in faith. Then he said you need to step out in obedience to the guidance of the Holy Spirit. That is often when you will actually have the experience of the Holy Spirit falling upon you, giving you the gifts and power you need. This was almost verbatim what he had done in 1984 in Taiwan!

I fully expected Archer to step forward and lead in ministry with laying on of hands, praying for people to be baptized with the Holy Spirit. But to my surprise he stepped back and said, "No, the anointing is on you two!" With that he walked to the back of the room! (Later, after the Holy Spirit was manifesting, Archer did lay hands on some people.) So, with Doug McMurry, I stepped forward. I know I had a moment of feeling abandoned, but then the Holy Spirit fell upon me. I knew Jesus was giving me the gift of mountain-moving faith. I knew that He would baptize with the Holy Spirit all who asked Him.

We first asked everyone to reaffirm their faith in Jesus Christ and recommit themselves to following Jesus. This was followed by a time of prayers of confession and words of forgiveness. Then we said that the people themselves needed to invite Jesus to baptize them with the Holy Spirit. Doug and I offered to lay hands on all who wanted to receive. As they came forward, the Holy Spirit started to fall in amazing ways. As we prayed for people, regardless of whether there were any obvious manifestations or not, we immediately asked them, as their first acts of obedience, to start praying for others. Soon there were groups all over the room in intense prayer. The Holy Spirit was falling upon people. Manifestations and gifts of the Holy Spirit were taking place all over the room. It was Pentecost! Many immediately experienced manifestations of the Holy Spirit like tongues, prophecy, or resting in the Spirit. Others had no experience at all but just received in faith. Many later reported that as when they went back to their places of work or ministry, as they stepped out in obedience, they had experiences of the Holy Spirit falling upon them for gifts, effective ministry, and witness to Jesus Christ. We could give many testimonies of those who were part of that Pentecost event whose lives and ministries were transformed, but one will suffice. Revs. Cindy and Steve Strickler have already been mentioned and have been so important in this ministry, that you need to hear more from her. Her experience is typical of many whom Jesus baptized with the Holy Spirit who did not feel anything but received in faith and then as they walked in obedience found new empowerment for ministry.

"Steve and I went to this conference after a time of being worn out from the burdens of ministry and parenting. Our two-year-old son, David, just was not sleeping. My parents made us an offer we could not refuse! They would keep David and pay for us to go to the Dunamis event so we could get some rest and refreshment. Mom had attended a PRMI event in Princeton and found out about the conference from the PRMI mailing list. I did ask my older sister Laurie, who had gone to seminary, if she knew anything about Brad. She just said that Brad was a classmate at Union Seminary in Va. In any event, this was a great Christmas gift! But on the way to

Lake George from New Jersey, we were horrified when we read the brochure and realized that this ministry was part of the charismatic movement. We decided to go anyway, and if it got too crazy, we could just skip out of the classes and spend some time as a couple.

When we arrived, we were surprised and relived to find that the people were not crazy, and the teaching was biblical. Even so, at the evening meetings we sat by the back door so we could make an easy escape if things got too out of hand. Finally on that last night, when the invitation was given Steve and I both went forward for prayer. I am not sure who laid hands on us, just that it was not any of the leadership team. We were both desperate for the empowerment of the Holy Spirit to do our work of ministry. When they laid their hands on both of us absolutely nothing happened! We were a little disappointed but also relieved. We recalled what Archer Torrey had said over and over again, "Ask! Receive in faith, and then step out in obedience!" It was when we got back to New Jersey that Steve experienced new empowerment for preaching every Sunday in both English and in Hungarian. He was also really good at pastoral work. For myself, I went back to the hospital where I was a Chaplain and for the first time I found a new power, freedom, and above all, the love of Jesus in my prayers for those who were sick. I even started praying for people to be healed! And they were! This launched me on this incredible and unexpected journey of cooperating with the Holy Spirit. I have taken part in igniting and sustaining moves of the Holy Spirit in many locations that I never could have imagined! It has been all Jesus and He gets all the glory!"

**Follow up and the Fruit of this Outpouring**

This was a true Pentecost event confirmed by having all five of the markers of such an event. Also there has been much fruit. Now, more than thirty years later, looking back at this outpouring in 1991, the fruit is obvious and verifiable. Many who prayed for the baptism with the Holy Spirit experienced the great result that Jesus had promised: They became His empowered witnesses and co-workers. A core group were called and anointed to become key leaders in PRMI's ministry and through them the Lord used the Dunamis Project to ignite outpourings of the Holy Spirit worldwide. From that time forward, invitations started to pour in, not just from the USA and Canada but also from New Zealand, Taiwan, Brazil, and around the world. The invitations were to "come over and help us! Bring the Dunamis teaching on the Holy Spirit." The rest of the story of moving from this outpouring event to Phase #3 Sustaining the Flame will be covered in a later chapter.

## How to Make the Transition from Phase #1 to Phase #2

I have found from long experience that moving from teaching, preaching, ministering, and all the other aspects of preparing the altar to seeing the Holy Spirit fire actually fall is often daunting. It is like facing an abyss with no bridge across it, but receiving the guidance from the Lord to, "Trust me! Just jump off!" It is much easier to keep praying or teaching or talking or worshiping or doing all the other things that prevent one from facing this abyss. What is the abyss we must cross to get to this igniting phase? It is that it is Jesus who baptizes us with the Holy Spirit. While we, of course, may be called to provide a lot of preparation, the actual Pentecost event cannot be manipulated or coerced.

In the example above of how the Holy Spirit fell at the first Dunamis, notice again that there was careful preparation which included a lot of prayer, wonderful worship, teaching, and so forth, but we knew that at some point we needed to move from these activities into the actual moment when Jesus was ready to pour out the Holy Spirit. This would be the shift from our activity to His activity—to the kairos moment, the moment of opportunity when God was ready to act.

Even though we announced that on Saturday night we would be praying for the outpouring of the Holy Spirit, I had no real idea of what to do. I knew we needed to take another step but there seemed to be a wall of impossibility blocking it. Archer Torey was the one who discerned the moment and announced that it was time. How did he know it was the right time?

When I asked him this question in the debriefing that followed, he said, "I just knew it was time! I heard Jesus telling me, "Now! Tell them that this is what I (Jesus) am ready to do, but they need to ask me!" When I said, "So Jesus just told you! Well, that is not real helpful! I mean how did He tell you?" Archer went on to say, "Well, you know I have had lots of practice with receiving guidance from the Holy Spirit. I have learned how He speaks. A good way to learn is testing the guidance by stepping out in obedience and trying it. When you miss it a bunch of times, after a while you start to learn what was your own thoughts or imagination and when it is the Lord speaking. Let me give you one example of missing the guidance. I had been to a healing meeting with Agnes Sandford.[95] I had watched her receive guidance that Jesus was healing the memories of those who had been rejected by their mothers. She said, "Right now Jesus is healing everyone who was hurt by being rejected by your mother. Jesus is calling you to stand up and forgive your mom for abandoning you." There must have been several hundred

---

[95]Agnes Mary Sanford (1897–1982) was an American Christian writer. She is most known for founding the Inner Healing movement, a process she described as the healing of memories.   https://en.wikipedia.org/wiki/Agnes_Sanford
She was the child of Presbyterian missionaries in China.  Archer and Jane Torrey were greatly influenced by her. They often referred to two of her many books, *The Healing Light* (1947) and *Sealed Orders* (1972).

people there. Many stood up and started to offer prayers forgiving them moms. There were lots of tears and it was clear that Jesus was at work. Well later, Jane and I were leading a prayer meeting and the idea that there were people in the group who needed to forgive their mothers just popped into my mind. I imitated Agnes Sanford and said, "If Jesus is healing you of memories of rejection by your mother, then stand up." No one stood up! I was amazed. Surely among the fifty or so people present, some of them had been hurt by their mom. I realized later that I had just acted on my own thoughts. Jesus was not working at that time to heal those wounds. After missing it like that several times, I learned to distinguish between the thoughts from the Holy Spirit and those that were my own. I also learned that it was not just the word itself, but the timing needed to coincide with what Jesus was doing. I had not discerned what is called a "kairos moment" when the Holy Spirit is moving over a group and giving us the word or action He is calling us to take. Further, I needed to discern any guidance I received by asking myself, "Does it give glory to Jesus? Is the guidance consistent with what the Bible teaches?"

So back to that moment at the first Dunamis event when we were preparing to pray for everyone after teaching on how to receive. I was asking the Lord urgently for guidance. As I looked at the gathered group, I could see expectancy and faith. The Holy Spirit was clearly priming the pump and getting them ready to ask for the baptism. I could see all that. Jesus could have just poured out the Spirit on everyone like he did in the home of Cornelius while Peter was speaking, but I knew that in this case the Lord wanted me to tell them that the time was right. I was just getting ready to give the invitation and invite everyone to come up for me to lay hands on them when the Lord stopped me dead in my tracks! He said, 'NO! I am not anointing you for that! I am ordering you to step back and you are to push Brad and Doug forward as they are my chosen servants for this outpouring of the Holy Spirit.' Wow! I did not like that guidance at all, but I knew that I would block the move of God if I disobeyed. You know, it's not about your ego or you become famous, it's about Jesus and Him getting all the glory."

So that was what was taking place within Archer at that decisive moment, but what about Doug and me? When Archer pushed us forward and we gave the invitation and started to lay hands on people, we experienced Jesus anointing us as fire starters. Doug and I were given an authority like Peter and John had received when they had come down from Jerusalem to pray for the Samaritans.

This anointing was not just for that moment in 1991 but has been upon us for the following three decades. Jesus empowered and called me to take this systematic teaching on the Holy Spirit to many locations worldwide. Everywhere I went the Lord used me to ignite Pentecost events. The same thing happened with Doug McMurry, who was given an additional anointing to lead in the work of intercessory prayer for revival and for a third great awakening. God also uses him as a great storyteller of past great moves of the Holy Spirit to inspire hope, faith, and intercession for this next great awakening.

Let's pause to provide a summary of the different elements of Igniting the Fire that are implicit in this account which we have experienced repeatedly in the many outpourings of the Holy Spirit that have followed. I believe they are consistent with the Bible and with the two Goforth foundations and the three R.A Torrey keys. These take place in venues where there is a physical address and where the Holy Spirit is preparing to fall.

## Within the Set-Apart Venue: Moving from Preparing the Altar to Igniting the Fire

A summary of these steps to prepare the altar:

- A dedicated group praying for Jesus to baptize with the Holy Spirit those whom He has called and prepared to become His co-workers.

- Preparing the venue i.e., the place and context, for God the Father to fulfill Acts 1:4-8 among a group of prepared people.

- Providing the biblical teaching on Jesus' promises of the baptism with the Holy Spirit and how to pray for and receive this outward work of the Spirit.

- Calling for a commitment or recommitment to follow Jesus Christ as Lord and Savior.

- Praying through the biblical steps of asking for the baptism with the Holy Spirit or being filled again with the Holy Spirit if one has already had that initiatory experience.

- Those anointed by the Holy Spirit as "fire starters" discerning that it is a moment of opportunity—a kairos moment—and that Jesus is ready to pour out the Holy Spirit.

- The fire starters receiving further guidance from Jesus of how He wants to do this work, and then stepping out in faith and announcing to the people what Jesus has told them about how they are to ask for and receive baptism or infilling.

After this initial outpouring at Lake George, we developed a total of six units of systematic biblical teaching on the Holy Spirit and how to cooperate with the Holy Spirit to do the work of Jesus Christ. These biblical teachings, as well as the context of the equipping events, have been, from their inception, used by God the Father for preparing the altar and then igniting the fire again and again, fulfilling Acts 1:4-8.

In the next chapter I tell the story (one of many) of how the Lord ignited a Pentecost event at a seminary in China which resulted in a major tributary in the river of the Holy Spirit advancing the kingdom of God.

# 12

# Igniting a Holy Spirit Move in China

I would like to illustrate the meta pattern with my own experience of how God used me as the ignitor in a great outpouring of the Holy Spirit that took place in China several years after the Tiananmen Square Massacre in 1989. I want to use this illustration for the following reasons:

First, this outpouring links our present prayer work for the next great outpouring of the Holy Spirit to the great move of the Holy Spirit that R.A. Torrey and Jonathan Goforth took part in igniting in Korea and China, which has continued to our present day as the Back to Jerusalem movement. With the latest (in 2023) assault on the Church of Jesus Christ and human freedom taking place through Chinese dictator Xi Jinping and the Chinese Communist Party, this continuing move of the Holy Spirit needs to be prayed into and supported. We believe God's plans are for this great wave of the Holy Spirit to overcome the demonic strongholds based on Marxism/Leninism that are blocking the Chinese church from fulfilling its full role of transforming Chinese society in accord with biblical Judeo-Christian values, and fulling their role in taking the gospel of Jesus Christ to the ends of the earth.

The second reason is that I did not intentionally implement any of these three keys, the two foundations, or the meta pattern, but the Lord did! He just called me to take part. I think this is a great testimony to the reality that God ignites revivals when we do our part in cooperation with the Holy Spirit. These events were obviously orchestrated by God and involved circumstances and people far beyond my control.

In what follows I think I experienced a little of what Peter must have experienced when he was unexpectedly dropped into God's master plan for the outpouring of the Holy Spirit upon the Gentiles in the home of Cornelius, the Roman centurion, because the Lord unexpectedly dropped me into His master kingdom plans for China.

## The Lord Igniting an Outpouring of the Holy Spirit in China

These events took place in a major city and in a seminary that must remain unnamed. I got to China through a long, convoluted process that started when I was a little boy and heard stories of the great missionaries in China. Also, my father had served in China and Burma in the Army Air Corp during World War II. I vividly remember hearing him tell stories about China. In 1980, Laura and I had been called to serve as Presbyterian Missionaries in Taiwan. Unlike most other missionaries sent to the Taiwan Presbyterian Church, we were required to learn Mandarin Chinese instead of Taiwanese because we were assigned to work at the Bible College. While in Taiwan as a missionary, I had a major visionary experience in which Jesus told me that I would be used to ignite waves of the Holy Spirit in China as well as in Japan.

In 1987 while I was the Vice President of the Presbyterian Bible College in Hsinchu, and the Director of the Presbyterian Lay Training Center which was located on the Bible College campus, Elder Howard Chow, who had been a co-worker during the outpouring of the Holy Spirit at the Bible College and in Taiwan, had taken me up to land which he owned on a high mountain. He offered to donate this large tract consisting of several hundred acres to the Lay Training Center to build a prayer mountain modeled after the prayer mountains in Korea. From that high mountain we could see across the Taiwan straits to China in the hazy distance. Suddenly the Holy Spirit fell on Elder Chow, and he prophesied that I would be used by God to ignite outpourings of the Holy Spirit in China. As he spoke, I was caught up into the heavenlies and saw a vision of this happening. We then looked north where, over the horizon was Japan. Again, Howard prophesied that the Lord would use me to ignite outpourings of the Holy Spirit, advancing the gospel in that land. This was very personal for Howard Chow, as his family had lost all their great wealth in Shang Hai when the communists took over China. Further, Howard had a great love for Japan as he had been educated in Japan and was fluent in Japanese.

I would have received this most generous gift of his land, but it was not God's plan for me to take part in building this prayer mountain in Taiwan. Rather, God called me out of Taiwan, and the prayer mountain vision has taken the form of the Community of the Cross in the mountains of western North Carolina, but the prophetic vision of both China and Japan have been and continue to be fulfilled.

After leaving Taiwan in 1989, I became the Executive Director of PRMI in 1990. In 1991, after the outpouring in Lake George which ignited the Dunamis Project, the Rev. Ted Ellis invited me to Wexford Presbyterian Church in Ontario, Canada. (Ted and Marilyn Ellis had been missionaries to Taiwan and a part of the move of the Holy Spirit there.) Ted invited me to lead the Prayer Mountain and to introduce the teaching on the baptism with the Holy Spirit that I had done in Taiwan. At that event the Holy Spirit was poured out upon the group gathered there. This launched a stream of the Holy Spirit that was to grow in the Presbyterian Church of Canada.[96]

At that event at Wexford, the Holy Spirit also fell powerfully on me as well as on Ted Ellis. While we were praying together the Holy Spirit gave me a series of powerful prophetic visions confirming the ones I had already received while in Taiwan on the mountain with Howard Chow. I believe I was caught up into the third heaven. The glorified Jesus revealed that He would use me to ignite a great move of the Holy Spirit which would advance the gospel all over China. He then showed me visions of how this would take place.

In the first vision, I was with Chinese co-workers whom I did not recognize but knew in the Spirit, meeting with the highest levels of

---

[96]That same year Jesus ignited another Pentecost event at the Maranatha Christian Reformed Church in Belleville, Canada. From these igniting events which were followed by many other events, the Lord in 2006 launched the Dunamis Fellowship Canada. https://www.dunamisfellowshipcanada.org/

the Communist Party and government officials. Under the anointing of the Holy Spirit, we were presenting to them the gospel of the kingdom of God through Jesus Christ and imparting to them the biblical Judeo-Christian values needed to replace the evil tyrannical system of Marxist Leninism.

The next vision was of a PRMI team from various nations preaching the gospel of Jesus Christ with signs and wonders before vast crowds of people in Tiananmen Square (天安門廣場) in Beijing. This was igniting great revival sweeping through the entire nation with millions upon millions of people born again through faith in Jesus Christ. I saw Jesus healing the nation of the woundings from their last two hundred years of oppression by Western powers, the Japanese, and the communists. I also saw the kingdom of God overcoming the tyranny of the Chinese Communist Party and making China a great missionary sending nation taking part in fulfilling the Great Commission.

I shared these visions with Ted as they were taking place. He witnessed to them, and we made a covenant together to pray until they were fulfilled. I also shared these prophetic visions with Elder Howard Chow in Taiwan who enthusiastically joined us in these prayers. I received these prophecies, not as predictions of what would happen, but as the Lord's invitation for me to pray and obey them into reality. A couple of years later Ted died of prostate cancer; however, the seeds that had been sown in agreement together in the name of Jesus were moving toward fulfillment.

So, for years I had been praying for the doors to open to go to China. The door opened with an unusual invitation while teaching a Dunamis event in Taiwan. A group of businessmen, after having been filled with the Holy Spirit at this event, secretly approached me and asked if I would be willing to take part in the seminary graduation ceremony that was to take place later that year. I said, "Yes!" I would be willing to go. They gave me the name of the city I was to fly to, the dates I was to be there, the address of the seminary, and the name of the large tourist hotel I was to check in to. I was to register with my English and Chinese name. And that was it! That was the last I heard from these businessmen!

208

So, it was a step of faith to invite another American co-worker who spoke Chinese to go with me, to pray in all the money needed for the trip, apply for a visa, and buy tickets. All of this came together, including gifts of over $15,000 US dollars from people who had been directed by the Holy Spirit to give to the China trip, even though I had made no public announcements about it. I had just asked a few key intercessors to start praying that the doors would open. I truly felt like we were both a little crazy and were stepping into a dangerous situation.

After long flights, we arrived, checked into the large Five Star tourist hotel, and waited to be called. Several days went by. On the morning of the graduation, the hotel room phone rang and a male voice with an odd accent in Chinese hastily said, "Dr. Long! Do not come to the graduation service. It is too dangerous." That was a real blow as it seemed that the entire reason for us being there had just been missed. So, we spent time in prayer, and I took a nice walk.

After lunch I was settling down for a nap when the hotel room phone rang again. The same odd voice said, "Come over right now!" Before leaving I picked up my Chinese English Bible, but then received a strong check from the Lord that I should not carry it through town. So, I said, "Lord what do you want me to prepare for?" He said, "I want to baptize them in the Holy Spirit so that I can comfort and empower them to be my witnesses and to raise up millions as my disciples." So, I hastily scribbled down in Chinese characters the texts from Luke and Acts where Jesus promises us the baptism with the Holy Spirit. Hiding that paper in the inner pocket of my jacket, we headed out on what was to be an extraordinary adventure.

## Outpouring of the Holy Spirit Upon the Volunteer Church Workers

We arrived at the address we had been given months before, which did not look like a seminary at all but dilapidated old buildings. We were greeted warmly by the president who seemed surprised that we were there. He pointed us to a door and said,

"Go in there; you are the speaker." Then he quickly left. We walked into the large room that was packed with about five or six hundred mostly aged men and women. Many were dressed in shabby clothes and many looked like they were farmers from the country. Most appeared desperately poor. We went to the front of the room. To my surprise a team from Taiwan was leading the worship. One of them, a lovely young woman who had been a part of the outpouring of the Holy Spirit in Taiwan, sat down with me and explained that these were what were called the "volunteer workers." They were not seminary students but the leaders, pastors, and teachers of churches of ten to even twenty thousand members, mostly in the poor, rural, undeveloped areas of China. Most had no education at all and no Bibles. They were at the seminary getting the very basics in Bible and Christian doctrine. The young woman from Taiwan then added that many of them had suffered terribly for their faith in Jesus under the communists. Amazed and humbled that I could have anything at all to say to those who had so suffered for their faith, I asked, "Well what do they expect me to teach on." She said, "Tell them about the baptism with the Holy Spirit Jesus has promised us in Acts 1:4-8. They are desperate for the power of the Holy Spirit to be witnesses to Jesus Christ."

She then said in passing, "By the way, it was good you did not come to the graduation ceremony. There were some other foreigners there and the students gave great testimonies to Jesus Christ. This alarmed the police who shut down the entire graduation ceremony. They took away the foreigners, no one knows where. All the seminary students and the entire faculty except for the president who were at the graduation were rounded up and taken down to the police headquarters for interrogation and reeducation. They are all there now." Then she asked, "Why did you not come over?" I told her about the strange telephone call. She said, "None of our group called you."

With that brief introduction, I was praying desperately for a word to give them. As I stepped up to teach behind a large bulky wooden podium, I took out of my pocket the notebook paper on which I had written in Chinese characters the Bible verses on the baptism with the Holy Spirit. I started to tell them about Jesus' promises in Luke 24:44-48 and Acts 1:4-8. Suddenly the Lord spoke to me, "Now hide! Order the young woman from Taiwan to take your place in the podium and tell her to talk about her mother. The police are coming!" This guidance was so clear as to be almost audible! So, I obeyed! I called the young woman up, "Quick! Tell a story of how you experienced your mother's love. And by the way, make sure you use a proper Beijing accent!" I looked around. There was no place to hide except inside the big wooden podium, so I crawled in. My American co-worker sitting in front, aware that something was up, had slid down on the floor. Suddenly there was a loud clamor in the back. I looked out through a small peephole in the wood. Apparently, I was not the first to hide inside the podium. A group of about twelve policemen came into the back. They were looking around with fierce, stern looks on their faces. However, all they saw was a lovely young woman telling a moving story about her mother. She had no trace of a Taiwan Mandarin accent. After a while they marched out the door and I stiffly crawled out from inside the pulpit. I was going to continue my teaching on the baptism with the Holy Spirit, but the Lord told me "No"; I was to pick up on the story of mother's love and talk about the love of God the Father who sent Jesus into the world. My text was one that I had memorized in Chinese, John 3:16. I was to call them to a total recommitment to following Jesus Christ. As I did, I was aware that the room was suddenly filling up with the manifest presence of God. The room was filled with the palpable love of Jesus Christ being poured out upon these people. Looks of awe, wonder and joy filled their faces. Suddenly it was like a wave of love washed over the room, and then the most astonishing thing started to happen. A wail of grief convulsed the room. People fell to the floor in spasms of grief and agony. They were weeping uncontrollably. My American co-worker, a large man, had stood up in the middle of the room. I could feel Jesus' love radiating through him. He stood there just praying in the Spirit with hands outstretched over the people. Soon a large group of both men and women, all old and wizened, were clinging to him, weeping loudly, drenching him with their bitter tears.

I could not figure out what was happening, so I waded out into the crowd of weeping people. They were pouring out their hearts mostly in Chinese dialects that I could not understand or in Mandarin with such strong accents and distraught emotions that it was incomprehensible to me. I asked someone to translate for me and was astonished to learn they were unleashing the grief of wounds going back decades, starting back with the Nan Jing Massacre by the Japanese in December and January of 1937-38. They were grieving seeing their mothers and sisters raped and murdered by the Japanese and their fathers and brothers tortured and beheaded. Then they moved to grieve all the horrors of the imposition of Communism upon the people and the disastrous programs imposed by Mao Tse-tung that destroyed millions of lives, wrecking families and society. Women were weeping over their babies lost to forced abortions. This continued even to the Tiananmen Square Massacre in 1989. Both men and women were screaming for their lost sons and daughters who had been crushed by the tanks. It was a heart-rending outpouring of suppressed grief that had been unleashed by the overwhelming presence of the love of Jesus.

As the room quieted down to muffed sobs, I stood up again and prayed for Jesus to have mercy on all and to give the grace to forgive. I started to name first the Japanese atrocities. Then, trespassing into the realm of the forbidden, I named the communist leaders who had afflicted such death and oppression upon the Chinese people. I said, "We forgive those Japanese soldiers in the name of Jesus, and we forgive those communist leaders who destroyed our families and killed our loved ones." As I did, the entire group responded with amens and their own words of forgiveness. Then I watched the literal fulfillment of Psalm 30:11: "You turned my wailing into dancing; you removed my sackcloth and clothed me with joy."

After the time of celebration and joy, Jesus said, "Now! I am going to baptize them with My Holy Spirit so they may be my empowered witnesses. Tell them to raise their hands to receive my gift." I spoke this out and immediately they all jumped up with hands outraised. The Holy Spirit was poured out on the entire group. It was truly Pentecost with tremendous manifestations of the Holy Spirit. There were expressions of the gifts of the Holy Spirit, the most obvious being tongues and prophecy. Then the Holy Spirit said to me. "You need to leave NOW before they start to give any of my glory to you. Also, if you stay any longer you are in danger of being caught." So, my American co-worker and I walked out the back door. It was Jesus doing all this work of giving the gifts and power to be his witnesses. I do not think anyone noticed we left. We went back to the hotel without incident, rejoicing and praising Jesus.

## The Holy Spirit Established the Two Goforth Foundations: The Bible as the Word of God and Jesus as King of Kings

As if all this was not enough, one little incident took place that made a huge impression on me, but to which I paid little attention at the time.

At one point, after I had spoken and the Holy Spirit had fallen, a very old man came creeping up to the pulpit. He snatched off the pulpit the notebook paper with my hand-scribbled Bible verses. Clutching the paper to his chest, he said, with desperation in his voice, "Please! Please! Please!  Let me have this!" I stammered, "Why? They are just my notes." He said, "NO! They are God's Word!  I am the pastor of a church with fifteen thousand people. We have not one Bible! This is God's Word! Please, may I have it?" I was stunned! "Sure!" I stammered. Their hunger and need for the Word of God was so great that my scribbled Bible verses on a piece of scrap paper were treasured.

I saw vividly that through the manifestation of the loving, kingly presence of Jesus Christ and, in this incident, the Bible as the Word of God, the two Goforth foundations were established. In this amazing Pentecost event, my role had been receiving the gift of faith and then stepping out in radical obedience. The Lord did all the rest in those whom He had prepared and gathered for this event. It is significant that the outpouring was started first by Jesus Christ manifesting Himself in love and as healer. This

213

was the preparation for the next step which was for Him baptizing them with the Holy Spirit. What about the follow up and sustaining the flame of this Pentecost event? I was not to have a role at that time in their continued equipping. However, through a series of miraculous manifestations of the kingdom of God that were to take place among the seminary students, the Lord was to provide this for them.

## Igniting the Outpouring of the Holy Spirit among the Seminary Students

We waited several more days at the tourist hotel. We were getting rather bored and just assumed that our time there was finished. Then early one morning, unexpectedly my hotel phone rang again and the same male voice with the odd Chinese accent, said, "Come over now! Alone!" and hung up. So, I hastily dressed and headed over. When I arrived, I was greeted by the President who said, "How did you know to come just as class was starting?" I told him about the call. With a quizzical look, he answered, "No one here called you, but never mind! You are here just in time! So go into that classroom. Now you are not allowed to teach or preach, or we will get in bad trouble with the government, but you can answer any questions." He quickly walked away leaving me before the closed door. I opened it and walked into a packed-out classroom full of students sitting at desks. There must have been thirty or forty students there. I introduced myself and gave my Chinese name. As I did a murmur went through the classroom. The students all looked surprised. They indicated that they had heard my name but had thought I was Chinese. They were surprised that I was a foreigner and that I could speak Chinese. After that brief introduction I asked, "Do you have any questions that you may want to ask me?" One of the students in the front stood up and said with utmost politeness, "Yes, Honorable Professor, Reverend Doctor Long (my name in Chinese), we all want to know how to be baptized with the Holy Spirit so we can be empowered to witness to Jesus Christ in the very difficult conditions we are called to." Not

214

knowing anything about my audience except that they appeared hungry for the Holy Spirit and had expectant faith, I started off on my basic teaching on the different works of the Holy Spirit as a foundation for teaching on how to pray for and receive the baptism with the Holy Spirit as Jesus has promised us in Acts 1:4-8. I had gotten into just a few paragraphs, when suddenly the Lord interrupted my teaching by pouring out the Holy Spirit upon the classroom. Once again there were manifestations. Students started speaking in tongues and moving in prophetic words. Some fell out of their chairs and rested in the Spirit. It was very quiet, decent and in order, but very powerful. Then the Lord started speaking through me giving prophetic words to many students as I laid hands on them. I do not remember most of what the Lord gave me except that He was calling these students to different ministries. I was surprised at how specific the prophetic words were and that He even gave me the names of some of the students, which of course I had no way of knowing as there had been no time for them to introduce themselves to me. I spoke them out anyway. After a time of this ministry, we heard a loud knock on the door. I was at first afraid it was the police, but it was the President. He motioned for me to come out with him. Without a word he pointed to another shut door down the hall. I walked in and there was another classroom packed with students, where the same amazing move of God took place, after they had asked the same question of how to be baptized with the Holy Spirit so they could be witnesses to Jesus in their difficult context. I never did get to do any of my teaching. Jesus just baptized these students with the Holy Spirit!

After a while the President knocked again, and even though tremendous ministry was taking place, said, "Let's go now!" As he walked me to the back gate to the seminary compound, he said, "Those two classrooms were our graduating class!" Then he said, "They have all done well." I asked what happens next. He said, "They just head off to their places of work, now empowered by the Holy Spirit." I then asked, "In Taiwan we always give the students and faculty a feast. Do you do that here?" He said no! When I asked why not, he said, "Well, we just do not have that much money to feed so many people." The Holy Spirit then gave me unexpected guidance—Jesus wanted to give them a feast as a foretaste of the Great Feast of the Lamb in the kingdom of God as an encouragement to them. The Lord said that I was to offer to pay for it. Then the Lord said, "Tell the President this and also tell him that it would need to be a real Chinese feast with many courses and lots of great local beer." (The city was famous for its excellent beer.) When I told the President this, he was most excited and grateful. He said that would be wonderful. I handed him about three hundred US dollars in Chinese currency and asked if it would be enough to feed the graduating students and the faculty. It was! The next day, we all gathered around noon for the great feast. This was a glorious time of fellowship. I was asked to make a speech, lead a prayer, and give some toasts. As I did the Holy Spirit fell upon me, and I found myself speaking Mandarin with the accent and pronunciation of that region. This would be like me, a southerner, speaking with a NY Bronx accent—something I do not naturally do. According to Chinese custom, I went from table to table toasting everyone, both students and faculty, and doing many "gan bei" which means "to dry the glass". I really enjoyed getting to know the students. Some stood up and gave testimonies of what they had experienced. We concluded with prayers, blessings, and singing hymns together. There were many hugs, and our pictures were taken with many students. It was just glorious, and no police showed up!

The next morning, we flew back to the United States.

I relate the long story of this series of outpourings of the Holy Spirit that ignited a move of God that continues to this day, because it illustrates the five markers of the Lord's work as well as the three R.A Torrey keys and the two Goforth foundations. Let's focus on just one—how the Lord prepared the people for this outpouring.

## Third Marker: A Gathered Group of Prepared People

Preparing the volunteer church workers and seminary students for the outpouring was a long process, most of which I was unaware. However, at the feast we offered the graduating class, I learned much as I followed the custom of going table to table toasting everyone. I found out why they had been surprised that I was a foreigner. They told me they had all read my book, *Passage Through the Wilderness*[97] written in Chinese (with a lot of help from Timothy Huang, my co-worker at the Bible College). They had also been exposed to the teaching on the Holy Spirit that I had written in manuals in Chinese brought to them by teams from Taiwan. Because of this they had no idea that I was not Chinese. Those teaching materials had prepared them to ask the question about the baptism with the Holy Spirit. They had also heard about the way signs and wonders had taken place during the persecution of the Cultural Revolution, but they had not experienced any of it. I also heard how God prepared them for what had happened in the classroom, increasing their hunger for the empowerment of the Holy Spirit through their first-time experience of persecution and "reeducation" similar to that of the Cultural Revolution, when taken to the police station. They had come out of that experience with a new awareness of the oppressive situation that they were being called into. They had heard about the Pentecost event that took place among the volunteer church workers. This also made them hungry for the Holy Spirit's empowerment.

As a group gathered around me asking to take their pictures, one student asked, "Well, how many years have you lived in our city? Your Chinese is perfect, and you are even speaking with our local pronunciation." I exclaimed, "Years!? I have only been here

---

[97]Zeb Bradford Long, *Passage through the Wilderness: A journey of the Soul* (Grand Rapids, MI: Chosen Books, 1998, available in English and Chinese). The original Chinese version was published by Olive Press while I was still in Taiwan.

217

for about ten days. Actually, my Mandarin is not that standard at all, and I have a heavy Taiwan and American Southern accent." The student looked up in amazement and said, "It really was the Holy Spirit empowering you!" It was.

As for the volunteer church workers, through the visits from people from Taiwan who had been filled with the Holy Spirit they had experienced worship empowered by the Holy Spirit, giving glory to Jesus Christ. Apparently, they had been given some basic teaching from the manuals I had written in Chinese for use in Taiwan. Above all they were prepared by the Holy Spirit Himself through the suffering and persecution they had endured, and then through facing the humanly impossible task of discipling thousands of people who were coming to faith with no Bibles, no curriculum, and just a minimum of education.

Another aspect of this preparation had been not just teams enabled by the Taiwan businessmen, but also their prayers for the outpouring of the Holy Spirit to take place in China. These prayers were no doubt mixed with the prayers of millions of others going back for centuries for the gospel to go forth in China.

Lastly, the preparation for the older group of volunteer church workers who had suffered so much was the teaching on the love of Jesus Christ and the amazing healing that took place from the wounds of the past. This prepared the way for the Holy Spirit to fall upon them in power.

## The Fourth Marker: Jesus Christ Baptizes People with the Holy Spirit

The four markers of a physical address, a time stamp, the prepared group, and Jesus doing the baptizing with the Holy Spirit all converged in the two instances just shared, first with the volunteers and then later with seminary students. With the volunteers, after pulses of the healing power of Jesus had swept over the entire group, they had been able to forgive their tormentors. We had moved into joy. As we did, I had discerned we were moving into a kairos moment, and the Lord was going to baptize them with the Holy Spirit. The Lord instructed me, "Tell them all to stand up, raise their hands, and I will pour out the Holy Spirit upon them." In this case my role was to discern the moment, declare what Jesus intended to do, and then invite them to embody their asking in faith by raising their hands. The Lord did the rest!

With the seminary students, it was much like what happened to Peter in the home of Cornelius. "While Peter was still speaking these words, the Holy Spirit fell on all those who heard the message" (Act 10:44). In the classroom while I was making some introductory remarks, Jesus just interrupted me and poured out the Holy Spirit upon them. My role was to stop teaching, get out of the way, and let Jesus do what He was doing. Later He called me to cooperate with Him in giving the prophetic words and words of knowledge that were manifested with such power and effect.

But there is a question that to this day leaves me with wonder! How did we arrive just at the right time when the Lord was sending the kairos moment for us to simply step into? Who was it who called us to show up at exactly the right time in these short, open windows of opportunity? No one knew who this was with the odd accent who had called with such exquisite timing. I really believe it was an angel with an accent from a phone that could not be traced.

## Following the Third Phase of Sustaining the Flame

We flew back to the United States the next day, so this third phase of sustaining the flame was truly in the Lord's hands. I was very concerned because I know that when outpourings of the Holy Spirit take place without follow-up and teaching, they usually fizzle out or move into heresy.

I really did not know how the Lord continued to nurture these leaders He had anointed as His witnesses. However, one night years later, the Rev. John Chang (張景祥) got a call from a man in China. He said that he was a student of Rev. Dr. Brad Long (羅學). This person had seen on the internet that we were teaching together in Taiwan. He said that for years he had wanted to contact me to let me know how he had been blessed. John asked, "How?" He told John the story of how he had been in that classroom when the Holy Spirit was poured out. He said that I had spoken a prophetic word to him saying that he was being called by God to start a great movement of the Holy Spirit in that part of China. Moreover, he was called to do this with the female student sitting next to him, whom I had apparently named. They were to be co-workers as husband and wife. He wanted to let me know that all this had happened—that they had married, and the Lord had given them effective ministry together. He further said that the outpouring of the Holy Spirit at the seminary had launched a wave of the Holy Spirit that had affected many parts of China. Those students had dispersed all over China and many had taken the fire of revival with them. These scattered embers of revival—and sometimes even the students themselves—later opened doors for John Chang and me to take many trips to China. We were able to spread the Dunamis curriculum to both official and unofficial church leaders, serving millions of Chinese Christians.

## Launching the China Initiative

After this extraordinary outpouring in China, the Lord raised up for me an anointed co-worker, the Rev. Dr. John Chang (張景祥), originally from Taiwan. After finishing at Princeton Theological Seminary, he founded the America Chinese/English congregation of Grace Christian Reformed Church in Staten Island, New York. In 1993, at a Chinese Conference in Nyack, New York, I was the keynote speaker. There was a major outpouring of the Holy Spirit. John Chang, whom I had never met, came forward as I was laying hands on people. As I prayed for him, not only did the Holy Spirit fall upon him filling him again for empowered preaching, but the Holy Spirit also fell on me. I suddenly recalled the vision I had seen in Canada of ministry in China. I heard Jesus say, "I have called and anointed this man to be your primary co-worker fulfilling the vision of witnessing to the communist leaders, igniting outpourings of the Holy Spirit all over China, and fulfilling the prophetic vision of seeing the vast revival with signs and wonders taking place in Tiananmen Square." With this word I saw us together teaching all over China as well as throughout the Chinese world. Then I heard the Lord say, "Now invite Rev. Chang to come with you on your trip to Taiwan." When friends from Taiwan heard that I had invited Dr. John Chang to come with me on the trip to Taiwan, they warned me that he was dangerous to work with because his commitment to Jesus Christ was too intense and he was driven to share the gospel everywhere. As I have also been accused of being too intense about just about everything, I took these well-meaning warnings as confirmation that the Lord had called us to be co-workers.

This launched us into an amazing partnership in Jesus in which we have not only introduced the Dunamis teaching in many Chinse and Taiwanese speaking congregations in North America but have also taken many teams to Taiwan, Hong Kong, Malaysia, Mainland China, and other locations. We're both able to preach, teach, and freely translate for each other in both Chinese and English. These missions were supported through intensive prayer, financial, and people support through PRMI, and also by the dynamic congregations founded by Dr. Chang, which have been through the intensive PRMI Dunamis equipping process. As this work grew, our number of co-workers grew as well and became a great way of equipping anointed leaders in PRMI as well as Chinese speakers from John's congregations. For me, Rev. Cindy Strickler was a key co-worker who joined in the teaching work. The Lord also uses her greatly in inner and physical healing ministry. Mary Ellen Conners, a gifted intercessor, would often come on the trips to provide prayer back-up and equip others in how to provide prayer support. The Lord also raised up some co-workers for John Chang, especially Dr. Shan Ji Dong (單繼東)who was raised in communist China by her parents who were fervent party members. They even named their daughter with characters which mean a "successor of Mao Tse-tung." She came to America to study, earned a PHD in genetics, and came to faith through an encounter with Jesus Christ in John Chang's congregation. She was a tremendous witness in China

221

being a scientist with her communist, atheistic background. Each of these missions ignited other outpourings of the Holy Spirit which launched successive waves of revival advancing the gospel of the kingdom of God. An entire book could be written about this amazing Chinese stream of the Holy Spirit which is in continuity with the revivals that were launched through R.A. Torrey and Johanthan Goforth from 1900 until about 1923. In many of these missions Rev. Chang and I were used as the fire starters. We were also able to introduce the rest of the Dunamis Project to enable people to grow in cooperation with the Holy Spirit.

One follow-up story of the seminary outpouring is in order just to demonstrate how the Lord continued to build on the initial event. In 2005 we took a combined team from the USA and Taiwan to China, once again to an undisclosed location where we had already been several times, teaching through the Dunamis Project equipping process.

At this event there were around 150 church leaders from both the house church movement as well as from the official government registered congregations. They had come from the far reaches of China. Some had traveled for weeks to get to the equipping event. We never knew how many of them had heard that we were providing this teaching. A few we recognized as having been part of previous events. These leaders represented vast networks of millions of believers. Providing these leaders with systematic biblical teaching, and also setting the context for Jesus to baptize them with the Holy Spirit was like lighting a fuse for revival fire to spread all over China. In addition to the basic biblical teaching on the Holy Spirit, we focused on the healing ministry of Jesus Christ. Most of the time, John Chang and I were in the role as fire starters, igniting outpourings of the Holy Spirit, but not this time. I share this story with you to demonstrate that there are times when the anointing shifts to others, and that we do not always get it right.

Rev. Cindy Strickler was teaching on healing with Su Chang (John Chang's wife) translating. Cindy is often used by God to impart gifts of healing. (It was so important to have anointed women on our teams as most of the Chinese church leaders are women.) As Cindy and Su were up front teaching, suddenly both came under demonic attack. It was as though a wave of evil hit them. Cindy felt like she was being stabbed in the back with a knife. Su looked confused and could not translate. I think this attack came because Dr. Chang and I failed to provide the prayer cover for them while they were in the upfront teaching role. Chang was off dealing with conflict that had arisen with another team member from Taiwan. I was in the front row but distracted, working on slides for the next teaching session and generally irritated with the person that John was dealing with. I felt awful about this because I had let down the prayer shield and failed in my role of providing cover for Cindy and Su. It was the two American members of the team who really stepped in—Mary Ellen and Tom who were in the back and watching what was happening to Cindy and Su up front. Later we realized that this demonic attack was just the first wave of Satan's counteroffensive against the work of the Holy Spirit. Later it included the police shutting down the entire meeting and all of us being detained and interrogated. That is another story.

After a while the attack against Cindy and Su lifted, and they continued announcing the love of Jesus and His authority to heal. We could see that the Holy Spirit was starting to move among the people. Jesus was reaching out His hand and healing them of various emotional hurts and physical ailments. Cindy and Su received guidance of what Jesus was doing or saying, such as healing backs or restoring broken relationships. Each time something was named when the Holy Spirit was moving, He would stretch out His hand and do the work. Mary Ellen and Tom were still providing prayer cover while I went out in the crowd and laid hands on people just to bless what the Holy Spirit was doing with them. This was wonderful! I could see up close Jesus' healing ministry taking place. I watched pain and tears give way to peace and joy. Some present still bore the emotional and physical scars of persecution. Words of forgiveness were spoken to those who had imprisoned or tortured them. For me, the most heart-wrenching of all were the younger women who had been forced to have abortions because of the One Child policy. They were weeping for their murdered children, and at the leading of the Holy Spirit were naming their names and commending their souls to Jesus. Many such manifestations of Jesus' healing and restoring love and presence occurred.

After a while the Holy Spirit's work shifted from healing and restoration to empowerment. Cindy received the guidance that Jesus at that moment wanted to baptize or fill each of them with the Holy Spirit so that they could be empowered to be His anointed witnesses and kingdom building co-workers. Then Cindy and Su were led to pray for the outpouring of the Holy Spirit.

As Cindy gave this word, she asked everyone to stand up and for each person to ask Jesus to baptize or fill them with the Holy Spirit. As everyone stood up it was a very intense, quiet moment in which, from the outside, it seemed that nothing much was happening. I had returned to my place just in front of the raised platform. I was entirely focused on praying for Cindy and Su, so was not looking back to see what was taking place. All I heard was a low murmur and I could not tell whether it was tongues or natural languages. I felt the love and presence of Jesus gently and sweetly manifesting around me. After a while Jesus' presence lifted and we took a break.

Immediately there came a counterattack. A member of the team from Taiwan criticized Cindy, saying that nothing was happening and that she had missed the guidance of the Holy Spirit and she and the American and Taiwan team should have laid hands on people. That really stirred up tension. However, when we gathered back together, I asked," Would any one like to report what Jesus did when you asked Him to baptize or fill you with the Holy Spirit." It seemed that nearly everyone had a testimony of Jesus touching them. Many had quietly received spiritual gifts of tongues and prophecy or had experienced the Holy Spirit falling upon them in physical expressions of warmth. Others had received visions of Jesus' majesty and power, and others received guidance for how Jesus was calling them as His witnesses.

It had truly been a Pentecost event with all five markers present! We realized later that Jesus had ignited this outpouring of the Holy

Spirit perfectly! We did not know at the time that we were being spied upon by the government religious police.

It would not have been good for any of the participants if we Westerners had laid hands on them or if there had been obvious or emotional manifestations. Also, it was totally clear to everyone that it was Jesus who had baptized them with the Holy Spirit. Jesus got all the glory; He cannot be shut down by the communist authorities.

After this outpouring in 2005, John Chang continued to take all-Chinese teams to China as it was no longer safe for us Westerners to go back. These trips continued to ignite outpourings of the Holy Spirit in multiple locations in China. Not only did the teams teach through the Dunamis Project units, but we had put the first three units on flash drives. These could be copied and widely distributed in the house church networks. Finally, the doors were closed to us by the increasing persecution of the Chinese Communist Party. However, we keep getting round-about reports from leaders of house churches and even large congregations that the Lord is using the video teaching and Dunamis teaching manuals on those flash drives to bring individuals and groups into experiencing Jesus fulfilling Acts 1:4-8. We are also hearing that this biblical and theologically Reformed systematic teaching is empowering the church for effective witness and avoiding heresy.

We have continued nurturing this stream of the Holy Spirit through the founding of the Double Grace Dunamis Theological Seminary (雙恩靈力事奉神學院 - 紐約) in 2019. Originally the plan was for it to be in China, but now because of recent oppression, it is located in Flushing, New York. The Seminary equips Chinese church leaders for Holy Spirit-empowered ministry. The core curriculum is the six Dunamis Project equipping units to which we have added a seventh unit, Growing the Church in the Power of the Holy Spirit. Further, for these church leaders there are also courses on church history, polity, pastoral care, and basic theology. We now have students from the Chinese diaspora in North America, and online students from all over China, Taiwan, and Hong Kong.

225

Two quick stories will illustrate how the Lord is using the Dunamis Seminary not just to provide academic knowledge, but as a context for Jesus to baptize the students with the Holy Spirit to be His empowered witnesses and co-workers. First, once a year those students and faculty located in the United States and Canada or even from Taiwan and Hong Kong, gather at the Community of the Cross in North Carolina for a face-to-face intense time of ministry in which they put into practice what they are learning about cooperating with the Holy Spirit. The most wonderful and amazing thing, however, is the Holy Spirit working online for those who cannot come to the Community of the Cross, which is all the students in China.

Dr. Ji Dung Shan (單繼東), reports,

"In my online class on the Gateways to Empowered Ministry, I always give the students a written test after each lesson to make sure they are learning the contents. They are good students, and all do well, but the really exciting thing is what happens when, instead of teaching online, I ask Dr. Chang to join me in praying for them all to be baptized or filled with the Holy Spirit. For most, this is the first time they have really asked Jesus to baptize them with the Holy Spirit. So, we virtually lay hands on each of them! This is just amazing! The Holy Spirit who is not bound by time and space will fall simultaneously on those gathered from all over the world, and just like in the book of Acts we hear and see them online speaking in tongues, prophesying or having other visible manifestations of the Holy Spirit upon them.

For some nothing seems to happen, but I always tell them that they need to ask and receive in faith and then expect the Lord to give them an opportunity to step out in obedience. Aways in the next online class, all the students come back with reports of how they have indeed experienced the gifts and power of the Holy Spirit and been used as witnesses to Jesus Christ. This is just amazing!"

In summary, the results for the kingdom of God of that outpouring of the Holy Spirit which took place in 1993 at that seminary in a city which I cannot name, have been far-reaching and incalculable. This revival movement, linking back to the days of R.A. Torrey and Jonathan Goforth, continues to grow and expand in China. We are praying and working toward the day that shall surely come that these streams of revival will grow to be a tsunami of the Holy Spirit, overcoming the demonic stronghold of the Chinese Communist Party and transforming China into a great missionary-sending nation doing their part in taking the gospel of the kingdom to all nations.

What I have described here of God's work in China, the combining of the five markers and three phases, is taking place all over the world. Praise God this is happening! Each phase is critical, but the one upon which all else hinges is the fire falling upon the prepared people, which is the altar composed of living stones. This requires those with the fire-starting anointing. We turn to this important topic in the next chapter.

# 13

# Becoming a Fire Starter—The First NGA COC Event

Fire starters start fires. In the realm of the Spirit, God calls and anoints some people to serve as fire starters.

We believe that we are at a turning point in the history of the advancement of the gospel of Jesus Christ. We are on the verge of major outpourings of the Holy Spirit which have the potential to converge and become the great, end-times global revival that Smith Wigglesworth "saw" in 1947—a revival fueled by the coming together of the Word and the Spirit. Doug McMurry studied past outpourings of the Holy Spirit and named what is coming "The Third Great Awakening." The present move of God has the potential to set the stage for Jesus' return in glory. "This gospel of the kingdom will be preached throughout the whole inhabited earth as a testimony to all the nations, and then the end will come" (Matt. 24:14).

In previous chapters we discussed dynamics related to Phase #1: Preparing the Altar. The hinge event that transitions individuals and groups from Phase #1 into Phase #2 (the application of R.A. Torrey's second key to revival) is the baptism with the Holy Spirit. We have already noted the critical importance of this baptism.

In 1904-1905, Jessie Penn Lewis, the anointed leader of the great Welsh Revival, declared,

**The Baptism with the Holy Spirit** is the "Essence of Revival," for revival comes from a knowledge of the Holy Spirit, and the way of co-working with Him which enables Him to work in revival power. The primary condition for revival is, therefore, that believers should individually know the

229

Baptism with the Holy Ghost. Such an infilling of the Spirit was the cause not only of the revival in Wales in 1904-1905, but also of all other revivals in the history of the world.[98]

The baptism with the Holy Spirit is essential because it results in power to serve as effective witnesses to Jesus Christ (Acts 1:8) and as His co-workers. Without it we falter for lack of passion and power. Our prayers become rote and self-centered, and we falter in our efforts to pass on a living, biblical faith to future generations. We have well established this role of the baptism with the Holy Spirit. The question that we must address in this chapter is the means that God has chosen to bring people into receiving it. In other words, who are the "fire starters" through whom Jesus ignites the kindling—thus passing on the baptism with the Holy Spirit so that Acts 1:4-8 is fulfilled repeatedly in a dynamic, synergistic manner resulting in biblical revival? This anointing of igniting the fire by bringing born-again believers into the experience of the baptism with the Holy Spirit is an expression of the apostolic anointing named by Paul as the first in the list of equipping anointings in Ephesians 4:11.

## New Testament Pattern for the Role of Fire Starters

Acts 8 introduces us to a gifted, Holy Spirit-empowered evangelist and teacher named Philip whose preaching of the gospel was accompanied by signs and wonders. Philip was clearly called and anointed to build Phase #1, Preparing the Altar. Apparently, however, he was not called or anointed for Phase #2, Igniting the Fire.

Now when the apostles in Jerusalem heard that Samaria had accepted the word of God, they sent **Peter and John** to them.

---

[98]Penn-Lewis, *War on the Saints*, 287.

**These two went down and prayed for them so that they would receive the Holy Spirit**. (For the Spirit had not yet come upon any of them, but they had only been baptized in the name of the Lord Jesus.) Then Peter and John placed their hands on the Samaritans, and they received the Holy Spirit. Acts 8:14-17

Peter and John had the Apostolic anointing needed to lead the Samaritans into experiencing the baptism with the Holy Spirit. They were called and anointed fire starters. In this way Jesus worked to fulfill His promise in Acts 1:4-8.

## The Lord is Raising Up Fire Starters

So far in this book we have told several stories about how the Lord used either Archer Torrey or me (Brad) as the means through whom He ignited Pentecost events. In recent decades a process of "ministry multiplication" has been occurring. Those of us who are presently anointed as fire starters are not being replaced, but we are being used by God to pass on an anointing to others whom Jesus is raising up as His fire starters. (As examples of multiplication, see Moses and the seventy elders in Numbers 11, and Jesus sending out the seventy-two in Luke 10.) In line with the model of Moses and Jesus, who did not step out until the right time, we are not stepping out, but stepping back, so that others whom the Lord is anointing may step forward and serve as Spirit-empowered fire starters. In the transfer of anointed leadership between Moses and Joshua there was a long period of overlap where Joshua was an apprentice to Moses. The transfer was complete when Moses went up Mount Nebo. Jesus' disciples had three years with Jesus before they received the Holy Spirit upon them at Pentecost.

I had over ten years of being mentored by Archer Torrey, even after he had pushed Doug McMurry and me into igniting the outpouring in 1991 at the first Dunamis Project event. At his invitation I launched a series of Dunamis equipping events at Jesus

231

Abbey to equip the ministry teams there. He continued to mentor and support me until he died in 2002. This is an important principle, because if the person with the apostolic anointing to ignite Pentecost outpourings is removed without sufficient overlap with the new fire-starters, they may not be mature enough to step into their anointing effectively. The other danger, of course, is that the anointed fire starters so enjoy being used by Jesus to ignite outpourings that they do not share this vital work with others.

In our present epoch, as we stand on the threshold of the next great awakening, the Lord is multiplying the number of fire starters. He is doing this not just in PRMI's tributary but in many different streams, including the Roman Catholic, Pentecostal, Jewish Messianic and many others who are part of God's master plans for bringing to completion the preaching the gospel of the kingdom to the whole world as a witness to all the nations and peoples on earth (Matthew 24:14, Mark 13:10). To accomplish this global gospel work, God the Father is releasing embers of revival to fall simultaneously in multiple locations around the world. Fanning the embers into flame will require a vast multiplication of those called into the apostolic role of fire starters. Also needed are those with the other callings— pastors, teachers, evangelists, prophets, and more who can prepare the altar and sustain the flame. However, 1 Corinthians 12:28 and Ephesians 4:11 make clear that there are "first apostles" because God works through apostles to ignite Pentecost events and provide the organizational expressions in which all the other gifts, callings, and vocations may find their place and means of expression. In this way those with an apostolic calling and anointing are Jesus' kingdom entrepreneurs.[99]

---

[99]We shall more fully develop this apostolic role of creating wineskins and containers in the next chapter.

# Summary Points for Becoming a Fire Starter and Stepping into an Apostolic Anointing

Through the examples of how God ignited Pentecost events in the Bible and through our own first-hand experiences within our Presbyterian and Reformed stream of the great river of God, we may derive some principles of how the Lord raises up people for this apostolic role of igniting outpourings of the Holy Spirit. There are two sides of this process. The first takes place in the person whom the Lord is preparing to call into this apostolic, fire-starting role. The second takes place in those who are already in this anointed role.

These principles may be summarized as follows:

## For the Person being Prepared by the Lord to Serve as a Fire Starter:

- Growing as a disciple of Jesus Christ.

- Having been baptized with the Holy Spirit.

- Sensing a call from God that is affirmed by mature, godly men and women to step into this apostolic anointing to serve as an ignitor of Pentecost events as well as a builder of forms and structures (new wineskins) to express the Holy Spirit's work.

- Participating on a team with other dynamic Christians.

- Growing in their ability to sense kairos moments and step into them (the dance of cooperation with the Holy Spirit).

- Being burdened to pray for outpourings of the Holy Spirit.

- Having suffered in the wilderness and died to their own dreams. Learning that the only way to work with God is "by Thy Spirit." They know that without the Holy Spirit, they cannot make anything happen.

- Turning away from enticements to serve as people-pleasers. Rather, they focus on Jesus and seek only His approval. They are no longer influenced by the fear of others or public opinion. This sets them free to become the means that Jesus uses to baptize people with the Holy Spirit (Galatians 1:10).

- Being mentored by another person who has the apostolic anointing for igniting Pentecost events and building containers to sustain the flame.

- Welcoming the wisdom and input of others, rather than being proud and unteachable.

## Role of the Apostolic Leader Already Anointed to Ignite Pentecost Events

- Participating in preparing the altar by creating the context for God the Father to fulfill Acts 1:4-8.

- Stepping back, but not out and making space for the new apostolic leaders the Lord is raising up. Supporting them through love, fellowship, mentoring, and prayer.

- Laying hands on people and praying in faith for them to receive the baptism with the Holy Spirit.

- Working to create the wineskins needed to sustain the flame—providing flexible structures and containers for the on-going work of the Spirit.

- Receiving the gift of faith to trust that as they step back and bless those whom God is calling to step forward, the Holy Spirit will work through the apprentice.

I think I need to add a personal note and observation from the perspective of those of us who are called to discern and mentor those people whom God may be calling and anointing as fire starters. It appears that sometimes the Lord uses the most unlikely people to be fire starters. An example is found in the movie, "Jesus Revolution."[100] Lonnie Frisbee was a hippie, and from what I've read, the Lord revealed Himself to Lonnie when he was high on drugs reading the Bible. Chuck Smith, the pastor of a traditional church, after some real struggle and soul searching, took the risk of letting Lonnie Frisbee speak and welcomed in his hippie friends. Being one of those "hippies" myself during my rebellious college days, whom God has used as an apostolic fire starter, I think it is entirely possible that in our present context and culture God is raising totally unlikely fire starters for today's revival. I am convinced that in our present culture in the USA, Canada, and the UK, that the Lord may well be choosing those coming out of the LGTBQ+ community, or those social justice warriors waving Black Lives Matter signs, or otherwise deceived into the Woke movement, that God is preparing as the apostolic fire starters today who will form the new wineskins needed for this present revival to become the next great awakening.

Our prayer must be, "Lord! Open our eyes to see who they are. Lord, give us the love and discernment needed to pray for them and to mentor them into the kingdom and into their anointed roles." For myself, I am seeking to do this with my own children and grandchildren and those young men and women whom the Lord is blessing at PRMI events.

---

[100] https://www.youtube.com/watch?v=8vmHFvnjPDw

## An illustration of God Multiplying the Fire Starter Anointing: The Next Great Awakening Concert of Prayer at the Community of the Cross, November 10-12, 2021

To model this process of one anointed apostolic fire starter stepping back to let other leaders step into their anointing, co-author Phil Noordmans will narrate the events that led up to the Pentecost event that took place at the Community of the Cross (COC) and will include the voices of other participants.

[**Phil Noordmans**] To illustrate how the Holy Spirit implemented these principles, consider the example of the PRMI "Preparing for the Next Great Awakening Prayer Concert" that took place at the Community of the Cross (COC) in 2021. This event set in motion within the Presbyterian Reformed stream of the Holy Spirit, a wave of the Holy Spirit which, if we persist in prayer and obedience, may become one tributary in a plethora of outpourings of the Holy Spirit that are beginning to happen simultaneously in many locations. At this event several PRMI leaders stepped more fully into their anointed and apostolic roles of igniting outpourings of the Holy Spirit.

The setting of this Concert of Prayer, the COC, is a 24-acre, wooded parcel which is situated beside a river on the side of a mountain in a beautiful valley in western North Carolina. Our purpose for gathering was to set in motion the meta pattern of the three phases of the outpouring of the Holy Spirit which we have described as:

- Preparing the Altar
- Igniting the Fire
- Sustaining the Flame

To accomplish this, we designed each day around one of R.A. Torrey's three keys for revival:

- Day 1: Evangelism
- Day 2: Baptism with the Holy Spirit
- Day 3: Prayer

## The Leadership Team

The Leadership Team included:

- Doug and Carla McMurry were there to lead us in harp-and-bowl worship and intercession. They have been praying for a great outpouring of the Holy Spirit to take place for about forty years, which put them in a spiritual grandparent role to all of us.
- Cindy Strickler participated in the event in her role as Director of PRMI and the PRMI Dunamis Fellowship. Cindy has been in anointed leadership and apostolic roles since 1991 when she was baptized with the Holy Spirit at the first Dunamis Event at Lake George.
- Martin Boardman serves as Prayer Mobilizer for PRMI and DFC (Dunamis Fellowship, Canada). He has a heart for praying in the next great awakening.
- Dave Westra and I (Phil Noordmans) are not only gifted teachers in the Dunamis Project but also anointed to nurture the working of the Holy Spirit within the context of local congregations.
- In addition, a team of onsite and online intercessors joined us in praying for an outpouring of the Holy Spirit to take place.
- David Pleuss led the worship team that, throughout the event, put our focus on exalting worship of the Lord.
- Brad was in overall anointed, apostolic leadership and spiritual authority and, with the team, was called to create the venue for the Holy Spirit to work.

Within this team were the fivefold equipping anointings as well as many other spiritual giftings, all expressed through different personalities and natural talents. We were knit together under King Jesus as a loving and supportive fellowship, grounded in the Bible as the Word of God and dedicated to receiving and obeying the guidance of the Holy Spirit.

## The Design of the Event

We are sharing these details so that others might have a pattern to follow loosely for designing events in their contexts.

### Day #1: *Preparing the Altar*

On Day #1, we emphasized R.A. Torrey's first key to revival, evangelism. We started with ourselves, recommitting ourselves to following Jesus Christ. We also prayed that there would be a great move of the Holy Spirit, like in Acts 8 with Philip, in which evangelism would take place with signs and wonders within our communities and nations.

### Day #2: *Igniting the Fire*

On Day #2, we focused on R.A. Torrey's second key to revival, the baptism with the Holy Spirit. Once again, we started with ourselves. We prayed that we would be baptized with the Holy Spirit, or in our case, because most of us already had that experience, would be filled again, and anointed for igniting the next great awakening. In time we shifted to praying for outpourings of the Holy Spirit in local congregations. We were especially burdened to pray for the next great move of the Holy Spirit to touch the younger generation. [Significantly, the Asbury Revival, which began on February 8, 2023, at Asbury University, engulfed 1000s of students.]

### Day #3: *Sustaining the Flame*

On Day #3, we focused on R.A. Torrey's third key to revival, prayer. We prayed for revival to take place in our churches and around the world. We prayed for people to be moved to pray. We also prayed that outpourings of the Holy Spirit would grow and be extended.

The whole event was wrapped in harp-and-bowl worship and prayer led by Doug and Carla. The Holy Spirit drew near to enable us to worship and pray with earnest sincerity.

### Loosely Structured

Although the above paragraphs give the impression that each day was tightly structured, that was not the case. We intentionally left open spaces for the Holy Spirit's on-the-fly guidance. We truly wanted Him to lead this dance.

**So, what happened?**

This was an amazing event! Each day was filled with the presence of God as well as manifestations of the Holy Spirit showing forth the Kingship and love of Jesus Christ.

However, I want to focus on the second day, November 11, 2021. To do this I will be bringing in each of the participants to tell their part of the story in their own words.

[**Brad Long**] I was so excited and ready to lead this day of preparing to receive the baptism with the Holy Spirit! I knew this day was a pivotal moment for launching PRMI's work in this next great outpouring of the Holy Spirit. To arrive at this culminating moment the Lord had taken me personally as well as the PRMI leadership team through a withering, refining fire. For me it consisted of strategic intercession as well as spiritual warfare. I had also cast the vision of the Next Great Awakening (NGA) which had been approved by the PRMI Board of Directors and whole-heartedly adopted by those called into leadership for the next phase of this ministry development.

I also knew that Jesus was preparing those of us who had been a part of the 1991 outpouring of the Holy Spirit that launched the Dunamis wave to share the mantle of anointed leadership with the next generation of leadership for the next thirty years.

I was earnestly praying for the Lord to pour out the Holy Spirit at the Community of the Cross and ignite the next great wave of the Holy Spirit. This was my passion! I was fully expecting that the Lord would use me in this location of the Community of the Cross to lay hands on people for igniting this next move of God. Most of the people in attendance had already been baptized with the Holy Spirit and were already empowered co-workers of Jesus Christ. So, we all realized that this was more of a time of praying for fresh infillings and for the Lord to call and anoint each of us for our parts in preparing for the next great awakening.

As I drove from my house to the Community of the Cross for the morning team meeting, I received a note from Earl Rutledge, President of the PRMI Board, who lives in Nicaragua. He and his wife, Bev, had been praying for an outpouring of the Holy Spirit to take place in Nicaragua. Their focus had been on prayers for repentance and salvation, the infilling of the Holy Spirit, and prayer for the church and the nation. The note said:

> Today I pray for a powerful outpouring of the Father's promise. "Ask and I will give the Holy Spirit."
>
> "Father, I ask that today there be a powerful filling and refilling of the Holy Spirit. Anoint... leaders as they lead us to this encounter with you, this filling of the Holy Spirit, this empowerment to be witnesses of Jesus Christ.
>
> Come Holy Spirit, come. Let Your fire fall upon us.
>
> Fill your people. Ignite your church. Prepare us to take coals of fire from the COC to our local churches and ministries and spread the fire, in multiple places, igniting a massive outpouring of the Holy Spirit in the world.
>
> Come Holy Spirit, come."

When I received this, my expectant faith was deepened. This was evidence that the Holy Spirit was stirring up a concert of prayer which was preparing the way for Jesus to work that day. Earl, as president of the PRMI Board of Directors, with them, had spiritual oversight and authority over PRMI, the entire global ministry. Earl had also sent this prayer to Cindy, which she shared at the team meeting.

[**Phil Noordmans**] When the leadership team met this rainy Thursday morning, I submitted the guidance I had received about leading a *Lectio Divina* exercise that focused on Psalm 63 and on key statements regarding baptism with the Holy Spirit. Dave Westra also submitted three areas of guidance including 'tarrying' [waiting] – something I heartily affirmed.

[**Dave Westra**] Before telling you about this morning I need to give a little background about how the Lord had been preparing me for what was to take place. It is important to know that for seven years I had been praying for revival. My wife Anne and I started praying together for it about two years ago. Around the same time, the Lord began highlighting the numbers 11:11 to me nearly every day. For a long time, I told the Lord, "You have my attention. What are you trying to communicate about?" When Brad phoned me earlier this fall to share the vision for the NGA event and invite my participation, I had a deep resonance because of my own personal prayers and yearning for revival, along with my sense that this is a 24/7 kairos moment. I also shared that the dates he was proposing fell over Nov. 11 (11-11), and I wondered if this is what the Lord had been pointing towards.

After accepting God's call to participate, I felt led by Him to fast from alcohol for the forty days leading up to 11-11, as I carried on my prayers for revival, and for an outpouring of the Holy Spirit. Because of a family vacation ahead of the event, I was able to arrive two full days prior to the event. I spent the majority of both of those days walking the trails at the COC and praying. Most of the prayer was personal preparation for whatever role God would assign me during the event. God took me to a place of deep and utter awareness of my/our complete inability to bring the revival/outpouring of His Spirit that we longed for, partnered together with a deep faith that He would do it as we followed Him in faith and obedience. I realized that while my story of extended preparation was unique to me, all the rest of the team had also gone through extended preparation. For instance, Cindy, Brad, and Martin were going through very difficult refining fire through conflict in PRMI. We all had been through extended periods of prayer and preparation.

On the morning of 11-11, I woke up at 4:30 with a splitting headache. The Holy Spirit gave me the ability to say joyfully, "This isn't getting in the way of what you are going to do today, Lord!" I made coffee and spent several hours in scripture and prayer. I felt led to fast that morning, and later learned that Phil had been led to fast as well. That provided extra time for more walking the trails and praying. I came away from these with three senses from the Lord:

1. This morning would look different from what we might expect.

2. That the Lord would have us "tarry" in his presence (not a word we normally use at PRMI!)

241

3. That at some point, I was to share some of my personal story of the last year and a half.

After coming in from walking the trails, Brad asked me what guidance I was getting, and I shared with him. He noted that Phil was getting some similar guidance, pulled together the team, who resonated and assigned us to lead. At this point, I didn't feel any of the nervousness that I often feel when I know I'll be "on point." It was like walking into something that had been long prepared in prayer. I knew the Lord would make a way, no matter how "bumbly" we might be. And He did!

[**Brad Long**] During the meeting in the morning, it was obvious to me that Dave Westra and Phil Noordmans, as well as Martin Boardman, were receiving guidance about how to conduct the time of prayer for the baptism and infilling with the Holy Spirit. It also turned out that both Phil and Dave had been in urgent prayer for this outpouring, even with fasting, for weeks before the event. However, I still thought that the Lord wanted me to be in the room as part of the team to support them and to take part in laying hands on people. I even thought that perhaps the Lord wanted me to be the primary fire ignitor as I had so often been in the past.

As we were preparing for the morning with worship, I had hoped that we could change our venue to pray for the outpouring of the Holy Spirit from the meeting room in the log house to the not-yet-completed Prayer House, where I had seen the vision of the flaming coals of the Holy Spirit fire falling, but it was pouring rain, so the team vetoed it. I gave up on that idea, which was part of the Lord working on me by calling me to surrender what I thought should happen.

No sooner had I accepted this than the Lord spoke another word to me which I really did not want to hear! He said, "Don't you remember what Archer Torrey did when I sent that great outpouring of the Holy Spirit at Lake George Silver Bay YMCA Retreat center in 1991? Remember he stepped back and pushed you and Doug forward to be the ones through whom I ignited that Pentecost event. Now I am calling you to do what I called

242

Archer to do; you are to step back and push Martin, Phil, and Dave forward!"

I had a moment of arguing with the Lord about this guidance. I reminded Him how much I had prayed for this and how the COC was the place where the outpouring was to happen. I offered some other unbecoming arguments reflecting my own ego needs, which I am embarrassed to put into writing, but you can imagine. With that I heard very clearly the Lord say, "Now, I want you to not only turn leadership over to them, but I am now commanding you to go out into the rain. You are to walk the COC trails and pray for those whom I am raising up with you in apostolic anointing and through whom I am now going to be pouring out My Holy Spirit. "

As I heard all this I repented of my silly, ego-centered arguments with Jesus Christ the King of Kings. I knew I had to obey; otherwise, I would block what He was planning on doing. I suspect that if I had not been so argumentative about releasing leadership, the Lord would have let me stay in the room and be a part of the marvelous manifestations of the kingdom of God that took place.

As we all gathered in the meeting room in the Log House, I felt the Lord saying, "Now tell the group what I have told you!" So, I announced to the group the guidance that I had received. I said that Martin was on point, with Phil and Dave on wing. I offered a quick prayer of blessing on them; then, feeling very alone and utterly miserable, promptly headed for the door. Before I could make it out the door, Cindy suddenly jumped up and walked out with me. She said that the Lord was calling her to join me. JuleAnn and Pauline received the guidance that they were called to be our prayer shield while we walked and prayed. I was so grateful to have Cindy's company and their prayer support. Together, Cindy and I left the meeting room and headed out into the rain. As we walked the trails, my role, with Cindy in a supportive role like Aaron upholding Moses' arms, was to hold back the powers and principalities that would close the doors of the open heaven. The Lord also gave us together the gift of faith that Jesus Christ was pouring out His Holy Spirit and launching an outpouring at this COC event through Martin, Dave, and Phil. Later we felt Jesus smiling at us!

That is my side of what happened. You can see some of the above listed principles of my role as an apostolic anointed leader being implemented by the Holy Spirit. His role was to give the guidance; my role was to follow Jesus!

**Meanwhile, back in the meeting room …**

So much happened that we need to hear from three voices to get a taste of how God moved.

[**Martin**] Before I can tell what happened next, I need to note that that Brad, the Executive Director, and Cindy, the Director of PRMI, the leaders of this event, demonstrated wise apostolic leadership by ensuring a seamless transfer of authority. Before leaving in response to the Lord's guidance to walk the trails and pray, they established me in the role of overall spiritual oversight, and Dave and Phil to serve together under me. This was announced publicly to the whole group. In this way Brad and Cindy ensured that the adversary did not have an opening to gain a foothold in our midst.

After Brad and Cindy both stepped out, I was aware of the Holy Spirit's anointing to be in authority over the whole event and ensure that we stayed on track with the Holy Spirit as a group. To do this, I was listening to the Spirit to get a sense of the direction He wanted to take us. At the same time, I watched the room to see what was happening, and checked with Dave and Phil to make sure we were in step together.

During the morning, I kept having a sense of the next step we needed to take. For example, I knew the next phase of the dance was to pray for the baptism, but I knew it was not quite time to take that step, so I was in a position of praying, watching, and waiting.

[**Dave**] After several minutes of worship, the Lord called Brad, who was interceding at the back of the room, to intercede from outside the room. Cindy felt called to join him. Personally, this was very helpful for me. Because I look up to Brad and Cindy so much, and have a bent towards "doing things right," and because I know that Brad so often senses exactly what the Spirit's doing, I can sometimes feel a pressure upon me when leading in his presence.

244

(Mostly this has to do with my own sanctification.) When Brad and Cindy left, giving us a prayer covering, I was able to settle even more deeply into a focus on what the Lord was doing.

[**Phil**] What a glorious morning! Dave offered impromptu, passionate opening comments; then, we went into worship. Several minutes later, leading a *Lectio Divina* exercise that focused on Psalm 63, I began to take the group through five scripture verses pertaining to baptism with the Holy Spirit. As soon as we read the third scripture, which included "John baptized with water, but you will be baptized with the Holy Spirit not many days from now," (Acts 1:5), Dave stepped over and whispered, **'Now! We pray for the baptism with the Holy Spirit now!'**

"Go for it," I replied, and Dave did.

[**Dave**] Phil and I had sensed that the Lord would have us listen and meditate, *Lectio Divina* style, upon Psalm 63 and four different passages from Acts. In time, we moved into Phil reading Psalm 63, followed by sensing the Lord calling us to express our thirst to him. As we began to do this, I began to discern that the time of inviting Him to pour out His Spirit might come much sooner than we'd anticipated. Phil moved from Psalm 63 into reading Acts 1:4-8, and as he was reading, I sensed the Lord saying, "**Now, ask me to pour out my Spirit!**" I hesitated for a moment, not wanting to interrupt Phil, but knew and could feel, immediately, what it would be like to miss this kairos moment. I put a hand on Phil's arm, whispered in his ear that I sensed now was the time, and received Phil's affirmation to move us into asking."

[**Martin**] Then, just before Dave stepped over to Phil, I was aware of something shifting. When Dave spoke, it confirmed that shift. There was a sense of "**Yes - now! Go for it**!' We were on track with the Holy Spirit. I got to watch the dance unfold before me and pray covering over what was happening."

It is difficult to describe what happened for the next 90 minutes. Waves of the Holy Spirit flowed over and through the group. Sometimes we stood in silence in the Lord's presence. Sometimes we cried out to Him with earnest and loud supplications. At one point the Lord prompted Dave to ask, "Who would like us to pray for you to receive the gift of faith?" Many hands raised; many voices cried out for faith. Dave and Phil moved around the room touching the hands and offering quick prayers, usually in tongues. The Lord prompted us to call out other gifts—miracles, healing, mercy combined with discernment—and a similar pattern followed.

[**Dave**] I began narrating the sense I had, being careful to name that we were asking God for something He was eager to give, that we were not in any way forcing His hand, but that we still needed to reach out to Him in faith, and then I began to call on the Holy Spirit to come, fall upon us afresh, come fill us afresh for witness to Jesus Christ. Almost immediately the Spirit began to fall upon people in various ways around the room. During this time, and for the next two hours, David Pleuss covered the room with worship on the keyboard, and this began a prolonged period of waiting upon and then receiving from the Lord in various waves. For a number of these waves of the Spirit, I felt led to go and lay hands on people, imparting gifts and praying for the fire of the Lord to fall upon them.

One of the other things the Lord prompted us to pray for was a "spirit of prophecy" to fall upon the group. One of the most amazing things that we learned in the debrief was that prior to my praying this, Doug McMurry had been receiving a prophetic word for Kristine Rand, but was unsure of what to do with it. As I prayed for a spirit of prophecy to fall upon the group, Phil was led to go to Doug, take him by the hand and lead him over to Kristine, saying, "I believe you have something for her." Doug was astounded. The Lord did just what we prayed for, right as we were praying for it. All without Phil and I talking to each other about it. ...

In the debrief that followed this amazing outpouring, we heard multiple other stories of the powerful ways the Lord was working in individuals during our two hours of waiting upon Him. This debriefing was so important because we were able to 'match" what was happening on the inside of people with what we had observed as external manifestations of the Holy Spirit.

For instance, as we were praying, I watched the Holy Spirit fall upon Barbara Koob. She had looked anxious and stressed, but then joy dawned on her face. Then she was overtaken by jubilant laughter which spread to the others sitting beside her. I knew something important was happening to her but was not sure what, until she reported during the debrief, that she had experienced a deep inner healing from Jesus who had just filled her with such joy. She heard Him saying to her, "I am bigger than anything the devil can do to thwart My purposes for your life. You belong to Me, and I will take care of everything that concerns you." This word from the Lord was given months before Barb's husband, Jim, suddenly and unexpectedly died. It was only then that this word took on its full significance and provided comfort for Barb in this time of sudden, devastating loss.

Another person I had seen being filled with the Holy Spirit with some evident manifestations was Brad's son-in-law, Josh Modrzynski. He had come with the many burdens from serving as Pastor of St. Giles Presbyterian Church in Richmond. After an initial wave of the Holy Spirit, while we were lingering in the Lord's presence and He was ministering to people, I saw Josh sitting quietly, writing in his journal. As we continued in prayer, the Lord gave me the word that I spoke out, "Jesus is placing in some of you a fiery passion to see the gospel of Jesus Christ go to the nations, and He is calling certain of you to be the carriers of that passion." I asked those who may be sensing this passion and calling from Jesus to raise their hands. Immediately I saw the Holy Spirit fall upon Josh. Interestingly, the two other people in Josh's row, Mary Sterenberg and Gina Dick, also raised their hands. Three of the six who responded were in one cluster. As we laid hands and prayed for the fire of the Lord to fall on them, Gina had the Spirit come on her and she began praying in all different tongues, moving from one to the next, with English interspersed. It became apparent to her that she was preaching the gospel in many different languages.

Later, Josh reported that before I was called to speak about Jesus placing a fiery passion to see the gospel spread, the Lord had already given him a vision of this. "I saw a vision of Jesus taking fiery coals from under the altar in heaven and hurling them to the earth. This seemed to be like the vision my father-in-law had seen, but I was not sure just what this meant for me, so I started to write the vision down in my journal. The moment I put my pen down, the Holy Spirit fell upon me, and I knew that the Lord was giving me this passion to spread the gospel of Jesus Christ and giving me this calling to ignite outpourings of the Holy Spirit, starting at St. Giles Presbyterian Church, but then moving beyond to the nations."

These connections between what the Lord was doing and speaking through the upfront leaders and what He was doing with those in the gathering, is an objective verification that the Holy Spirit is the one actually directing the ministry. One person commented, "It was such a diverse move of the Holy Spirit, and yet it was in no way chaotic. It was so peaceful!" The dynamic synergy of this dance of the Holy Spirit among the different participants, however, is often not obvious until afterwards during the time of debriefing.[101]

Additional testimonies came from people who were listening and watching online. In the room, Jesus was healing people, restoring hearts, re-affirming and deepening callings, giving new gifts, and refreshing us in His presence. It was glorious! Afterwards we found out that the Lord was also working in similar ways with the participants online who were scattered all over the world. Truly God was manifesting His glory and working to prepare people to participate in some aspect of the next great awakening.

I can tell you from my perspective, it was an incredible joy to get to share in what Jesus was doing by leading together with Phil. One last thing...these paragraphs are my attempt at a summary, but they are in no way detailed or complete. It's just what I can give now, hoping to be helpful. To the glory of God!

---

[101]It is the practice of PRMI always to do a debriefing (or what in military terms is called an After-Action Review (AAR)) after there have been manifestations of the Holy Spirit. This enables us to discern carefully what has been from the Holy Spirit, what has been human responses or emotions, or if any of the manifestations were from evil spirits. This practice has enabled us not only to grow in understanding how to cooperate with the Holy Spirit but also helped us to discern emotionalism as well as demonic deception.

[**Brad**] While it is premature to evaluate the long-term results of this particular Pentecost event, what we can confirm is that it provides a model for how Jesus is calling us to cooperate with Him in His work of calling, equipping, and sending people into their spheres of activity as His co-workers with the apostolic anointing for igniting Pentecost events. As of March 2023, when I was reviewing this chapter, what we can say with certainty is that this outpouring of the Holy Spirit, that took place under the framework of this meta pattern, the five markers, the three keys and the two foundations, has been followed by other outpourings of the Holy Spirit.

One aspect of this event with profound consequences must be noted: The physical address of the Pentecost event and the prepared group of people gathered needs to be expanded to include cyberspace. We were gathered in "one place" just like at the first Pentecost outpouring in Jerusalem, but through the internet this one place was vastly expanded to include people in scattered, multiple geographical locations. This demonstrates that Jesus may use the internet to baptize His born-again disciples with the Holy Spirit in multiple locations simultaneously. That opens up unprecedented opportunities for igniting revival worldwide.

I earnestly pray that we will look back years from now and see that it was this event that set in motion one tributary in the great outpouring of the Holy Spirit that became the next great awakening.

## Reflections on the Multiplication of Anointing that was Taking Place.

Before we focus on Dave who stepped into the kairos moment, we need to be clear that he was part of the team of three surrounded by an even larger support team of intercessors and worship leaders. These teams were like concentric circles, all working together, with each member doing his/her part in the dance of cooperation with the Holy Spirit. This provides us with a model for how the Lord works through an apostolic anointing to raise up fire starters.

## The Holy Spirit was Working through a Team to Create the Context for Fulfilling Acts 1:4-8

Jesus rarely uses a one-man or one-woman show. He usually works through a team of anointed leaders with different gifts. Notice that in Acts 8 Peter and John came as a team of two to lay hands on the Samaritans. In Acts 19:6, Paul laid hands on the twelve men who received the baptism with the Holy Spirit and spoke in tongues and prophesied (Acts 19:6). It appears that Paul did this alone. However, Paul always traveled with a team; Acts 19:22 says, "So he sent into Macedonia two of those who ministered to him, Timothy and Erastus, but he himself stayed in Asia for a time." And Acts 19:29 mentions, "Gaius and Aristarchus, Paul's travel companions." So, although Acts 19:1 only mentions Paul, it isn't unreasonable to suggest that he had a team with him, though he was the fire starter. The text does not say this, but I suspect that it was those twelve who then did, indeed, become the anointed team who continued to support Paul's work in Ephesus. They may have been the disciples who went with Paul out of the synagogue as he was every day speaking and teaching in the "lecture hall of Tyrannus" (Acts 19:9). In I Corinthians 12-14, Paul certainly presents the team model— "What should you do then, brothers and sisters? When you come together, each one has a song, has a lesson, has a revelation, has a tongue, has an interpretation. Let all these things be done for the strengthening of the church" (1 Corinthians 14:26). This team approach, which includes many different gifts and expressions, is critical for how Jesus is working in this epoch to prepare the altar, ignite the fire, and then sustain the flame of outpourings of the Holy Spirit.

Martin Boardman, Phil Noordmans, and Dave Westra were all part of the upfront leadership team taking part in this outpouring. Behind them providing the context were the intercessors, the worship team, and others. Each person gathered at this location and online, as part of the prepared group of people upon whom the Holy Spirit fell, had a unique story of how the Lord had prepared them and called them to be there at that strategic moment.

Through them the context was created for God the Father to fulfill Acts 1:4-8 in that particular location and at that specific time.

## The Kairos Moment when Dave sensed the Lord saying, "Now, ask me to pour out my Spirit!"

Let's focus here on the moment when Dave sensed the Lord saying, "Now, ask me to pour out My Spirit." This is indeed the turning point when the shift took place from our part of the dance to where Jesus stepped in and did His part. This is often the most difficult step to take.

What is described above of Dave getting the guidance that it was now time, confirms that it is not that we light the fire, but that Jesus tells us, "NOW I am going to baptize or fill these people with the Holy Spirit." Usually this does not happen as a team, but rather with one person who discerns the kairos moment, names it, and steps into it. The team may be in the role to confirm the guidance, but in all my experience it has usually been one person, and often it has been the one with the apostolic fire-starting anointing, who hears Jesus say, "Now I am ready!" This knowing that now is the time is then followed by either the fire starter or another anointed person on the team receiving the guidance as to how Jesus intends for us to cooperate with Him as He does His work. In this case Dave's role was to narrate the guidance he was receiving of what Jesus was doing.

There is a great diversity of ways that the Lord may call a person to work. Perhaps it is to offer to lay on hands, or to ask people to come forward, or to pray through the R.A. Torrey conditions for asking for and receiving the baptism with the Holy Spirit, or "everyone get into groups of three and lay hands on each other," or "go outside on the prayer trails alone and ask Jesus to baptize you with the Holy Spirit." There is a vast variety of ways the Lord may decide to pour out the Holy Spirit. Whatever the guidance may be, receiving and acting upon it in faith becomes the turning point when everything shifts from us to Jesus, who is the only One qualified to baptize people with the Holy Spirit.

I cannot teach you how to do this as I am convinced that this comes from the sovereign action of King Jesus the Baptizer with the Holy Spirit and fire, who chooses the "who", the "where", the "time", and the "how" He will pour out the Holy Spirit. Much of this, however, comes from learning the dynamic dance steps in cooperating with the Holy Spirit. I have written about these extensively in other books and this is a major theme of Dunamis Project teaching.[102] We cannot fully develop that dynamic of cooperation here, but I do want to focus on one key part: This is learning to discern the moment of opportunity and then trusting Jesus as He gives the guidance to step into it. This requires a total and complete surrender to Jesus and a radical commitment to do His will, which is accompanied by astute gifts of discernment in knowing when Jesus is actually speaking. This hearing Jesus' guidance and stepping out in radical obedience is also accompanied by the gift of mountain-moving faith. Adding one more element to this already complicated dynamic, is that one must be totally free from the fear of man and set only on pleasing Jesus Christ, no matter what the cost. (Galatians 1:10)

## Example from the History of D.L. Moody

I [Brad] think it is important to add an historical example demonstrating this dynamic of discerning the kairos moment, knowing that Jesus is going to baptize people with the Holy Spirit, and then getting the guidance of how Jesus is calling us to cooperate with Him. One may rightfully ask, "Where do you see this dynamic in the Bible?" My answer is that you do not. All you have is the report. For instance, Peter and John, or Paul laid hands on people and Jesus baptized them with the Holy Spirit. The focus there is on the condition of those disciples of Jesus who had not yet had the Holy Spirit come upon them for power. We do not find anywhere a report on just how Jesus led the apostles to lay hands

---

[102]See the Dunamis manual #2 *In the Spirit's Power* where we introduce this dynamic. Also, in the book I coauthored with Cindy Strickler and Paul Stokes, *Growing the Church in the Power of the Holy Spirit*, we go into greater depth in this dynamic.

on people at that very moment. We do find the report of Philip who was given the guidance step by step which led to the conversion of the Ethiopian. We may assume that the others also received guidance in similar ways, which is by "an angel of the Lord spoke..." (Acts 8:26) or the "Spirit said" (Acts 8:29). I recognize that because there is no chapter and verse in the Bible confirming these principles illustrated in Dave receiving the guidance "Now!" that what we have presented here may seem speculative. However, it is not contrary to the way God works with us as His friends and co-workers. For support for this dynamic of knowing when Jesus is ready to baptize or fill people with the Holy Spirit and gives directions as to how He intends to do this, I cite an historical example of another apostolic team of fire starters – D.L. Moody and R.A. Torrey. R.A. Torrey tells the following story:

"There is an afternoon that I shall never forget. It was the eighth day of July 1894. It was at the Northfield Students' Convention. I had spoken that morning in the church on How to Receive the Baptism with the Holy Spirit. As I drew to a close, I took out my watch and noticed that it was exactly twelve o'clock. Mr. Moody had invited us to go up on the mountain that afternoon at three o'clock to wait upon God for the baptism with the Holy Spirit. As I looked at my watch, I said, 'Gentlemen, it is exactly twelve o'clock. Mr. Moody has invited us to go up on the mountain at three o'clock to wait upon God for the baptism with the Holy Spirit. It is three hours until three o'clock. Some of you cannot wait three hours, nor do you need to wait. Go to your tent, go to your room in the hotel or in the buildings, go out into the woods, go anywhere, where you can get alone with God, meet the conditions of the baptism with the Holy Spirit and claim it at once.' At three o'clock we gathered in front of Mr. Moody's mother's house; four hundred and fifty-six of us in all, all men from the eastern colleges. (I know the number because Mr. Paul Moody counted us as we passed through the gates down into the lots.) We commenced to climb the mountainside. After we had gone some distance, Mr. Moody said, 'I do not think we need to go further. Let us stop here.' We sat down and Mr. Moody said, 'Have any of you anything to say?' One after another, perhaps seventy-five men, arose and said words to this effect, 'I could not wait until three o'clock. I have been alone with God and I have received the baptism with the Holy Spirit.' Then Mr. Moody said, 'I can see no reason why we should not kneel right down here now and ask God that the Holy Spirit may fall on us as definitely as He fell on the apostles at Pentecost. Let us pray.' We knelt on the ground; some of us lay on our faces on the pine-needles. As we had gone up the mountainside, a cloud had been gathering over the mountain, and as we began to pray the cloud broke and the raindrops began to come down upon us through the overhanging pine trees, but another cloud, big with mercy, had been gathering over Northfield for ten days and our prayers seemed to pierce that cloud and the Holy Ghost fell upon us. It was a wonderful hour. There are many who will never forget it..."[103]

Notice several key elements in this report which are consistent with what we have been teaching.

### Preparing the Altar Through Biblical Teaching on the Baptism with the Holy Spirit

R.A. Torrey was a great Bible teacher. So, when he provided teaching on how to receive the baptism with the Holy Spirit, we can be sure that this was well grounded in the Bible. I am sure that Torrey must have presented to those young men, many of whom were destined for the ministry, his teaching of the necessity of the baptism with the Holy Spirit:

"It is evident then that the baptism with the Holy Spirit is absolutely necessary in every Christian for the service that Christ demands and expects of him. There are certainly few greater mistakes that we are

---

[103] R.A. Torrey, *The Person and Work of The Holy Spirit As Revealed in the Scriptures And in Personal Experience* (New York, Chicago, Toronto, London and Edinburgh: Fleming H. Revell Company, 1910), 185-186.

making to-day in our various Christian enterprises than that of setting men to teach Sunday-school classes and do personal work and even to preach the gospel, because they have been converted and received a certain amount of education, including maybe a college and seminary course, but have not as yet been baptized with the Holy Spirit. We think that if a man is hopefully pious and has had a college and seminary education and comes out of it reasonably orthodox, he is now ready that we should lay our hands upon him and ordain him to preach the gospel. But Jesus Christ says, 'No.' There is another preparation so essential that a man must not undertake this work until he has received it. 'Tarry ye (literally 'sit ye down') until ye be endued with power from on high.'"[104]

He most likely would have presented to this group of young men his seven steps for receiving the baptism with the Holy Spirit. These calls for action are listed with full scriptural backup in his great book *The Person and Work of the Holy Spirit*. Just to demonstrate what those young men may have heard on that day, here they are in summary:

1.The first step is to accept Jesus Christ as our Savior (Acts 2:38).

2. The second step in the path that leads into the blessing of being baptized with the Holy Spirit is renunciation of sin.

3.The third step is an open confession of our renunciation of sin and our acceptance of Jesus Christ.

4.The fourth step is absolute surrender to God. This comes out in what has been already said, namely, that we must accept Jesus as Lord as well as Saviour. It is stated explicitly in Acts 5: 32, "And we are His witnesses of these

---

[104]Ibid., 152-153.

things; and so is also the Holy Ghost, whom God hath given to them that obey Him." That is the fourth step, "obey Him," obedience.

5. The fifth step is an intense desire for the baptism with the Holy Spirit. Jesus says in John 7: 37-39, "If any man thirst, let him come unto Me and drink..."

6. The sixth step is definite prayer for the baptism with the Holy Spirit. Luke 11: 13

7. The seventh and last step is faith. We read in Mark 11:24, "Therefore I say unto you, 'What things soever ye desire, when ye pray, believe that ye receive them and ye shall have them.'"[105]

This conference in the set-apart location with the prayer, worship, fellowship, and the teaching of R.A. Torrey was all part of Phase # 1 Preparing the Altar.  The hearts of those young men were prepared for the fire to fall. In PRMI's Dunamis Project, we have adapted Torrey's seven steps for receiving the baptism with the Holy Spirit.  His principles are based on biblical revelation. Jesus has continued to use these steps to prepare the altar for the fire to fall and ignite a Pentecost event.

### Teamwork!

First, D.L. Moody and R.A. Torrey were working as a team, with Torrey being the main teacher. He had presented the steps on how to receive the baptism with the Holy Spirit, with D.L. Moody taking part later when the students arrived at his mother's home.  Beyond this team of two, there was no doubt an expanded team of intercessors also at work.  I can guess this because prayer was the major key to

---

[105]Ibid., 161-179.

revival which R.A. Torrey incorporated in all his events. While Torrey was teaching perhaps D.L. Moody was praying.

## R.A. Torrey Giving Two Ways that Jesus May Pour Out the Holy Spirit

Torrey gives two options for the young men to respond to the presentation on the necessity of the baptism with the Holy Spirit and how to receive this preparation for empowered witness. The first was to go up the mountain at 3:00 pm. The second option was to, "Go to your tent, go to your room in the hotel or in the buildings, go out into the woods, go anywhere, where you can get alone with God, meet the conditions of the baptism with the Holy Spirit and claim it at once." In doing this, Torrey gave the option for people just to ask Jesus Himself to baptize them with the Holy Spirit. He needed to speak it out and give the option and have the faith that if they just went alone and asked, then Jesus would baptize them with the Holy Spirit. From the reports, there were many who did indeed ask and receive the baptism. These were individual Pentecost events.

Many times, when I have been a part of preparing the altar for the fire to fall, I have given people the option to go out alone and ask for the baptism with the Holy Spirit if it is the first time, or for the infilling if they are stepping into a new phase of ministry. There usually are a few whom Jesus calls out alone to fill with the Holy Spirit. When we are at the Community of the Cross in North Carolina, it is just wonderful to watch them coming off the prayer trails filled with joy or the excitement of having been given a vision or receiving one of the gifts of the Holy Spirit.

## D.L. Moody Received the Guidance from Jesus that It Was a Kairos Moment.

When the group of men gathered and started up the mountain, it was part of the preparation for asking Jesus to baptize them all with the Holy Spirit. Apparently, those who had already received started to share testimonies of what had happened. D.L. Moody discerned that then was the moment and he made this announcement:

"I can see no reason why we should not kneel right down here now and ask God that the Holy Spirit may fall on us as definitely as He fell on the apostles at Pentecost. Let us pray."

As they did, the Pentecost event took place. We do not have any details, but it was a profound "unforgettable experience." Moody did not call this a "kairos moment," but it was, and he received the guidance to step into it.

This dynamic of D.L. Moody cooperating with the Holy Spirit and Dave Westra cooperating with the Holy Spirit are parallel. Both took part with an anointed team in preparing the altar, both were doing the work of prayer, both discerned the exact moment when Jesus said, "Now I am ready to work." Both, in faith and radical obedience to Jesus Christ, had to speak this guidance out to the group gathered. When they did, the great transition took place—Jesus stepped forward and did the work that only He could do which was baptizing and filling His friends and co-workers with the Holy Spirit.

These two experiences separated by over a hundred years, in different locations and with different audiences and actors, confirm that the "hinge point" between Phase #1 Preparing the Altar and Phase #2 Igniting the Fire, is the person, usually in a team, with the apostolic anointing discerning the moment and then stepping into it. These are the fire starters who are the vanguard of outpourings of the Holy Spirit which may become revivals, and under certain conditions, earth-shaking great awakenings. Without these fire starters, these dynamic moves of God do not take place.

# 14

# Critical Component: Inner Healing and Deliverance

## Growing in the Apostolic Anointing of a Fire Starter

To get to the point of being used by the Lord in this apostolic anointing of starting fires and building the structures, we need not only to keep the fire going, but spread it so that it becomes a movement of the Holy Spirit. In addition to receiving the power of the Holy Spirit and learning the dance steps of cooperation with the Holy Spirit, this requires two other factors related to our sanctification—going through spiritual wilderness and being healed of inner wounds, including the removal of any demonic spirits.

### Jesus' Wilderness School of Apostolic Leadership

A first requirement for anyone whom Jesus calls to be the means through whom He will pour out His Holy Spirit and build the containers to sustain it will be a session in the same wilderness school that Jesus Christ Himself went through.

Our consolation is, if we are in the wilderness or needing to be sent there, that Jesus Himself went through this time of wilderness testing as preparation for His anointed ministry. If Jesus, the second Person of the Trinity Himself in human form required such testing and refinement, how much more do we need the same preparation?

After Jesus was baptized with the Holy Spirit, which was when the Holy Spirit started falling on Him for power, He was driven into the wilderness to be tested by Satan. Mark gives a terse description of this event:

> "The Spirit immediately drove him into the wilderness. He was in the wilderness forty days, enduring temptations from Satan. He was with wild animals, and angels were ministering to his needs." Mark 1:12-13

Notice that it is the Holy Spirit who drove Jesus into the time of wilderness testing. The Greek here is the same word used for casting demons out of people. This suggests not a genial leading by the Holy Spirit but an aggressive forceful sending of Jesus into this time of testing by Satan. It was there that He learned to be totally submitted to God the Father. It was after having been in the wilderness that Jesus could say, "Amen, amen I tell you, the Son cannot do anything by Himself. He can do only what He sees the Father doing. Whatever the Father does, the Son does likewise" (John 5:19 TLV). It is after this wilderness testing which galvanized His total submission to the Father, that the Gospel of Luke reports, "...Jesus, in the power of the Spirit returned to Galilee, ..." He is anointed for proclaiming the kingdom of God and calling for repentance, calling disciples, preaching, teaching, casting out demons and healing. (Mark 1:15, Luke 5:17)

Likewise, for us to move into this role cooperating with God the Father, Son, and Holy Spirit in this apostolic fire-starting anointing, we must, like Jesus, learn that we can do nothing in ourselves, but that we can only do what Jesus is doing. That happens in the wilderness where, through the refining fire of temptations, we die to ourselves. Our new birth through faith brings us, Jesus' friends, the baptism with the Holy Spirit, which brings the empowerment to become Jesus' co-workers. It is in the wilderness where we, like Jesus, learn with our whole hearts, that it is "Not I, but Jesus." And He, not us, even when He has chosen to work through us, is still the one who is pouring out the Holy Spirit.

Wilderness testing and refinement is the Lord's cure for the sin of pride which often leads to the downfall of fire starters and leaders whom God has called and anointed for igniting and growing revival movements. I know this from the personal experience of having been driven into the wilderness three terrible times. One particularly severe time of wilderness testing was when the Holy Spirit was using me to ignite outpourings of the Holy Spirit in Taiwan after Archer Torrey had ignited the movement in 1984 at the Bible College in Hsinchu. For a season everywhere I went, most often with a team, there were moves of the Holy Spirit accompanied by amazing signs and wonders, especially of healing and deliverance. During these events, Jesus would baptize and fill many people with the Holy Spirit. I became quite famous on that small island of Taiwan. There was growing in me the sin of spiritual pride and the delusion that somehow it was me and not Jesus who was doing it all. Also because of the intense expectation of the people, I was being more and more tempted to start manipulating people. There was also the growing danger of temptations from the many lovely and needy women who were part of this movement. I have told this story of the wilderness in another book, so will not repeat it here,[106] but suffice it to say that before Jesus could continue using me, He sent me into a period of extreme wilderness testing. He did this in Taiwan, but then again recently as I relate in the next section on our need for healing.

Jesus is our model for this wilderness testing that we will also be called to endure. His example gives us some pointers as to how we may come through this ordeal—for instance, by tenaciously clinging to the Word of God and resisting Satan. I found all this helpful when I was personally going through times of wilderness

---

[106] Zeb Bradford Long, *Passage Through the Wilderness: A Journey of the Soul* (Bloomington, Minn.: Chosen Books, 1998). There is also a version in Chinese, 曠野的經歷 作者羅學川 譯者: 黃輝爵 出版社: 橄欖出版有限公司出 版 日期: 1990/02/28l  https://www.eslite.com/product/1001125032871076

testing, but one help which is not obvious from Jesus' example, is the role of a mentor or mentors who have also been through the wilderness training themselves. With their friendship and support, these brutal times of testing may become productive rather than simply debilitating. For me (Brad), my mentors have been those great saints like Rees Howells, R.A. Torrey, Jonathan Goforth, William Wilberforce, Dietrich Bonhoeffer, and others whose lives and writings Jesus used to mentor me. Jesus also used Archer Torrey and Doug McMurry for decades to mentor me in this role as an apostolically anointed leader.

I pray the same for each of you reading this book! If not in person, then perhaps the Lord will use what we have written to raise you up as His anointed fire starter.

Frankly, I know of no one either in history or in my own experience who has been greatly used by God to ignite outpourings of the Holy Spirit and to nurture them into kingdom-advancing movements, who has not been through such times of wilderness testing. So, all who are praying for revival and are offering ourselves to be used as the answers to our prayers, let's be prepared for Jesus to say, "Come follow me! I want to anoint you to be a fire starter, but first, come with me into the same wilderness school that I had to endure."

## Without Healing and Deliverance, Fire Starters May Become Arsonists

I was ready to conclude this chapter on becoming a fire starter which has gotten long, but then, Barb asked, "Have you seen the movie, *Jesus Revolution*?" I admitted that I had not seen it yet but knew the story. She continued, "Well you know that Lonnie Frisbee was a great fire starter! Through him God poured out the Holy Spirit upon those hippies, igniting the Jesus movement, but sadly, it did not end well for him. It appears to me that he had never been healed of his inner childhood wounds or set free from the demonic spirits that tormented him. Wasn't that an open door for Satan's deception? Plus, it not only hurt Lonnie, but it had the potential to wreck the entire movement that Lord had ignited through him. I wonder if one of those apostolic leaders should have stood in the gap as a loving spiritual father to Lonnie so that he could have been healed. I also think experiencing Jesus' healing and deliverance oneself should be one of the conditions for being an anointed apostolic fire starter and structure builder. How many movements of the Holy Spirit have been destroyed by the same anointed leader God used to ignite them? Surely, the ignitor of the movement of God, or for that matter any one of us, can be used by Satan to become an arsonist, wrecking the very movement that God has built."

## It Must Start with Us! With Me!

As I pondered this suggestion, I realized that Barb was right! But we did not need to use Lonnie Frisbee as an example. We do not really know the entire story from his inner perspective, but there is one story that I do know intimately: it is my own! I have always been an apostolic, anointed fire starter and structure builder. This book demonstrates that I have a long history of being used by God, not just to ignite outpourings of the Holy Spirit, but to build the structures to nurture them to become sustainable movements of revival for decades—movements that have the potential to become the next great awakening which may fulfill the conditions for Christ's return in glory. However, as hard as it may be to admit it, I need to confess here in print that I needed deep inner healing and deliverance so that Satan could not use me to destroy all that the Lord has done through me over the last thirty years. I really dread telling this story, but I must. Otherwise I would not be faithful to Jesus Christ in passing on to future leaders all that is necessary to be used by God to ignite this next great move of the Holy Spirit.

These principles are so important for leaders of revival movements to understand, that rather than just give a summary of what happened, I want to include here the report from the issue of *Discerning the Times* where I told as much of the story as I can without breaking confidences.

## Pruning and Refining Preparation for a Great Outpouring of the Holy Spirit

God prepares people and groups for His kingdom's purposes through the work of pruning and refining. Brad shares a recent journey of personal refining and healing as an example of the Lord's preparation for great outpourings of the Holy Spirit. A guide with steps to walk personally with Jesus through the refining fire is included.

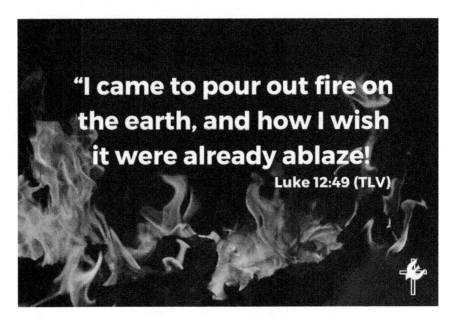

Recently we have reported to you about the outpourings of the Holy Spirit that have been taking place in our **PRMI** stream.[107]**See these reports**! [108] These confirm that we are at a most

---

[107] https://www.prmi.org/

[108] https://discernwith.us/healing-is-a-part-of-the-great-outpouring-of-the-holy-spirit

extraordinary epoch when the Holy Spirit is being poured out, igniting the fires of revival worldwide. This move of God to advance the kingdom of Jesus Christ has already started, and I believe PRMI has been given a strategic role in preparing for it. That is the exciting part! However, historically, pruning and refining fire have been part of the preparation for every outpouring of the Holy Spirit which advances the kingdom of Jesus Christ.

## Refining and Pruning

We all know what Jesus says about pruning:

"I am the true vine and my Father is the gardener. He takes away every branch that does not bear fruit in me. He prunes every branch that bears fruit so that it will bear more fruit. You are clean already because of the word that I have spoken to you. Remain in me, and I will remain in you. Just as the branch cannot bear fruit by itself, unless it remains in the vine, so neither can you unless you remain in me, "I am the vine; you are the branches. The one who remains in me – and I in him – bears much fruit, because apart from me you can accomplish nothing. John 15:1-5

"I came to pour out fire on the earth, and how I wish it were already ablaze! Luke 12:49 (TLV)

John the Baptist tells us that:

"I baptize you with water, for repentance, but the one coming after me is more powerful than I am – I am not worthy to carry his sandals! He will baptize you with the Holy Spirit and fire. His winnowing fork is in his hand, and he will clean out his threshing floor and will gather his wheat into the storehouse, but the chaff he will burn up with inextinguishable fire!" Matt. 3:11-12

Further, Peter notes that the trials we go through test and refine both our faith and us:

These trials are so that the true metal of your faith (far more valuable than gold, which perishes though refined by fire) may come to light in praise and glory and honor at the revelation of Messiah Yeshua. 1 Peter 1:7 (TLV)

So, the implication is that both the preparation for the outpouring of the Holy Spirit and the result will be a refining fire that prepares us to be more fit vessels for participating in God's kingdom. This will lead us to repentance, confession, healing, deliverance, and pruning so that we may be prepared to be Jesus' friends and co-workers to bear fruit for the kingdom of God.

This is a process for individuals and the corporate expressions of the body of Christ—the Church. This refining process is necessary for participation in the next great wave of the Holy Spirit. Thankfully, by His grace, Jesus has seen fit to include PRMI and us in this refining process.

## Pruning and Refining within PRMI

I am so thankful that the Lord has recently sent PRMI through a terrible time. (This was from 2019-2022.) I believe this was part of the refining fire to prepare us to fulfill the mission that Jesus has given us to prepare for the next great awakening in the power of the Holy Spirit, so that the things I have been talking about (igniting outpourings of the Holy Spirit) can be fulfilled.

Going through refining fire and pruning is never fun. It is awful! However, I believe we already see good fruit in the outpourings and manifestations of the Holy Spirit that we have been experiencing.

## A Demonic Stronghold Within the Ministry

The short version of what happened is that a demonic stronghold had been formed within PRMI's ministry. A high-level evil spirit had taken root that was twisting communications. Gossip and rumors were destroying our fellowship amongst those in anointed leadership. Many people were getting hurt, and there were all sorts of misunderstandings. No matter how hard other leadership team members and I tried to work on solutions, everything just got worse.

I am sure those on the other side had the same experience. Their efforts to reach out to me and the leadership team were also being twisted through miscommunications energized by this high-level demon. It was a challenging time and led to the possibility of splits in the ministry and our fulfilling our kingdom purposes and mission being blocked.

I do not need to go into all the gory details. I just need to tell you what the Lord did to me—how the Lord pruned and refined me. Others can tell their story; I am being led here to share my story mainly because I contributed to the situation in my role as Executive Director. I did so because, while I clearly saw the specks in everyone else's eyes, I could not see the logs in my own.

In doing so, I contributed to the formation of the demonic stronghold, but I really could not see it until several of the PRMI Board and team members suggested that I had contributed to building that demonic stronghold.

## My Contribution

My initial response was, "What me!??" I do not need to confess all my sins here, as I have already done that, but I want to tell you one of them. When I feel betrayed by someone, I find I lash out in anger and go into "attack mode," even when they are not betraying me at all!

This is uncomfortable to talk about but true. I have struggled with the tendency for a long time and have mostly learned to control these inappropriate responses. However, I realized that I had wounded a lot of people! That was where I contributed to the demonic stronghold being formed in PRMI.

## Spiritual Wounding

As I wrestled with all this, I also had to face the reality that I had sustained some spiritual wounding from the strategic intercession and spiritual warfare that I had been through over the last several years. I have written about these strategic level prayer engagements in two recent books.

The first involved praying for the kingdom of God to overcome the violence of the Marxist and occult groups around BLM and ANTIFA seeking to deceive the Church of Jesus Christ and destroy the common grace structures of government and society in America. These structures give the Church the freedom and means to fulfill its gospel mission.

The second was what many other intercessors and I experienced as a demonic invasion of the United States between November 3, 2020, and January 6, 2021. Satan's intention in this invasion was to bring tyranny into society once again and to usurp and/or destroy the expressions of God's kingdom on earth.

Both involved engagements, in cooperation with the Holy Spirit, to overcome high-level demonic powers. There was the breaking of witchcraft curses and being called by Jesus Christ to be His means of engaging high-level demons who had entered our human and earthly sphere where we have dominion.

These protracted spiritual battles and prayer engagements had left me spiritually exhausted and wounded. Frankly, as anyone who has been through the experience of deliverance and exorcism knows, such encounters with evil, even when entirely led and covered by King Jesus, sear one's soul.

The result was that I had become a very defensive and difficult person to be with. I knew I needed healing and restoration from these strategic engagements. I know for sure that it was the wounding and battle fatigue in me from these prayer battles that Satan also used to contribute to building this destructive demonic stronghold within PRMI.

*a Gary Hixson in Seville Spain doing prayer.*

## Receiving Prayer Ministry

As I wrestled with this, I decided to reach out to a friend with similar experiences in strategic intercession and spiritual warfare—Gary Hixson. I introduce him in this issue of **Discerning the Times on witchcraft.**[109]

Gary is incredibly experienced in deliverance ministry and dealing with high-level demonic spirits. So, I set up a prayer time with him over Zoom as he lives in Seville, Spain. [110]

We had an amazing two-hour healing and deliverance prayer session. We dealt with the arrows of demonic curses and wounding from these prayer battles. I needed an extensively experienced prayer warrior who, like me, had been on the frontlines of strategic level engagement with the "...rulers, the powers, the world rulers of this darkness, the spiritual forces of evil in the heavens." (c.f. Eph 6:12) Open doors to flaming dart attacks were healed and closed, curses spoken against me and PRMI were broken, and I was set free from harassing demonic spirits. Praise God! Through this prayer time with this anointed man of God, Jesus spoke to me, reaffirming my calling as an apostolic leader called to advance the kingdom of God, a warrior to defeat Satan's schemes, but also as a healer restoring those who are broken.

All this was part of the refining fire Jesus was putting me through, as had been the prayer engagements. It was a good start,

---

[109] https://discernwith.us/defending-against-witchcraft-attacks-an-interview-with-rev-dr-brad-long-and-rev-gary-hixson

[110] DEEP HEALING INTERNATIONAL A Christian Ministry of Inner Healing and Deliverance  https://www.deephealing.eu/en/

but there was still something in me—my lashing out in anger when I felt betrayed. I just could not seem to get past this tendency, which really worried me. It was a sign that a deeper level of wounding needed to be dealt with, but I did not know what it was.

## A Word of Knowledge

As I struggled with all this, during one of the PRMI Board Executive Meeting conference calls, a board member, Becki Newman, with gifts of healing, said, "You know I keep seeing you as a boy on the school playground." I said, "Well, thanks, but that does not mean anything to me."

Then Cindy, PRMI Director, who was also on the call, said, "You need to think about that because I am getting the same guidance. Something that happened to you on the playground really hurt!"

I had already dealt with the wounding and rejection that I had received in school because of my dyslexia which meant that I could not spell or, at that time, read or write. This was different and seemed to point to a deep root of feeling betrayed as a leader.

## Uncovering the Wound

The Lord used the words of these two sisters in Christ to start working on me. To make a long story short, I asked those who had received the guidance about me on the playground to pray for me. This took place over a Zoom meeting. I was wrapped in love and the presence of Jesus.

I just want to say that Jesus was right there with me, manifesting His unconditional love and acceptance of me and affirming my calling and anointing as a leader in His kingdom. During the prayer time, suddenly, a deep memory from my elementary school days came back to me, a memory that had been buried and forgotten for decades.

## The Baseball Game

What we did all summer long when I was in elementary school in Charlotte, North Carolina was play baseball. Each neighborhood would have its own team, and I was the captain of our neighborhood team. At the end of summer, just before school started, all the teams would gather for a weekend championship match.

For this grand event, the fathers of the team captains would often buy nice uniforms for the kids, but my father was too stingy to do that for my team. He also thought playing baseball was a waste of time, which hurt. He did not realize how important it was to me. Because of my dyslexia, I could not spell, could hardly read, and was a complete failure in school, but I could play baseball; and I was a natural leader.

Above is an odd picture of me on the far right with my little sister Lucy, with what appears to be a double exposure of my mother in the background. This captures well the appearance of our team—barefooted, with my little sister Lucy as one of the girls on the team. (The picture was taken in Montreat, North Carolina while wading in the mountain stream.)

We showed up for the great championship final game. My team was mainly barefooted in shorts and tee shirts, and the other teams were all dressed in new uniforms and special baseball shoes with cleats.

We could hear the jeers and laughter of the crowd as we lined up. What got the most laughter and ridicule was that I had several girls on my team. My little sister Lucy was too young to play, but tagged along with me, her big brother. (Actually, she was good at throwing rocks and catching.)

We also had the two girls in my class from across the street; their fathers had taught them to play ball. The other teams were all boys, and the girls were in their proper place as cheerleaders. Except for my mother and the fathers of the two girls, we had no one to cheer for us. One of the lads shouted, "Look, girls! They can't even throw a ball right. They can't win!" Do you get the picture?

In the last inning, we were tied. We had the bases loaded, and I was up to bat. Standing there barefooted, with no fancy baseball shoes, I was already feeling humiliated, but what made it worse was that someone noticed that I was holding the bat wrong! I had gotten my right and left hands mixed up, as I still do today. They shouted, "Look, he can't even hold the bat right." Everyone laughed. Now that made me angry, but I was also asking God to help me.

Then the pitcher pitched. I swung and missed twice. On the third pitch, the ball came in, and I remember it felt almost supernatural! As the bat connected with the ball, I felt like one of those huge Scottish catapults that could hurl huge stones to smash castle walls. The ball took off and flew, not just out of the baseball field, but out of the park completely! We won the championship. I was the hero.

The father of one of the girls on the team shook my hand and shouted to the crowd, "Slugger!" That became my nickname. My father was not even there, and that hurt. There was great celebration and astonishment, and everyone thanked me.

## Fists on the Playground

The next day, on the school playground, the boys on the team all ganged up on me. They had been humiliated enough that we had not had nice uniforms and that I had invited girls to join the team but having me be the hero was just more than they could take.

I am sure I contributed to their hostility by not handling my fame very well. So, I had to fight them all; and of course, I won, giving them bloody noses and black eyes, but their betrayal really hurt.

While walking home, when I was sure no one was looking, I broke down and cried. This hurt by these boys and by my father for not being there became a place of deep wounding in my heart.

It was so deep that whenever I felt betrayed, or my leadership rejected or ridiculed, I just wanted to give people bloody noses and black eyes. I cannot do that with my fists as I did in elementary school on the playground, but I can certainly do it with my words, which are far more effective at hurting and destroying people than my fists.

That event had been suppressed and forgotten for at least six decades. Over the years, the Devil had used that anger at being betrayed to hurt many people. It was one of the open doors the enemy had used to establish a demonic stronghold in PRMI.

## The Healing Ministry of Jesus

In the prayer time I remembered all this and relived it vividly and totally, but Jesus was right there with me, giving me the grace to forgive those boys who had betrayed me, even though I, as their leader, had led them to victory.

I also forgave my father, who had betrayed me by not buying us nice baseball shoes with cleats, and by not even showing up for my day of triumph. The immediate result of this prayer of confession of my sin and receiving healing by forgiving those who caused those deep distant hurts is that a door was closed to flaming dart attacks

273

of anger and betrayal. I suspect, too, that an evil spirit that had been attached to me for many years just left me.

I was also able to forgive and release to Jesus for His blessing all those who had taken part in forming that demonic stronghold in PRMI and who had caused hurt to the ministry.

This experience of recalling and facing my own sin and seeking help from Gary for the wounding from the prayer battles was a refining fire for me. It was a painful process of pruning by Jesus, but what took place in this experience of healing and deliverance was that Jesus Christ was more fully established as King in my life.

## Restored for Kingdom Service

This began a restorative healing process, which of course, is not finished. It also set in motion the preparation for me to continue to lead PRMI in preparing for the next great awakening in the power of the Holy Spirit (which has included writing this book). It all had to start within my own heart where Jesus Christ had to be fully King.

So, what I have learned from this entire experience is that true revival begins in our hearts. It often starts when we welcome Jesus, who loves us, to lead us through His refining fire so He may be our King to whom we are totally submitted!

My word to all of us praying for a great outpouring of the Holy Spirit is to ask Jesus Christ to do His refining work within us, in His love and mercy. We can take the risk of doing that because we are confident He will never let us go! After the refining fire has done its refining work, Jesus will use us to ignite outpourings of the Holy Spirit for His glory. – End of the Discerning the Times article.

A few months after this healing and deliverance took place in me, Doug and Carla McMurry came down to Black Mountain to lead an event with me at the Community of the Cross. I was led by the Holy Spirit to share the report above of how Jesus had sent me through the refining fire, had healed me of the deep inner wounds and also had cast out of me some demons of anger and revenge. Later, after being in ministry together for four days, Doug privately told me, "You know I had always been concerned about you as my brother in Christ. It seemed to me that you had an irrational, angry part of you that lashed out at people. Actually, I was worried that Satan would use that tendency in you to destroy all the good that the Lord has done through you over all these decades. I need to tell you how relieved I am to see that tendency is completely gone! You are different now! I am sure that by taking you through that healing and deliverance ministry, Jesus is now ready to use you to take part in igniting this next great awakening."

While I feel very vulnerable sharing this, let it be a lesson to all of us who would take part in this great outpouring of the Holy Spirit. Ask the Lord to show you those areas where you need inner healing. You also, like me, may need to have some evil spirits cast out of you! You must do this not only if you are to take part in this great outpouring of the Holy Spirit, but if you are not to end up being the means that Satan uses to derail or quench this wonderful, gracious work of God.

With that sober word of warning to all those who are called to be fire starters, let's turn to the other aspect of the anointing to ignite outpourings of the Holy Spirit—creating the wineskins so that these movements may grow, flourish, and truly advance God's kingdom. This is all critical for moving to Phase # 3, Sustaining the Flame.

# 15

# Phase #3—Sustaining the Flame

The third phase in the meta pattern—sustaining the flame that has been ignited through the Pentecost event—is necessary if the outpouring of the Holy Spirit is to bear the good fruit of growing the Church of Jesus Christ and expanding the kingdom of God. To sustain the flame requires that Jesus' empowered co-workers and witnesses have some means or medium through which to express their calling and the anointing that has been placed upon them. Further, there must be some way for those people who have been born again because of their empowered witness to be integrated into the church, which is the human and earthly expression of the kingdom of God.

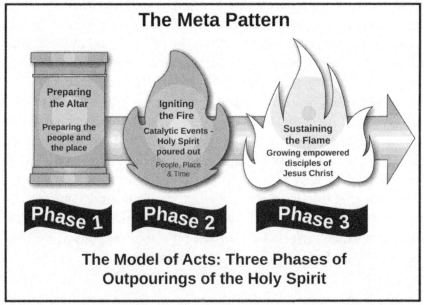

**The Meta Pattern**

Preparing the Altar — Preparing the people and the place

Igniting the Fire — Catalytic Events - Holy Spirit poured out — People, Place & Time

Sustaining the Flame — Growing empowered disciples of Jesus Christ

Phase 1

Phase 2

Phase 3

**The Model of Acts: Three Phases of Outpourings of the Holy Spirit**

Some of you may find this chapter on Phase #3 - Sustaining the Flame to be confusing. I find it confusing! My confusion is that as I reviewed the biblical examples, studied revival history, and reflected on my own experience, I realized that Phase #3, while distinct, flows out of the anointing of those who have enabled

Phases #1 and #2. This is especially true of what I have identified as the apostolic anointing of the fire starter, which, if the fire is to be sustained in Phase #3, must include the anointing to create the wineskins or containers for the fire. The apostolic anointing has two integrated manifestations: igniting the outpouring of the Holy Spirit and creating the wineskins in order for it to be expressed. It will be shown that the apostolic anointing is the one that enables the three phases to continue as a repeatable cycle.

## Apostolic Role of the Fire Starter Includes Building the Containers

In Acts chapters 2 and 3 right after Pentecost, we observe the apostles putting in place the structures needed to enable Phase #3 Sustaining the Flame. After the 120 had been baptized with the Holy Spirit, they gathered in a fellowship which formed the base from which they launched out in the preaching of the gospel accompanied by signs and wonders. The result was that thousands of Jews received Yeshua the Messiah and were born again into God's eternal kingdom. The entrance into this spiritual reality is expressed within the human and earthly sphere, as, "So those who accepted his message were baptized, and that day about three thousand people were added" (Acts 2:41). What were they added to? This was the fellowship of born-again and Holy Spirit-empowered believers, which was the new wineskin or the container that the Holy Spirit was creating for Jesus' kingdom to be expressed on earth. Essentially this new wine skin was the church, or in Greek the "ecclesia," a term with the connotations of a called-out group as a fellowship and a governing assembly. [111]

---

[111] Fenton John Anthony Hort, "Christian Ecclesia: A Course of Lectures on the Early History and Early Conceptions of the Ecclesia and One Sermon," https://www.ccel.org/ccel/h/hort/ecclesia/cache/ecclesia.pdf

These containers are the means of sustaining and passing on the fire of Pentecost, and of nurturing its fruit to maturity.

Following igniting Pentecost events, the role of those with apostolic anointing is then to establish these containers for God's work which are concordant with God's Word, governed by Jesus as King, and in the service of advancing God's kingdom on earth. We see this very clearly after Pentecost where, under the leadership of the apostles, the Jewish social structures governing their lives and ways of being God's covenant people were adapted into the new wineskin of the early church. The development of the new wineskin for the new wine of the resurrected Messiah and the outpouring of the Holy Spirit upon all believers did not consist of a total rejection, invalidation, or replacement of the original Jewish wineskins. Rather, they were built upon and added to. Jesus the Messiah started this process Himself by, for instance, adding to the celebration of Passover the understanding that He is now the Passover lamb who has been sacrificed, the bread is now his broken body, and the wine is his blood shed on the cross instituting the new covenant (Luke 22:7-23). After Pentecost with the Holy Spirit falling upon them giving great power for witness, and with the kingdom of God being manifestly present in signs and wonders, there was an exponential, quantum leap forward in the movement and the number of people being brought in. We see the beginning of the new wineskin being adapted from their Jewish foundations in the following summary:

> They were devoting themselves to the apostles' teaching and to fellowship, to the breaking of bread and to prayer. Reverential awe came over everyone, and many wonders and miraculous signs came about by the apostles. All who believed were together and held everything in common, and they began selling their property and possessions and distributing the proceeds to everyone, as anyone had need. Every day they continued to gather together by common consent in the temple courts, breaking bread from house to house, sharing their food with glad and humble hearts,

279

praising God and having the good will of all the people. And the Lord was adding to their number every day those who were being saved. Acts 2:42-47

The elements in this short summary provide the contours of the Holy Spirit-empowered fellowship that is centered in the presence of the resurrected Jesus Christ as King. There was empowered preaching and teaching as well as prayer and praise. They gathered together in the temple courts for their public meetings, which must have consisted of prayer, praise, and preaching, and in their homes for sharing in deeper fellowship together in breaking bread—which could mean the celebration of the Lord's supper as instituted by Jesus, but also just having meals together as families of born-again believers. They were overflowing with love for each other and suddenly needing to feed and take care of many people. All this together was the fulfillment of the prophecy of Ezekiel following his vision of the valley of dry bones.

"I will put My Ruach (Holy Spirit) in you and you will live. I will place you in your own land. Then you will know that I, Adonai, have spoken and that I have done it." It is a declaration of Adonai. Ezekiel 37:14 TLV

The dry bones of the Jewish forms were all around them—not just in the stones of the temple courts which now echoed with worship of their risen Messiah, but also in the traditions that had all been shaken and transformed with this new reality of the kingdom of God manifesting in their midst. The temple was now being built with living stones of born-again disciples of Jesus Christ who were filled with the Holy Spirit and who now worshiped in spirit and in truth (John 4:23).

As time went by, this process of forming wineskins to contain the new reality of the first Pentecost event continued. We see the anointed apostles leading the way. For instance, the selection of the seven deacons or "servants" in Acts 6:1-4, (with the qualifications for this service role given in 1 Timothy 3:8-13), seems to be a new addition to the Jewish forms of life that needed to be put in place to deal with the transformative effects of the Pentecost event. The original Old Testament model is of Jethro advising Moses to call men of good repute to help govern the people (Exodus 18:25). The new addition included works of compassion birthed because of the love of Jesus Christ infused throughout the fellowship of believers. They have the Holy Spirit not only falling upon them for power but within them for the fruit of the Spirit, most of all love.

Because the movement continued to grow and expand with Jesus working through the fire starters (the apostles who continued to ignite Pentecost events) the continual need arose for their apostolic work to include putting in place the structures or "wineskins" needed to sustain and express that move of the Holy Spirit. We see this structure-building work through Paul in Lystra, Iconium, and Antioch. The text says of Paul and Barnabas:

> "They strengthened the souls of the disciples and encouraged them to continue in the faith, saying, 'We must enter the kingdom of God through many persecutions.' When they had appointed elders for them in the various churches, with prayer and fasting they entrusted them to the protection of the Lord in whom they had believed." Acts 14:22-23

This appointment of elders who could provide for the governance and care of the believers was part of that structural and organizational building work necessary for the Church to embody the kingdom of God. Without such forms that gave shape as well as order to those who had been transformed by the movement of the Holy Spirit, the harvest could have been lost.

The essential work that was taking place with these organizational structures, whether we identify them as wineskins or containers or means, was the formation of the "spiritual house" to express God's kingdom on earth. "You yourselves, as living stones, are built up as a spiritual house to be a holy priesthood and to offer spiritual sacrifices that are acceptable to God through Jesus Christ" (1 Peter 2:5).

It does seem that all down through history (and it certainly is our recent experience) that those with an apostolic, fire-starting anointing leave in their wake not only empowered witnesses, but also the new wineskins suitable for expressing this new reality.

## Growing Outpourings of the Holy Spirit Through Implementing New Wineskins.

An historical example is the Moravian Pentecost that took place August 13, 1727, in Herrnhut, Germany. Jesus Christ poured out the Holy Spirit upon those gathered in prayer without human mediation. However, Count Zinzendorf, with an apostolic anointing, was able to give the new movement the effective wineskins which are the organizational structures, or roles for the people to fit into—a flexible Holy Spirit-led authority/accountability system. These forms such as the Love Feasts, the 24-hour prayer meetings, regular Bible studies, the missionary calling, sending, and supporting systems, enabled the movement to become a global kingdom movement.

Both R.A. Torrey and Jonathan Goforth, through whom Jesus ignited the Pentecost events which became great revival waves of the Holy Spirit, were also anointed to put in place these containers. These consisted of systematic teaching of the Bible, the establishment of prayer groups, and ways of discipling new believers. R.A. Torrey created lasting institutions like the Montrose Bible Conference, the Bible College of Chicago which became Moody Bible College, and the Bible College of Los Angeles (where Torrey was the academic dean) which became BIOLA University.

The charismatic movement of the Holy Spirit started in the late 1950s. In 1966 the founders of PRMI not only had an apostolic anointing to ignite outpourings of the Holy Spirit but also to create new structures to express and grow the work of the Holy Spirit. For instance, they started first by forming what was called the Presbyterian Ministers Charismatic Fellowship and later what was called Presbyterian Charismatic Communion[112] as a way to express what could not be expressed within the traditional forms of the established Presbyterian and Reformed denominations that they were a part of. Rather than leave the Presbyterian stream and start an entirely new denominational expression, as many in that movement did, they were called to stay and work for renewal of the Presbyterian Church.

This group of anointed leaders were able to introduce into local congregations certain forms that would enable the transformation of the entire congregation. They developed prayer and praise services, healing services, and taught on the work of the Holy Spirit through programs such as Spirit Alive for first igniting and then nurturing the move of the Holy Spirit in local congregations. During this era materials were developed for growing into maturity these born-again and Holy Spirit-empowered disciples of Jesus Christ.[113]

After I became the Executive Director in 1990, I built on the firm foundations of their igniting and building work. After the outpouring of the Holy Spirit that took place in 1991 at Lake George New York, the Lord gave us the Dunamis Project as a way to build in all three phases of this dynamic process: Phase #1 Preparing the Altar, Phase #2 Igniting the Fire, and Phase #3 Sustaining the Flame. The result has been that this movement of the Holy Spirit continues to grow and flourish and has developed a global reach.[114] We shall

---

[112]Presbyterian Charismatic Communion (PCC) was founded in 1966 and later was renamed Presbyterian Reformed Renewal Ministries International (PRRMI). Then, with another name change, became just Presbyterian and Reformed Ministries International (PRMI).

[113]Each stream of charismatic renewal developed its own materials and approaches for growing disciples. In our Presbyterian Reformed stream, the Rev. Douglas McMurry wrote the Bread Books series which could be used by lay people in small groups gathered in the homes, business, and churches. These materials are still available through PRMI at www.prmi.org

[114]https://www.prmi.org/about/history-of-prmi/

return to the Dunamis Project in a later chapter as a model of how to grow these phases into a repeatable cycle.

## When Fire Starters Become Arsonists Destroying the Congregations

Along with these positive examples we could add the very negative experiences of what takes place when those who are anointed to ignite outpourings of the Holy Spirit are not able to build those structures for sustaining the flame. This was our experience in Taiwan which was emblematic of other times of revival. A Presbyterian pastor was baptized with the Holy Spirit and was greatly anointed for evangelism. He was welcomed into many Presbyterian congregations where he was able to present the gospel of Jesus Christ, often accompanied by signs and wonders, especially of physical healing. There were also manifestations of evil spirits as people accepted Jesus Christ. This was just wonderful and upbuilding to the churches who welcomed the people being born again. This anointed man of God was in a role very similar to that of Philip in Samaria in Acts 8 with the gospel of the kingdom being preached with signs and wonders. But then he went to Korea and came under the influence of a famous Korean Pentecostal leader. He insisted that to this work of evangelism there needed to be added the laying on of hands for people to receive the Baptism with the Holy Spirit, with the initial physical evidence of speaking in tongues. On several occasions, the Presbyterian Pastor was accompanied by his mentor from Korea. When this took place there were indeed authentic outpourings of the Holy Spirit—Pentecost events with the five markers all in evidence. However, neither of these anointed and well-intentioned men had the apostolic anointing of being able to build the structures to provide the context for sustaining the flame and growing people in how to cooperate with the Holy Spirit. Further, they brought in the unbiblical expectation that everyone who received the baptism with the Holy Spirit would speak in tongues. It was not long before what had been a great blessing for the building up of the congregations became a disaster. They moved from being evangelistic and constructive fire starters to arsonists who were destroying congregations.

Thankfully, before too much damage could be done, the Pentecostal evangelist had to return home to Korea and the Presbyterian pastor came to the Presbyterian Lay Training Center and took part in an equipping event.[115] His theology was corrected, and he became a powerful member of our team. In that context, he could do the work of evangelism (still often accompanied with signs and wonders) and I could prepare people to pray for and to receive the baptism with the Holy Spirit. Together we then provided the teaching and equipping to sustain the flame and grow the movement within those Presbyterian congregations.

This example demonstrates the necessity of our working together as teams where all the different equipping anointings and spiritual gifts may be expressed.

## Igniting Outpourings in Taiwan AND Building Structures

During this period of great revival in Taiwan in the 1980s, the Holy Spirit especially moved among the Presbyterian aboriginal congregations in the isolated mountain areas of the island. Groups of lay people who had been filled with the Holy Spirit, started visiting other congregations carrying the fire of revival with them. They gave empowered testimonies. The Lord graciously worked through them in signs and wonders, lots of people were born again, and many people were baptized with the Holy Spirit. Genuine miracles of healing, deliverance, and supernatural provision started to take place. The great tragedy was that the British, American, and

---

[115]I worked with a team at the Presbyterian Bible College in Hsinchu Taiwan to found the Presbyterian Lay Training Center in 1984.
https://www.prmi.org/history-of-the-dunamis-project/

Canadian missionaries who had prayed for this revival to come among the aboriginal people were horrified at what was happening. Their Western materialistic worldview had no room for either the manifestations of the Holy Spirit or for the demons that were leaving people with the advancement of Jesus' kingdom. They ended up rejecting the very people among whom they had labored for so many years. The result, for the people abandoned by the missionaries, was the absence of biblical teaching and a lack of discernment. Soon a number of the revival locations fell into heretical notions and extreme emotionalism.

There was one great exception that made a difference. A godly couple sent by the Canadian Presbyterian Church named Clare and Grace McGill had labored with aboriginal people for years. They lived on the campus of the Presbyterian Bible College in Hsinchu. They had especially worked among one of the tribal groups called the Tayal and translated the Bible into their native language. The McGills had been baptized in the Holy Spirit themselves while on home assignment back in Ontario, and had been praying for revival. When the Holy Spirit started to fall, they invited me, with my teaching team, to take several trips into the mountain areas to teach on the work of the Holy Spirit.

## The Holy Spirit Falling Upon a Large Crowd Followed by Teaching

I could fill up a volume with stories, but one will suffice. Once we traveled over potholed and perilously steep roads for nearly five hours to come to the location where the Presbyterian congregations had scheduled a five-day revival meeting. They were following the Pentecostal Korean example of fasting for the whole time. I was the keynote speaker to launch this entire event. I was to preach in Mandarin Chinese which the younger people all understood, but then this had to be translated into Japanese as the language that was understood by the older people who had lived under the Japanese occupation. These aboriginal people had been headhunters up until the end of World War II. When a man had taken a head (often a Japanese or a Taiwanese head), the women in his family were allowed to have a certain decorative tattoo on their faces. These people had come to know Jesus Christ through the wonderful love and empowered preaching of Presbyterian missionaries like the McGills from Canada who were followed by American Missionaries like Don and Virginia McCall (馬好留). [116] The headhunters, through Jesus Christ, had become Presbyterians!

By the time I arrived at the gathering place in a high mountain valley I was terribly sick. Perhaps it was car sickness or the awful food that we had eaten at the village we had stayed in the night before. We arrived very late and the several thousand people who had gathered had been singing hymns and praying for hours. As we got out of the Land Rover and walked out on the bamboo platform, I asked the Lord, "What do you want to do?" The guidance came, "I have prepared their hearts. Right now, I want you to first call them to follow me, and then I will baptize them all with the Holy Spirit! You and your team will do the teaching about what all this means later." I was so sick, fighting not to throw up, all I could manage was to stand on the platform and ask, "Is Jesus here?" There was a roar of joyful affirmation! "Do you all accept him as your Lord and Savior?" I paused as I could see the Holy Spirit moving over the crowd like the wind in a Kansas wheat field. I asked, "Lord what now?" Jesus answered, "Tell them to stand up if they want to affirm their faith in Me." As I shouted this out, the entire crowd stood up! I looked down in amazement at their faces all looking up, not at me, but to Jesus. There were many young people, but also, I was blessed to see so many older women with the tattoos from their head-hunting days. I then, according to the guidance that I had received, without the usual teaching or explanation, announced, "Now Jesus is ready to baptize you with the Holy Spirit just like He did those first disciples at Pentecost, so you can be His witnesses. If you want to receive this equipping of

---

[116]http://www.laijohn.com/archives/pm/Mccall,R/brief/TCN.htm

the Holy Spirit now, just reach out to Him with both your hands and ask Jesus to baptize you with the Holy Spirit." I had hardly gotten this word out when the crowd of several thousand all raised their hands. The Holy Spirit fell on them, but because I knew that I was going to throw up, I quietly turned to the native pastors and the team who had come with me and said, "Ok, now you are in charge." I briefly laid hands on them, bolted off the platform, and, in the back, violently threw up again and again, but no one heard me as there was a great chorus erupting of praying in tongues, words of prophecy, and joyful shouts of praise. Later some of my co-workers from the Bible College who were worried about my strange behavior, came back and found me. They carried me back to the Land Rover and took me up to the church where we would be staying. I was very sick for the rest of that day and night.

The ministry went on for hours. I saw none of it. I was told later that signs and wonders had taken place with people who could not walk getting healed. A number of the native pastors had stepped into an amazing anointing of casting out demons. Many demons of murder and vicious head-hunting spirits as well as many others left with blood-curdling shrieks. The Lord made sure that He got all the glory by having me vomit behind the platform instead of being upfront. The next day the entire crowd gathered back. Word of what had happened had gotten out, so the crowd had doubled. By noon I was feeling better and so started to give the Bible's teaching on the Holy Spirit. I also told everyone that they did not need to fast anymore as they needed to be able to really pay attention to the teaching about what they had experienced. This went on for five days, with new outpourings taking place every evening. Now the native pastors were leading ministry teams where the Lord was fast-tracking people into ministry in the Holy Spirit. The signs and wonders continued.

A distinctive part of these days following Jesus baptizing them with the Holy Spirit was moving into extended periods of confession of sins, often with weeping with remorse. Many egregious, terrible sins were confessed publicly—incest, selling

288

their daughters into prostitution, adultery, drinking, witchcraft, murder and more. This is not the normal order. Usually, the confession and repentance is preparation for accepting Jesus Christ as Lord and Savior: the first R.A. Torrey Key which is Evangelism. Also repentance is one of the steps in asking for and receiving the baptism with the Holy Spirit. This time it was different; it followed it. I think the reason was that these people needed first to see the amazing love and presence of Jesus. Secondly, Jesus needed empowered co-workers among the native church leaders themselves to provide the deep inner healing ministry for those whose sins were being exposed. There was especially the need for casting out evil spirits who had gotten in and were tormenting the people and holding them in bondage.

This Pentecost event with all five of the markers contributed to the revival move of the Holy Spirit that had already started. Now was added the biblical teaching to help this movement stay on track. The result was great blessing and growth among these aboriginal Presbyterian congregations. Also, the Holy Spirit fire started to spread to other ethnic groups in Taiwan. We were able to continue to nurture this movement of the Holy Spirit through intensive seminars for the aboriginal church leaders at the Presbyterian Lay Training Center at the Presbyterian Bible College in Hsinchu.[117] These were glorious times! The gospel was going forth, the Holy Spirit was falling and igniting revival, and the result was growing congregations.

The above short review of the book of Acts and some recent revival history, (as well as dealing with the negative example) leads us to the conclusion that every outpouring of the Holy Spirit that has been ignited by Jesus through a fire starter with an apostolic anointing that has survived past the initial burst of power and life in the Pentecost event has developed these new wineskins. After this fire is ignited and these structures are in place, the other

---

[117]With a team I founded the Presbyterian Lay Training Center on the campus of the Presbyterian Bible College in 1984 after Jesus used Archer Torrey to ignite that outpouring of the Holy Spirit.

fivefold equipping anointings named by Paul in Ephesians 4:11-16 will have their role in sustaining and growing this dynamic. For instance, the role of the evangelistic office is to populate these forms with born-again people. The prophet's role is to speak the word of God and to provide guidance so that these forms may be constantly adapted to the changing times while staying faithful to God's intentions and the Word of God. The teachers provide the instruction for passing God's intentions on to others and making sure that everyone is grounded in the Word of God as well as helping people grow as Jesus' disciples. Those in the pastoral office help to nurture and sustain the people in relationships with one another and with God the Father, Son, and Holy Spirit that form this living organism which embodies the kingdom of God and God's presence on earth. [118] Further, within these forms created and sustained by the fivefold equipping anointings, is the organizational structure in which all the other gifts and callings of the Holy Spirit may be expressed. For instance, those with the functional gifts of mercy and administration now have a context in which to express their giftings. All of this works together in the vision given to us by Paul of the body with many parts, each of which is essential.

---

[118] It needs to be noted that when these structures are governed by "power and might" instead of "by thy Spirit" and move out of synch with the word of God revealed in the Bible, and Jesus Christ as the only way of Salvation, they will depart from being means of expressing the kingdom of God and God's sovereign rule on earth. When this happens, they may become demonic strongholds in the service of Satan building his empire of evil on earth.

Now you are Christ's body, and each of you is a member of it. And God has placed in the church first apostles, second prophets, third teachers, then miracles, gifts of healing, helps, gifts of leadership, different kinds of tongues. Not all are apostles, are they? Not all are prophets, are they? Not all are teachers, are they? Not all perform miracles, do they? Not all have gifts of healing, do they? Not all speak in tongues, do they? Not all interpret, do they? 1 Cor. 12:27-30

Apostles are named first by Paul because they are the ones through whom Jesus sets in motion the entire dynamic by pouring out the Holy Spirit and then forming wineskins to express the outpouring so that everyone who has been born again into the kingdom of God may have a medium through which to express the diversity of their calling and giftings.[119] Without these structures being put into place, it is very easy for Satan to enter in and use the transformative nature of the baptism with the Holy Spirit for his own evil purposes of bringing division and confusion.

## Summary of the Components Needed for Sustaining the Flame.

The following seem to be the basic structures and practices that are needed to sustain the flame after a Pentecost event. These are based on the core practices already noted after the first Pentecost and the outpourings that have followed.

- Preaching and teaching based on the Bible and presenting Jesus Christ as Lord and the way of salvation.

---

[119]In a future chapter we will explore further how the fivefold equipping anointings of the Holy Spirit—the fivefold ministries of apostles, prophets, evangelists, pastors, and teachers (Ephesians 4:1-16)—have a role in creating and growing the three phases as a repeatable cycle.

- Building in ways for born-again believers to grow as disciples of Jesus Christ, and for those who have been baptized in the Holy Spirit to grow in discernment and in cooperating with the Holy Spirit.

- Growing in loving, supportive fellowship where the ongoing life of prayer, worship, teaching, ministry, and care of one another takes place.

- Providing the context where people may grow together in discerning and cooperating with the Holy Spirit in worship, prayer, ministry, and mission outreach.

- Engaging in outreach by sending out anointed evangelists and those anointed as fire starters and container builders. This point of taking part in outreach helps keep the expression of the gifts and power of the Holy Spirit focused on their true purpose which is enabling the witness to Jesus Christ to go out to all people (Acts 1:8).

These practices and their routinized expressions will take specific forms that will be unique to the needs of the people and their overall context. Sustaining the flame is essentially putting in place the different elements needed for growing the Church in the power of the Holy Spirit. With Cindy Strickler and Paul Stokes, I have written a book with this title that goes into detail on how to implement the above practices. Please refer to this work for the details of how to do this in your own context.[120]

Some of these elements have already been identified in historical outpourings of the Holy Spirit, such as the 24–7 prayer meeting and the Love Feasts of the Moravian Revival, the home Bible study groups, and the prayer, praise, and healing services of

---

[120] Brad Long, Cindy Strickler and Paul Stokes, *Growing the Church in the Power of the Holy Spirit: The Seven Principles of Dynamic Cooperation* (Grand Rapids, MI: Zondervan, 2009).

the Charismatic Renewal movement, or in the case of PRMI, the intensive teaching and equipping process of the Dunamis Project. Here is one simple example of sustaining the flame which was also part of Phase #1 Preparing the Altar.

## Phil Noordmans, Pastor of the Chinese Community Church in San Diego, CA

Let me give an example of how I was called to sustain the flame in the congregational context. While serving as the senior pastor of the Chinese Community Church in San Diego, CA, I wanted to pass on some of the things the Lord was teaching me through PRMI about:

- The empowering work of the Holy Spirit.
- The dance of cooperation with the Holy Spirit – staying in step with the Spirit (Galatians 5:16, 25).

Deep within I knew that I knew that the Holy Spirit is not merely an idea or an impersonal force but the living and active third Person of the Trinity who empowers people to serve as Jesus' witness.

As I prayed, the thought came to mind, "During the next year, devote one Sunday per month to teaching on some aspect of the empowering work of the Holy Spirit." So, I did.

Did it matter? Did it make a difference? Although I do not have objective data on changes in people's attitudes, perspectives, and behaviors, my subjective sense is that by the end of the series people were much more open and freer to talk about the Holy Spirit's work in their lives and ministries. For example, during baptisms—and, by God's grace, there were many—brother Kwan joined me in praying over the person (usually a student) who was being baptized, calling on Jesus not only to protect them and nurture them, but also to activate the gifts He was giving them and empower them for the ministries to which He was calling them. Essentially, we were asking Jesus to baptize them with the Holy Spirit.

Could more have been done? Of course. Nevertheless, I believe that we were in step with the Spirit for that phase of our life together.

We could provide many more examples of sustaining the flame in the local congregation and will do so in a later chapter. The reason for offering the models is based on the following caveats.

The first is that Phase #3 Sustaining the Flame does not fully take place unless it becomes part of the three phases of the meta pattern, becoming a repeatable, sustainable cycle. So, this focus on ways of sustaining the working of the Holy Spirit, while valuable, is none-the-less not the complete picture.

The second caveat is that this repeatable cycle of the meta pattern will need to have embedded in it the other basic patterns that God has chosen to work through for Pentecost events to become revival movements of the Holy Spirit. These are the five markers of authentic Pentecost events, the three R.A. Torrey keys to revival and the two Goforth foundations. Holding all this together and having the anointed people needed to implement these patterns will require the three phases becoming a repeatable cycle which in turn requires the full expression of the equipping anointings as well as the dynamic interplay between the different expressions that God has created for the healthy growth of the body of Christ as well spreading the fire of revival. We explore these topics in the next chapter.

# 16

# The Three Phases Becoming a Cycle

In this chapter and the next we address the question of how Pentecost events grow into revival movements that persist over time and expand into more and more locations. What must happen for these movements to produce good fruit in the church, embody the kingdom of God, and fulfill our mission of making disciples of Jesus Christ? In the pages that follow we will be providing the guidance that the Lord is giving us for how to cooperate with Him to grow these outpourings of the Spirit into kingdom-advancing revivals.

## How God calls us to sustain and grow movements of the Holy Sprit

This process of praying in and igniting Pentecost events and then sustaining the flame is not just so we can have exciting events or fill up an empty church. It is to take part in God's master plan of seeing these events become movements of the Holy Spirit which advance the kingdom of God. Such movements may become revivals with the potential to become great awakenings which will overthrow colossal and insidiously growing demonic evil, bringing entire societies into alignment with God's kingdom purposes. This awakening will, above all, lead to the completion of the condition for Jesus' return, which is the gospel of the kingdom being preached to all nations. (Matthew 24:14)[121]

For this to happen, these five markers, three keys, and two foundations must be embedded within the meta pattern of preparing the altar, igniting the fire, and sustaining the flame. In addition, if a Pentecost event is to become a sustainable movement and spread to more and more people and places, then these three phases must become a repeatable, transferable cycle, in which more and more people are brought into the kingdom of God, are nurtured as disciples of Jesus Christ, are filled with the Holy Spirit, and go out as witnesses to Jesus. The result of this dynamic is that not only do fellowships and congregations grow as expressions of the new life in the kingdom, but they also grow in fulfilling their mission of evangelism and missions. A derivative will be that revival movements continue and spread.

---

[121]What I am speaking of here may seem a little contradictory. There is a stream of Christianity that sees the church in total opposition to evil fallen society. A biblical view, however, sees the kingdom of God embodied in the Church functioning to constrain human and demonic evil, but also transforming the rest of society with kingdom values. These in turn provide the human means for the church to express its life and mission. Paul tells us in Romans 12:2 not to be conformed to this world, but to have our minds transformed, which then will have a transforming effect on society. This engagement in society starts with praying for those in authority (1 Timothy 2:1-4). This is necessary so that we may have the context of peace, prosperity, and freedom to live our faith and to fulfill the mission mandate of extending the gospel of Jesus Christ. Often the objection is made that the church flourishes under oppression and persecution. This is true to a degree. However, when this oppression and persecution takes place under an antichrist system of totalitarian control like Islam from its inception with Muhammad (570-632), in the rule of Hideyoshi in Japan in the 1500s, that has chosen the subjugation and extermination of Christians, then the church does not flourish but is simply obliterated or reduced to a scarcely surviving, hidden remnant with no opportunity to impact that oppressing society except through hidden prayer and witness. This is rapidly becoming the situation in communist China under Xi Jinping.

## Anointed Leaders Returning to Sustain the Cycle

To sustain and grow this cycle within a particular context such as a local congregation or a movement like PRMI requires that a certain number of anointed and gifted people are always available to provide the leadership for each of the three phases.

This need for gifted and experienced leaders who embody the values of the movement or institution coming back to sustain the system is not unique to this move of the Holy Spirit. This is necessary for sustaining any movement or institution past its initial founders. For instance, to sustain a college or university a certain number of its top graduates, after proving themselves, must return to provide the core faculty and administration.

I have seen this dynamic taking place in the United States Army firsthand in my son-in-law, LTC Adam Schultz. After proving himself a very capable officer and leader on the battlefields of Iraq and Afghanistan, he is now in the training command where his knowledge and experience are enabling both individuals and units to grow in their war-fighting skills. Also, as a student of history and as a patriot, he is in a key position to pass on to others the core values of America and the US Army.

An aspect of this work of growing leaders for growing the movement of the Holy Spirit has been demonstrated all through the history of the Church. In the family of God, anointed leaders, become, not just "brothers and sisters" but also "mothers and faithers" who first nurture, and then release their spiritual children into their own kingdom roles.

In PRMI this process of anointed, proven leaders coming back to equip others is taking place. For instance, I spent nearly twenty-five years constantly teaching at Dunamis Project events as well as being used by God in multiple nations and locations to ignite outpourings of the Holy Spirit. However, now that a global network of teachers and leaders has been raised up, they are doing this teaching and traveling. The Lord has called me to stay here in North Carolina and focus on the equipping of other leaders. This takes place at the Community of the Cross, located on twenty-four acres, by a river on a mountainside here in western North Carolina. This is our set-apart place for encounter with Jesus Christ, for prayer, equipping, and sending.

Frankly this has been difficult for me! Stepping back so that others may step forward takes putting one's ego aside as well as the great joy of being used by God in power ministry, and encouraging others to do what one not only loves doing but have become very good at doing. But this is my role now—enabling others to move into the great dance with the Holy Spirit. The key is to step back, but not out! This is what my mentor, Archer Torrey, did for me, and now I am called to do for others.

This dynamic of well-seasoned anointed leaders coming back to equip others requires the organizational structures to enable this to take place. We will give examples of these structures being put in place in a local congregation in this chapter and will return to how they are developed for missional organizations like PRMI in a future chapter.

## Anointed Witnesses and Co-Workers Must Keep Being Sent Out

To keep this cycle alive and focused on advancing the Kingdom of God requires that in addition to leaders returning to sustain the system, anointed witnesses to Jesus Christ must constantly be being sent out. The Church of Jesus Christ has been raised up by Jesus not just to embody the Kingdom of God but to extend the Kingdom of God. We see this in the book of Acts after the first Pentecostal outpouring in Jerusalem. The believers in the upper room became a close-knit, cohesive fellowship who could pray in one mind and heart. However, the immediate result of the outpouring on the day of Pentecost was that their community expanded to include three thousand more new believers. That no doubt presented enormous challenges to remaining a close fellowship. We see these struggles reflected in Acts chapters 5 and 6—the deception of Ananias and Sapphira, unequal distribution of food to the widows, and increasing persecution. I suspect that

298

meeting these challenges resulted in them becoming an even closer dynamic, Spirit-empowered community. However, with the martyrdom of Stephen, they came under persecution.

And Saul agreed completely with killing him. Now on that day a great persecution began against the church in Jerusalem, and all except the apostles were forced to scatter throughout the regions of Judea and Samaria. Act 8:1

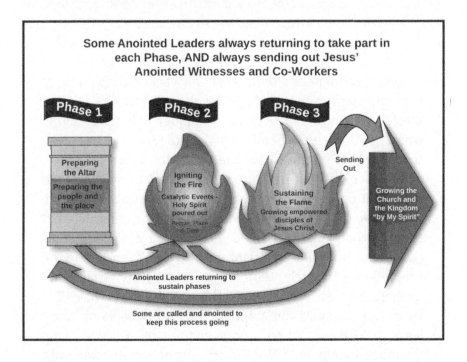

The result was that the team was scattered, and the reach of the Kingdom was expanded. "Now those who had been forced to scatter went around proclaiming the good news of the word (Acts 8:4). The result was new outpourings of the Holy Spirit which expanded the Kingdom. This sending out is not only essential for the expanding of the gospel but for keeping the cycle vital and alive. If there is the constant pouring in but not going out, it becomes like the Dead Sea; it dies. It is the same with the church. Once again, like the leaders returning to support the system, organizational structures are needed to enable the process of sending out.

## A Season when the Cycle was Not Sustained at St. Giles

There are many examples where the altar was prepared, the fire fell, and the flame of revival was sustained for a season. However, this was not nurtured as a repeatable cycle bringing more and more people into the dance of the Holy Spirit. An example of this is St. Giles Presbyterian Church in Richmond VA. Art Thomas, a biblical historian and author who grew up at St. Giles had this to share with me:

St. Giles experienced a remarkable revival and outpouring of the Holy Spirit in the 1970s under the ministries of Dr. Earl Wesley Morey and Dr. Louis Alexander Skidmore during which hundreds were baptized in the Holy Spirit and received spiritual gifts such as tongues, discernment, prophecy, deliverance, healing, etc. Although the revival was hindered by cessationists who instigated an investigation by the presbytery, the St. Giles leaders stood fast and defended that the spiritual gifts continued to the present (known as continuationism) and the right for Holy Spirit renewal in the Presbyterian Church USA. After presbytery trials and deliberations, St. Giles received this permission. In May 1979 there was a remarkable revival led by the leaders of Youth with a Mission, Loren Cunningham, Joy Dawson, and Campbell McAlpine. YWAM is still strongly connected with this church."

For a season this cycle was maintained, bearing great fruit for the Kingdom of God which included introducing Laura and me to the Charismatic Renewal. While we were students at Union Theological Seminary in Virginia, starting in 1974, we would go and visit St. Giles Church and take part in their amazing prayer and praise services. Their anointed pastor, Earl Morey, provided dynamic, empowered preaching and Bible teaching. Many people had been baptized with the Holy Spirit and were growing in the gifts and power of the Holy Spirit. All the manifestational gifts were in evidence—tongues, prophecy, healing, casting out of demons, and more. We participated in dynamic Holy Spirit-led praise, prayer, and worship. Loving, healing, prayer ministry was taking place. Among those taking part at St. Giles was an older fellow seminary student, David Partington. David had had the experience of being baptized with the Holy Spirit amid a successful career as a church musician and orchestra conductor. This experience led him into preparing for the pastoral ministry. Art Thomas, who had been a part of the initial outpourings of the Holy Spirit, was our graduate instructor at the seminary. They and others welcomed us. However, despite their warm welcome, neither Laura nor I were very open to all this. Not only did these supernatural manifestations of the presence of God not fit our worldview, but they also did not seem consistent with the sound biblical and reformed faith that we were being taught at seminary. I must confess that when we went to the St. Giles prayer, praise, and healing meetings, we would sit as close to the door as possible and mock these "overly emotional" people. However, seeing these clear manifestations of the power, presence, and love of Jesus Christ made us very hungry. These born-again and Holy Spirit-empowered people, many of them our own age, were obviously alive in Jesus Christ and were experiencing a level of effectiveness in ministry we envied. They also had a passion for Bible study and for God speaking to them through the Bible that made our seminary study of the original languages seem very dry and lifeless.

To make a long story short, taking part in those charismatic worship services at St. Giles sowed the seeds for what God had in mind for us later. While still in seminary as part of the degree program, we took a year to go to South Korea (this was in 1976-77) where we were both baptized with the Holy Spirit. When we returned to seminary, after an opening Chapel service, David Partington approached us with a big smile said, "Something happened to you in Korea, right?" When we hesitated for fear of being misunderstood, he said, "You both were baptized with the Holy Spirit! I can tell because both of you exude the joyful presence

301

of Jesus!" He invited us to his apartment on campus for a small prayer group in which he mentored us in expressing the gifts of the Holy Spirit. He also urged us to return to St. Giles. We returned to St. Giles, not as skeptical observers but as enthusiastic participants. It was there with the solid Bible teaching and dynamic fellowship that we continued to grow in the gifts and power of the Holy Spirit. St. Giles Presbyterian Church in Richmond Va. was one among many Presbyterian and Reformed congregations scattered throughout the United States, Canada and the United Kingdom that had been ignited by outpourings of the Holy Spirit. They were a core part of what was then called the Presbyterian Charismatic Communion. This growth and dynamism was sustained for several years with great impact, not only on the city of Richmond, but on many other congregations. During this period, they were also a major part of PRMI with the pastoral leaders of St. Giles being the keynote speakers at our larger charismatic conferences. At that time in the 1970's and 1980's, St. Giles was held up by PRMI as a model congregation which experienced an outpouring of the Holy Spirit and then continued, not just to keep the fire going, but to take part in extending the move of the Holy Spirit to other congregations.

After two years in parish ministry and nine years on the mission field in Taiwan where we were part of the great outpouring of the Holy Spirit that took place there, we returned in 1990 from the mission field, and I took up this role as Executive Director of PRMI. In this capacity, I found that most of the charismatic renewal had not only died down but that in several locations the movement had gone off the rails with church leaders having fallen into immorality or apostasy. Abuse of spiritual authority in some movements like the Shepherding movement also had a damaging impact on individuals. All of these things brought division to congregations.

I will never forget the shock I had when I was invited back to St. Giles to lead a conference on the Holy Spirit. Only a small group of older people, who still had the embers of renewal burning in them, attended. In the contemporary service, which was sparsely attended, there were only a few older people who had been a part of the first Pentecost outpouring events, who raised their hands or seemed to engage in the worship. The rest, mostly a younger group, were distant and uninvolved. The healing prayer ministry and the other contexts for expressing the gifts of the Holy Spirit had continued mostly in small groups led by a faithful few who remembered and had taken part in the glory days of the past. Specifically, Dr. John Harler, a St. Giles elder and physician had rekindled the healing ministry at the church and people were blessed.[122] However it seemed from my outside perspective that while the flame was being sustained, there was no longer the dynamic of the church growing in the power of the Holy Spirit.

Apparently, since the initial outpourings, younger generations and new members of the congregation were not being brought into the into the experience of the baptism with the Holy Spirit. I found out later that there were many reasons why this had happened. First, for a season there was no longer any clear biblical teaching provided by the leadership on the baptism with the Holy Spirit. Also, apparently with the exception of an occasional special speaker, opportunities to be prayed for to be baptized or refilled with the Holy Spirit were not offered in the regular life of the congregation. Another reason why this cycle had not been implemented was that the church had experienced massive spiritual warfare in which anointed leaders were removed and those who were brought in to replace them were faced with the overwhelming task of just holding the fractured and wounded congregation together.

As I traveled about the United States and Canada to what had been the flagship congregations in the charismatic renewal from the 1960s to the 1980s, I found that the situation at St. Giles was common to almost all of them. I would find a dwindling remnant, mostly of older people who were part of the original outpouring, who desperately sought to sustain the flame of life in the Holy

---

[122] Arthur Dicken Thomas, Jr., "The St. Giles Presbyterian Church Revival: Evangelical and Charismatic Spirituality, Theology, and Reform in Richmond, Virginia, 1937-2023." Unpublished manuscript.

Spirit. There were one or two exceptions, but for the most part the landscape was very bleak. Partly because of the excesses of the charismatic renewal movement, congregations had split into fragmented remnants. These divisions and conflicts however were not always the fault of those on-fire Christians dedicated to following Jesus, moving in the gifts of Holy Spirit and receiving the Bible as the Word of God. In many cases, including my own, they had experienced a contemptuous and fire-quenching rejection from the denominations that they were a part of. Now, nearly four decades later, we can clearly see the real root cause, as well as the results of this rejection of the Charismatic Renewal movement by the leadership of these mainline denominations such as the Presbyterian Church in the USA. They are on the slippery slope of apostasy away from their own creedal affirmations of the authority of Scripture and that Jesus Christ is the Way, the Truth, and the Life, and the only way to God the Father.

Frankly, in those days, it was not just these congregations and entire denominations but also PRMI itself that had lost the fire of the working of the Holy Spirit. We too had lost the cycle, especially of igniting the fire which can only take place through providing contexts for fulfilling Acts 1:4-8. For instance, when I first returned from the mission field in August of 1989, I attended a pastors' retreat sponsored by PRRMI. [123] This was led by a well-known, anointed speaker. Not that many pastors were in attendance, and what was worse, following a nice inspirational talk, there was no ministry and no opportunity to pray for and receive the baptism or infilling with the Holy Spirit. Instead of times of prayer ministry,

---

[123] In 1966 this ministry was founded as the **Presbyterian Charismatic Communion (PCC)**, but because the charismatic renewal movement had fallen into disrepute in many places and because we had so many participants from the Reformed Church of America, the name was changed to **Presbyterian & Reformed Renewal Ministries International (PRRMI)**. This was such a tongue twister that we later just became **Presbyterian & Reformed Ministries International (PRMI)**.

prayer, or Spirit-led worship, we had an "ice cream social" each night of the retreat.

It turned out that this ministry was no longer overtly teaching on the baptism and infilling with the Holy Spirit because that was no longer politically acceptable. Our larger conferences that in the 1970s and 80s had drawn thousands, had dwindled down to small groups or closed altogether. One conference in Southern California and another at Messiah College in Pennsylvania had kept the fire going, but these eventually were discontinued for lack of attendance. There were other PRRMI events and programs, like Spirit Alive for local congregations, where the flames were still being sustained, but once again much of the fire had gone out. This cycle had not been sustained.

So, what went wrong? First, was the role of Satan's massive counterattacks against outpourings of the Holy Spirit. This attack resulted in key anointed leaders being morally compromised and removed from leadership. These devastating counterattacks had taken place, not just in once thriving congregations, but also within PRMI itself.

Second, no doubt as a part of the spiritual warfare counter-attacks, false, unbiblical teaching infected some parts of the movement. Abuse of authority and manipulation by anointed leaders had occurred. This had brought division within congregations as well as dishonor to Christ and to the movement. In fact, the term *charismatic* was so poisoned that this organization had to change its name from Presbyterian Charismatic Communion (PCC) to Presbyterian Reformed Renewal Ministries International (PRRMI) which later became Presbyterian Reformed Ministries International (PRMI).

Third, and most often, there were no "wineskins" that would enable this threefold meta pattern to become a repeatable, sustainable cycle. This was the case, not just for local congregations, but within PRMI itself, which God had called to embody this movement of the Holy Spirit. At the root of this problem of being able to sustain this cycle was the lack of anointed leaders who were mature and able to step back from upfront, anointed ministry (which was often exhilarating and rewarding), to take part in sustaining this cycle in either the local congregations or in the trans-congregational movements like PRMI. This was not always the leader's fault. There were often no built-in ways for these anointed leaders to step back, but not out, where they could express their wisdom and experience in ways that would nurture others into anointed ministry. There were often no effective ways for the equipping process to be extended to younger generations.

Fourth, there was no body of biblically grounded, theologically sound teaching materials that was being consistently taught by PRMI. The result was that we were ourselves contributing to the confusion and division over such terms as the baptism and infilling with the Holy Spirit. A major issue in those days was the issue of the gifts of tongues as the initial, physical evidence of having been baptized with the Holy Spirit and normative for everyone. Further, there was not a clear understanding of the Bible having authority over contemporary prophetic words.

Fifth, a dynamic that was often hidden or unnoticed in a number of these instances, is that the larger congregations had tried to maintain the dynamic of growth completely within themselves, rather than staying connected to revival streams that transcended the local congregations. The result was that in many cases they could not sustain the flame. Biblical, orthodox teaching and preaching, and Christ-centered discipling of believers had not been enough to keep the dynamic cycle going forward. As I looked at these situations, I found it was Phase #2 (Igniting the Fire through catalytic events) that had been neglected or in some cases outright rejected, which meant that born-again believers were no longer being baptized with the Holy Spirit, and older, more mature believers were no longer experiencing the infilling, empowering work of the Holy Spirit needed to meet the constantly changing opportunities and challenges. The reason for this was that in these cases there was no connection to revival streams that transcended the local congregations. We shall examine this reality later.

To sustain this repeatable cycle with some leaders returning and some being sent out, the full implementation and operation of the foundational components of the body of Christ is required. One of these components has been revealed to us in Ephesians 4:11, "And he himself gave some as apostles, some as prophets, some as evangelists, and some as pastors and teachers ..." These have often been identified as the "fivefold ministries" or what we will be naming as the "five equipping anointings." In the next chapter we shall demonstrate that the active expression of these five equipping anointings is essential for preparing for, igniting, sustaining, and extending movements of the Holy Spirit which advance the gospel of the kingdom of God.

# 17

## The Five-Fold Equipping Anointings for Revival

I believe the Lord has given us a model to address this problem of being able to sustain the cycle of the three phases with the three keys for revival and the two foundations all embedded within them, and to have leadership being raised up constantly with the gifting to sustain and expand this cycle. Much of this has been assumed throughout this book, but let's pull these concepts together in two steps: First is the role of each of the fivefold equipping anointings as all are needed to sustain the cycle of the movement of the Holy Spirit.

The second step will be covered in the next chapter and has to do with the dynamic relationship between two redemptive structures which are modeled in the local congregation and the special mission group, which is connected to, but transcends the local gathering. Together these two encompass the body of Christ.

[Phil Noordmans] Let's focus here on the first part of this process, which is developing the full expression of all five of the ministry giftings mentioned by Paul in Ephesians 4:11-13, which have often been described as the "fivefold ministries" or as the "vocational gifts of the Holy Spirit." Each will have a role in each phase of preparing for, igniting, and then sustaining outpourings of the Holy Spirit. Before we do this, we need to elaborate on what I will be identifying as the fivefold equipping anointings. Seeing these as different anointings of the Holy Spirit for the equipping of the saints, will enable us to include but transcend these expressions as rigid established offices in the church. This approach helps us appreciate and grow in these expressions of the Holy Spirit as dynamically functioning in ministry or leadership teams, which are practically needed for igniting and expanding revivals. We will pay special attention to the apostolic anointing through whom Jesus will baptize His disciples with the Holy Spirit (thus repeatedly fulfilling Acts 1:4-8) and create the "wineskins" or "containers" for expressing all the works of the Holy Spirit.

## The Equipping Gifts of the Holy Spirit.[124]

"He gave some as apostles, and some as prophets, and some as evangelists, and some as pastors and teachers, for the <u>equipping of the saints</u> for the work of service, (Ephesians 4:11-12, NASB). (Underlining mine.) The five gifts listed above—often aptly called the "fivefold ministry"—are not capacities given by the Holy Spirit to individuals; rather, they are individuals given by Jesus to the Church. The person himself or herself is the gift, and Jesus gives these people to the Church "to equip the saints for the work of ministry, for building up the body of Christ," (Ephesians 4:12, ESV). Not every Christian is gifted to equip others, but some are.

Remember Bezalel in the Old Testament? The Lord chose him and filled him "with the Spirit of God, with skill, ability and knowledge in all kinds of crafts—to make artistic designs," (Exodus 35:31-32, NASB). God also chose Oholiab to serve as Bezalel's co-worker, and God gave both Bezalel and Oholiab "the ability to teach others," (Exodus 35:34, NASB). They were not only artisans; they were also equippers: they could teach others. Likewise, the apostles, prophets, evangelists, pastors, and teachers in Ephesians 4 are not only able to function well personally in their respective capacities; they are also anointed to teach and equip others for the work of ministry.

---

[124]Philip J Noordmans, *A Primer on Spiritual Gifts*, (Kindle Direct Publishing, 2019), 101-131. https://www.amazon.com/Primer-Spiritual-Gifts-Philip-Noordmans/dp/1077036299

## Fivefold Ministry: Structuring the Church for Spiritual Health

A student went off to college in a distant city and began looking for a church that understood and practiced the fivefold ministry. During a service at one of the churches she visited, the pastor announced, "We offer the fivefold ministry. If you need healing, come to the altar and I will pray for you. If you need to hear a prophetic word, come and I will prophesy over you. If you need deliverance, come and I will set you free."

That is not the way God designed the fivefold equipping anointings to work. The fivefold ministry is not one person functioning in five offices or capacities. Rather, it is five or more people working together, each of whom has a specific anointing and gifting. When the right people are in each office, the "wineskin" or "container" [the organizational structure] is ready for Jesus to fill it with the oil of the Holy Spirit. The outcome will be that the church will move toward greater spiritual maturity (Ephesians 4:13-16). Where oil flows, the church grows.

The background to the concept of "containers" reaches back to the story of Elisha and the widow in 2 Kings 4:1-7. The oil did not start flowing until the containers were in position to receive it, and it continued to flow as long as containers were in place.

When a leadership team, such as an Elder Board or a Consistory includes an apostle, prophet, evangelist, pastor, and teacher, the team becomes a "container" into which Jesus may pour the oil of the Holy Spirit. If the container remains essentially whole and holy, the oil of the Spirit continues to flow freely. Godly leaders build spiritually healthy congregations, and the oil of the Spirit flows into them as well.

Generally, Jesus will not pour the oil of the Holy Spirit into containers with holes in them. We must present to Him suitable containers before the oil of the Spirit will flow.

(For more teaching on all the equipping gifts of the Holy Spirit I recommend the PRMI Dunamis Equipping Unit# 2 *In the Spirit's Power,* [OBJ] and my book *A Primer on Spiritual Gifts.*)

## Apostle

Terry Shanahan's nickname is "ApCat," apostolic catalyst. Terry served in the Northeast as the Regional Pastor for the Conservative Congregational Christian Conference, interfacing with churches and pastors in that area. When I asked him to tell me a story about how he became aware that he might have an apostolic anointing on his life, he replied, "I never saw that in myself. Rather, when others noticed the ways God used me to link leaders and champion new ministries, I guess they just decided I was 'apostolic.'" Indeed, he is.

The word "apostle" is the result of the merger of *apo* ("from") and *stello* ("send forth"). It signifies "one sent forth by another with a special commission to represent the other and to accomplish his work."[125] We translate the verb *apostello* as "to send" and the noun *apostolos* as "apostle", meaning "one who is sent." An apostle is like an ambassador who is sent out on a mission and bears the authority of the one who sent him or her.

As soon as we begin to talk about apostles, someone protests saying, "Apostles no longer exist in our day because no one in our day fulfills the criteria of Acts 1:21-22 for replacing Judas, which is, "Thus one of the men who have accompanied us during all the time the Lord Jesus associated with us, beginning from his baptism by John until the day he was taken up from us—one of these must become a witness of his resurrection together with us." Further no one is writing documents that are on par with Scripture. Scripture is complete. As New Testament believers we look to it, not to present day apostles and prophets for revelation of true doctrine.[126] Nevertheless, we must ask, "In our day is God calling,

---

[125] http://preceptaustin.org/ephesians_411.htm#4:11  See also DNTT, I, 126.
[126] For example, S. Michael Houdmann champions this view on GotQuestions, http://www.gotquestions.org/five-fold-ministry.html

equipping, gifting, appointing, and anointing some men and women to serve as apostles?"

The original twelve, plus the Apostle Paul are unique and stand alone. However, the New Testament records Jesus sending out seventy-two additional apostles in Luke 10, Barnabas is called an apostle in Acts 14:14, and Andronicus and Junia are mentioned as being "of note among the apostles" in Romans 16:7. Those kinds of apostles are still being called and sent! Men and women cannot appoint themselves to this role as Robert Duvall did in the movie, *The Apostle*. Neither can a congregation make someone an apostle by a democratic vote. Rather, apostles must be called, appointed, and anointed by God Himself to wear this mantle. Alert congregations will affirm God's anointing.

I find it helpful to delineate three tiers of apostles:

1. Jesus – in a class all by Himself.

2. The twelve Apostles plus Paul.

3. Historical and modern-day apostles—called by God and anointed to function in roles and capacities similar to those of the original twelve. These people are "small a" apostles. These are the type of apostles raised up for the equipping of the members of the body of Christ which Paul names in Ephesians 4:11.

Apostles are initiators. They launch ministries and they launch people into ministries.

The work of an apostle (literally, "one sent") is that of laying foundations, that is, establishing new leaders, ministries, and congregations.

Several years ago, while riding with three men to a denominational meeting, one of them mentioned that he was thinking about planting a church. In the course of the conversation, I commented that the most effective church planters have an apostolic anointing. He looked at me with a puzzled expression like I was speaking a foreign language. The conversation quickly shifted to a more palatable topic. He went on to plant a church, but for several reasons it did not go well.

Even though the average denomination sends out teachers and worship leaders to plant churches, by God's design we would be wiser to send anointed apostles and prophets to launch new works (Ephesians 2:18-22).

Modern day apostles function with a high degree of spiritual authority. In addition to evangelizing, preaching, teaching, speaking prophetically into people's lives, and exercising authority in the Name of Jesus over demonic powers, they wield significant authority in matters pertaining to church order, church discipline, and church government. They advance the King's agenda in the field in which God assigns them to serve (1 Corinthians 3:9; 9:2). They also set in order existing ministries (Titus 1:5). Their powerful words are often authenticated by powerful works including miracles (Romans 15:18-19).

## The Responsibility Stops with the Apostle

God appoints apostles to serve as primary founders and often leaders of ministries, churches, and denominations. Every ministry must take seriously the hierarchy of leadership prescribed by God who appointed in the church first apostles, second prophets, third teachers … (1 Corinthians 12:28, ESV).

Jesus expects apostles to work together with prophets, evangelists, pastors, and teachers—like five fingers on a hand—to equip people in the congregation, ministry, or movement for the work of service. The Holy Spirit orchestrates the synergy. They are mutually accountable to scripture, to Jesus Christ, to one another, and to the church where they serve. If the church leadership, such as the Council or Session, becomes ingrown or morphs into a good-ol'-boys club, Jesus will send a "Nathan" to rebuke and correct them.

The biblical assumption is this: When a godly apostle is in place, he will properly "order" the remainder of the church. In cooperation with prophets, evangelists, pastors, and teachers, as well as the congregation, apostles will manage resources in a manner that honors God, builds-up the church, and advances the King's agenda in our needy communities and world.

These different anointings generally work together in each of the three phases of the meta pattern, in which are embedded the three R.A. Torrey keys and the two Goforth foundations. These are very fluid and dynamic with a lot of overlap, but they seem to be associated with each phase.

## Phase #1 Preparing the Altar

This requires the work of the evangelist to bring people into being born-again through faith in Jesus Christ, which is a precondition for becoming a disciple of Jesus Christ and receiving the baptism with the Holy Spirit. Recall that in the book of Acts all those whom Jesus baptized with the Holy Spirit were already born-again disciples or that these two events took place concurrently as in the case of Cornelius the centurion.

In this phase, the anointed preaching and teaching will have the critical role of providing the biblical foundation needed for born-again disciples to understand the work of the Holy Spirit and the promises that Jesus has given concerning the baptism and infilling with the Holy Spirit. The role of the apostolic, prophetic, and evangelistic anointings will be, first, to cast the vision for the fellowship to take part in extending the Kingdom of God beyond itself to fulfill the great commission of making disciples and to transform society according to Kingdom values. Second, they must present the reality that the wider mission can only be accomplished, not by "power and might," but "by my Spirit," which means people and programs that are led and empowered by the Holy Spirit.

## Phase #2 Igniting the Fire

We have already established that those through whom Jesus works to call the prepared people to ask Him for and to receive the baptism with the Holy Spirit are those with an apostolic anointing. The role of those who have a prophetic anointing will be to discern the kairos moment. Generally, the fire starters will involve both the prophetic and apostolic anointings together to create contexts for God the Father to fulfill Acts 1:4-8 again and again, so that Pentecost events may continue to take place within the life of individuals as well as within the church. In this way, Jesus will have a growing body of empowered co-workers through whom He may work.

## Phase #3 Sustaining the Flame

This requires the role of those with an apostolic anointing to put in place "wineskins" and structures so that all the gifts and ministries of the Holy Spirit express the reality of Jesus Christ as Prophet, Priest and King working on earth. The role of teachers is to continue to provide biblical teaching so that people can grow in the dance of cooperation with the Holy Spirit, and in applying the Word of God to their lives. The role of those with a pastoral anointing is nurturing the loving, caring community of Christ and walking with people in faith to bring the comfort and joy of living in Christ. This will create the context for the healing ministry of Jesus Christ to take place. Pastors also are responsible for the spiritual discipline of believers who may wander into error or sin.

In summary: All of these anointed offices of apostle, prophet, evangelist, teacher, and pastor, along with the other gifts and manifestations of the Holy Spirit, must work together to enable this to be a repeatable cycle. This is what we see in the book of Acts in which God was daily adding to their number those who were becoming disciples of Jesus Christ. When these fivefold equipping anointings are fully functioning, they will build the two foundations of the Bible as the Word of God and Jesus as King. Further, the three R.A Torrey keys of evangelism, the baptism with the Holy Spirit, and the work of prayer will be taking place. And further, these equipping anointings will also encourage others to share in this anointing. In other words, pastors not only "pastor people" they equip people to "pastor people." The work of the evangelist is not only to evangelize, but to equip the saints to evangelize, and so on.

This all forms a dynamic synergy in which the church continues to grow, embodying the kingdom of God and fulfilling the mandate to take the gospel of the kingdom to all nations. This synergy provides the basis for sustaining and expanding revivals which in turn may become great awakenings.

## The Key to Sustaining this Dynamic Cycle

The key to sustaining this dynamic cycle is the constant process of raising up and equipping these leaders with the anointing and gifts through whom Jesus constantly baptizes or refills people with the Holy Spirit. After receiving this empowerment, the new believers must be nurtured into the dynamic of cooperation with the Holy Spirit. The key foundation stone in all this is having those people who are the anointed fire starters expressing this anointing within the context of constantly preparing the altar and then sustaining the flame.

The keystone will be those with apostolic anointing, but the groundwork to sustain the movement within the context of the congregation will be the vetting, equipping, and raising up of those individuals and groups with the anointing to fill each of the fivefold equipping ministries.

In the model of Acts, we see this process of equipping those newly born-again disciples into these anointed roles taking place under the direction of the apostles. They were devoting themselves to the apostles' teaching and to fellowship, to the breaking of bread and to prayer (Acts 2:42).

This teaching takes place within the context of fellowship, breaking bread, and prayer. We might also add worship and the full manifestation of the gifts of the Holy Spirit in their life together as well as being a mission base for those going out as witnesses. In other words, this was not just an academic process of teaching, but rather the teaching was taking place within the context of the ongoing, vibrant life of the church, which was embodying the Kingdom of God.

There are practical ways that this dynamic of the fivefold equipping anointings, supporting the meta pattern as a repeatable cycle, can be sustained within a single congregation.  A model of what is possible is described in the next chapter.

# 18

# A Congregation Sustains the Meta Pattern

In our experience there have been a number of congregations where this dynamic has been sustained for an extended period of time. Often these are congregations that are larger and diverse enough to contain within themselves, not just the fivefold equipping anointings, but also the rigorous process of vetting and equipping leaders who can take part in sustaining the three phases as well as implementing the two Goforth foundations and the three R.A. Torrey keys. These congregations are composed of many overlapping groups and subgroups. I have already mentioned the on-fire, charismatic congregation of St. Giles in Richmond, VA, which sustained this dynamic for at least two decades during the 1970-90s. We shall return to that congregation in another chapter. Rather than pointing back to the glory days of that historical model, I would like to provide a contemporary model congregation that is leading the way and modeling how this may be accomplished in our present epoch.

## Gold Avenue Christian Reformed Church in Grand Rapids, MI

I have chosen this congregation because it is not a large church, but rather a church of about one hundred members. We have already introduced Dave Westra as an anointed fire starter in the context of the Community of the Cross. Igniting outpourings of the Holy Spirit and then sustaining the flame within the local congregation is an entirely different challenge than in a set-apart location. Let's go to the other context that Dave is called to minister in—the Christian Reformed Congregation called Gold Avenue CRC. In this context he is joined by co-pastor, Rev. Gina Dick. Together they form an apostolically anointed team through whom the Lord is preparing the altar, igniting outpourings, and putting in place those programs and structures that enable sustaining the flame. Together they are also putting in place what is needed for the three phases to become a cycle. The key is developing the internal processes for systematically discipling believers, providing opportunities for them to be filled with the Holy Spirit, and then equipping them for cooperating with the Holy Spirit and moving into their different areas of gifting. In addition to this internal work, the congregation, through small, is active in sending out witnesses. This is done in their neighborhood but also by forming mission teams and providing prayer support for ministries beyond themselves. The result is that the fivefold equipping anointings are being cultivated to enable the sustaining of the three phases within their congregation.

Here then are Rev. Gina Dick and Rev. Dave Westra to tell their own story of how they came to develop effective wineskins for fulfilling each of the R.A. Torrey essentials.

## How We were Led to Develop the Two Programs of Empowered for Witness and the Gospel Tool.

[Gina Dick and David Westra] Many of us have probably experienced attending a conference only to return home to have the recently ignited fire go out rather quickly and unintentionally. This has happened to us after returning from a PRMI Dunamis Project event or a Growing the Church event. It is wonderful being in the set-apart context where the fire falls, but then we return to the local congregation where in our role as pastors we must minister to people at many different levels of spiritual growth. It is difficult for pastors and church leaders to keep the fire going but it is even more difficult for lay people who have experienced the baptism or infilling with the Holy Spirit to return to a congregation where there is no support. I would say that our primary motivation as we returned to our local congregation was twofold: First, seeking to lay/deepen within our own congregation the two foundations for growing the church (leaders who embody the kingdom and congregations growing to embody the kingdom), [127] AND obedience to Jesus' guidance as we prayed. In hindsight, we can see that it also functions to prepare an altar, ignite the fire, and sustain the flame.

We were both on the teaching team of a marvelous Growing the Church in the Power of the Holy Spirit Conference in 2019.[128] At this event many pastors experienced powerful works of the Holy Spirit. At its conclusion we felt prompted to offer a follow up opportunity to keep fanning the flames, helping people learn to cooperate with the Holy Spirit. We offered this course at the Gold Avenue CRC Church where we are pastors.

We taught the biblical and theological framework for the empowering of the Holy Spirit, adapting PRMI's Dunamis materials with permission. We called the course **Empowered for Witness** (EFW) **101**. This was the basic teaching on the person and work of the Holy Spirit in the Dunamis Unit #1 course *Gateways to Empowered Ministry*. Local leaders invited teams to come along to learn together. 150 people registered, which included about 35 local pastors. One gentleman drove six hours from his home in Wisconsin to Michigan to attend every week!

Meeting one evening a week for six weeks, we experienced wonderful times of fellowship, worship, teaching, and small group "lab time" to apply the teaching. One of the memorable moments came as we prepared to pray for the empowering/baptizing work

---

[127] This concept of the two foundations comes from the book *Growing the Church in the Power of the Holy Spirit*  https://www.amazon.com/Growing-Church-Power-Holy-Spirit/dp/B00320NLXI

[128]Intro to the conference offered in the UK and USA, http://growingthechurch.org/   Intro to the video course by Paul Stokes, https://www.prmi.org/coursesId/growing-your-church-in-the-power-of-the-holy-spirit/

of the Holy Spirit. Across the front of our sanctuary, about fifteen pastors came forward to repent publicly for quenching or resisting the Holy Spirit in their churches and in the denomination that many represented. There were tears of grief followed by incredible joy as together we received God's forgiveness and publicly welcomed the Holy Spirit's ministry in our lives and churches.

There were many stories of life and worldview change as a result of the way the Holy Spirit worked at EFW101. One pastor used what he had learned to preach a sermon series leading up to Pentecost. In response to requests, we established a webpage empoweredforwitness.org offering the course online.

The following year we offered **EFW 102** on the Gifts of the Holy Spirit focusing on 1 Cor. 12-14. The Holy Spirit poured out gifts on those in attendance, as we intentionally included activation exercises. Many experienced how His gifts are useful for building up the body and equipping for more effective witness to Jesus Christ. There was great joy in learning to cooperate with Him!

(For a complete description of the Empowered for Witness program which may be implemented in your own congregation go to their website: https://goldavenuechurch.org/empowered-for-witness/)

### The Gospel Tool Bible Study

Empowered for Witness 101 and 102 were used greatly by God to lead people into the empowering work of the Holy Spirit and then teach them how to cooperate with the Holy Spirit. However, there was more needed to truly sustain the flame. We had heard Jesus' command to "Go and make disciples!" After years of praying and studying discipleship methods and resources, we sensed God leading us to develop a new tool to help us comply with Jesus' command.

We wrote a 40-paragraph, peer-reviewed summary of the gospel of the kingdom, which some are calling a new catechism. Forty inductive style Bible study lessons were written, which intentionally focused on gospel literacy and deepening intimacy with the Lord through prayer and spiritual disciplines.

Small groups met for discussion, learning skills for sharing the gospel, and praying for one another and those who don't yet know Jesus. We preached sermons that went along with the weekly topic, and 85% of our congregation enthusiastically participated in The Gospel Tool Bible Study!

Our hope was to see each person:

- Mature as a beloved disciple—investing significant time establishing practices that would deepen their intimacy with the Lord.
- Understand the gospel of the kingdom—seeing how Jesus' life, death, and resurrection fits into the bigger picture of the Kingdom of God.
- Grow passion for making disciples—gaining skills and experience in sharing the gospel and then use these tools to help others begin and grow in their faith.

We had a celebration at the end of the forty weeks and heard exciting testimonies of people's joy, expectation, eagerness, and urgency about sharing the gospel. Campus pastors were using it with college students. Grandfathers were using portions of it for family gatherings. People had grown in their prayer lives. Others who had never been in a Bible study before were eager to go through it again and invite their friends. When churches who heard about it began to ask if it could be available for use in their congregations or small groups, the Lord led us to a wonderful Kingdom-minded printer who has helped make it available for purchase online. We believe God will continue using The Gospel Tool Bible Study for preparing the altar, inviting empowerment, and mobilizing evangelism as we pray for revival and spiritual awakening. For a complete description of the Gospel Tool and to order go to gospeltool.org.

[Brad] In summary, the Gospel Tool is a great way to grow new believers for preparing the altar, but then offering follow up to those who have been baptized with the Holy Spirit to continue to grow as followers of Jesus Christ. Also, the Empowered for Witness courses are a very important supplement to the basic disciplines that all Christians need for preparing for the baptism in the Holy Spirit, receiving this experience, and then continuing to grow in the dynamic of cooperation with the Holy Spirit. The result is that people are being equipped and receiving anointing for fulfilling the fivefold equipping ministry roles needed to sustain and grow the cycle of preparing the altar, igniting the fire, and sustaining the flame.

This is taking place at Gold Avenue CRC. This cycle is continuing because they are continuing to equip people to step into anointed roles in the fivefold equipping ministries needed to sustain this process over time. This can work and has been working in the local congregation for an extended season because the leadership of the congregation put in place these programs such as the Gospel Tool and the Empowered for Witness Courses which have been specifically developed to be embedded in the normal life of the local congregation. However, you will see in Gina's and Dave's descriptions, the programs that were developed were partly inspired by the events and teaching that came from the ministry of PRMI, which is an organization and a movement that transcends their local congregation. This points to a larger dynamic taking place beyond the local congregation. We shall show in the next chapter that while local congregations can and do enable this process to continue, the biblical model will be that they will be supported by another expression of the body of Christ—the special mission group.

## Pondering the Problem of Congregations Starting in the Spirit but Ending in the Flesh

As already mentioned regarding the St. Giles congregation, usually outpourings of the Holy Spirit have been followed by a season of effectively sustaining the equipping of the fivefold equipping anointings, which in turn can keep the three-fold cycle going. However, history shows that it is difficult to sustain the movement of the Holy

Spirit within congregations and denominations. The history of outpourings of the Holy Spirit and their long-term fruit is not very hopeful. How many began with a focus on Christ alone in the power of the Holy Spirit but then lost their center in Christ and the Bible as the word of God and ended in "power and might"?

For the most part, we see the constant repetition of what Paul found taking place with those who experienced the outpouring of the Holy Spirit and formed the church in Galatia.

> You foolish Galatians! Who has cast a spell on you? Before your eyes Jesus Christ was vividly portrayed as crucified! The only thing I want to learn from you is this: Did you receive the Spirit by doing the works of the law or by believing what you heard? Are you so foolish? Although you began with the Spirit, are you now trying to finish by human effort? Galatians 3:1-3

In congregation after congregation, we find that it is very difficult to sustain the full expression of all five of the equipping anointings to keep the cycle going for very long after the initial outpouring of the Holy Spirit has taken place. There are, no doubt, a multitude of reasons for this tendency. Without taking time to do a complete study of these reasons, we suggest a few.

### Spiritual Warfare, in which Satan Does Everything Possible to Block the Empowering Work of the Holy Spirit

Many congregations that have experienced a move of the Holy Spirit have then endured major spiritual warfare in many ways, blocking the work of the Holy Spirit. Satan has an entire arsenal of means to disrupt and destroy vital growing congregations. This should not surprise us as it was the experience of Jesus Himself. After receiving water baptism by John, in continuity with the Old Testament, the Holy Spirit fell upon him for empowerment to fulfill his mission. Then the text says, "The Spirit immediately drove him into the wilderness. He was in the wilderness forty days, enduring temptations from Satan. He was with wild animals, and angels were ministering to his needs" (Mark 1:12-13). This "being driven into the wilderness for testing by the Devil," has been the

325

experience of many after having received the baptism with the Holy Spirit. This is not just for individuals, but for those groups that have experienced a Pentecost event.

The first disciples experienced it with Ananias and Sapphira lying to the Holy Spirit, arguments over equally sharing provisions, and later in deadly persecution from the religious and government authorities. The reality of casualties during the times of wilderness testing is confirmed by our first parents Adam and Eve who failed their first time of being tested by Satan in the garden of Eden. Then when God led the Hebrews out of bondage in Egypt, many perished during the forty years of testing in the wilderness. Only a few of the original group were able to enter the promised Land.[129]

This testing in the wilderness is to be expected; it is a normal part of growing in empowered ministry. Sadly, many individual leaders, congregations, and even movements do not survive this ordeal. Those that do come through the refining fire are better prepared to be a part of God's kingdom plans.[130]

## Those with Apostolic Anointing to Ignite Fires and to Create Containers Are Often Called to Other Fields After a Season

It seems that it is especially difficult to have as part of the congregation or a denomination those with the apostolic anointing to fulfill Phase #2 Igniting the Fire. The main reason is that usually after those with apostolic anointing have completed their work of igniting the fire, putting in place the wineskins for sustaining the flame, and nurturing people into the dynamic of cooperation with the Holy Spirit, they are called out to establish other kingdom projects. We see this in the ministry of Paul.

---

[129] Num 14:32-33 But as for you, your dead bodies will fall in this wilderness, (33) and your children will wander in the wilderness forty years and suffer for your unfaithfulness, until your dead bodies lie finished in the wilderness.
[130] See my book, Zeb Bradford Long, *Passage Through the Wilderness* (Ada, MI: Chosen Books, 1998).

After they had proclaimed the good news in that city and made many disciples, they returned to Lystra, to Iconium, and to Antioch. They strengthened the souls of the disciples and encouraged them to continue in the faith, saying, "We must enter the Kingdom of God through many persecutions." When they had appointed elders for them in the various churches, with prayer and fasting they entrusted them to the protection of the Lord in whom they had believed. Act 14:21-23

Then the text says that Barnabas and Paul continued their evangelistic and church planting mission to other cities. Often when those with the apostolic and evangelistic anointing are called to move on to other fields, the roles needed to sustain the work of the congregation or to just hold the community together shift to those who are pastors and teachers. These by nature often are not fire starters through whom Jesus baptizes with the Holy Spirit the new disciples who are being brought in.

## The Nature of the Congregation Itself is Not Conducive to Sustaining the Fire Long Term on their Own.

I suspect that part of the problem is that in God's plans the local congregation was never intended to stand alone to keep the cycle going. This has already been hinted at by Gina's and Dave's testimony of the role played by PRMI's ministry connected with the development of programs and ministry in their congregation. While PRMI is an expression of the body of Christ, it is a ministry movement transcending the local congregation. We also see this inclusion of movements beyond the local congregation in the letter that Paul wrote to the Galatians. The local congregation, or more likely a group of congregations in the province of Galatia, were part of the whole body of Christ, which included a relationship with Paul's apostolic team. Paul, not bound to the local church, had the authority as well as freedom as an outside observer to help keep the local expressions of the body of Christ faithful to their biblical foundations and walking by the Holy Spirit.

The fivefold equipping anointings are essential for the church, but they are not the only thing that is needed to ignite Pentecost events, sustain moves of the Holy Spirit, and see movements of revival grow and expand to new geographic areas. Paul's missionary team, and the interactions with the local congregations provide us with a way to understand how God the Father has formed the body of Christ to embody His Kingdom on earth and to extend the gospel to all nations. We will find that through the full expression of the fivefold equipping anointings, the Holy Spirit has created not just one expression of the body of Christ but many which the Lord intends to be in dynamic relationship with one another. These expressions of the body of Christ together are the key to igniting and sustaining revivals that advance the gospel of the kingdom. It is to this topic that we turn in the next chapter.

# 19

# The Two Expressions: Modality and Sodality

To address the challenging issue of sustaining all the elements needed for a revival to grow and expand, we need to understand the nature of the Church that Jesus Christ has raised up to embody and extend the Kingdom of God. Often, we tend to think of the "church" in whatever form we came to accept Jesus as Lord and Savior and then were nurtured in the faith.

For me, this was first Presbyterian Church in Charlotte, North Carolina. There as a child I experienced the love and fellowship of my own family, but also the extended church family, and particularly with Miss Sally, my Sunday school teacher, all through elementary school. She loved me like my mother, even when I was naughty most of the time. Later, in Sunday worship services and special events, I would look up to the choir loft where my mother was part of the great choir accompanied by an ancient pipe organ. The huge, pre-civil war, gothic sanctuary echoed with the great hymns of the faith. I also heard many wonderful biblical sermons, at least when my little brother George and I had not escaped from the morning service to explore the maze-like nooks and passages of that old building. There was also the fellowship hour with hot donuts and pastries, where we were surrounded by old family friends as well as some of my mother's Bradford and McCauley relatives. One was the doctor who had been present when I was born. This was the place where I was baptized as an infant, confirmed when I was twelve years old, and then nurtured in the faith. To me, this local loving congregation filled with my extended family and family of faith was the Church.

But this local congregation is not the only expression of the body of Christ! Another model was experienced by my son-in-law, Josh Modrzynski. Rebecca met Josh while a student at Fuller Theological Seminary. When Rebecca first brought him home to introduce him to us, we had the talk where Josh asked if he could marry Rebecca. Laura and I were of course delighted to say, "Yes!" As part of these conversations with my future son-in-law, I asked him to tell me about his church experience where he met Jesus and grew in faith. His answer surprised me.

> "Well, I grew up Catholic. What do you expect with my Polish background? But that is not where I met Jesus Christ or grew in faith. I grew in faith through the Navigators while attending the University of Tennessee. This was a wonderful, close group of students who would meet to study the Bible. That is where I really met Jesus as real and accepted Him as my Lord and Savior. That is where I had great friends and was nurtured as a disciple of Jesus Christ. We were also committed to witnessing to other students, and to bringing them to faith in Jesus Christ and into our loving fellowship, centered around learning the Bible. So, for me, church was sitting around in the dorm room, having great discussions, reading the Bible, sharing our personal struggles, praying for each other, and witnessing to others. For me, this was Church!"

For Josh his experience of "the church" was a very different reality from what I experienced. Our different experiences of how we were nurtured in faith point to two different expressions of the body of Christ that we rudimentarily find in the book of Acts and the letters from Paul. First, we find local congregations, which is the equivalent to what I experienced growing up at First Presbyterian Church. For example,

> All who believed were together and held everything in common, and they began selling their property and possessions and distributing the proceeds to everyone, as anyone had need. Every day they continued to gather

330

together by common consent in the temple courts, breaking bread from house to house, sharing their food with glad and humble hearts, praising God and having the good will of all the people. And the Lord was adding to their number every day those who were being saved. Acts 2:44-47

When they arrived in Jerusalem, they were received by the church and the apostles and the elders, and they reported all the things God had done with them.  Acts 15:4

"To the church of God that is in Corinth," 1 Corinthians 1:2; 2 Corinthians 1:1, ESV

Second, we see another model represented by Paul as he traveled with a small team from place to place to preach the gospel to unbelievers and to strengthen newly established churches. This is equivalent to what Josh experienced with the Navigators, that special mission group who were doing evangelism and growing as disciples.

When they [Paul and Barnabas] had preached the gospel to that city [Derbe] and had made many disciples, they returned to Lystra and to Iconium and to Antioch, strengthening the souls of the disciples, encouraging them to continue in the faith, and saying that through many tribulations we must enter the Kingdom of God. And when they had appointed elders for them in every church, with prayer and fasting they committed them to the Lord in whom they had believed. Acts 14:21-23, ESV

Only Luke is with me. Get Mark and bring him with you, because he is a great help to me in ministry. 2 Tim 4:11

These two models, first the local stable fellowship and second, the mission team, have different qualities and characteristics, enabling them to have different functions to embody the Kingdom of God on earth.  They are essentially working together to fulfill the gospel

331

mission. We shall see later that together these two expressions are needed to prepare, to ignite, and to sustain revivals.

## Ralph Winter Introduces the Concepts of Modality and Sodality

Based on the biblical witness and the history of the expansion of Christianity, the late Presbyterian missiologist Ralph Winter identified two redemptive structures that form the body of Messiah and are essential to the fulfillment of its mission. These are, first, the local congregation or groups of congregations, which he identified as a "**modality**." The most common dictionary meaning of "modality" is: "*Modality* shares its root with the word *mode*, meaning "the way in which something happens or is experienced." …. In general, a modality is a particular way in which something exists." [131] Winter has filled this term with its own specific meaning for the redemptive structure within the body of Christ. He said that modality is a church with a hierarchy and vertical structure that has people of all ages and stages of life who are involved in the life of the church at many levels. Some people are very committed, while others due to life stages, beliefs, and choice are nominally involved." [132]

---

[131] https://www.vocabulary.com/dictionary/modality

[132] https://en.wikipedia.org/wiki/Sodality - This is a very good article written from the Roman Catholic perspective.

The second redemptive structure we see in the New Testament is the missionary band, (usually headed by Paul), which moved around from place to place. Winter named this structure a "**sodality**." The term comes from the Latin word sodalist which means "companion." A sodality is an organization of companions or friends.[133] Within the Roman Catholic tradition these have been highly developed in the orders. In contrast to modalities (local congregations), "sodalities on the other hand are much more narrowly focused. They are usually very task and relationally focused, where belonging to the community means deep and multiple commitments. It is almost impossible to be a nominal part of a sodality as they define themselves by high commitment levels."[134]

Both are the body of Messiah or the Church of Jesus Christ and together they enable the advancement of the gospel of Jesus Christ. Further, working together in dynamic tension, they will enable outpourings of the Holy Spirit to grow and to expand.

A biblical, historical, and missiological informed ecclesiology acknowledges that both sodalities and modalities are equally "church." They are part of the same body but with different functions and structures. Apostolic expressions of the body of Christ are just as legitimately "church" as the parish, diocese, or congregation. These two redemptive structures are mutually

---

[133] https://en.wikipedia.org/wiki/Sodality

[134] Ralph Winter--
https://frontiermissionfellowship.org/uploads/documents/two-structures.pdf

beneficial only if there is separation and tension between them. The sodality needs freedom to operate and to focus on its mission, while the modality needs to be able to focus on nurturing its community and meeting the diverse needs of its members.

The following is a summary of Dr. Winter's core concepts of modality and sodality, augmented with my own observations of how these two "redemptive structures" function in practice. This is based on his seminal article "The Two Structures of God's Redemptive Mission."[135]

---

[135] Ralph D. Winter, "The Two Structures of God's Redemptive Mission" 1973. https://frontiermissionfellowship.org/uploads/documents/two-structures.pdf

| MODALITY | SODALITY |
|---|---|
| Congregational redemptive structures to fit people of all ages and seasons of life | Committed companions highly focused on a specific mission |
| Modalities are complex, structured, and diverse fellowships (old and young, rich and poor, with different levels of commitment). | Sodalities are second-decision communities. They often sit alongside or within modalities but require a much deeper level of relational commitment to the group. |
| The modality of the local congregation is essentially a first-decision structure which includes people who have accepted Jesus Christ as Lord and Savior. In our Reformed and Presbyterian view, modalities also include "children of the covenant," that is, the children of believers. | A sodality is a structured fellowship in which membership requires a second decision beyond modality membership and is limited by either age, sex, marital status, and/or calling and commitment to a shared Kingdom-focused vision. |
| Terms like denomination, local congregation, parish, or diocese all refer to forms of modalities. Modal communities are relatively stable and make low demands on their members. | Examples of sodalities include missionary organizations, men's / women's / student groups within local churches and across entire denominations, monastic orders, and house church groups. Church planters tend to start off as a sodality (a highly focused and committed team) that eventually grows into a modality. |

The modality of the body of Messiah requires an organization that nurtures all this diversity of different levels of commitment and spiritual growth and enables people to enter the life of the Church through many ways. The great thing about the modality of the local congregation is that they provide the context for nurturing and growing disciples of Jesus Christ within the context of daily life.

Modalities may also last a long time: they become institutionalized. There is a tendency for denominations (such as the United Methodist Church, the Episcopal Church, and the Presbyterian Church in the United States), to lose their biblical grounding and centeredness in Jesus Christ and fall into apostasy. Then they are no longer in the service of God's Kingdom.

The life span and life cycle of a sodality is typically longer than a modality because the sodality can enforce discipline. People can be "fired" from a sodality for not doing their job. That is a standard that the church in its local form rarely attempts. Catholic orders such as the Benedictines, have lasted over 1500 years. In the Protestant stream, different mission agencies like China Inland Mission or special mission groups like PRMI which was founded in 1966 have lasted because they have remained faithful to their founding vision.

| | |
|---|---|
| The default mode of modalities is to look inwards towards maintenance. | The default mode of sodalities is outward and missional. |
| It is easy to criticize modalities for this introversion and the accompanying appearance (or reality) of compromise, but it is because of this emphasis that they tend to be inclusive, family-friendly, and safe. | As a result, sodalities are often exciting, envisioned, and have a deep sense of community. However, they must always beware of the tendency towards exclusivity, a sense of superiority, and an unhealthy work-ethic which can cripple any visionary group. |
| Modalities are sustained by those with the anointing of pastors and teachers. They also benefit greatly from including within their midst the role of the prophet who calls the modality to faithfulness to the Word of God and to God's vision. | Solidities are generally formed around the ministries of those with an apostolic or evangelistic anointing. Embedded within them are people with a prophetic anointing which keeps them on track with the Word of God and God's vision for their work and mission. Sodalities need to have organization that give them shape but allow the flexibility to respond to the guidance of the Holy Spirit. |
| Practically speaking, some modalities like the Roman Catholic Church have been able to include the sodalities of religious orders. | Sodalities are identified as apostolic movements because they are essential in establishing congregations and ministries that advance the kingdom of God. |

| | |
|---|---|
| | Practically speaking, for sodalities to survive they must have within them certain modality functions such as administration and organization. |
| In order to remain vital, the modality of the local congregation / denomination must welcome sodalities through which the Holy Spirit can bring renewal and the means of expressing missions. | Further, to keep them from simply becoming cults or sects, sodalities must be connected to the modality structures of the body of Christ. |

## Modality and Sodality in Creative Tension Enable the Body of Christ to Advance the Gospel

This cooperative tension between the two is well illustrated in the relationship between the missionary bands of Paul and the congregations that they founded. This relationship is seen in the following ways: Paul, by expressing the gift of evangelism, gathered born-again people into a fellowship. He served in the apostolic role of praying for them to be baptized with the Holy Spirit but also of shaping their life together and establishing the leadership structure. The relationship between the church and Paul and the missionary band was one of love, but Paul was not part of the congregation.

Paul continued to nurture the faith of the congregations and especially to mentor some of their leaders through letters and through occasional visits. By these means Paul sustained his relationship with the congregations and provided teaching and correction.

The local congregation, "the modality," and Paul and his missionary team, "the sodality," were connected through mutual prayer support.

Paul was praying for the churches and the members. Paul asked for and received prayer support from the congregations.

While the sodality of Paul's mission team seemed to have had its own means for support (Paul was a tentmaker) there were times when the congregation did provide financial support. The Holy Spirit sent out Paul and Barnabas on their mission to Cyprus, but He did this *through* the church in Antioch. The mission teams were sent out from the congregations.

> Now there were these prophets and teachers in the church at Antioch: Barnabas, Simeon called Niger, Lucius the Cyrenian, Manaen (a close friend of Herod the tetrarch from childhood) and Saul. While they were serving the Lord and fasting, the Holy Spirit said, "Set apart for me Barnabas and Saul for the work to which I have called them." Then, after they had fasted and prayed and placed their hands on them, they sent them off.  So Barnabas and Saul, sent out by the Holy Spirit, went down to Seleucia, and from there they sailed to Cyprus. Acts 13:1-4

These verses demonstrate how the Holy Spirit was working through both the sodality of the mission team and the modality of the church at Antioch to advance the gospel. From this we may make the following generalizations about how the sodality interfaces with the modality.

### Summary of How Sodalities and Modalities Interface

- Sodalities are primarily task-oriented and focus on a shared sense of mission, often narrowly defined. They often help modalities be healthy and create new modalities.

- Sodalities frequently multiply modalities as well as sodalities.

- While sodalities can form within denominations in the Protestant movement, they are frequently transdenominational. In the Catholic Church sodalities have been welcomed within the church as religious orders.

- The impetus for renewal and spiritual vitality most commonly flows from sodalities into the modalities.[136]

It is our contention that the fivefold equipping anointings, as well as the patterns essential to prepare for igniting, sustaining, and extending revival movements, take place through the dynamic interface between these two redemptive structures. This requires that both structures are healthy, both are submitted to the Lordship of Jesus Christ, and both are empowered by the Holy Spirit. This at least is the ideal that has been revealed in the book of Acts and confirmed through the historical advance of the gospel.

A well-known contemporary example of the positive cooperation between local congregations and a mission society are the Billy Graham crusades conducted by the Billy Graham Association. Local pastors and their churches of various denominations participate in the crusades as counsellors and altar workers, providing a link for new converts into a modality for discipleship, while the Billy Graham Association, a sodality, provides the dynamic of global vision and evangelistic outreach.

In our own Presbyterian and Reformed stream, this partnership is confirmed. The great R.A. Torrey evangelistic missions igniting revivals worldwide were conducted by Torrey and his team—a

---

[136]This excellent summary is from the web page (this page seems to no longer be functional) - http://www.undertheiceberg.com/2006/06/03/characteristics-of-apostolic-structures-an-overview/ .

sodality working together with many different modality expressions of the Church in the form of congregations.

The great expansion of missions through the Presbyterian churches in America can trace their beginnings to 1837 with the establishment of the Board of Foreign Missions. The purpose was "Spreading the gospel through the heathen and anti-Christian world." The British Christians were way ahead of the American churches in advancing the gospel through independent mission societies. The London Missionary Society was founded in 1795 with the purpose of proclaiming, "the glorious gospel of the blessed God."[137] In 1865 Hudson Taylor founded the China Inland Mission with the purpose of taking the gospel of Jesus Christ to the rest of unreached China. These mission agencies functioned as independent sodalities but were connected to the various modalities of congregations and denominations which provided prayer, financial support, and recruitment of workers for the mission field. By being sodalities, these missionary societies were truly "second decision" groups, often run by those on fire with the vision for missions. These missional sodalities in the sending countries were managed by the missionaries themselves and those who had returned from the field. For the modalities of the denominations and congregations, these missional sodalities provided a way to express Jesus' mandate to take the gospel to the ends of the Earth. The result of this symbiotic relationship was both the vast extension of the gospel as well as spiritual vitality for those modalities that were participating in this great work.

When Laura and I were first called as short-term missionaries to Korea in 1976-77 and later to Taiwan in 1980, we were sent by the Presbyterian Church in the United States PC(USA). In Korea and Taiwan, we were known as the Southern Presbyterian Church. The mission board still had the flavor of and functioned as it had as an independent but connected missionary society. Most everyone on the PC(USA) Mission Board in the 1970s when we were sent out had been on the mission field themselves, and now had returned

---

[137]https://www.britannica.com/topic/London-Missionary-Society

to help others. Our mission board as well as the United Presbyterian Church's mission board, with their founding roots before the American Civil War, still had the focus of advancing the gospel of Jesus Christ, which, with our biblical, Reformed kingdom framework, included all dimensions of reality. So, in addition to doing evangelism and founding congregations, we also started schools, colleges, universities, and hospitals as well as implementing biblical justice by liberating those living under oppression. This took place in multiple locations around the world. Our Presbyterian form of government was introduced wherever these missionaries established congregations and institutions. They provided a model of how a democratic representative form of government can function to give everyone voice and constrain the human tendency toward tyranny, thus having transformative impact far beyond the church.

I participated in this great missionary enterprise in Korea, Taiwan, China, the Middle East, Africa, Latin America, and Brazil. All this, I believe, was the fruit of a focus on fulfilling the Great Commission in the power of the Holy Spirit, which brings people to be born-again into the Kingdom of God, which in turn transforms society. This focus was sustained for many decades, even during the massive disruptions of war, revolutions, changing geopolitical circumstances, and the encroachment of non-biblical ideologies like liberalism, largely because of the dynamic tension between the sodalities of the missionary sending societies and the modalities of local congregations and denominations. These missional sodalities were able to keep their focus on Jesus Christ even when the modality structures lost their way.

The sodality/modality tension is God's way of curing the perennial tendency for the body of Christ to fall into "power and might" and instead, to continue to work, "by My Spirit." Whenever this dynamic relationship was lost, usually through the modality structures (which were being captivated by liberalism) absorbing the sodality missional structures, so too was lost the dynamic of vital Holy Spirit-led and empowered, Jesus Christ-centered, biblical faith which upheld the driving vision and devotion needed to fulfill the Great Commission.[138]

The following chart describes this relationship.

## The Body of Christ Consists of Two Interconnected Redemptive Structures

**Modality**

Local Congregations and Denominations

Established by those with Apostolic & Evangelistic Gifts and Anointings

Nurtured by the Pastoral, Teaching, Prophetic Gifts and Anointings

Eph. 4:11-12

Working together in dynamic tension, both will enable outpourings of the Holy Spirit to grow, expand and advance the Kingdom of God

**Sodality**

Special Missions Groups

Birthed by those with Apostolic, Prophetic & Evangelistic Anointing

Eph. 4:11-12

This is a mutually beneficial relationship, but the benefits are lost if the following take place:

They become so distant that they no longer have a relationship. This has often taken place when the apostolic mission group no longer has a relationship with the modalities of the local

---

[138] I experienced firsthand this absorption of the missionary work as a vital sodality in the denominational structure of the Presbyterian Church in the USA. This corresponded with the liberal takeover of denominational leadership which was accelerated by the denomination's exclusion from its leadership structures of evangelical and charismatic-based sodalities of the Presbyterian Lay Committee, Presbyterian Pro Life, and Presbyterian Reformed Ministries International. I tell the story of this bitter history of PRMI at first being welcomed and then excluded in Chapter 20. It is beyond the scope and purpose of this book to provide the historical confirmations of these statements, but they are written in the tragic demise of the once great "mainline" denominations as well as in the corresponding loss of their involvement in advancing Jesus' gospel of the kingdom in their own neighborhoods and the world.

congregations or the denomination. When this happens, the sodality usually just becomes a modality or drifts off into becoming a sect or cult promoting unbiblical doctrines.

The modalities, like a local congregation, a denomination, or a megachurch become completely self-centered and insular. They no longer welcome a connection beyond themselves with the viable missional sodalities.

PRMI as a sodality has often faced the attempt of the modality of a larger church or a denomination to exert control over the mission group and absorb it into itself, or, in order to have a "place at the table," the missional sodality must give up its distinct mission focus and become constrained by the modality.

In any of these cases the mutually beneficial dynamic that we see in the biblical example of Paul's missionary band and the congregations is lost.

## The Key to Sustaining Revivals: Sodality and Modality Together

The key to the constant equipping and deployment of people for sustaining the repeatable cycle of preparing the altar, igniting the fire, and sustaining the flame is the two redemptive structures of modality and sodality in dynamic relationship and tension together. This is not the place to go into the rich history of vital Christian faith and Holy Spirit revival being sustained by the dynamic between modalities and sodalities, but it is most helpful to give some recent well-known examples:

- Samaritans Purse, led by Franklin Graham,[139] is a sodality that has focused on proclaiming the gospel through disaster relief. They have provided the context for thousands of congregations, as well as denominations, to express compassion through practical help for those in need.

- Alpha International[140] is the sodality that offers the Alpha course, a means of evangelistic outreach and an introduction to the person and work of the Holy Spirit. This program, which grew out of the Anglican congregation of Holy Trinity Brompton in England has helped to ignite and sustain vital Christian faith in thousands of congregations worldwide. Alpha is an effective evangelistic tool for bringing people into being born-again into the Kingdom of God. This movement has spread from the Anglican world into many other streams.

We could name many more missional sodalities that have effective, dynamic relationships with modalities of local congregations and denominations. Here we want to explore more deeply the one sodality that we are most familiar with: Presbyterian-Reformed Ministries International. This is the topic of the next chapter as we review how PRMI, a sodality, has connected with local congregations and denominations to sustain outpourings of the Holy Spirit.

---

[139] https://www.samaritanspurse.org/

[140] https://alpha.org/

# 20

# PRMI Sodality Ignites and Sustains Revival

Presbyterian Reformed Ministries International (PRMI), a sodality, was founded in 1966 as Presbyterian Charismatic Communion and has the distinctive purpose and focus of bringing Christians into the empowering work of the Holy Spirit as promised by Jesus in Acts 1:4-8, so that the Church may be empowered to do all that Christ commands, to the glory of God the Father.

Through PRMI Jesus has brought many thousands of church leaders and lay people into the empowering work of the Holy Spirit Jesus promised in Acts 1:4-8 so that they would be Jesus' witnesses. As this has happened, the Lord has used us to ignite and sustain the movement of the Holy Spirit within congregations and even denominations.

PRMI has been able to embody and extend this movement of the Holy Spirit by staying focused on our core mission which means first creating the contexts for God the Father to continue to fulfill Acts 1:4-8, and then, when the Pentecost events take place, offering them the equipping needed to continue learning to cooperate with the Holy Spirit.

### How has PRMI been Able to Keep the Three Phases Going?

There are some key factors that may be distilled from our founding in 1966 until the present that have been critical for God using this ministry to continue to ignite and to sustain outpourings of the Holy Spirit. Here I want to get to the essence of what it is that has kept this dynamic of the three phases going within the sodality of PRMI. The

347

reality is that if PRMI had not been able to sustain this constant cycle, or if we had ceased to be a vision-driven missional sodality, we would not have been able to have impact upon these modalities.[141]

Since 1991 the primary program expression that has enabled PRMI to combine the four patterns of igniting outpourings of the Holy Spirit and to develop them into a sustainable expanding cycle has been the Dunamis Project. Dunamis is the Greek word for "power" and comes from Acts 1:8, "But you will **receive power** when the Holy Spirit has come upon you, and you will be my witnesses in Jerusalem, and in all Judea and Samaria, and to the farthest parts of the earth." I have already described how the Dunamis Project was launched in 1991 with the outpouring of the Holy Spirit that took place at Silver Bay in Lake George, New York, in which Archer Torrey, Doug McMurry and I served on the teaching team. This initial five-day teaching event was attended by about 140 people and ignited a movement of the Holy Spirit. We continued to follow up with a series of other equipping events in the same set-apart location. The other five-day equipping events are built on the teaching on the Holy Spirit in the Gateways event. The entire series became as follows:[142]

**Unit #1 Gateways to Empowered Ministry** – Provides the basic biblical teaching on the person and work of the Holy Spirit, with a focus on Acts 1:4-8 and leads participants to pray for and receive the baptism with the Holy Spirit.

**Unit #2 In the Spirit's Power** – Introduces the dynamic of cooperation with the Holy Spirit in doing the ministry of Jesus and includes teaching on spiritual gifts as the way that Jesus Christ will

---

[141]The challenge in doing this is to keep from getting lost in the weeds of the details of the different program expressions that we have been called to. You can see that from our web pages and other documents. See also the appendix for our various program expressions.

[142] For more details on topics covered and how to register see the PRMI web page. https://www.prmi.org/program-descriptions/the-dunamis-project/

work through us in prophetic, priestly, and kingly roles, growing the Church and extending the Kingdom of God.

**Unit # 3 The Power of Prayer** – The first way we cooperate with the Holy Spirit is through prayer, through which we receive guidance. Our praying, "Thy Kingdom come, thy will be done on earth as it is in heaven" calls us into the work of intercessory prayer through which we may shape history according to God's kingdom plans.

**Unit #4 The Healing Ministry of Jesus Christ** – We address all six of Jesus' healing works starting with spiritual healing and including inner and physical healing and corporate healing of the nations. We do not present a method or a technique but the dynamics of cooperation with the Holy Spirit in Jesus' healing ministry. Jesus is the healer!

**Unit #5 Spiritual Warfare for Kingdom Advancement** – As we take part with Jesus Christ in all His work, we will find that we meet with demonic opposition. In Unit #5 we deal with the nature of personal spiritual attacks. We learn the basics of discerning the presence of evil spirits, and the steps in the process of deliverance ministry. We introduce the basics of strategic level spiritual warfare.

**Unit #6 Listening Evangelism** – Here we focus on missions and evangelism in the Power of the Holy Spirit. Unit #6 pulls all the teaching of the Dunamis Project together for the purpose that the Holy Spirit has been sent, which is witnessing to Jesus Christ. The term "listening evangelism" comes from the basic teaching of the entire Dunamis Project. As we listen to the Holy Spirit and to the person we are addressing, we will receive guidance about how we are called to cooperate in the work of Jesus Christ to share the gospel.

Each of these units is accompanied by a several hundred-page manual of systematic Bible teaching from a Reformed theological perspective illustrated with practical experience. Each event is led by a team of anointed leaders who provide systematic teaching leading into practical lab times where people experience first-hand the work of Holy Spirit. Each event is wrapped in prayer and worship. At each event there are Gateways Makeup sessions in which all newcomers are provided the foundational teaching they missed by entering the series after the initial event. At each event there is an opportunity for people to reaffirm their faith and commitment to Jesus Christ. Always the opportunity is presented for people to pray for and receive the baptism with the Holy Spirit. The series of six events generally takes place in a set-apart retreat or conference setting. Usually there is a six-month gap between each unit, and each occurs in the same location.

The three phases of the meta pattern are always embedded into each five-day equipping event. What is more, the two Goforth foundations of Jesus as King and the Bible as the Word of God are included, as well as the three R.A. Torrey keys, namely, evangelism, baptism with the Holy Spirit, and the work of prayer. To make these relationships explicit, each Dunamis equipping event may be organized around each of the phases.

**Phase #1 Preparing the Altar**—The context of teaching, sharing meals together, worship, praying together, and building fellowship are all part of Phase #1, Preparing the Altar. An important part of this is the biblical and practical teaching on the Holy Spirit and His ministries, in which participants gain a rational understanding of what the Bible teaches on these topics. As part of this preparation, there is always the call to repentance of sin and the opportunity to make a recommitment to Jesus Christ as Lord and Savior. At nearly every event there is much healing prayer ministry, during which past hurts and other blocks to following Jesus may be healed and removed. The entire preparation for the event is covered in intercessory prayer and at the event itself there is always a team of intercessors.

**Phase #2 Igniting the Fire**—This takes place by giving the invitation for people to pray for and receive the baptism or infilling with the Holy Spirit. This opportunity is offered at every event by those on the team with the apostolic anointing of cooperation with Jesus Christ, who is the one who baptizes or fills us with the Holy Spirit.

This usually takes place on the final night of the equipping event, but may take place any time after the people have been prepared.

**Phase #3 Sustaining the Flame**—This takes place at the event and in the events that follow through continued teaching on how to cooperate with the Holy Spirit. There are also resources available for continued study as well as materials and models of how to cooperate with the Holy Spirit. Just as important for follow up and sustaining the flame is the wonderful fellowship that develops between the participants.

When we first launched the Dunamis Project we were not aware of these three phases, but in retrospect I realized that the Holy Spirit led us not only to structure the equipping events around the phases, but also to include the Goforth foundations and the R.A. Torrey keys as well as the five equipping anointings. By making these dynamics explicit we may be more intentional in cooperating with the Holy Spirit to create the contexts where God the Father continues to fulfill Acts 1:4-8. Also, when the underlying dynamics are made explicit, as we have done throughout this book, they may be more effectively transferred to others and adapted for implementation in different contexts.

The fruit of this process since 1991 has been multiple series of the Dunamis equipping events conducted in many locations around the world with thousands of people having experienced the baptism with the Holy Spirit and growing in cooperation with him. At nearly every Dunamis equipping event the three phases have been implemented, with Pentecost events taking place in which all five markers have been present. When these Pentecost events take place within the context of ongoing teaching and practices, they produce a cascading effect in which more and more people are brought into the movement with more and more influence on local congregations and networks of congregations. When this same dynamic of the three phases has been put in place at other PRMI set-apart events, such as Growing the Church in the Power of the Holy Spirit, and more recently, the events at the Community of the

351

Cross for preparing for the next great awakening, we see the Holy Spirit equipping and empowering people to serve Jesus with greater effectiveness. The result is that not only has PRMI grown to ignite and sustain movements of the Holy Spirit in many diverse locations and cultures worldwide, but there has been a vast multiplication of ministry through the thousands of people who have gone out as empowered witnesses to Jesus Christ.

Each event has its own story of how this cycle has been sustained, how the outpouring took place, and how those involved have been empowered to take part in their local churches and in other mission groups. Let me provide one vivid example which took place at our first track in the United Kingdom. This may serve as a typical example of what has happened at nearly every Dunamis track that has taken place worldwide which has maintained this cycle.

## The Outpouring of the Holy Spirit at the First Dunamis Track in the UK at High Wickham

The first series of Dunamis events in the United Kingdom took place at a conference center in the town of High Wickham in 2000-2003. The first introductory unit, Gateways to Empowered Ministry, was attended by about forty people, mostly from a few United Reformed Congregations. The preparatory work for this had included some prayer events at the City Temple Church in London, and by Elder James Gray bringing over to the United States a few key people to introduce them to PRMI and to the Dunamis teaching. James had been baptized with the Holy Spirit in his congregation in Durban, South Africa, which had been touched by the charismatic renewal through listening to teaching tapes from PRMI (then called Presbyterian Charismatic Communion).

In this first five-day Dunamis event we taught the Old and New Testament foundations for Jesus' promises of the baptism with the Holy Spirit. While we had a supportive team from the United Reformed Church congregation of City Temple in London and wonderful worship led by Karen and Rob Woods, we had to bring in all the teachers and prayer ministers from the United States. Rob and Karen Woods had been a part of PRMI as worship leaders and teachers in the United States but had accepted a call to pastor City Temple. Frankly, the fact that we had forty people sign up for this high-commitment, five-day event must be attributed to the work of James Gray, who was its tireless salesmen and advocate. In addition, we had the expense of bringing teachers from the USA.

This first event was very quiet. I did most of the teaching. It was well received, but the participants, especially the pastors, had many theological and biblical questions. There were two key issues they were wrestling with. First was the idea that Jesus Christ, while being 100% God and 100% man, had conducted his miracles not out of His divine nature but out of his human nature empowered by the Holy Spirit. The second big issue was that of overcoming the Pentecostal framework of the baptism with the Holy Spirit, namely, the holiness Pentecostal teaching that one had to have what was called a second grace experience of entire sanctification before qualifying for the baptism with the Holy Spirit. Further there was the traditional Pentecostal teaching that the initial physical evidence that one had received the baptism with the Holy Spirit was speaking in tongues.

We spent a lot of time on the biblical teaching. When it came time to pray for the baptism with the Holy Spirit, I first walked them through R.A. Torrey's steps to receive the Holy Spirit, feeling that it would be better hearing this from his perspective instead of my own. They were very receptive, especially when I shared that this is what Torrey had taught in his 1903 and 1904 trips to England when he had packed out Royal Albert Hall in London and had contributed to igniting the great Welsh Revival. Then, the other Americans and I laid hands on each of them. It was a very quiet Pentecost event and very appropriate to the audience. As far as I could see, except for joy and peace, there were almost no manifestations. I told everyone that this did not depend upon them having any type of emotional experience but that they were to just receive in faith. I alerted them to expect opportunities for stepping out in obedience later, because that is when they would actually experience the empowering and gifts of the Holy Spirit. What was significant about this first event was building the trust, love, and fellowship between those of us coming from the United States and those gathered from the UK.

Six months later we returned to the same location to offer the next event, Unit #2, In the Spirit's Power, which focuses on how to cooperate with the Holy Spirit and His gifts. The Rev. Larry Selig joined me in teaching on the gifts. He fit the British milieu perfectly, being very reserved but with a deep, loving faith as well as being personal and systematic in his teaching style. Also, he did not have a Southern accent like I did, which I think helped. Larry was a successful associate pastor in a large Presbyterian congregation in Pittsburg.

Almost everyone who had been at the first Dunamis event returned for this second event. They had indeed experienced the empowering work of the Holy Spirit in their places of work and ministry. Further they had brought their friends and members of their congregations, so our numbers nearly doubled. We again provided systematic teaching on the dynamic of cooperating with the Holy Spirit, including receiving guidance, discernment, and spiritual gifts. All of this was somewhat abstract and intellectual until Larry Selig taught on the healing gifts of the Holy Spirit. He then was led by the Holy Spirit to offer a practice time of praying for all those who needed physical healing. The room was filled with the wonderful manifest presence of Jesus Christ, marked especially by love and peace. It did seem that Jesus was doing some quiet, physical healing work.

All this was very quiet and in order when suddenly a pastor's wife, while being prayed for regarding some physical issue, started to manifest evil spirits.[143] Larry was immediately concerned that this would get disruptive and so I took her out to the next room for continued ministry with several of the other American team. I instructed the ladies who had accompanied me to pray that the Lord would reveal the reason why the evil spirits had gotten attached. I suggested to her that she may need to go through a time of confession and to take the risk of naming her sins to the other ladies. I pointed out the Word of God, "Confess your sins to one another and pray for one another so that you may be healed. The prayer of a righteous person has great effectiveness," (James 5:16). I left them to have some confidential space for this deep personal work to take place. I went back to the group where Larry was continuing to lead in very quiet but deep, love-filled, healing prayer ministry.

There were now groups all over the room quietly praying for one another and asking the Lord for the gifts needed. This was lab time in which the participants were moving from the academic knowledge of the gifts to the personal knowledge that comes from firsthand experience. Suddenly this quiet ministry was interrupted by loud shrieks coming from the other room. One of the ladies leading the prayer with this pastor's wife came rushing out asking for help. I handed off the authority over the whole room to Larry and went back to help. She was obviously manifesting a powerful demonic spirit. I commanded the evil spirits in the name of Jesus to stop manifesting. As they quieted down, I was praying for guidance. I knew we needed more prayer support and that we should take her to another location so it would not disrupt the ministry in the meeting room.

---

[143] I have withheld her name for several reasons. One reason is to protect her, but the other reason is that this report while factual in the details in the context of the UK Dunamis equipping event, has in broad outlines taken place at many Dunamis events in diverse places. So, this is a composite of several actual events when the Holy Spirit manifested the power, presence, and authority of Jesus Christ. Therefore, this "pastor's wife" could be "Everyman" or "Everywoman" who has provided a public manifestation of the reality of the working of the Holy Spirit, which then builds the faith and expectation for Jesus to continue working in signs and wonders.

Suddenly I receive the frankly uncomfortable and unexpected guidance from the Holy Spirit that this was a kairos moment of opportunity and the Lord wanted to show forth His glory, power, and presence. I was to invite the entire group into the deliverance ministry and their role was to back us up with prayer. I was very concerned about protecting this person from any embarrassment. I shared with her the guidance and asked her permission. She said "Ok, let's just get this over with." I went back to the group, who looked startled and anxious and told Larry about this guidance. He reluctantly agreed. Further there was no other place to go for the ministry without disrupting the other groups who were at the conference center.

As this pastor's wife walked in, suddenly the evil spirits manifested again. We were in battle for about an hour. The Lord had told me to forbid the demons from hurting her or anyone in the room, but to show themselves in such a way that everyone could see that there really were evil spirits present and that they really were under the authority of Jesus Christ. The whole group was engaged in urgent prayer. I found out later that for some this was when they moved into actually experiencing the gift of praying in tongues, receiving words of prophecy, and also gifts of discernment to know the names of the demons. As I, in the name and authority of Jesus Christ, commanded the demons to separate from her body and personality, which they did, she manifested some behavior that very clearly was not her. She ended up retching on the floor as I commanded the evil spirits out.

When the evil spirits left, everyone in the room could see the Holy Spirit manifesting His love and presence with joyful tears, not just of the pastor's wife but of the ministry team too. For some this was the first time that they had ever been in deliverance ministry, and they went out to spend time processing what they had just witnessed. The pastor's wife came back with her luxuriant black hair combed; she was radiantly beautiful and exuding a heavenly joy, but looking around the room I could see that there were also many questions in people's minds. Some people looked disturbed by the outbreak of the supernatural in their midst. Others had themselves experienced Jesus at work in ways new to them.

356

It is our practice at PRMI events to pause the teaching, prayer, or worship after periods of ministry, or when there is a clear manifestation of the Holy Spirit or of evil spirits. We then move into a time of debriefing.[144] Larry and I led this debriefing session in which we addressed all the questions that people had. We gave this lovely pastor's wife a chance to share from her 'inside' experience what we had only seen from the outside. While keeping confidential the exact reasons why the evil spirits had gotten in, she shared some of the inner struggles and the experience of the demons separating from her own personality in the presence of Jesus Christ. She then gave a glorious testimony of how Jesus had worked to set her free and the experience of the evil spirits leaving her. Further the team shared what they had experienced. As we went through this process, it turned out that many other people who had been a part of the healing prayer exercise had also themselves experienced Jesus' healing work.

Larry and I debriefed with the group for several hours. We shared our experiences and insights, and helped everyone to discern what manifestations were authentic from the Holy Spirit and what may have simply been human emotional reactions or expressions of evil spirits. This was a profound learning experience for everyone, and we all gained a much deeper understanding of how the Holy Spirit works among us. We were also able to dispel some misconceptions about the experience, such as the idea that it was simply an out-of-control emotional experience or the result of manipulation.

This obvious manifestation of the presence of demons and of Jesus overcoming evil, had given almost all the participants, including the ministry team, a firsthand experience of the reality of the Holy Spirit's work. It had expanded our Western materialistic worldview to include biblical paradigms and spiritual realities, revealing how God is at work in the world. When it came time to pray for the baptism with the Holy Spirit and a fresh

---

[144] We have followed the model of the US Army and called these analytical review sessions, "After Action Reviews" or AARs.

infilling for those who had already had this initiatory experience, the Holy Spirit fell upon the group. Once again, it was all decent and in order, but there were many clear manifestations of the Holy Spirit's power and gifts.

This event contributed greatly to igniting the movement of the Holy Spirit in the United Kingdom, which led to the Dunamis Project being offered in other locations. There is now a branch of the PRMI Dunamis Fellowship called the Dunamis Fellowship in Britain & Ireland (DFB&I).[145] They continue to keep the cycle going by constantly equipping their own leaders and offering new venues for the outpourings of the Holy Spirit. They have had a major impact on a number of local congregations in the UK, and further have taken part in extending the Dunamis equipping process in Africa and Europe.

While this account may seem somewhat dramatic, it is typical of most Dunamis Project series, no matter where in the world they take place or in what cultural setting they have been conducted. At some point in the series of six, and often at each equipping event, clear manifestations of the reality of the Kingdom of God like what was demonstrated by Philip in Acts 8 with conversions, healing, and deliverance take place. This then gives the context for biblical teaching and builds the faith to pray for and experience the baptism and infilling with the Holy Spirit. Acts 1:4-8 is fulfilled again and again in these Pentecost events. When the five markers are in place, the Holy Spirit moves! These moves have continued within the expressions of PRMI, the sodality, but now, through the people who take both the fire and the teaching with them, these moves are spread to their local congregations, the modalities, and to other sodalities such as special mission groups.

---

[145] https://www.dunamis.org.uk/

# How Have the Dunamis Project Events Been Sustained Over the Decades?

I hope that by providing you with this overview of the Dunamis Project, you have a better understanding of how it works, but also that you are wondering how we have been able to keep this cycle of three phases going for decades.

It requires a highly committed fellowship of people through whom Jesus Christ can express not only the five vocational anointings (apostles, prophets, evangelists, teachers, and pastors), but all the other gifts of the Holy Spirit as well. The greatest challenge we have faced is the constant repetition of Phase #2, where people are baptized in the Holy Spirit and then grow as Jesus' co-workers to sustain the cycle so that revival continues and spreads. The answer to this question lies in the constant implementation of ingredients needed to sustain this three-phase cycle, which are anchored by the two Goforth foundations and the three R.A. Torrey keys.

These ingredients are as follows:

## The Ongoing Work of Intercessory Prayer

As constantly noted, the secret of all outpourings of the Holy Spirit is the work of prayer. Jesus tells his first disciples, and I believe commands us as well, to pray, "... Thy Kingdom come, thy will be done on earth as it is in heaven..." He also commands us to pray, "Ask the Lord of the harvest to send laborers into the fields which are white unto harvest." Jesus tells us to ask Him for the empowering of the Holy Spirit and, from the example of the disciples, we may pray for the Lord to work in signs and wonders and that we would be able to proclaim the gospel with boldness. This is prayer which invites the Holy Spirit to move, and which is also asking for guidance and direction for how the Lord is calling us to take part in His work. It is also essential to pray constantly for the provision of people and finances, and for open doors of opportunity. In addition, we pray for the Kingdom of God to overcome Satan's empire of evil which holds people in bondage.

359

As a ministry we have focused on this work of prayer as well as offering equipping in prayer. Over the years this has been a constant feature in our work and the main reason why God has been able to keep us on track.

## The Constant Equipping of Anointed Leaders Who Can Embody the Culture of the Movement and Keep the Programs Going

For decades, we have been constantly working to vet, equip, and deploy anointed leaders with the different anointings and giftings needed to continue to create the venues for God the Father to fulfill Acts 1:4-8. This essentially requires that they are stepping into anointings that include the manifestational gifts listed in 1 Corinthians 12, the functional gifts listed in Romans 12, and the vocational gifts—or the fivefold equipping anointings—listed in Ephesians 4. The Dunamis Project described above is essentially an equipping process which is available to all whom the Lord is calling into this stream of revival. However, a more intensive equipping process is required in order to have the equipped and anointed people through whom Jesus does the work of intercessory prayer, as well as all the other roles needed to create the context for fulfilling Acts 1:4-8. In this ministry of PRMI we have been very intentional about equipping our leaders. This has taken the form of different program expressions. The first is the Dunamis Project itself, our basic course. Then we have created a special course called Exousia, specifically designed for equipping those who will do the teaching and provide the leadership of the Dunamis Project. Advanced courses on intercession and other critical topics are available. These can be viewed on our web page www.prmi.org. Here let us provide just one example of the intensive equipping that is required for raising up the leaders who can constantly return to provide the teaching of others so the cycle may be sustained.

## The Year Long Advanced Healing and Deliverance Course

In 2003 The Rev. Cindy Strickler, the Director of PRMI, and I worked together to launch a year-long process for providing deeper equipping in the areas of healing and deliverance. The teaching in the Dunamis Project Unit # 4 on the Healing ministry of Jesus Christ and Unit #5 on Spiritual Warfare were good introductions to these topics. A number of people who attended these equipping events were called by Jesus into these areas of anointed ministry. They needed a way to continue to grow in mastering the content, but also a context where they could grow in expressing their gifts. They needed to learn from and be mentored by teachers who had mastered the teaching and were also experienced in cooperating with the Holy Spirit in all forms of Jesus' healing ministry, including casting out demons. This course designed by Cindy met all these criteria. The course is unique in that it covers the six spheres of Jesus' healing ministry—spiritual, emotional, relational, physical, healing of the nations and deliverance/exorcism, in which Jesus removes the demonic spirits which block this redemptive healing process. We do not present a specific method but rather focus on the dynamic of cooperating with the Holy Spirit which is the key to the effectiveness of all methods and approaches.[146]

The fruit of this course over the past twenty years is hundreds of students who have been through this course stepping into various forms of healing and deliverance ministry in their own congregations and special mission groups. Thus, Jesus' healing ministry has expanded into many different locations with incalculable results of people healed of emotional wounds or physically restored and set free of evil spirits. Additionally, the Rev. Cindy Strickler has been most gifted in identifying those among the students who have the potential to join in the teaching and mentoring of others in the course or providing leadership in PRMI's

---

[146] For the details of this course please go to our web page: https://www.prmi.org/program-descriptions/advanced-healing-and-deliverance/.

Dunamis Project. These people anointed for the practice of healing and deliverance returning as teachers and mentors has been essential to sustaining this equipping process.

This course has provided another critical element. In the outpouring of the Holy Spirit manifesting the Kingship of Jesus and advancing the Kingdom of God, the vanguard has often been Jesus healing people and setting them free from demonic bondage. We see this first in the ministry of Jesus who sent out His disciples to do the works that He had been doing.

> After Jesus called the twelve together, he gave them power and authority over all demons and to cure diseases, and he sent them out to proclaim the Kingdom of God and to heal the sick... Luke 9:1-2

When persecution forced Jesus' disciples to disperse, they advanced the gospel of the kingdom everywhere they went. Healing, deliverance, signs, and wonders were a part of this advance. Philip going to Samaria is a typical example.

> The crowds were paying attention with one mind to what Philip said, as they heard and saw the miraculous signs he was performing. For unclean spirits, crying with loud shrieks, were coming out of many who were possessed, and many paralyzed and lame people were healed. So, there was great joy in that city. Acts 8:6-8

Healing and deliverance ministry as the vanguard of the advance of the Kingdom of God on earth is not just for Jesus and those first disciples but for all of us called today to take part in the preparing for, igniting, and sustaining moves of the Holy Spirit. So, this year-long equipping course has been truly strategic for preparing for this present-day great move of the Holy Spirit. Jesus is not only healing those wounded who are living in a fallen world, but He is also healing the earth itself. He is doing this through those He is calling, anointing, and sending to reach out to a hurting world.

## Building in the Organizational Structures to be a Vision-Driven Sodality.

If any organization or movement is to be sustained over decades or generations, a process of equipping its leaders with not only the content and skills but, most of all, the DNA of the institution's or movement's culture must be built in. Some of the Catholic religious orders like the Benedictines have survived for over 1500 years. The Benedictine order is the quintessential model of a living sodality, a "band of brothers" which has withstood the vicissitudes of time and fashion and held fast to its core vision and mission. Ever since I was called into this apostolic role of igniting outpourings of the Holy Spirit and creating the wineskins to express the working of the Holy Spirit, I have been a serious student of those movements that have lasted beyond their founders.

I have also had the opportunity to study those movements that failed to move past their founders. Indeed, I have had first-hand experiences of those failures. My first failure was my own when I was Vice-President of the Presbyterian Bible College in Taiwan. During the season of the great outpouring of the Holy Spirit that I have already described, with a team I founded the Presbyterian Lay Training Center on campus. After the original founding team and I left, the vision of this being a place for equipping Holy Spirit-empowered witnesses to Jesus Christ was lost. The buildings are still there and there is, no doubt, good work taking place, but it is not the original vision that was birthed with the outpouring of the Holy Spirit that took place in 1984 through Archer Torrey. In short, we failed to continue to be a sodality and were merely incorporated into the modality of the Taiwan Presbyterian Church in Taiwan.

From this study and the leading of the Holy Spirit in which He constantly has given my co-workers and me new vision submitted to and discerned by the PRMI Board, we have been able to put in place some key structures needed for a sodality to remain true to its mission, and vital and alive in advancing the Kingdom of God.

We learned that beyond equipping leaders and teachers in whom is embedded the DNA of the Holy Spirit movement, we must intentionally build the structures required to be a sodality. In general, these organizational structures have been common to all missional sodalities that have been used by God for centuries to advance His Kingdom purposes on earth. These are not unique to PRMI but have been a part of every movement that has lasted beyond its original founders.

Let me summarize these to show some of what is required to sustain a vital sodality that can be in the vanguard of advancing waves of the Holy Spirit.

- ***Dunamis Fellowship International***

This is an apostolic network of people who share the vision of PRMI. They have been through the Dunamis equipping process, and are committed to fulfilling the common vision of PRMI, which is:

**Exalting Jesus Christ! Igniting the Church in the Power of the Holy Spirit, Under the Authority of the Holy Bible as the Word of God through—Prayer, Equipping, Growing the Church, and Mission Outreach so that the Church may be Empowered to Do All that Christ Commands for the Glory of God the Father.**

This vision statement is Trinitarian and includes the two Goforth foundations of Jesus as King and the Bible as the Word of God. The middle phrases establish the means by which we are called to fulfill this vision—with the priority being prayer.

To join the DFI requires a commitment to 10 tenets of basic orthodox biblical faith, as well as assent to three areas of contemporary challenge to biblical faith. Active membership in the Dunamis Fellowship International is required for all who are in leadership roles in this ministry. The Dunamis Fellowship International has regional expressions in various locations and these are how these ministries may be offered in multiple locations. The key to keeping this fellowship, as well as the entire ministry, vital and on track with God's Kingdom purposes is the requirement that a person must renew their membership each year. This provides for a way to report if their beliefs change or if they have been compromised. They can remove themselves or be removed.

- **The Dunamis Institute**

Every movement that advances the Kingdom of God that has lasted beyond its initial founding has created a body of teaching that is based on the eternal truths of the Bible and is passed on to others. Usually this has been the role of the "academy" which is not just an academic endeavor but one where the master teachers not only pass on information but also shape the character of the students. The model for us is Jesus' teaching, mentoring, and sending His disciples out into practice. This is the role of the Dunamis Institute, which is responsible for maintaining the equipping and for ensuring that we do not depart from our foundational teaching on the person and work of the Holy Spirit. A primary and essential task of the Dunamis Institute is the constant equipping of the teachers and leaders who then provide ministries of PRMI.

- **The Community of the Cross**

Jesus makes it clear that true worship of God does not need to be located in a particular geographic place, but rather in Spirit and in truth (John 4:21-24). This does not mean that places cannot have special significance. Throughout history set-apart places where people gather have become the home bases of prayer, worship, living the life of faith, and equipping, the place from which people are then sent out. The Lord has given PRMI such a set-apart place. Located on twenty-four acres beside a river in the mountains of western North Carolina is the "Community of the Cross: A Place of Encounter with Jesus Christ for Prayer, Equipping and Sending." This is the spiritual home base for the Dunamis Fellowship where members may return for spiritual refreshment, healing prayer ministry, and for equipping. It is the location of the PRMI office which provides administrative support for the international ministries. This set-apart location is also the site where the

Dunamis Institute offers intensive equipping for those members of the DFI who are called and anointed to provide leadership for ministries of PRMI. Above all it is a set-apart location for the ongoing work of intercessory prayer.

In all the functions listed above, the Community of the Cross (COC) enables this ministry of PRMI to function as a sodality that takes part in igniting, sustaining, and bringing others into this present great move of the Holy Spirit. The specific role of the COC in igniting and sustaining outpourings of the Holy Spirit was confirmed in 2021 while I was caught up in prayer in the PRMI Prayer House while it was still being constructed. This was after going through withering attacks of spiritual warfare which functioned as a refining fire. I was caught up in a vision in which I saw Jesus Christ reaching into the altar in front of the throne of God the Father, taking blazing coals, and then casting them upon the earth. In each place where the coals landed, Pentecost events took place, igniting waves of the Holy Spirit and advancing the Kingdom of God. The coals were landing also at the Community of the Cross. Then the word came to me that PRMI was called to take part in preparing for the next great awakening that would advance the Kingdom of God worldwide and complete the Great Commission. The guidance also came that the COC was to be a 'landing pad' for these coals of Holy Spirit revival, and to be a launching pad for Holy Spirit-anointed and equipped people to take the fire of revival worldwide.

### The Formation of a "Literary Tradition" Based on the Bible, Sound Theology and Experience.

Every great movement of God that has been able to last for generations has had in written form the foundational elements that define the distinctives of this movement. These written documents are in addition to, but never as a replacement for the Bible as the Word of God. For instance, the Methodist movement has as a core literary tradition of writings and hymns of John and Charles Wesley. The Presbyterian and Reformed movement has the writings of John Calvin as our basis. These writings often provide a distinctive interpretative framework for both understanding the Bible as well as God working his purposes out in human history. They also contain the ongoing defining, unique stories of how God has worked among a specific group of people who are one tributary in the great river of the Holy Spirit.

If these extra-biblical writings are to function as the foundations for movements which are embodying God's Kingdom on earth, they must be in accord with the essential revelations of the Holy Bible as the Word of God. If the Bible remains the foundational revelation of true doctrine, morality, and the ways of God working with humanity, this literary tradition provides the basis for constant updating and revision that ensures that the movement stays vital and relevant to changing times.

In this movement of the Holy Spirit embodied in Presbyterian Reformed Ministries International, our foundation is the Bible as the Word of God. Second are the writings of John Calvin and Abraham Kuyper, reflecting Presbyterian Reformed roots, but regarding the teaching on the Holy Spirit, our literary basis is the writings of R.A. Torrey. My role, starting first with Doug McMurry and then other co-authors like Cindy Strickler and Paul Stokes, has been to build on R.A. Torrey's teaching. We have done this through a series of teaching manuals and workbooks, as well as published books and articles. By writing things down and having complete manuals to accompany our events we provide a standardization of the foundational principles. We also provide a basis in which future generations can adapt our writing to their own unique circumstances without losing the essential principles.

We have found from bitter experiences that when this written core of materials has not been made available, perhaps by being translated and adapted to the language or cultural context in which an outpouring takes place, then it usually does not last or easily falls into deception.

### The Sodality (PRMI) Intentionally Connecting to Modality Expressions of the Church.

One other element that is essential to sustaining and growing this movement of the Holy Spirit embodied in PRMI is the intention of being a sodality: The commitment to stay connected to and supportive of the modalities of congregations and denominations.

I am writing this entire book from the perspective of the leader of a sodality and not as a pastor or leader of a modality. I did not do well as a pastor of a local Presbyterian congregation. As a Presbyterian missionary sent to Korea and to Taiwan, I was part of the vital "sodality" expression within the larger modality of the Presbyterian denomination. From this perspective I can attest that much of the problem with sodality movements has been within the movements themselves, in not doing a good job connecting to the modality structures. These missional movements have tended to become isolated from congregations and denominational structures, and in some cases have so separated from the church of Jesus Christ that they have become sects or in the worst cases cults. Often what happens is that the full God-intended benefits of both redemptive structures in a dynamic relationship is not realized for either expression.

PRMI so far has avoided this danger by initially committing to being a sodality, and at the same time committing to relationship with and support of the local congregations. Where we are welcomed, we formally connect with denominations. This commitment is first expressed in the requirement that all members of the PRMI Dunamis Fellowship be an active and supportive member of a local congregation. Or, if they are church leaders within a denominational structure, then faithful and active within that structure. PRMI is not a replacement for these modality expressions of the body of Christ.[147]

This commitment to connect with congregations has also taken the form of adapting our teaching and ministry programs to ignite and sustain the renewal movement of the Holy Spirit within congregations. This has been through our Spirit Alive program as well as more recently the Ignite programs.[148] We have also offered a series of events and teaching that adapts the Dunamis Project teaching for local congregations. With Cindy Strickler and Paul Stokes, I wrote a book specifically applying the teaching on the Holy Spirit to the local congregational context. The title is, *Growing the Church in the Power of the Holy Spirit: The Seven Dynamics of Cooperation*. We have also offered a set-apart event just for pastors and church leaders by the same name. Recently we have developed materials that can easily be used within the local congregation.[149]

This intentional connection to the modalities of the Church is not just so that we can promote our programs; it is necessary for the continued fulfillment of our mission. If this ministry of PRMI becomes disconnected from these modalities, especially the local congregation where biblical faith is practically lived, then we would no longer play a strategic role in advancing the gospel of the kingdom.

These factors have enabled PRMI, this one small tributary in the great river of God, to remain a vital sodality that has been able to sustain the moving of the Holy Spirit from our founding in 1966. Keep in mind that these organizational structures or wineskins, while giving the means of expression, do not in themselves guarantee that the

---

[147]This is among the Ten Tenets of the PRMI Dunamis Fellowship International that all members must agree to on an annual basis.  See https://www.prmi.org/ministries-of-prmi/dunamis-fellowship-intl/

[148]Ignite provides opportunity for a congregation to catch the Holy Spirit's flame and grow in faithfulness to Jesus Christ.  https://www.prmi.org/program-descriptions/ignite/

[149]These are all listed on our web page.  www.prmi.org.

sodality will be in the service of God's kingdom. These structures must be built of "living stones" who embody the kingdom of God in their own lives—people who are born-again, committed to following Jesus Christ, growing as His disciples, grounded in the Bible as the Word of God, and who are themselves filled with the Holy Spirit. In our system the key to keeping this ministry on track with God's purposes is the Dunamis Fellowship International—an apostolic network, second-decision fellowship made up of such people. We must keep the meta pattern going as a sodality so that we may continue to be a blessing to the entire body of Christ.

There is one other element which has been alluded to throughout this book. While being intentional about being a sodality, we have consistently attempted to stay connected to the modality expressions of the body of Christ.

In the next chapter, we make this connection explicit as it is in the dynamic, mutually supportive relationship between modalities and sodalities that this move of God will be able to continue and may be expanded into the next great awakening.

# 21

## Modality and Sodality Together Sustain Revival

From the example of the book of Acts, we may deduce that it is God's design that these two redemptive structures described by the terms modality and sodality are together needed to prepare for, ignite, and sustain Kingdom-advancing revival waves of the Holy Spirit. Indeed, it is by this dynamic interface that the body of Christ can continue to advance the gospel of the Kingdom God's way, which is "by My Spirit," and resist the relentless gravity of human sin which inevitably leads to "power and might." Or simply put, the only way for movements of biblical faith that start in the Holy Spirit not to end in the flesh, is by these two redemptive structures being fully operative and in a dynamic, mutually beneficial relationship with each other.

This dynamic interface between the redemptive structures together in the body of Christ provides the suitable wineskin for the full expression of the five-fold equipping gifts, the three R.A Torrey keys, the Goforth foundations and the meta pattern. This is God the Father's master plan to ignite and sustain waves of revival. This plan not only reforms and enlivens the Church of Jesus Christ, but it also may release great awakenings that may transform entire societies and advance the gospel of the Kingdom to all nations.

Each vital stream of the Holy Spirit that is advancing the Kingdom of God, will have its own distinctive interface between modality and sodality structures. [150] Here let us provide two examples of this interface from my own Presbyterian and Reformed stream. The first example is the relationship between the Presbyterian Church in the USA denomination (the modality), and PRMI, a missional group (the sodality). This turns out to be a parable, warning of the dire consequences to the advancement of the Kingdom when this dynamic relationship is dissolved. The second example is the interface between the St. Giles Presbyterian congregation in Richmond, VA (the modality) and PRMI (the sodality). This one is a model of the blessings to the Kingdom when this dynamic is sustained.

## First a Cooperative and then a Severed Relationship with the PC(USA)

In 1966 the five Presbyterian pastors who established Presbyterian Charismatic Communion (PCC) decided not to follow the trend of the day of starting independent charismatic congregations, but to remain within the Presbyterian denominations that they were a part of. The PCC was set up as an independent organization, not directly under the authority or control of the denomination. However, in those days formal ways for special mission groups or sodalities to be connected to the denomination were built into first the UPC(USA) and the PCUS and later, after reunion in 1984, the PC(USA). This meant that we would report to the General Assembly, as well as have open doors into congregations as well as a place at the table during the General Assembly. This was under what was called Chapter 9 Organizations. This term was used because it was Chapter 9 of the Book of Order that

---

[150]For some traditions, most notably the Roman Catholic stream, this dynamic has been well developed and institutionalized in the relationship between the religious orders "sodalities" and the institutional church the "modalities." While these two structures have often been in tension and sometimes violent conflict, together they have insured that biblical Christian faith has flourished over the centuries.

defined this collegial and mutually supportive relationship. This included several different sodalities—evangelical groups like Presbyterians Prolife, Presbyterians for Renewal, the Presbyterian Lay Committee, Knox Evangelistic Fellowship, the Outreach Foundations, and PRMI. In addition, there were some special organizations who were under the same framework of reporting and accountability that were promoting abortion, gay rights, and other unbiblical causes.

For an extended period, the prophetic witness, the prayer, and work for renewal of biblical faith by the evangelical and charismatic missional groups was welcomed within the denomination. We had a very positive effect both of sustaining renewal and constraining the unbiblical movements which were leading the denomination into apostasy. As the leadership of the PC(USA) was more and more taken over by the liberal wing of the church, we were called to speak and act prophetically against the apostasy that we saw coming. Over time, with the liberal takeover of the denominational leadership structures, these evangelical organizations were no longer welcomed. Finally, after the liberals gained the upper hand, the means of connection and accountability were completely removed. The long sad history of how this happened is beyond the scope of this book but is told elsewhere by the past head editor of the Presbyterian Lay Committee.[151] The end result, however, was what happens any time the church silences and disenfranchises those people and movements with prophetic and apostolic gifting. In other words, the church no longer embodies the Kingdom of God and the manifest presence of King Jesus. It calcifies into a dead orthodoxy or falls into apostasy.

---

[151]Parker T. Williamson, *Broken Covenant: Signs of a Shattered Communion* (Isle of Lewis, Scotland, UK: Reformation Press, 2007).

## The PC(USA): A Story First of Dynamic Cooperation with PRMI and Later Rejection

This relationship was illustrated at the annual General Assemblies where this ministry, as well as many others under the framework of Chapter 9 of the Book of Order were welcomed to present their special callings to the rest of the church. These groups included not just evangelical and charismatic mission groups but also some other sodalities like the More Light groups and Voices of Sophia that were advocates for movements that were departures from biblical faith and morality.

During this period PRMI would always send teams of intercessors to pray for the General Assembly (GA) proceedings. We also offered a charismatic prayer and praise service which was always well attended with hundreds of participants who were attending the GA. We had offered these prayer and praise services since about 1970. It was at this well-attended GA worship service that the Holy Spirit would fall. Many GA participants were baptized with the Holy Spirit, or they would be filled with the Holy Spirit. Throughout the multi-day GA, we would offer prayer ministry, love, and support for hundreds of church leaders and laypeople who often were serving in difficult locations. At the GA we would often receive invitations to come into the local congregations to bring teaching on the Holy Spirit and to help nurture healing prayer teams.

During this period, we also had mutually beneficial partnership agreements where the GA Mission Board confirmed PRMI's role in igniting outpouring of the Holy Spirit in Brazil, Korea, Taiwan, China, and Uganda. In those locations we intentionally connected empowered church leaders and on-fire congregations back into the already established congregational and denominational modalities in those nations. We also supported the PC(USA) mission programs through prayers and by encouraging congregations who had come alive in the Holy Spirit to express their mission outreach through the mission agency of the PC(USA).

## Igniting a Pentecost Event at the General Assembly which had a Role in Pushing Back the Apostasy.

One incident that took place illustrates this healthy sodality/modality dynamic, but first I must introduce to you a great man of God who was part of the renewal groups which were the sodalities in tension with the modality of the PC(USA) denomination—The Rev. Bob Pittman.

After serving the strong evangelical charismatic congregation of the Presbyterian Church in San Mateo, California, Bob founded the Knox Evangelistic Fellowship. This sodality was dedicated to helping the PC(USA) do the work of evangelism. Bob was empowered by the Holy Spirit and always insisted that the baptism and infilling of the Holy Spirit and the gifts of the Holy Spirit were for equipping the church to be witnesses to Jesus Christ.

Over the years when PRMI was conducting the Prayer and Praise Services at every General Assembly, Bob Pitman and others from Knox Fellowship were always there supporting us and joining in the prayer for the outpouring of the Holy Spirit. Bob would always join in praying for the baptism and infilling with the Holy Spirit, especially for the many pastors and elders to be empowered for evangelism. Like R.A. Torrey, Bob had a passion for souls!

Once, during one of the big controversies over the radical feminist and gay agenda that was rending asunder the denomination, we conducted our annual GA Prayer and Praise service. This was at the June 1994 General Assembly in Wichita, Kansas. Dr. Jim Logan, an African American, anointed Presbyterian, who was on our PRMI Board of Directors at the time, was the keynote speaker.[152] The large ball room was packed with hundreds of people, many standing along the sides. The atmosphere was oppressive with demonic presences. It was as though a palpable presence of evil was hanging over the entire group. Jim and I were up on the platform with the worship team from First Presbyterian Church in San Mateo. We were somewhat overwhelmed with the presence of evil; we literally were having trouble breathing. We could see the source of the evil in the back of the room where there was an entire row of gay and radical feminist activists. Some women in that group, who had been at the 1993 Reimagining God conference, seemed to be muttering witchcraft curses. Jim and I, standing up in front of the packed-out room, were overwhelmed with confusion and waves of nausea. We were essentially paralyzed in front of the waiting crowd, so much so that we could not even do the normal welcomes and introductions, or even ask the worship team waiting behind us to start.

Right then Bob Pitman, stepped up from the crowd, came onto the stage and took the microphone from my hand, and said, "Please let me pray for you!" He then launched out in the most amazing Holy Spirit-anointed prayer. He gave glory to Jesus Christ as the Way, the Truth, and the Life, and the only way to God the Father. Then he proceeded in the name of Jesus Christ to bind and cast out of the room all demons. He named demons of witchcraft,

---

[152]For a report on this Assembly which took place right after what was called the Reimagining God Conference that took place in 1993. This conference, supported by PC(USA) mission monies, had rejected the atoning work of Jesus Christ as the of way of salvation. PRMI had joined with the other PC(USA) evangelical and charismatic renewal groups (sodalities) in opposing this apostasy. For more background on this event see the following reports from the official news agency. https://history.PC(USA).org/blog/2018/06/wabash-valley-hears-1994-ga From the Presbyterian Lay Committee, which was in the frontlines of exposing the heresy, here is a retrospective summary of that watershed event. https://layman.org/news2e37-2/

Jezebel, and many more. As this prayer continued, like a dawn breaking over the crowd, oppression started to lift. The hostile crowd in the back started to look very uncomfortable. Bob persisted in his prayer, giving glory to Jesus Christ and binding the evil spirits. He then said, "Now in the name of Jesus, I command all demons in this room, including those that are hiding under the chairs and in some of these people, to leave now!" He repeated, "You guys hiding under the chairs OUT NOW!" Honestly, it was so funny that I started to laugh, but I guess that naming and commanding the evil spirits under the chairs to leave completed it! Or, it was just too over the edge. Suddenly the entire group of gay and radical feminist activists along with those casting curses got up and hastily left the room. With that, we moved into glorious praise. I do not remember if Jim Logan ever got to speak or not because the Holy Spirit fell upon the whole group like at Pentecost! During that amazing outpouring, Bob stood up again, and like an anointed Peter, quoted Acts 1:8, and said, "The baptism and infilling of the Holy Spirit is so that we may be empowered witnesses to Jesus Christ." He also prayed a powerful prayer of anointing, for many in the room were being called into evangelism.

Extraordinary outpourings like this took place at our Prayer and Praise services at each General Assembly that I was part of starting in 1990 until 2001. Not only did these events provide a context for hundreds of Presbyterian leaders to receive the baptism with the Holy Spirit, but they also assisted in igniting and growing moves of the Holy Spirit in their local congregations. We did this through various programs such as Spirit Alive, Ignite, the Dunamis Video Courses, and others designed for congregations.

## Strategic Intercession Defeating Strongholds and Upholding Biblical Faith

It must be noted that in addition to these public events with manifestations of the Holy Spirit and preaching of the gospel, teams of intercessors were at these General Assemblies, often hidden away from the public eye. Doug and Carla McMurry for two decades (1991 – 2021) led this intercessory prayer work. For hours while the GA Committees met or the plenary sessions (where attendees debated and voted) were taking place, this vanguard team of intercessors were engaged. They were able to sustain this intensity through what is called "Harp and Bowl." This is a combination of worship and prayer led by the Holy Spirit—a joining in what is revealed to be taking place in heaven by the twenty-four elders around the Father, Son, and Holy Spirit, in which "...each of them had a harp and golden bowls full of incense (which are the prayers of the saints)" (Rev. 5:8).

This work of prayer was usually conducted by a small team of three to twelve people who had learned to pray together. Their work was like that of Moses, Hur, and Aaron at the battle with the Amalekites in Exodus 17:8-17. They were on the mountain supporting Joshua who was fighting down in the valley.

Often this work of prayer included intense engagements with high-level demonic spirits, in which the Lord Jesus Christ would prevail. Often these engagements corresponded to decisions made by the governing bodies that were consistent with biblical faith and morality.

This dynamic partnership ended with the liberal takeover of the denominational leadership. When this happened, not only PRMI but the other evangelical missional sodalities were intentionally cut off from and no longer given any room at the General Assembly. On the other hand, those sodalities that were consistent with the liberal ideology continued to be welcomed. The result has been that the PC(USA) has fallen more and more into apostasy, away from their own biblical and orthodox creedal foundations.

Although many faithful and anointed individuals and even several congregations have not fallen into apostasy, the denominational leadership definitely has. While we have no official connection to the PC(USA) as we once did, there are still many members of PRMI and those on our leadership team who are a faithful remnant. Through their prayers and faithful witness, there is hope for an outpouring of the Holy Spirit to take place to restore the denomination to biblical faithfulness. If that does happen, it will take place out of interaction with a faithful sodality. We are most excited that even now we are seeing outpourings of the Holy Spirit taking place within the modality of the PC(USA).

Many of us are doubtful that a denomination (a modality) whose leadership and governance structures depart from biblical faith can be restored to biblical faith. Often those who have departed from the orthodox Christian doctrine that Jesus Christ is Lord and Savior, and the Bible is the Word of God, have built a culture and organizational structure based on "power and might." This corporate culture often grows to become demonic strongholds that not only quench the working of the Holy Spirit but often actively work against and exclude those who still hold to biblical faith and are led and empowered by the Holy Spirit. However, even within the most apostate denominations there is still a faithful remnant of people, pastors, and congregations through whom Jesus is at work. There are many who have been called by God to stay within the apostate structure to pray for true revival. Most often we find that these courageous individuals and congregations are only able to fulfill this difficult mission within the modality by cooperating with a sodality like PRMI or the Alpha Couse, which stands outside their structure.

One such person is Rev. James Cubie who has remained within the Presbyterian Church in the USA. He serves the over 300-year-old Mattituck Presbyterian (PC(USA)) congregation on Long Island, New York, USA. Rev. Cubie has been a part of our Dunamis Project as well as a member of the Kingdom Congregations Development Team, and most recently has been taking part in what is called the Next Great Awakening Catalyzers Prayer Team (NGA Catalyzers).[153] The purpose of this NGA Catalyzers team is to fulfill R.A. Torrey's mandate of gathering a few people to pray for revival until it happens. We are doing this work of prayer. We also are helping one

---

[153] This prayer team was formally launched in 2021 by the PRMI Board of Directors under the leadership of Martin Boardman. Our purpose is to pray for revival and to support one another in our different spheres as we seek to follow the guidance of the Holy Spirit.

another discern the guidance of the Holy Spirit as to how we are called to implement these patterns for revival within our context.

### An Interview with Rev. James Cubie, A PC(USA) Congregation Where the Holy Spirit Has Just Fallen.

[Brad] I was so excited to hear your report at our NGA Catalyzers meeting about how the Holy Spirit had fallen at a recent event with your congregation. Tell us a little bit about what happened.

[James] Yes! For the past two years we've hosted two equipping events focused on the gifts and power of the Holy Spirit. They have averaged sixty participants. This second year we experienced the presence of the Holy Spirit in a profound, unexpected way.

[Brad] Were there some specific manifestations of the Holy Spirit?

[James] At our Summer 2023 event (called "Onward and Upward") the most obvious and significant manifestation was several people getting rested in the Spirit–people who had not sought or had that kind of experience before. That this took place in our Presbyterian congregation was just wonderful! We Presbyterians, of course, are not known for that sort of thing.

[Brad] Was this a new experience for your congregation?

[James] Yes. We are an evangelical congregation in the PC(USA), and we have a lot of members and people in leadership who come out of Spirit-filled non-denominational backgrounds. Many of them became Presbyterian because something went wrong in those charismatic churches (leadership failures, etc.). So, we have folks who have experienced this kind of thing elsewhere, sometimes many years ago, but not here.

The striking thing about the Summer of 2023 was that several new people who had been tracking with us for the past two years—

people who had not had this kind of experience—were baptized with the Holy Spirit.

Our church experienced several very rocky years before I began as pastor in 2021. A very successful, faithful pastor led the church for almost thirty years, and retired in 2015. Then, after an interim pastor, two pastors lasted less than two years each. Put COVID on top of that, and the church was really hurting and in need of healing when I arrived.

I came to the church full of hope because I knew that it was a diamond in the rough—an evangelical and charismatic congregation in the PC(USA)! After arriving, I sought the Lord in prayer, first, to ask what He wanted for us. Several months later, I received this word: "Build me an altar in the North Fork and begin with yourselves."

The North Fork is the part of Long Island we live in, and I believe this call was to press into the works of intercession, evangelism, and seeking the baptism with the Holy Spirit (the "altar" part of this work), and that a significant part of creating a people for the Lord to use in this work would be for us to return to the disciplines of holiness (the "begin with yourselves" part). This "build me an altar" word was consistent with another word that I received several years ago, which has become a watchword for me and my ministry: "The wood must be dry for my fire to descend."

[**Brad**] It seems like this outpouring has fit the meta pattern of the three phases?

[**James**] Yes, indeed! My sense is that we are at the beginning of Phase #2.

In Phase #1, in addition to the "Onward and Upward" event I mentioned, we began to do basic teaching on the baptism with the Holy Spirit at a four-week event called "SpiritFire," held for the past two years, just before Easter. We also identified our prayer warriors, and Mary Ellen blessed us by leading them in an online training for Intercessors. I also began to preach and teach in a more evangelistic way: Messages and classes that met people who did not know God and called them to faith. Finally, in this first phase, we also began to experience a kind of unity we had not had for many years: Many people who left—or took a long break—from church, returned, and have experienced the Spirit's joy in fellowship.

It really took two seasons of doing this before we began, as a church and in our leadership teams, to experience Phase #2: Receiving the Spirit in power, which included the resting in the Spirit experience I described earlier.

[**Brad**] What about the third phase of sustaining the flame? What happens next to keep the fire growing in the congregation.

[**James**] One of my heroes is John Kilpatrick. I love what he and his team did to lay the groundwork for revival in Brownsville. In an interview with Michael Brown, he shared that he was at Brownsville for 11 years before revival came. It was a 300-member church when he arrived. And over the next several years, he built trust and did the basic things a pastor should do to shepherd his people.

That's how I, personally, imagine moving forward: I want to continue to build trust with the people God has given me to shepherd, and to press into the three disciplines of intercession, empowerment, and evangelism with our leadership teams.

We've also expanded our life groups ministry and have done a 12-week training for the life group leaders to know better how to disciple people from baby-Christians to spiritual mothers and fathers. As we connect more fully with the Holy Spirt, and— hopefully—If He comes and does an awakening work in and through us, we want there to be dedicated teams (life groups) who can receive and help those who are new—or returning—to The Faith, to grow in the fruit of the Spirit.

[**Brad**] How about the R.A Torrey keys for revival? I know you were doing the work of prayer, as well as teaching on and making opportunity for people to be filled with the Holy Spirit, but what about the role of evangelism?

[**James**] Very early on, we created an evangelism team to develop containers/events for the Holy Spirit to come and do His work among us. At those events, the structure has been to introduce basic teaching about the Holy Spirit, his power, and gifts, and finish with an evening of worship and prayer for healing and empowerment, which have sometimes included prophetic words. We intentionally develop the teaching and preaching that accompanies these events to answer basic questions and objections about the Holy Spirit, His gifts and power. It's evangelistic (almost a kind of apologetics) in that sense.

We've also done basic training in individual evangelism and structure our worship and our posture toward the surrounding community in an evangelistic way: I preach to reach people who do not know God; we offer Sunday School for adults and children that introduces the Christian faith from the ground, up.

I would say that we are just now beginning to draw these programs and personal disciplines more fully into their rightful dependence on the Holy Spirit. I found it very helpful not to search for a "perfect beginning" where we were all on the same page about every point of teaching on the Holy Spirit. Instead, we just began all these ministries, and I layered in my personal example and the teaching to that stage and/or that ministry.

[**Brad**] Tell us how your association over the years with PRMI has been helpful to you as you have worked in your congregation?

[ **James**] It is hard to put it into words—I have received so much in terms of fellowship and equipping!

I've been a member of the Kingdom Congregations team for five years, so I have a good sense of what it looks like when congregations cooperate fully with the Holy Spirit. I generally know what it takes for them to get from A to B, and all the things that can go wrong in the attempt.

I also just completed PRMI's Advanced Healing and Deliverance course.[154] For my final project, I wrote about the refining work that the Holy Spirit is doing, specifically in ministers of Word and sacrament during this time. Ministers have a lot of inner healing, and even deliverance, that needs to take place so that we can be used by God in the next move of the Holy Spirit. I learned this through three years of trying to plant a church during COVID. PRMI's course on healing and deliverance was just essential for me to sweep away all the non-biblical images of the work of a pastor and return to the disciplines of becoming a Spirit-filled shepherd.

My sense, too, is that as the Spirit does His work in this season of what we hope will be the next great awakening, that healing and deliverance will be a significant part of how Christ transfers people out of the kingdom of darkness, and into the Kingdom of God. To that end, we hope to create healing and deliverance teams here, at our church.

[**Brad**] How has this taken place within the context of the PC(USA) and do you have any hope for this once great denomination?

[**James**] We are in a Presbytery that still respects our right to self-determination. For example, several years ago, we spoke publicly about our commitment to keep to biblical standards of marriage and ordination. Our General Presbyter, while personally differing, went on the record in the local newspaper to defend our decision. A lot depends on the Presbytery you are in. Our hope is that our next General Presbyter will be an honest broker and respecter of our rights.

It's no secret the PC(USA) is in dire straits, and that one of the chief problems it has is that so many of its churches forgo the work of evangelism, never mind intercessory prayer and seeking

---

[154]For more information on PRMI's Advanced Healing and Deliverance Course go to: https://www.prmi.org/program-descriptions/advanced-healing-and-deliverance/advanced-healing-and-deliverance-course-application/

empowerment from the Holy Spirit. That unwillingness to evangelize, of course, comes from a low Christology: Jesus is at best a teacher, but not the Savior—not God. When that's your mindset, the stakes change, and God cannot bless churches who proceed in that way.

My sense is that it's a matter of time until we get to the point where the PC(USA) is no longer "connectional" in the way that it currently is. The PC(USA) will, likely, become more congregational in style of governance and focus. God may be doing all this to refine and preserve a remnant who can prepare the way for the next great awakening. Please pray that God will protect our little Zion here, in the North Fork of Long Island!

[**Brad**] One, final question—Do you have any advice or recommendations for other pastors like you who have been filled with the Holy Spirit and are working to advance the gospel of Jesus Christ in a denominational context that is not supportive.

[**James**] If I can end with a frank word, it would be this: God does not promote shepherds and churches to the work of awakening before they do the basic, faithful things well. So, press into the "ordinary" work of shepherding and being a church, and then begin to layer in teaching about the Holy Spirit. Always do that work of "layering" by invitation, not command, and always in an apologetic/evangelistic posture—that is, always ready to answer basic questions and objections.

To the extent that you can, maintain close, cordial relationships with your Presbytery and your colleagues in ministry—if they know you and your heart for your people, you at least have the chance to avoid misunderstanding.

Finally—but perhaps, first!—get plugged in at PRMI: Here you will find brothers and sisters in the same journey, with decades of experience, who will love, support, and equip you.

## Example of St. Giles Presbyterian Church in Richmond, and PRMI

I have already given the example of the St. Giles Presbyterian Church in Richmond VA. There was a season when the dynamic of sustaining the vital move of the Holy Spirit was not entirely lost but certainly hindered through spiritual warfare as well as the needed inward focus of restoring the congregation from the divisions and wounds that were sustained. Through the perseverance of the St. Giles leadership and many faithful people in prayer as well as commitment to the gospel of Jesus Christ, this dynamic has been restored within the congregation itself.

A part of this restoration was leaving the non-supportive and often hostile PC(USA) Presbytery and joining the ECO. The ECO is "A Covenant Order of Evangelical Presbyterians." [155] This Presbyterian denomination was formed in January of 2012 and at this point has the dynamic feel of a "modality" which has provided accountability as well as spiritual support for its member congregations. This has been a very upbuilding and supportive denominational context for St. Giles to function in and be able to grow. That is a worthy story, and a useful model for other evangelical or charismatic congregations that are finding themselves constrained by being a part of a denominational structure that is departing from core biblical faith and morality.

What I will speak to here is the relationship that has existed for decades between PRMI and St. Giles. PRMI played a vital role in helping them sustain the flame of the Holy Spirit's work, especially before they were able to be freed from the PC(USA). St. Giles' people and leadership were always supportive of PRMI and other renewal groups like the Presbyterian Prolife. At the PC(USA) General Assembly we joined together in the work of intercessory

---

[155] ECO | A Covenant Order of Evangelical Presbyterians,  https://eco-pres.org/about-eco/

prayer for renewal of the PC(USA) and in the battles that resisted the encroaching apostasy. Members of the early leadership of St. Giles were the keynote speakers and anointed teachers in PRMI. Also, members of St. Giles were strong financial supporters of PRMI and served on our board of directors.

What has been most significant is the deep personal friendships in Jesus Christ and shared common vision of the Kingdom of God. These relationships are always the key to igniting and sustaining movements of revival. They are also the key to bridging and connecting the two redemptive structures of modalities and sodalities. This is always the case, just as we see that it was the deep love and friendships that connected the missionary Paul with the congregations. These relationships were based on love, deep friendship, and trust that enabled the type of dynamic flexible, mutual connections between modality and sodality. Just to illustrate, it takes a lot of trust for a pastor or a local governing board to welcome into the congregation, a speaker, teacher, or program from an outside, potentially disruptive force of a sodality like PRMI.

This dynamic "sodality/modality" partnership has been expressed in two ways.

### First, PRMI People Being Invited to Offer Seminars and Teaching to Nurture the Gifts of the Holy Spirit.

Over the decades I have often been invited to St. Giles Presbyterian Church to preach or teach. At the request of the church's leadership, I would teach various aspects of the work of the Holy Spirit, usually to a small but eager group, going deeper into issues like intercession, prophecy, healing, or spiritual warfare. For the most part, these were people who had been touched by the first moves of the Holy Spirit in the 1970s-1980s, and so were older. This was always about equipping their own leaders to offer ministries. Often these invitations would come during times when the congregation was facing challenges or in crisis.

One example may serve to illustrate this dynamic relationship. Right after a period of intense conflict, I had been invited for a weekend teaching event to address the topic of discerning the presence of and overcoming demonic strongholds that can take root in a congregation. Not being a part of the congregation but a trusted friend from outside, everyone seemed to be free to tell me their side of the story. It was obvious that there was much confusion as well as hurt and misunderstanding. My role was just to listen and to pray for healing and restoration.

At an evening healing service which was very full, I was to preach and to pray for the outpouring of the Holy Spirit. As we moved into worship, the large sanctuary room was filled with tension. I could feel the brokenness in the group. I could feel the disunity like a corrosive acid destroying the warmth of fellowship. It seemed that there were barriers everywhere to moving into Christ-exalting worship. I was praying for guidance and asking the Lord to please show up and break through this tension and heal these fractures. The worship finished and it was my turn to step into the pulpit. I really had received NO guidance of even how to begin! I learned long ago not to manipulate people or the Holy Spirit by faking it. So, I admitted to the gathered crowd that I had no guidance from the Lord and had no idea how to proceed. I just said, "Everyone, let us wait upon the Lord." The silence started to last too long, and it was becoming awkward, when an African American member of the congregation stood up and in a deep bass voice spoke a message in tongues. This tongue in a heavenly language with a sternness and authority as if spoken from God Himself on Mount Sinai, resounded through the whole sanctuary. I could feel and see in the people's faces the brooding presence of God settle over the congregation. I asked, "Does anyone have the interpretation?" For what felt like forever, we all waited in a deepening, heavy silence. Finally, Katie, whom I knew very well from the many General Assembly prayer gatherings where she and her husband had been intercessors, stood up and came forward. In stark contrast to the one who gave the tongue, Katie is a petite, meek white lady. She said "I think the Lord is giving me the interpretation. But I am afraid to give it." I handed her the microphone and responded, "Please step out in faith and obedience and give it. I am praying for you for boldness!" In a quivering sweet voice she said, "I, the Lord am calling y'all to repent now! Forgive each other and get reconciled! Now! Otherwise, I will not be able to keep working at St. Giles!" Trembling, she handed back the microphone. The instant she gave the interpretation an amazing thing took place. People all over the sanctuary stood up and started to go to one another and ask forgiveness. There were hugs and other signs of people being reconciled. This was followed by an extended period in which the Holy Spirit moved in our midst in healing ministry not just of individuals but of the fractured fellowship. It was a glorious evening.

This took place because someone they trusted, who was part of a trusted sodality, provided the context for the Holy Spirit to work through them. My role was just to help prepare the venue for the Holy Spirit to work. That can sometimes only happen through someone who is not completely enmeshed in the congregation and its conflicts. The gift that I brought, besides helping to set the venue for the Holy Spirit to work, was that I left on Monday morning! I also continued to pray for them as they carried on being led by the Holy Spirit to be restored as a congregation.

I need to say that PRMI and I were not the only ones who were brought in during this period to help. There were many others!

### Second, People from St. Giles Taking Part in PRMI Events, Being Equipped, and Taking It Back to the Congregation—an Interview with Rev. Rebecca Modrzynski

The other way this dynamic modality/sodality partnership has been expressed is PRMI people attending a St. Giles event and then participating in their groups in the congregation. To get into this dynamic of this relationship, I interviewed one of their pastors, the Rev. Rebecca Long Modrzynski. Here, a disclaimer is in order. This is my daughter! She was born in Taiwan while Laura and I were missionaries. When we moved to Black Mountain, North Carolina in 1993, she was nurtured in the faith in the context of PRMI events and mission trips where manifestations of the Holy Spirit were normal. She was also a part of the Montreat Presbyterian Church in Montreat, North Carolina, where Pastor Richard White preached Jesus Christ-centered, biblically grounded sermons Sunday after Sunday. He was filled with the Holy Spirit at a PRMI Dunamis Project which resulted in greatly empowered Jesus Christ-exalting sermons. Further, Rebecca was part of a dynamic, loving youth group led by Shawn Stewart, who was also filled with the Holy Spirit. After Rebecca and her husband Josh finished at Fuller Seminary, he worked for nine months at Montreat Presbyterian Church (Now called "Christ Community Church which is no longer PC(USA) but is now a member of the Evangelical Presbyterian Church (EPC) denomination.) Then Josh spent three years on staff at PRMI developing our Dunamis Institute curriculum before he served as pastor of the Riceville Presbyterian Church. During this time, besides being a mom with two children, Rebecca worked with PRMI in developing our healing prayer ministry. Rebecca was also ordained to the ministry by the Evangelical Presbyterian Church Presbytery. Afterwards they were called to serve at St. Giles Presbyterian Church in Richmond, VA.

## An Interview with Rev. Rebecca Long Modrzynski

[**Brad**] Rebecca, how have you found working with a congregation like St. Giles compared to what you experienced at the events in PRMI or the mission trips that I took you on to Brazil, Uganda, and the UK where the Holy Spirit was poured out?

[**Rebecca**] Well, that is a hard question to answer without it sounding like one is better than the other. At a PRMI event, you have this special set-apart group of people who have all gathered for a very compressed period. In that context, the Holy Spirit seems to build koinonia quickly and deeply. There is also expectation and faith that the Lord will move, and He often does so in powerful ways! I have seen the Holy Spirit move in our congregation too, but it just looks different. The Lord uses the weekly rhythms of Sunday worship, Bible studies, and prayer times to build koinonia, expectation, and thirst for God. We have seen the Holy Spirit move in gentle ways in our Sunday morning service, such as a tangible sense of His presence in worship and the Lord ministering His hope and truth through the preaching of the Word. We have a monthly healing service and extended prayer sessions in which God has healed both physically and emotionally. Yet, the overall tone is still gentle. I would say the wonderful aspect of a PRMI event is being immersed in what God is doing, and the challenge of being in the local church is that you cannot stay in that set-apart space. There are schedules and daily life to attend to; parents have children to care for, jobs to go to and just the day-to-day responsibilities.

However, I think this is where discipleship comes in. When I worked as the Coordinator of Healing Prayer at PRMI, it was always a concern when I made a follow-up phone call after a prayer session and asked, "Do you have a local church where you are plugged in and can grow in your faith?" When they said, "No," I'd often have no idea what happened to that person.

And so, Josh and I aim to be extensively involved in discipleship. It can feel slower than being at a PRMI conference (which can be like a fire hose), but it is a joy to walk with people and see their long-term growth and transformation. It is awesome when we see breakthroughs in healing and faith, and then we are able to watch the person live it out in the day to day. Truly it is a gift that we get to be a part of!

[**Brad**] How has your relationship with PRMI helped you in this pastoral context?

[**Rebecca**] First, PRMI has helped both Josh and me in our leadership abilities. One great example is the ability to recognize a kairos moment. The upfront leadership (worship team, Josh, and I) is growing together in how to take our congregation into these Holy Spirit-initiated moments. We sense the Lord is at work and is

391

inviting us to go deeper. So, we ask Him what He wants to do. There have been corporate times of confession, a lingering time of prayer and offering words of worship and adoration.

For sure, PRMI has given us the tools to go deeper. We want to be in the river, in the flow of the Holy Spirit. PRMI has helped us experience that real transformation is possible and for this reason, we have a big vision for St. Giles. Since we have tasted of the Kingdom of God, we pray and long for His Kingdom to advance at and through St. Giles.

Besides big vision, PRMI has taught me several specific tools for ministry. For example, how to listen to the leading of the Holy Spirit in a prayer session or a pastoral care visit. We have used PRMI's Dunamis materials to teach on empowerment, gifts, prayer, and healing. Recently, we had several St. Giles prayer ministers attend the *Intermediate Course on Healing and Deliverance*. Like ripples, PRMI is impacting our congregation and helping us to grow in cooperating with the Holy Spirit.

[**Brad**] What are the challenges of nurturing the work of the Holy Spirit in the context of a well-established congregation as St. Giles?

[**Rebecca**] One big challenge is to persevere in-season and out-of-season. When we are in-season, it is exciting because things are happening. However, during those out-of-season times everything seems to move slowly. Last year we had a prophetic word about the Lord doing His work in increments, and in the last three years, we have seen those steps of increments, but then, there is the between time when the Lord calls us to be faithful in the day-to- day.

Our church has a heritage and a past move of the Spirit, and that has been a gift. There is already a hunger to go deeper and a longing to see God move. So, we have the joy of building on this amazing foundation. However, it is also a challenge to make sure that we are in step with the Holy Spirit and that we are faithful to how He desires to move in this time and season. And it may not look like the past.

[**Brad**] How are you working to overcome those challenges?

[**Rebecca**] We are so very hopeful! In September 2023, it will be three years since we arrived at St. Giles. Oddly, it seems like we are just starting, but we know that only God can do this and that we are called to be faithful. Josh and I preach gospel-centric messages and strive to model a reliance on the Holy Spirit. The joy of being in ministry together is that we encourage each other, pray together, discern together, and struggle together. Honestly, prayer is something we can do more of.

Fortunately, we are very supported. We have a session that is behind us and who desires to walk in step with the Spirit and is willing to take risks. In addition, we have a prophetic group that meets on a regular basis to practice growing in the prophetic gifts. They will listen for prophetic words for the church, and we've had several very encouraging words. We know there are people praying for us. We even have an intercession group that meets on Wednesday evenings, and we have an outside network of support such as PRMI, family, and our ECO denomination.

[**Brad**] As I understand it, besides PRMI, you have also had experience with other special mission groups and with your own denomination the ECO. How have they been helpful to St. Giles in growing as a Christ-centered evangelical congregation?

[**Rebecca**] So, at our last National Gathering with ECO there was a focus on discipleship. We came away very encouraged to pursue a deeper level of discipleship at St. Giles. There is also an openness to the Holy Spirit with an overall aim to follow Jesus and submit to His lordship.

On the more local level, we have partnered with other ECO churches in wonderful ways. We did a VBS this summer and we shared Holy Week services. This is a wonderful support network with a united vision to pursue Christ in Richmond.

[**Brad**] Is there anything you would like to say to help or encourage church leaders who are seeking to follow Jesus Christ within the setting of a local congregation?

[**Rebecca**] Yes, my suggestion is to learn and grow in how to cooperate with the Holy Spirit and seek opportunities to do this often. Build your prayer support and seek out others who can join you in the work of prayer to encourage you when you are in a hard and dry season.

## Sustaining Synopsis

After reading the two interviews with the Rev. James Cubie and the Rev. Rebecca Long Modrzynski, can you see how the Lord nurtures and sustains the movement of the Holy Spirit in the body of Christ? It is through the longer term, mutually supportive relationship between a modality like a local congregation and a sodality like PRMI, and this relationship must be based on a mutual trust.

Without doubt, PRMI has given these local congregations the tools to go deeper to sustain the flame. Church leaders are learning how to listen and grow in the power of the Holy Spirit so that they will disciple believers, be fruitful, and multiply. The body of Christ is greatly encouraged and supported to do the work of the Holy Spirit, to advance the Kingdom of God through worship, intercessory prayer, Bible studies, life groups, pastoral care, and so on. Therefore, we must learn how to work together—both modality and sodality—totally relying on God *by His Spirit*.

# 22

# Every Revival: A Child of Prayer

In this final chapter of this book, I must return to this work of prayer, which as R.A. Torrey notes, is the basis of all revivals, and which he affirms as the means of advancing the gospel of the kingdom on earth through the body of Christ.

Throughout this book we have repeatedly returned to this foundational concept that every revival is a "child of prayer." Here is very good summary that I found just to reaffirm the importance of prayer in relationship to igniting outpourings of the Holy Spirit that may become revivals advancing the Kingdom of God.

## Never A Revival Without Mighty Praying by R.A. Torrey

Prayer will do more to bring a deep and lasting and sweeping revival, a revival that is real and lasting and altogether of the right sort, than all the organizations that were ever devised by man.

If you study the history of the living Church, you will find it has been very largely a history of revivals. Humanly speaking the Church of Jesus Christ owes its very existence today to revivals. Time and time again the Church has seemed to be on the verge of utter shipwreck, but just then God has sent a great revival and saved it.

If you study the history of revivals, you will find that every real revival in the Church has been the child of prayer. There have been revivals without much preaching; there have been revivals with absolutely no organization; but there has never been a mighty revival without mighty praying....

# A God-Sent Revival

What we need more than anything else today in our own land and in all lands, is a real, mighty outpouring of the Spirit of God. The most fundamental trouble with most of our present-day so-called revivals is *that they are man-made and not God-sent*. They are worked up by man's cunningly devised machinery— not prayed down. Oh, for an old-time revival, a revival that is really and not spuriously of the Pentecostal pattern, for that revival was born of a fourteen days' prayer-meeting. But let us not merely sigh for it. Let us cry for it, cry to God, cry long and cry loud, if need be, and then it will surely come![156]

**We have been Doing the Work of Prayer! And the Lord is Sending Outpourings of the Holy Spirit!**

This work of prayer is a given! Prayer is the essential foundation for implementing and sustaining the cycle of each of the three phases of preparing the altar, igniting the fire, and then sustaining the flame. R.A. Torrey suggests that this is not just general prayer, but urgent, earnest prayer in the name of Jesus Christ within small groups of people who are meeting Jesus' conditions for Him to answer our prayers. These are:

1) being in connection with Jesus Christ—abiding in the vine,
2) asking in faith,
3) according to God's will,

---

[156]This summary by R.A. Torrey was found on two locations on the web, https://www.heraldofhiscoming.org/index.php/93-past-issues/2015/jun15/950-never-a-revival-without-mighty-praying-6-15
   Also this compiled and led by Robert Hill PUBLISHED May 11th 2004 https://bible.org/seriespage/6-topical-prayer-revival
These seem to be gathered from various books that Torrey wrote. I have not been able to identify all their sources.

4) in the name of Jesus Christ, and

5) in agreement with one another. (John 14:14, John 15:7,
   1 John 5:14-15, Matthew 18:19)

Prayer that brings outpourings of the Holy Spirit preceded the first outpouring of Pentecost. "All these continued together in prayer with one mind, together with the women, along with Mary the mother of Jesus, and his brothers" (Acts 1:14). After Pentecost this work of prayer continued but with the addition of strategic level intercession and spiritual warfare:

When they heard this, they raised their voices to God with one mind and said, "Master of all, you who made the heaven, the earth, the sea, and everything that is in them, who said by the Holy Spirit through your servant David our forefather, 'Why do the nations rage, and the peoples plot foolish things? The kings of the earth stood together, and the rulers assembled together, against the Lord and against his Christ.' "For indeed both Herod and Pontius Pilate, with the Gentiles and the people of Israel, assembled together in this city against your holy servant Jesus, whom you anointed, to do as much as your power and your plan had decided beforehand would happen. And now, Lord, pay attention to their threats, and grant to your servants to speak your message with great courage, while you extend your hand to heal, and to bring about miraculous signs and wonders through the name of your holy servant Jesus." When they had prayed, the place where they were assembled together was shaken, and they were all filled with the Holy Spirit and began to speak the word of God courageously. Acts 4:24-31

This prayer is the wellspring of all revivals as well as the means of sustaining them and igniting new outpourings. It is also the means that God uses to remove the human and demonic threats to the advancement of His Kingdom. As Torrey says, "Every true revival has been a child of prayer." This has been true in the past, is proving to be true in the present, and will be in the future. Prayer is what undergirds all the patterns that Jesus is calling us to implement in cooperation with his Holy Spirit. Without prayer these programs will be empty of God's power and effectiveness and become expressions of human power and might. With prayer they will be used by God for igniting and sustaining wave upon wave of revival moves of the Holy Spirit, advancing the gospel of the kingdom to all nations, continuing the final preparation for Jesus' glorious return.

For decades, many of us in this ministry of PRMI have joined with countless Christians worldwide who have been doing this Holy Spirit-empowered prayer, matched with radical obedience to follow Jesus and be His witnesses. Many of us who were part of the past great outpourings of the Holy Spirit that took place in the charismatic renewal, or in the wave of the Holy Spirit that took place with John Wimber and the Vineyard movement, have been urgently praying, "Lord, do it again, in our epoch! And Lord, especially bring into your Kingdom those younger generations who have not had the experiences of your manifest presence."

A vast concert of prayer is taking place globally within all the great streams of Christianity. We in PRMI have only been one small tributary in this great river of God. However, I believe that over the last years, coming out of the refining fire of the Covid 19 pandemic, we are seeing that God is indeed answering those prayers. He is indeed raising up fire starters, and Pentecost events are taking place all over the world. We are so excited and encouraged that the outpouring of the Holy Spirit is already taking place. These are taking place within the stream which is embodied in PRMI. Outpourings are taking place at our PRMI/DFI events in the USA, Canada, UK, Korea, the Spanish speaking world, in China, the Chinese diaspora, and other locations. These are joining other tributaries of revival that we have seen at Asbury University and many other locations. These outpourings are all harbingers of what God is doing as a counter to the rise of evil that is casting such an ominous shadow over the Church and the world.

Currently the Lord is calling us all to take part in this great move of God that has already begun. Each of us must ask the Lord how He is calling us to be in cooperation with the Holy Spirit. The basis for our saying YES to this invitation is who we are in Christ, and above all, who Christ is.

Let's fix these great passages in our hearts and minds:

But God, being rich in mercy, because of his great love with which he loved us, even though we were dead in transgressions, made us alive together with Christ—by grace you are saved!—and he raised us up with him and seated us with him in the heavenly realms in Christ Jesus, to demonstrate in the coming ages the surpassing wealth of his grace in kindness toward us in Christ Jesus. Eph. 2:4-7

We say yes to this call from the Holy Spriit to do his work of prayer from the position of sitting with Jesus Christ in the heavenly place, which means we share in the authority that Jesus Christ has received.

The one we sit with in the heavenly places is revealed in the vision that John received while on the island of Patmos.

I turned to see whose voice was speaking to me, and when I did so, I saw seven golden lampstands, and in the midst of the lampstands was one like a son of man. He was dressed in a robe extending down to his feet and he wore a wide golden belt around his chest. His head and hair were as white as wool, even as white as snow, and his eyes were like a fiery flame. His feet were like polished bronze refined in a furnace, and his voice was like the roar of many waters. He held seven stars in his right hand, and a sharp double-edged sword extended out of his mouth. His face shone like the sun shining at full strength. When I saw him, I fell down at his feet as though I were dead, but he placed his right hand on me and said: "Do not be afraid! I am the first and the last, and

399

the one who lives! I was dead, but look, now I am alive—
forever and ever—and I hold the keys of death and of Hades!
Revelation 1:12-18

This vision of Jesus Christ in glory as sovereign Lord over all is the basis for our saying yes to this call to pray in the great revival, and to step out in obedience as led by the Holy Spirit to implement the biblical keys that have been given us. He is the one who is sending this great revival which will not only defeat Satan's ominous plans but will spread the gospel of the kingdom from individual human hearts to all the nations on earth. Jesus will accomplish all this, but He is calling us as His friends and coworkers to join Him in this great work which will prepare for His return in glory.

# Epilogue

To conclude this book, we must return to the prologue where I provided the context for this book consisting of two events which were both revelatory and catalytic.

The first event was the October 7th, 2023, Hamas invasion of Israel from Gaza, in which Islamic jihadis committed the worst atrocities against the Jewish people since the Nazi Holocaust. This terrible event, and the many expressions of hatred of the Jewish people taking place around the world, exposes for all with eyes to see the colossal evil that is virulently growing in the world right now. Their plans were exposed, which is not just the destruction of the state of Israel but of the extermination of the Jewish people. The hatred of the Jewish people and overt attacks against them is a sign of the emergence of the demonic evil and the confirmation that it has gained the military and political means to implement the Devil's agenda. The October 7 invasion and the evil that has been set in motion will continue to shape the epoch in which we are in and will expose the forces of evil that are aligned against the kingdom of God and the advancement of the gospel of Jesus Christ.

Recall too, the second revelatory catalytic event that also took place from October 10-15, the Mountain Top Equipping Camp at the PRMI's set apart prayer and equipping center in western North Carolina, the Community of the Cross. At this event we experienced extraordinary outpourings of the Holy Spirit. Also, at the guidance of the Holy Spirit, we joined with Jesus in the work of constraining the spirit of the antichrist, praying for the demonic strongholds and their leaders to be exposed and removed. By the time you are reading this book, it is our hope that the Lord has indeed overturned Satan's plans. Our hope is that God, working through the wise decisions by political leaders, and the expression of military might by Israel, and other nations who align with God's promises of blessings for humanity based on their treatment of the Jewish people, that a catastrophic, global war has been avoided. Our deepest hope is that there may still be the time and the conditions for the next great awakening, which would bring the fulfillment of God's plans for the gospel of the kingdom to be carried to all nations on earth, including those through whom Satan is working to block those redemptive actions. Constraining and defeating demonic evil is, however, just one aspect of this work of prayer to which Jesus Christ is calling us.

The second part of this work of prayer is revealed in the vision of the flaming coals from heaven falling all over the earth igniting revival. Here is the vision which I saw which I believe is both prophetic and an invitation to all of us:

"I could see the Word of God going forth and the fiery coals from the altar before God the Father [c.f. Isaiah 6], landing on the locations as they were named and identified on the map. Everywhere they landed, I could see the heavens opening, the fire of the Holy Spirt falling, and revivals being ignited. Everywhere these revival fires were falling the Lord was stirring up in His born-again people earnest and empowered prayers for revival. A great host of people from all nations were joyfully saying yes to Jesus' call. In the power of the Holy Spirit, they were implementing the keys that the Lord has given us for preparing for, igniting, and sustaining these great moves of God, these transformative outpourings of the Holy Spirit.

"These fires of revival were being ignited across America, in Israel and the entire Middle East, in China and the Chinese-speaking world, in the United Kingdom and in Canada. Other nations and areas were mentioned but these seemed to be the ones where, at that particular moment, God had chosen to pour out revival fire.

Everywhere these flaming coals landed, it was as if I was there. I saw these flaming coals igniting in these locations with tributaries of mingled Holy Spirit fire and living water. I saw the Word of God and the Spirit all meeting and becoming a river of a great global awakening with millions upon millions of people being born again and brought into the kingdom of God. I also saw the nations and peoples aligning themselves either with or against God's biblical plans, which have always started with His people, the Jews. God's blessings were being poured out upon those people and nations who blessed His people, and His judgement was falling upon those individuals and nations who were aligned with Satan against His people."

These prophetic visions of a great global awakening have already been set in motion by the prayers of countless people for generations. The revelatory event of October 7 reveals that Satan is working to oppose this great move of God that has begun and is growing. Already the nations are raging! It is imperative at this time in our epoch, that we receive these contemporary prophetic visions not as "done deals" insured by God's sovereign power, but as the Lord's invitations to us to steadfastly keep up our work of earnest prayer, and at the same time to step out in obedience and apply the biblical keys that the Lord has given us to ignite and sustain outpourings of the Holy Spirits.

At the guidance of the Holy Spirit, I have written this book to help all whom Jesus is calling as His friends and coworkers to be able to do our part in fulfilling God the Father's plans of sending this great awakening which will complete the Great Commission and usher in the return of Jesus Christ. To God be all the glory!

.

# Appendix A: Biblical Keys for Great Moves of God

Here we want to gather all this together and provide you with a summary of the core concepts presented in this book in a distilled format without the narrative surrounding them. These are biblical keys for great moves of God which can assist you in applying these essential concepts in your local context.

## Blueprint for Igniting Outpourings of the Holy Spirit

From the study of Acts, a review of the decade of revivals 1900-1910, as well as my own practical experience in this ministry, the blueprint of how God has been at work to prepare for, ignite, and sustain moves of the Holy Spirit emerge. We have observed this blueprint and taken part in implementing it within the tributary of the river of God where Presbyterian-Reformed Ministries has functioned for over fifty years.[157] They are as follows:

1) **The Five Markers of a Pentecost Event**
    o A prepared people (individual or group)
    o A physical address
    o A time stamp
    o Jesus (mediated or unmediated) baptizes or refills with the Holy Spirit
    o Empowered disciples who are witnesses to Jesus Christ

---

[157]This includes the United States, Canada, the UK, members of the British Commonwealth of Nations especially in Africa, the Reformed stream starting in the Netherlands, Indonesia, Europe, Korea, Japan, and China. We are in the Spanish-speaking world and Brazil, following the charismatic move of the Holy Spirit. In recent years we have made significant connections with the Roman Catholic and the Messianic Jewish portions of the body of Christ.

2) **The Biblical pattern of Igniting Revivals – Based on the Three R.A. Torrey Keys**
   o Evangelism
   o Baptism with the Holy Spirit
   o Empowered Prayer

3) **The Two Goforth Foundations**
   o Jesus as King
   o The Bible as the Word of God

4) **The Meta Pattern – (in which is embedded all the above)**
   o Preparing the Altar
   o Igniting the Fire
   o Sustaining the Flame.

This blueprint describes the fundamental and practical "dance steps" for how we are called to cooperate with the Holy Spirit in igniting these Pentecost events. We are then called to take part in nurturing these outpourings of the Holy Spirit through creating the context for Pentecost events to become waves of revival which involve us embodying the Kingdom of God on earth and extending the gospel to the ends of the Earth.

This blueprint also shows us the building blocks that Jesus is calling the apostolic leaders to utilize to create the "wineskins" for preparing for, igniting, and then growing this present great outpouring of the Holy Spirit.

While all outpourings of the Holy Spirit come from the sovereign acts of God the Father, as we walk in faith and obedience to the guidance of the Holy Spirit, these revival waves may become the next great awakening that enables the gospel of the Kingdom to be preached to all nations, meeting the condition that Jesus has set for His return in glory.

## Meta Pattern Fundamentals:

- Anointed Fire Starters and Apostolic Leaders

- Inner Healing and Deliverance

- The Three Phases Becoming a Cycle

- Five-Fold Equipping Anointings

- Modality and Sodality Working Together

# Appendix B: Resources to Grow
## Presbyterian-Reformed Ministries International

PRMI was founded in 1966 to pray and work for the spiritual renewal of Presbyterian and Reformed churches. Over the past fifty years, we  have grown to include other parts of the body of Christ in many nations and continue to have a distinctive role in the world-wide movement of the Holy Spirit advancing the gospel of Jesus Christ for the fulfillment of the Great Commission.

Presbyterian-Reformed Ministries International offers many resources for igniting and growing outpourings of the Holy Spirit which grow the church and advance the gospel of the kingdom.

Go to the following web sites to access this wealth of information, to receive our newsletters, and to register for events and courses.

## www.prmi.org

Receive **Discerning the Times**, an email digest of blogs written by Dr. Zeb Bradford Long, offering discernment on current events and educating people on issues that face the Church today for the purpose of mobilizing intercessors for advancing the Kingdom of God and fulfilling the Great Commission.

## www.discernwith.us

# Books for Preparing for Holy Spirit Outpourings

**Receiving the Power** for
the Holy Spirit
By
Zeb Bradford Long &
Douglas McMurry
Chosen Books

By Brad Long &
Cindy Strickler
Zondervan

**Prayer that Shapes the Future**:
How to Pray with Power and
Authority
By Brad Long &
Doug McMurry
Chosen Books

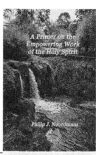

## Books by Phil Noordmans

FireStarter
Kindle Direct Publishing
Amazon

A Primer on Spiritual Gifts
Kindle Direct Publishing
Amazon

A Primer on the Empowering Work of
the Holy Spirit
Kindle Direct Publishing
Amazon

Why Pray? Because Sometimes God
Relents!
Kindle Direct Publishing
**Amazon**

Order through www.amazon.com or for bulk rates contact the
PRMI USA office  prmi@prmi.org  or call at 828-669-7373

**"...you will receive power when the Holy Spirit has come upon you, and you will be my witnesses in Jerusalem, and in all Judea and Samaria, and to the farthest parts of the earth." Acts 1:8**

Learn how to cooperate with the Holy Spirit to be a witness to Jesus Christ by effectively engaging in ministries of prayer, healing, spiritual warfare, and evangelism for growing the Church and advancing the Kingdom of God.

Dunamis can help you deepen your walk with the Lord and prepare you for effective ministry wherever the Lord has called you. "Dunamis" is the Greek term for "power."

With the Dunamis teaching, you'll discover.

- **Solid biblical theology about the person and work of the Holy Spirit in the life of the believer.**
- **Teaching forged from the scriptures, proven in ministry, and informed by 200 years of renewal and revival movements.**
- **Your spiritual gifts and how to use them effectively in the Kingdom of God.**
- **How to recognize God's guidance for ministry in a given moment through the experience-based lab times and review debriefings.**

The Dunamis Project consists of six units, each taught over five days six months apart in the same location. Each event consists of intensive biblical teaching and practical application in the context of prayer and worship. These events are designed to enable every believer to grow in their faith and personal relationship with God and participate in the ministry of the Holy Spirit. For more information, go to www.prmi.org.

# Timeline: People and Events

| | |
|---|---|
| 1509-1564 | John Calvin, Geneva. Reformed theologian. |
| 1514 - 1572 | John Knox, Scotland. Reformed theologian. |
| 1727 | Count Nicolaus Zinzendorf and the Moravian Pentecost |
| 1739 | The Love Feast in Fetter Lane, London, New Year's Day, 1739.<br>Participants included John Wesley, Charles Wesley, Mr. Hall, Charles Kinchin, Benjamin Ingham, George Whitefield, and Hutchings. |
| 1730s – 1770s | First Great Awakening. Jonathan Edwards, George Whitfield. |
| 1795 - 1835 | Second Great Awakening. James McGrady, Charles Finney, Cane Ridge Camp Meetings. |
| 1837 - 1899 | D.L. Moody, evangelist. |
| 1837 - 1920 | Abraham Kuyper, Netherlands. Reformed theologian. |
| 1857 - 1859 | Third Great Awakening. Jeremiah Lanphier, Fulton Street, NYC |
| 1890 - 1910 | World-wide outpourings of the Holy Spirit. Two key figures God used were American evangelist and teacher of the Holy Spirit, R.A. Torrey (1856-1928), and the Canadian Presbyterian missionary to China, Jonathan Goforth (1859-1936). Their streams of revival ran through the English-speaking world as well as Korea and China. |
| 1900 | The Boxer Rebellion broke out in China with attacks against foreign missionaries. |
| Dec. 1901 | R.A. Torrey's first international tour began. |

| | |
|---|---|
| 1903 | The Wonsan, Korea Revival, which sprang from the prayers of Methodist missionary Mary C. White, Presbyterian missionary Frances McCully, and station chief, Dr. R.A. Hardie. Great moves of God came in waves in Korea in 1903, 1905, and 1907. R.A. Torrey embarked on global tours which included Great Britain, China, Japan, Australia, and India. |
| 1904-1905 | The great Welsh Revival. Key leaders included Jessie Penn Lewis and Evan Roberts. |
| 1905-1906 | Azusa Street revival. – Ignited through William J. Seymour an African American preacher. |
| 1907 | Jonathan Goforth visited Korea to view firsthand the great outpouring taking place. The great Pyongyang, North Korea, revival of 1907 heavily influenced him. His participation in this outpouring in Korea sparked the fire in Goforth that he took back to China. |
| 1907 - 1908 | God used Canadian Presbyterian missionary Jonathan Goforth (1859-1936) to ignite the great Manchurian Revival (northeastern China) of 1907-08. |
| 1918 | R.A. Torrey III (Archer) was born in China. |
| 1937-1938 | Nan Jing Massacre in China by the Japanese in December and January of 1937-38. |
| 1949 | Communists took over China. |
| 1951 - | Zeb Bradford (Brad) Long born. |
| 1957 - 1964 | Archer Torrey was called to reestablish the Anglican seminary in Seoul. He served as director of the seminary from 1957 to 1964. |
| 1965 | Archer and Jane Torrey establish Jesus Abbey as a prayer community, on the east coast of South Korea. |
| 1960s | Charismatic Renewal movement. |
| 1966 | In January Brad Long, with his family make their first trip to Jesus Abbey. Brad and Ben Torrey become brothers. |
| 1966 | Rev. Brick Bradford and four other Presbyterian pastors establish Presbyterian Charismatic |

| | |
|---|---|
| | Communion (PCC). Later it became Presbyterian Reformed Ministries International (PRMI). |
| 1973 | Billy Graham in Seoul, Korea conducted his largest crusade ever. Archer Torrey with Presbyterian missionary David Ross equipped "personal workers" by teaching on the baptism with the Holy Spirit, which was R.A. Torrey's requirement for effective personal evangelism. |
| 1974 | Brad Long spends summer at Jesus Abbey in preparation for starting Union Seminary in VA. |
| 1976-1977 | Laura and Brad Long spend a year as short term PCUS missionaries in South Korea teaching at the Presbyterian Theological Seminary in Seoul. |
| Feb. 1977 | While staying at Jesus Abbey, Brad Long receives the baptism with the Holy Spirit, as well as a calling by Jesus to advance the Kingdom of God worldwide. This took place when Archer and Jane Torrey, with other members of the Abbey community, laid hands on him. |
| Mar 1977 | At a prayer meeting in the home of Presbyterian missionaries David and Ellen Ross, Jesus directly baptizes Laura Long with the Holy Spirit. |
| 1978-1980 | Brad and Laura are ordained and serve Presbyterian congregations near Pilot Mountain, North Carolina. |
| Aug. 1980 | Brad and Laura are sent to Taiwan to serve as Presbyterian missionaries. They spend two years in language school in Taichung, and then move, in 1982, to serve at the Presbyterian Bible College located south of Taipei in the city of Hsinchu. |
| 1982- | Brad starts to take small groups of Bible College faculty, then Taiwan Presbyterian Church pastors and then missionaries, to Korea to visit Jesus Abbey where they all receive the baptism with the Holy Spirit. |

| | |
|---|---|
| | He also took groups of Bible College students to the Prayer Mountain where they were filled with the Holy Spirit. |
| June 1984 | Archer Torrey traveled from Jesus Abby in Korea to Taiwan to teach on the Holy Spirit at the Presbyterian Bible College in Hsinchu. Result: A great outpouring of the Holy Spirit among over 120 Taiwan Presbyterian Church and other denominations pastors, as well as Canadian, American, and UK missionaries. |
| 1985 | Out of this outpouring, Brad Long and a Bible College team including President Wang and Board Member Howard Chaw founded the Presbyterian Lay Training Center on the campus of the Bible College. For the next four years they conducted many major equipping events with hundreds of church leaders at the Lay Training Center. They brought in major teachers on the Holy Spirit from the United States. They also sent teams all over Taiwan and beyond, igniting outpourings of the Holy Spirit in many congregations in Taiwan. |
| June 1989 | Ten Nan Men (Tiananmen Square) massacre. |
| Aug. 1989 | Brad and family returned to the United States. |
| Jan. 1990 | Brad began serving as the Executive Director of Presbyterian Reformed Ministries International. |
| March 1991 | The first Dunamis event at Lake George, New York, at the Silver Bay YMCA Conference Center. This was led by Archer Torrey, Doug McMurry, and Brad Long. This was when the core leadership of PRMI for the next 30 years was engrafted into the movement, especially Cindy and Steve Strickler, Linda and Larry Ruby, Tom and Raylene Wilcox, Allan and Debbie Kemp and many others. |

| | |
|---|---|
| 1991-2002 | The Dunamis Project equipping tracks go viral throughout the USA and Canada, and Brad Long takes teams to multiple locations around the world to teach on the Holy Spirit, igniting moves of the Holy Spirit. Dunamis Tracks were implemented in China, Korea, Hong Kong, Taiwan, New Zealand, Brazil, Uganda, Central America, and other nations. |
| 1993 | Rev. Dr. John Chang (張景祥) and Brad Long become an anointed team after a trip to Taiwan igniting outpourings of the Holy Spirit. |
| 1993 | The outpouring of the Holy Spirit takes place at the seminary in China, launching the wave of the Holy Spirit that resulted in many teams going to China. These were led by Brad Long and John Chang until after 2005, when just Dr. Chang took teams of Chinese co-workers to multiple locations in China. This work lasted until 2019 when the oppression and the pandemic made it no longer possible. |
| 2002 | Archer Torrey **BIRTH** 19 Jan 1918 China<br>**DEATH** 6 Aug 2002 (aged 84) South Korea.<br>Archer was the one who launched the movement of the Holy Spirit in June of 1984 in Taiwan. In 1991 he was the primary teacher launching the Dunamis Project at Lake George, New York. I had invited him to return from Korea to take part in launching the PRMI Dumanis Fellowship, but six weeks before this event, after doing a service at Jesus Abbey in Korea, he fell, hit his head, and went into a coma. Ten minutes before starting the founding meeting of the DFI, Ben called me from Korea to tell me that he had died. (We felt him there in the Spirit!) |
| 2002 | PRMI establishes the Community of the Cross: A place of Encounter with Jesus Christ for Prayer, Equipping and Sending. |

| Aug. 6 2002 | The Founding of the PRMI Dunamis Fellowship International at the Blue Ridge YMCA Conference Center in Black Mountain, NC. |
|---|---|
| 2004 – 2023 | Under the Leadership of Rev. Cindy Strickler, the Dunamis Fellowship expands with outpourings of the Holy Spirit.  DFI branches are formed to nurture and expand these streams of revival.<br>2002 – Dunamis Fellowship International (DFI)<br>2004 – Dunamis Fellowship Alaska (DFAK)<br>2005 – Dunamis Fellowship Britain and Ireland (DFB&I)<br>2006 – Dunamis Fellowship Canada (DFC)<br>2015 – Dunamis Fellowship Korea (DFK)<br>2018 – Dunamis Fellowship Northwest US (DFNWUS) |
| 2019 | First Dunamis event sponsored by PRMI at Hallelujah Church near Seoul, Korea. |
| Sept. 2020 | Double Grace Dunamis Theological Seminary – NY 紐約雙恩靈力事奉神學院 founded by PRMI and Grace Christian Church.  The original Team establishing the Seminary was Rev. Dr. John Chang (張景祥), Dr. Ji Dung Shan (單繼東) Rev. Dr. Brad Long and Rev. Cindy Strickler. |
| June 2021 | Prophetic word through Doug McMurry that the Lord had prepared PRMI to be a key player in the Third Great Awakening. |
| Nov. 2021 | A vision through Brad Long regarding Jesus casting handfuls of blazing coals to earth that ignited revivals. |
| Feb. 2023 | The Next Great Awakening Concert of Prayer at the Community of the Cross. |
| Feb. 2023 | Outpouring of the Holy Spirit at Asbury University in Wilmore, Kentucky. |

# Index of People and Relationships

| | |
|---|---|
| D.L. Moody, 1837-1899 | Evangelist. Founder of Moody Church and Moody Bible Institute. Co-worker with R.A. Torrey. |
| R.A. Torrey, 1856-1928 | American evangelist and teacher on the Holy Spirit. D.L. Moody's Associate Evangelist. Took over Moody's ministry upon his death in 1899. |
| Jonathan Goforth, 1859-1936 | Canadian Presbyterian missionary to China. R.A. Torrey's friend and co-worker. |
| Rosalind [Bell-Smith] Goforth, 1864-1942 | Jonathan Goforth's wife. |
| R.A. Torrey, Jr. | Missionary to China, and later when the communists took over in 1949, went to South Korea. |
| Reuben Archer Torrey III (Archer), 1918 -2002 | <ul><li>R.A. Torrey's grandson.</li><li>Born in China.</li><li>Returned to the USA to attend Davidson College.</li><li>Married Jane</li><li>Friends with Brad Long's parents.</li><li>Called to reestablish the Anglican seminary in Seoul. He served as its director from 1957 to 1964.</li><li>Founders of Jesus Abbey in Korea and the Fourth River Project.</li></ul>Brad Long's spiritual father and mentor. |
| Ben Torrey, 1950 - | Archer Torrey's son.<ul><li>Brad Long's friend.</li></ul> |
| Peyton Johnson | Archer Torrey's nephew. |

| Rev. Brick Bradford and Rev. Carter Blaisdell | Rev. Brick Bradford and his associate Rev. Carter Blaisdell gave leadership to the Presbyterian Charismatic Communion (PCC) in 1966, which became PRMI. |
|---|---|
| Zeb Bradford Long, 1951 - | Was grafted into the R.A. Torrey, Jonathan Goforth, and China-Korea stream, first through friendship with the Archer and Jane Torrey and later in 1977 by being baptized with the Holy Spirit while at Jesus Abbey. |
| Rev. Laura Long | Brad Long's wife, also engrafted into the R.A. Torrey stream through visits to Jesus Abbey and receiving the baptism with the Holy Spirit while in Korea. An ordained Presbyterian minister. |
| Rev. Rebecca Modrynski | Laura and Brad Long's middle daughter born in Taiwan, and an ordained Presbyterian minister. |
| Rev. Doug and Carla McMurry | Co-founder with Brad Long of the PRMI Dunamis Project. Co-author of the first three Dunamis Manuals on the work of the Holy Spirit and Prayer, and of several published books with Brad Long. An anointed intercessory prayer leader, and author of the *Glory Through Time* books telling the stories of revivals throughout church history. |
| Rev. Dr. John Chang (張景祥) | Brad Long's Chinese friend and co-worker. |
| Rev. Su Chang | John Chang's wife. Accompanied John and Brad on early trips to China and also translated the first three Dunamis Project manuals into Chinese. |
| Rev. David Westra | Ordained CRC pastor. Has taken part in mission trips to Korea to work with the Chinese and is the pastor of the Gold Avenue CRC congregation. Used by God to ignite |

| | |
|---|---|
| | outpourings of the Holy Spirit through the Growing the Church program and developer of the Gospel Tool and the Empowered for Witness course based on the Dunamis Project. |
| Rev. Cindy Strickler | Engrafted into this stream of the Holy Spirit through being baptized with the Holy Spirit at the first Dunamis Project event in 1991 taught by Archer Torrey, Director of the PRMI Dunamis Fellowship International and Director of PRMI. Took part in the development of the PRMI Dunamis Project. Teacher and minister on many PRMI mission trips to Hong Kong, China, Korea, Taiwan, Japan, United Kingdom, Brazil, Canada igniting and sustaining moves of the Holy Spirit. |
| | |

# About the Authors

**Rev. Dr. Zeb Bradford Long** was born in Charlotte, NC into a family with vital Christian faith. During high school, he was exposed to different cultures and cross-cultural missions when his family accompanied his father to his State Department posting in South Korea. In the 1970s-80s, Brad and his wife Laura served as evangelistic and educational Presbyterian missionaries, first in South Korea and later in Taiwan where they were part of Holy Spirit outpourings in those nations.

Brad is the Executive Director of Presbyterian Reformed Ministries International (PRMI) and founder of the Dunamis Project—a series of six intensive equipping events providing systematic biblical and Reformed theological teaching, which has provided the context for God the Father to fulfill Acts 1:4-8. Conducted in multiple national and international locations, thousands have experienced the baptism/infilling with the Holy Spirit, becoming Jesus' Holy Spirit-empowered friends and co-workers growing the Church and extending the gospel of the Kingdom worldwide. To support this worldwide movement of the Holy Spirit, PRMI established the Community of the Cross (COC) under Brad's leadership. The COC is a place of encounter with Jesus Christ, located on twenty-four acres in Black Mountain, NC, in the beautiful Blue Ridge Mountains. It is a center for prayer, equipping, and sending, to see the Kingdom of God transform all dimensions of reality. For a list of books and publications by Zeb Bradford Long, go to PRMI.org.

**Rev. Dr. Philip J. Noordmans** was raised on a dairy farm in west-central Minnesota. Jesus dramatically called 11-year-old Phil to Himself through a traveling evangelist at his family's home church. Eventually he graduated from Wheaton College (B.A., History) and Fuller Theological Seminary (M.Div. and D.Min.).

In the year 2000, Jesus initiated a new learning curve in Phil's life. Jesus used His Word, His Spirit, and trusted friends at PRMI to open his mind and heart to understanding and experiencing the empowering work of the Holy Spirit. This journey continues to this day as he endeavors to "keep in step with the Spirit," (Galatians 5:25, ESV).

Phil and his wife Teri have served full-time for over forty years in various churches in the Midwest and west coast. Currently Phil is serving as a Regional Pastor for the Conservative Congregational Christian Conference. In this role he interacts with 30 churches and 130 pastors in the western USA.

Phil has self-published eight books, available on Amazon, including *FireStarter: The Holy Spirit Empowers* which chronicles his theological and experiential journey from being a rigid dispensationalist to a balanced charismatic.

**Barbara Koob** is a "globe-trottin' mama" who is on a mission to share the love of Jesus Christ through the gospel wherever she goes. Barb has a heart for discipleship, loves to travel, and has served as a short-term missionary in several countries, nurturing, encouraging, teaching, and interceding for others. She yearns to see the Lord ignite revivals in the power of the Holy Spirit. Barb is the Writing Project Manager for Rev. Dr. Brad Long. She is also an author and speaker. Her book *Dream Discoveries* encourages readers to hope and dream with God's purpose for their lives, using His gift of biblical dream interpretation.

Printed in Great Britain
by Amazon

37159918R00255